Cordon Bleu Cookery

Cordon Bleu Cookery

Rosemary Hume & Muriel Downes

TREASURE PRESS

Introduction

Many people tell us that they want to learn how to cook 'the Cordon Bleu way'; to know about the basic methods used in the preparation of good French food, just as we teach them to our students at the London Cordon Bleu Cookery School. In this book, we have gathered together many of our main lessons, each one dealing with a specific cooking technique, each fully explained, with clear photographs, where necessary – for it is important to know exactly how a dish should look – and with enough varied recipes for you to practise your new-found skills while cooking to suit the family and yourself.

We have included some more specialised dishes for the experienced cook to add to her repertoire, and warn of any likely pitfalls on the way.

After all, we feel that cooking should be fun. Learn with us, to enjoy it too.

First published in Great Britain in 1975 by
Octopus Books Ltd in co-operation with
Phoebus Publishing Company

This edition published in 1984 by
Treasure Press
59 Grosvenor Street
London W1

© 1968/81 Macdonald Phoebus Ltd

ISBN 0 907812 92 9

Printed in Hong Kong

Contents

All the recipes have been tested at the London Cordon Bleu Cookery School. Quantities given are for four servings and spoon measures are level – unless otherwise stated.

Hors d'oeuvre

The name hors d'oeuvre, literally 'outside of the main work', means a selection of individual dishes to be eaten hot or cold before the main course. There is almost no limit to the choice of dishes and many can be made for a small party from what is in your store cupboard. All the recipes overleaf allow for four portions, and some of them may be served singly as a first course, in which case double the quantity. Alternatively, a selection of hors d'oeuvre can be served for a set lunch or buffet lunch, with the addition of salads, recipes for which are given on pages 196–199.

COLD HORS D'OEUVRE

With a little imagination, you can invent new salads and different combinations of fish, meat and vegetables. The hors d'oeuvre course should consist of two or three 'straight' dishes – slices of salami, garlic or liver sausage, pickled herring or fillets of anchovy – together with two or three salads dressed with a mayonnaise or vinaigrette dressing. In fact you go through the fish, meat and vegetable courses in miniature. The number of dishes served depends on the number of guests, but for a party of six you can have up to eight or ten.

The traditional hors d'oeuvre dish is rectangular, about 2½ inches deep and usually in white china. You can use any convenient dishes or you can buy a tray set fitted with curved dishes.

Hors d'oeuvre may also be arranged in scallop shells. Put two varieties in one shell, set these on a plate and serve one for each person. For a small party, or when time is short, this method of serving is often more convenient than having a selection of different dishes.

To save time, have French dressing and a thick mayonnaise ready-made and stored, covered, in a jar or container. This can be kept for a week or two in a cool larder. If you must keep mayonnaise in the refrigerator, be sure to take it out at least 2 hours before use and leave at room temperature; should it curdle or separate, add 1 tablespoon of boiling water and whisk well.

Tunny fish and prawn salad

1 small head of celery
1 small can (approximately 7 oz) tunny fish
2–3 oz prawns (shelled)
French dressing (to moisten)
1 dessertspoon parsley (chopped)

Method
Cut celery stalks first into 1½-inch lengths, then down into bâtons (sticks). Soak these in iced water for 30 minutes, then drain and dry thoroughly.

Drain oil from tunny fish and break it into large flakes with a fork. Add to the prawns with the celery. Moisten well with the French dressing and add parsley.

Eggs mayonnaise

3–4 eggs (hard-boiled)
¼ pint thick mayonnaise (using lemon juice instead of vinegar to sharpen it)
2 dessertspoons parsley (roughly chopped)
few prawns (shelled) – optional

A curry-flavoured mayonnaise, as used for the curried potato salad, overleaf, may be substituted.

Method
Split the eggs in half lengthways. Arrange in dish, rounded side up. Coat with the mayonnaise and sprinkle well with the parsley.

Prawns can be scattered over the eggs before coating them with the mayonnaise.
Watchpoint When coating eggs with mayonnaise make sure it is really thick, otherwise it will slide off the whites and spoil the appearance of the dish.

Cucumber salad
(see photograph, below)

Peel 1 medium-size cucumber and slice thinly; salt lightly, then press slices well between two plates and leave in a cool place for 1 hour before draining. Pour over French dressing or spoon over a little sour cream or yoghourt. Sprinkle with snipped chives.

Cucumber salad with chives

Couronne of shrimps in aspic (see recipe on page 18) provides an attractive and accomplished starter to a meal

Rice, tomato and black olive salad, with button mushrooms

minutes in the water with a good squeeze of lemon juice. Cook quickly, uncovered, so that liquid is well reduced by the time mushrooms are cooked; shake and stir well.

Mix all ingredients with a fork, season well and moisten with French dressing.

Potato mayonnaise

¾ lb potatoes (old or new)
French dressing (to coat potatoes)
about ¼ pint mayonnaise
pickled walnuts (sliced)
paprika pepper

Method
Boil potatoes in their skins, then peel and toss them in French dressing while still hot. Small new potatoes can be kept whole; old potatoes should be sliced. When cold, mix potatoes with a little thick mayonnaise. Season well; put on serving dish.

Dilute 2 tablespoons mayonnaise with 1 dessertspoon hot water to a coating consistency. Spoon over the potatoes. Garnish round with sliced pickled walnuts, sprinkle with paprika.

Curried potato salad

about ¾ lb small new potatoes (cooked), or 1 small can
French dressing (to coat potatoes)
scant ¼ pint thick mayonnaise

For curry mixture
1 shallot, or ½ small onion (sliced)
2 tablespoons olive oil
2 dessertspoons curry powder
1 teaspoon paprika pepper
½ cup of tomato juice, or 2 teaspoons tomato purée mixed with ½ cup of water
1 slice of lemon
1 dessertspoon apricot jam, or redcurrant jelly

Method
To make curry mixture: soften shallot or onion in oil, then add the curry and paprika; cook for 1 minute, then add tomato juice or purée, lemon, and jam

Vinaigrette salad

3 medium-size beetroots (cooked and diced)
4–5 medium-size potatoes (cooked and diced)
1 small head, or 2–3 sticks, of celery (diced)
1 large apple (peeled, cored and diced)
1 pickled dill cucumber (diced)
salt and pepper
1 cup of peas (cooked)
1 large cup of cooked meat, or fish (shredded, or flaked)
¼ pint French dressing
½–¾ pint mayonnaise

This is one of the best salads and ideal for using up odd leftovers. In addition to the basic mixture of vegetables you can use meat, chicken, fish or shellfish.

Method
Peel the beetroot and cut into dice. Cook potatoes in their skins, peel and cut into dice while still warm. Dice celery, apple and dill cucumber. Mix together and season very well.

Fork in the peas and meat or fish. Moisten well with French dressing. Cover bowl and leave 2–3 hours or overnight. To serve, pile up in a dish or salad bowl, coat well with the mayonnaise.

Decorate, if you wish, with sliced dill cucumber, curled celery, prawns, slices of salami or garlic sausage.
Watchpoint Unless using shellfish it is best made the day before so that flavours can blend well together. It will keep for 2–3 days in a covered bowl in a refrigerator.

Rice, tomato and black olive salad

3 tablespoons rice
¼ lb tomatoes (ripe and firm)
2 oz button mushrooms
2 oz black olives (halved and stoned)
2 tablespoons water
squeeze of lemon juice
2–3 tablespoons French dressing (made with dry white wine instead of vinegar)
salt and pepper

Method
Boil rice, drain, refresh and dry. Scald and skin tomatoes, quarter, and flick out seeds, then cut away the stalk. Cut each quarter in half lengthways.

Wash and trim mushrooms, quarter and cook for 2–3

or jelly. Cover, simmer for 7–10 minutes, then strain. Keep this mixture in a small jar or covered container until wanted.

Have the potatoes ready, cooked and tossed in French dressing (see potato mayonnaise). If using canned potatoes, drain them thoroughly and season with lemon juice, salt and pepper. Add enough curry mixture to flavour the mayonnaise to taste. Put potatoes on a serving dish and coat with the mayonnaise.

Tomato salad with lemon dressing

½ lb tomatoes (ripe and firm)

For lemon dressing
1 tablespoon lemon juice
2 tablespoons oil
2 tablespoons single cream
½ teaspoon salt
1 rounded teaspoon sugar
pepper (ground from mill)
rind of ½ lemon

Method
Scald, skin and slice tomatoes, then put them in a serving dish.

To prepare lemon dressing: beat all the ingredients (except rind) together and adjust seasoning. Cut lemon rind into fine shreds, blanch, drain and dry them; sprinkle over the dish.

Sweetcorn, pepper and pickled onion salad

1 large can sweetcorn kernels
salt and pepper
2 caps of canned pimiento
   (coarsely chopped)
1 tablespoon small pickled onions
   (quartered, or thinly sliced)
French, or lemon, dressing (as
   for tomato salad)

Some brands of canned sweetcorn already contain sweet pepper, in which case do not add pimiento.

Method
Drain sweetcorn well from its

Sweetcorn, pepper and pickled onion salad, with dressing

liquid; put it into a bowl, season well and add the pimiento and the onions. Moisten sweetcorn mixture with the chosen dressing and turn into a serving dish.

Mushrooms Philippe

4–6 oz button mushrooms
1 large tablespoon olive oil
1 shallot (finely chopped)
1 wineglass red wine
1 teaspoon thyme (freshly
   chopped)
1–2 tablespoons French dressing
   (preferably made with red
   wine vinegar)
salt and pepper

Method
Wash and trim mushrooms (cut off stalks level with caps, slice stalks lengthways and put with mushroom caps).

Heat oil in a small frying pan, put in the mushrooms and the shallot. Fry briskly for about 3 minutes, turning and stirring them all the time.

Lift out mushroom mixture with a draining spoon into a

bowl. Pour wine into the pan and boil until it is reduced by half. Add to the mushrooms with the herbs and French dressing. Season well, cover, and leave until cold.

Russian or vegetable salad

1 large beetroot (cooked and
   diced)
1 carrot (diced)
2–3 tablespoons peas
1 potato (diced)
French dressing (to moisten)
2–3 tablespoons mayonnaise

Method
Put beetroot into a bowl. Cook carrot in pan of boiling water until barely tender, then add peas and cook for a further 2–3 minutes, or until both vegetables are tender. Drain and refresh.

Cook diced potato in boiling water until just tender (5–6 minutes). Drain it and add to the beetroot with the peas and carrot. Moisten with French dressing. Leave until all is cold, then stir in 2–3 tablespoons thick mayonnaise.

Watchpoint The combined amount of carrot, peas and potato should be half that of the beetroot.

13

There are quite a number of unusual cooked salads that may be served, including bean salad (left), leek and egg salad (centre), and artichoke and tomato salad (right)

Bean salad

4 oz dried brown beans, Italian or
   Dutch (soaked overnight)
bouquet of 1 bayleaf, 1 stick of
   celery and 4–5 parsley stalks
1 medium-size onion (finely
   sliced)
2 ripe, firm tomatoes
2 oz Dutch cheese (sliced and cut
   in shreds)
1 dessertspoon parsley
   (chopped)
salt
black pepper (ground from mill)
¼ pint lemon cream dressing

Method
Drain beans and put into a pan
of fresh, slightly-salted water.
The beans must be brought to
the boil very slowly, taking not
less than 40 minutes. When
they have boiled, add the
bouquet, cover pan and simmer
for 1 hour.

Cool slightly in the liquor,
then drain. Simmer onion in a
pan of salted water for 3–4
minutes or until just tender, and
drain. Scald and skin tomatoes,
cut in half, remove seeds and
hard core, and slice each piece
into four. Put beans into a bowl
with onion, tomatoes, cheese,
parsley and seasoning to taste.
Moisten well with the lemon
cream dressing.

Leek and egg salad

4–5 leeks (according to size)
salt
little French dressing
3 hard-boiled eggs
¼–½ pint mayonnaise
paprika pepper

Method
Wash the leeks thoroughly.
Split in half lengthways and tie
together to form a neat bundle.
Boil in salted water until just
tender (about 12 minutes),
drain and refresh. Untie, put in
dish and pour over a little
French dressing.

Cut white of eggs into strips
and scatter over the leeks.
Sieve yolks through a wire bowl
strainer. Thin the mayonnaise,
if necessary, with 1 tablespoon
of boiling water. Spoon this
over the salad to coat leeks,
and sprinkle sieved yolks on
top. Dust with paprika pepper
and serve lightly chilled.

Artichoke and tomato salad

1½ lb jerusalem artichokes
salted water
squeeze of lemon juice
4–5 tomatoes (according to size)

For dressing
1 carton plain yoghourt
2–3 tablespoons thick cream
salt and pepper
1 teaspoon sugar
squeeze of lemon juice
1 dessertspoon chives (snipped),
   or parsley (chopped)

Method
Peel artichokes and cut into
walnut-size pieces. Cook in pan
of salted water with a good
squeeze of lemon juice until
just tender (about 7–8 minutes).
Drain, rinse in cold water and
drain again. Put in a bowl with
tomatoes (skinned, seeds removed, flesh shredded).

To prepare dressing: turn
yoghourt into a bowl, whip the
cream lightly, add to yoghourt
with the seasoning, sugar and
lemon juice. Add chives or
parsley. Mix together with artichokes and tomatoes.

Arrange in a salad bowl or
hors d'oeuvre dish, and serve
with brown bread and butter.

The following recipes are
for hors d'oeuvre salads and
the quantities given are
enough for two servings.

Herring and dill cucumber salad

2–3 herring fillets
1 Spanish onion (sliced)
2 dill cucumbers (sliced)
French dressing (made with dry
   white wine instead of vinegar)

In many delicatessens herring
fillets preserved in white wine
may be bought quite cheaply.
These, cut into strips diagonally
and sprinkled with grated horseradish or mixed with horseradish cream, make an excellent
hors d'oeuvre.

Method
Cut fillets into strips diagonally.
Set aside. Push onion slices out
into rings. Blanch for 5–6
minutes, then drain and refresh.

Arrange herring fillets in
centre of serving dish, surround
with the cucumber and place
the onion round that. Spoon
over enough French dressing
to moisten well.

Anchovy and bean salad

2–3 oz haricot, or buttered, beans (well soaked and simmered until tender), or 1 can butter beans (drained from their liquid)
1 small can anchovy fillets

For dressing
½ teaspoon onion (grated)
½ tablespoon white wine vinegar
2 tablespoons oil
1 teaspoon anchovy essence
2 tablespoons double cream
1 dessertspoon parsley (chopped)

Method
Combine all ingredients for the dressing, mix with the beans. Put salad in serving dish. Have ready the anchovy fillets, split in two lengthways. Arrange these lattice-fashion over salad.

Anchovy and bean salad decorated lattice-fashion

Frankfurter and ham salad

1 pair of Frankfurter sausages
¼ lb ham (cooked and thinly sliced)
¼ lb tomatoes
1 red, or green, pepper (shredded and blanched)

For dressing
1 tablespoon white wine vinegar
1 teaspoon tomato purée
3 tablespoons oil
salt and pepper
sugar (to taste)

Method
Poach the sausages in boiling water for 5–6 minutes; then drain and cool. Shred the ham. Scald, skin and quarter the tomatoes; flick out the seeds and cut away the stalk. Slice each quarter into three.

Slice sausages diagonally and put into a bowl with the ham, tomatoes and pepper. Combine the ingredients for the dressing, season to taste, mix well and fork lightly into the sausage mixture.

Italian salad (pasta shells, ham and olives) with mayonnaise

Italian salad

2 oz pasta shells
¼ lb ham (cooked and sliced)
2 oz black olives (halved and stoned)
2–3 tablespoons thick mayonnaise
1 teaspoon French mustard

Method
Simmer pasta shells in pan of boiling salted water for about 7 minutes or until just tender. Drain and refresh them.

Shred the ham and mix this with the olives and pasta. Add mustard to mayonnaise and stir enough into the salad to bind it together.

COLD APPETISERS

A platter of home-made appetisers: stuffed grapes on sticks, Argenteuil tartlets (left) and smoked salmon roulades (right)

Argenteuil tartlets

4 oz quantity of shortcrust
   pastry

For filling
1 bundle of asparagus (about
   16 spears)
1 packet of Demi-Sel cheese
salt and pepper
2 tablespoons French dressing
1 teaspoon mixed chopped herbs

16 small boat moulds

Method
Roll out the shortcrust pastry, line the boat moulds with it and bake blind. Leave them to cool, then turn out of the moulds.

Cook the asparagus, refresh and leave to drain on a piece of muslin.

Season the cream cheese and fill into the pastry cases, levelling it with a palette knife. Trim each asparagus spear to the size of the boat moulds and spoon over the French dressing and herbs. Arrange a spear of asparagus on top of the cheese in each pastry case.

Roulades of smoked salmon

1 small brown loaf
about 4 oz butter
½ lb smoked salmon
juice of ½ lemon
black pepper (ground from mill)

Method
Cut the crust lengthways from the top of the loaf; butter and cut thin slices from the length of the loaf. Cover each slice with smoked salmon and season with lemon juice and pepper. Trim away crust and roll each slice the length of the loaf like a swiss roll. Then cut each roll in thin slices.

Watchpoint If the bread is crumbly, it will be easier to slice the rolls if they are first wrapped in greaseproof paper and chilled.

Stuffed grapes

1 lb large black grapes
4 oz cream cheese
salt
black pepper (to taste)
2 tablespoons finely chopped
   salted almonds

Method
Wipe the grapes and carefully take them off the stem. Split each one at the stalk end and carefully lift out the pips with the point of a knife.

Work the cream cheese with salt and black pepper to taste, put it into a cone of greaseproof paper and fill the grapes, allowing the cheese to come well above the top of each grape. Dip them into the salted almonds and serve on cocktail sticks or in small paper cases.

Cassolettes of cucumber

3 or 4 cucumbers (according to size)
croûtes of toast, or fried bread
pimiento, or strips of chilli skin (to decorate)
1 pint aspic jelly
small cress (to garnish)

Fluted and plain cutters

Method
Cut the cucumbers in 1-inch thick slices, stamp into cases using a fluted cutter for the outside and a smaller, plain one for the inside; do not cut all the way through as cases must have bases. Discard seeds. Cook cucumber cases in boiling salted water for 5 minutes, then drain and refresh them. Prepare the fillings (see below).

Then place each cucumber case on a croûte and fill with the chosen mixture, doming it slightly on top. Decorate with rounds of pimiento or crossed strips of chilli skin and baste with cold liquid aspic. Garnish cases with cress and serve them well chilled.

> **Cassolettes** are individual containers (casseroles) and this recipe is so called because the cucumber cases take the place of true cassolettes.

CASSOLETTE FILLINGS

Mushroom filling

4 oz mushrooms
1 oz butter
1 teaspoon flour
3–4 tablespoons milk, or stock
salt and pepper
1 teaspoon chopped mint

Method
Wash mushrooms and chop finely. Melt butter, add mushrooms and cook until all the moisture has been driven off. Draw pan aside, stir in the flour

and milk (or stock). Season and bring mixture to the boil. Add the chopped mint and allow mixture to cool before putting it into the cucumber cases.

Cheese and shrimp filling

1 packet of Demi-Sel, or cream, cheese (2–3 oz)
salt and pepper
4 oz shelled shrimps

Method
Work the cream cheese with seasoning to taste and add the shelled shrimps.

Chicken and ham or tongue filling

2 oz cooked chicken (minced)
2 oz cooked ham, or tongue (minced)
1 anchovy fillet (minced)
mayonnaise (to bind)
salt and pepper

Method
Mix the chicken, ham (or the tongue) and anchovy together, bind with the mayonnaise and season well.

Tomatoes bruxelloise

8 even-size tomatoes
salt and pepper
1 small clove of garlic
8 oz frozen prawns, or shrimps (chopped)
2 tablespoons double cream
1 bunch of watercress (to garnish)

For mayonnaise
2 egg yolks
salt and pepper
mustard
½ pint olive oil
about 1½ tablespoons tarragon vinegar

Method
Scald and skin the tomatoes, slice off the tops, scoop out and discard the seeds; season the insides and set aside.

To prepare the mayonnaise: cream the yolks well with the seasonings, add the oil slowly, beating well between each addition, and add the vinegar when it begins to thicken.

Crush the garlic with a little salt and add it to the mayonnaise with the chopped prawns

and cream. Fill tomatoes with the mixture, replacing the tops. Dish up and decorate with the bunch of watercress.

Danish tartlets

For shortcrust pastry
4 oz flour
2½ oz mixed lard and butter
1 egg yolk
1 tablespoon water

For filling
1 small jar of smoked cod's roe
2 oz unsalted butter (creamed)
salt and pepper
lemon juice
2 small firm tomatoes (skinned and sliced)
2 tablespoons finely chopped browned almonds

8–9 tartlet tins

Method
Make up the pastry, line on to tin and bake blind. Leave to cool, then turn out.

To prepare the filling: sieve and work the cod's roe with the creamed butter; season to taste and add a few drops of lemon juice. Fill the pastry cases with this mixture and arrange a slice of tomato on top of each. Finish with chopped almonds around the outside edges.

Stuffed avocado pears

3 avocado pears
1 packet of cream cheese (2–3 oz)
1–2 teaspoons anchovy essence
6 black olives (chopped)
juice of 1 lemon
lettuce leaves (to garnish)
¼ pint vinaigrette dressing

Method
Work the cream cheese with the anchovy essence and add the chopped olives. Halve, skin and remove the stones from the avocados. Fill the cavities with the cream cheese mixture and re-shape. Roll each avocado quickly in the lemon juice and wrap in transparent wrapping paper (Saran wrap) or wet greaseproof paper to exclude the air. Keep them refrigerated until ready to serve.

Arrange crisp lettuce leaves on a serving platter, slice the avocados in rounds, place on the lettuce and spoon over the vinaigrette dressing.

Eggs en gelée (eggs in aspic)

4–5 small eggs (new-laid)
2 pints chicken aspic (cool but liquid)
4–5 slices of ham (wafer-thin)
1 small lettuce, or chopped aspic (to garnish)

4–5 oval dariole moulds (about 2½ inches deep)

These are soft-boiled eggs (eggs mollet) rolled in slices of ham and set in individual moulds.

Method

Soft boil eggs, peel carefully and keep in cold water until wanted. Have ready the aspic, pour enough into each mould to cover the bottom by a good ¼ inch; leave to set.

Drain eggs and dry them thoroughly, wrap each one in a slice of ham and put into a mould. Fill to the brim with cool aspic, then leave it to set.

Turn out eggs, arrange them in a serving dish, garnish with lettuce leaves or chopped aspic.

Watchpoint These individual tin moulds are known as deep oval darioles. The eggs must be small (from pullets) so that once in the moulds they do not rise over the edge. Otherwise they will not sit flat when turned out.

Seafood cocktail

8 oz frozen prawns, or scampi
1–2 tablespoons water with squeeze of lemon juice (for scampi)–optional
1 medium-size jar of mussels
1 small can crab claw meat
1 small can tunny fish
1 head of celery
1 small lettuce
French dressing

Prawns can, of course, be used alone for this type of cocktail.

Method

Open and drain mussels, rinse if preserved in brine. If using scampi, poach in oven with 1–2 tablespoons water with a squeeze of lemon juice. Cool in the liquid. For prawns, thaw out overnight in the refrigerator. Divide crab meat into 4–6 pieces, and tunny fish into large flakes.

Cut celery into bâtons (short match-shaped pieces). Soak in iced water for 30 minutes. Wash lettuce well, tear in small pieces.

Make French dressing and season very well. Turn fish into a bowl, drain and dry celery and add to fish. Mix with enough dressing to coat mixture well. Pile into goblets with the lettuce for serving.

Couronne of shrimps in aspic

6 oz shrimps or prawns (shelled)
4 tomatoes
1 head of celery, or 1 bunch of watercress
¼ pint mayonnaise

For aspic jelly
1½ pints well-seasoned fish, or light chicken stock
1½ oz gelatine
2 egg whites
¼ pint white wine
squeeze of lemon juice

Ring, or border, mould (1½–1¾ pints capacity)

Method

First prepare aspic jelly: put the stock and gelatine into a scalded pan and dissolve it over gentle heat. Whip the egg whites to a froth and add them to the pan with the wine and lemon juice; whisk over steady heat until boiling point is reached, then allow liquid to boil to the top of the pan undisturbed. Draw pan aside without breaking the crust on top and leave jelly to settle. Then boil it up twice more in the same way, leave it to stand for 5 minutes, pour it through a scalded cloth and reserve. Scald and skin the tomatoes, cut them in four, scoop out the seeds into a small strainer and reserve the juice.

Line the mould with a little cool aspic, arrange the quarters of tomato on this, rounded side down, and with the points towards the outer rim of the mould. Spoon over enough cold but still liquid aspic to hold the tomatoes in position and leave to set. Fill the mould alternately with shrimps (or prawns) and cool aspic, and leave to set.

Cut the celery into 2-inch lengths, then shred them into julienne strips. Leave these to soak and curl up in ice-cold water for about 30 minutes, then drain thoroughly.

To turn out the mould dip it into warm water, put your serving plate or dish over it, quickly turn it over; the jelly should slide out easily. Fill the centre with the celery curls (or washed sprigs of watercress). Mix the mayonnaise with the juice strained from the tomato seeds and serve this separately, and brown bread and butter.

Peach salad

1 white-fleshed peach per person
lettuce leaves (for serving)

For dressing
1 teaspoon curry powder
2 tablespoons port
1 tablespoon apricot jam
¼ pint double cream

Method

First prepare the dressing: warm curry powder, port and jam together until the jam has melted, then strain mixture through a piece of muslin. Whip cream until it begins to thicken, then stir in the strained dressing mixture.

Scald and peel the peaches, cut them in half and remove the stones. Arrange these peach halves on the lettuce leaves and spoon dressing over them.

Roulades of ham

8 thin slices of ham
4 tablespoons long grain rice
1 can tunny fish (7½ oz)
2 caps of pimiento (chopped)
good ¼ pint thick mayonnaise
about 1¾ pints chicken, or veal, aspic (cool)

Method

Boil the rice until just tender (about 12 minutes), then drain, rinse and dry. Break tunny fish into flakes with a fork, mix into the rice, add the chopped pimiento and enough mayonnaise to bind. Season well.

Spread out the ham slices on a board, divide the mixture between them and roll them up like fat cigars. Arrange in a deep dish, then chill.

Have ready the cool aspic, then pour it carefully into the dish to cover the roulades completely. Leave it to set.

Seafood cocktail is a popular favourite

Unusual cold appetisers shown above are grapefruit and green grape salad, and pears in tarragon cream dressing

Grapefruit and green grape salad

3 large grapefruit
6–8 oz green grapes
little sugar

For dressing
3–4 tablespoons olive, or salad, oil
about 2 tablespoons lemon juice
caster sugar and salt (to taste)
pepper (ground from mill)
1 teaspoon fresh, or bottled, mint (chopped)

Choose thin-skinned and heavy grapefruit.

Method
Cut the grapefruit in half and prepare by segmenting in usual way. Dip grapes in boiling water, then peel and pip. To remove pips easily, flick them out with pointed end of potato peeler. Put 1 dessertspoon of grapes in the centre of each grapefruit half. Dust with sugar and chill.

To make dressing: combine all the ingredients, whisk well. Taste and correct seasoning.

Pour tablespoon of dressing over grapefruit before serving.

Crab ramekins

8 oz white crab meat
1 teaspoon tomato purée
1 glass sherry
1 can consommé (about 10¾ fl oz)

8 ramekin dishes

Method
Mix the tomato purée with the sherry and gently stir in the consommé. Lift the crab meat with a fork into the ramekin cases; this is to make sure that the crab meat does not get tightly packed.

Spoon over the prepared consommé and put into refrigerator to set for at least 1 hour.

Pears in tarragon cream dressing

3–4 pears
lettuce leaves (optional)
paprika pepper (optional)

For tarragon cream dressing
1 egg
2 rounded tablespoons caster sugar
3 tablespoons tarragon vinegar
salt and pepper
¼ pint double cream

Use ripe, juicy pears such as Comice (one half per person).

Method
First prepare dressing: break egg into a bowl and beat with a fork. Add sugar and gradually add the vinegar. Stand bowl in a pan of boiling water. Stir the mixture until beginning to thicken, then draw off heat and continue to stir. When mixture has consistency of thick cream, take basin out of pan, stir for a few seconds longer; season lightly and leave till cold.

Partially whip cream and fold into the dressing.

Peel pears, cut in half and, with a teaspoon, scoop out cores and fibrous threads which run from core to stalk. If using lettuce leaves, lay one or two on individual serving plates, breaking spines, so that they lie flat. Place half pear in centre of each, rounded side up. Before serving coat each pear with 1 tablespoon of dressing. Shake a little paprika over the top.

The dressing can be made up (without cream) in large quantities and stored, when cold, in a screw-top jar in the refrigerator. It will keep for 2–3 weeks. When needed, take out required amount and add cream.

HOT APPETISERS

Mushroom beignets and devil sauce dip

¾ lb firm button mushrooms
fritter batter 1, or 2 (see recipes on page 99)
deep fat (for frying)
fried parsley (to garnish)

For devil sauce dip
½ pint mayonnaise, or boiled dressing
1 tablespoon finely chopped pickles
1 tablespoon finely chopped parsley
1 clove of garlic (crushed)
1 teaspoon grated onion
1 tablespoon chopped capers
1 tablespoon chopped olives
salt and pepper

Method
Trim the stalks of the mushrooms, wash quickly in salted water and dry well. Prepare the fritter batter, cover and stand in a warm place for 30–40 minutes. Combine ingredients for dip and season well. Dip each mushroom into the batter and fry in deep fat. Drain on absorbent paper and serve on cocktail sticks. Garnish with fried parsley and hand devil sauce dip separately.

Mushroom tartlets

4 oz quantity of shortcrust pastry (see Danish tartlets, page 17)
½ lb firm mushrooms
1–2 oz butter (to sauté)
salt and pepper
1 tablespoon tomato chutney
dash of Tabasco sauce
2 oz anchovy butter

8–9 tartlet tins

Method
Prepare the pastry, line tartlet tin and bake blind. Leave to cool, then turn out.

Slice the mushrooms thickly and sauté in the butter. Season well, add chutney and Tabasco.

Put a spoonful of the hot mushroom mixture in each pastry case. Just before serving put a pat of anchovy butter on top of each tartlet.

Shrimps Mariette, served hot, make an unusual appetiser

Asparagus nordaise

1 bundle of asparagus
2 oz mushrooms
1¼ oz butter
salt and pepper
½ oz flour
5 fl oz top of milk
1½ oz grated cheese
hot buttered toast (for serving)

This quantity makes approximately 8 servings.

Method
Trim, cook and drain the asparagus. Wash and cut the mushrooms into thick slices, add to ¾ oz of the butter, melted, season and cook slowly with the pan lid on for 5–6 minutes.

Melt the remaining ½ oz butter in a pan, add the flour, mix together, then pour on the milk. Stir sauce until boiling; add the cheese and seasoning.

Arrange the mushrooms, and then 1–2 asparagus tips, on fingers of hot buttered toast. Spoon sauce over each one and glaze them under the grill.

Shrimps Mariette

4 oz shelled fresh, or frozen, shrimps
round croûtes of bread (1–1½ inches in diameter)
salt
pinch of pepper, or cayenne pepper, or Tabasco sauce
½ oz butter

For cheese cream
½ oz butter
½ oz flour
¼ pint creamy milk
1½ oz cheese (grated)
salt and pepper
English mustard

Method
Heat some oil or butter and fry the croûtes until golden-brown, drain and keep warm. Toss the shrimps over the heat with the seasoning and butter and, when this mixture is thoroughly hot, pile it up on the croûtes. Put these in a flameproof dish and keep warm while preparing the cheese cream. Proceed as if making a white sauce; finish by gradually beating in the grated cheese. Season lightly and add mustard to taste. Spoon this cheese cream over the prepared croûtes and brown well under the grill. Serve very hot.

Curried fish croquettes

½ lb fresh haddock fillet
1 blade of mace
1 oz butter
1 shallot (finely chopped)
1 teaspoon curry powder
1 oz flour
4 fl oz milk
salt and pepper
½ egg (beaten)
deep fat (for frying)

For coating
1 egg (beaten)
dried white breadcrumbs

Method
Poach the haddock, with the mace to flavour, in moderate oven at 350°F or Mark 4 for 10–15 minutes or until tender, then drain, remove skin and bones, and flake flesh. Melt half the butter, add the shallot and cook for 2–3 minutes. Add the curry powder and cook a further minute. Blend in the flour and milk, stir over heat until boiling and allow to simmer for a minute or so. Put flaked fish into the sauce a little at a time. Season to taste and add beaten egg. Turn mixture on to a plate and allow it to get quite cold. Divide it into dessert-spoonfuls and roll into croquettes (cork shapes) on a floured board. Coat with the whole beaten egg and crumbs and fry in deep fat until crisp.

Scampi with Alabama dip

This recipe for scampi with a tasty Alabama sauce makes an extremely appetising dip for a party.

1 lb scampi (shelled)
fritter batter (see page 99)
deep fat (for frying)

For Alabama dip
½ green pepper (chopped)
4 sticks of celery (chopped)
1 clove of garlic (crushed)
½ cup boiled dressing
1 cup tomato chilli sauce
1 tablespoon grated horseradish

Method
Mix together all ingredients for the dip and set aside. Coat the scampi in batter and fry in deep fat until golden-brown; drain well. Serve on cocktail sticks

PATES AND TERRINES

When terrine maison is cold remove fat from around the sides (see recipe opposite)

Pâtés are savoury mixtures made principally from either chicken, calves or pigs liver with the addition of other meat, poultry or game. They can be smooth and velvety, or coarse in texture. They are served cold as a first course, either scooped from the pot with a spoon or cut in slices, and should be served on indi-vidual plates, with hot toast and pats of fresh butter served separately.

A more substantial pâté (similar to a galantine) is served as a main course with salads, or as a dish for the buffet table. This type is some-times called a terrine after the glazed earthenware casserole in which it is cooked. A terrine can have sliced meat or game between the farce and all pâtés of this sort are lightly pressed after cooking to make them easier to slice.

The meats for both pâtés and terrines should be well seasoned and have a pro-portion of fat, a dash of brandy or sherry being added for additional flavour and also in order to help them keep.

Pâtés should be cooked tightly sealed to see that the mixture fills the casserole, and a luting paste used to seal it well. This is a paste of flour and water mixed together to a soft, putty-like consistency and spread with the fingers on the join between the lid and casserole. The casserole is then put into a roasting tin half-filled with hot water, ie., a bain marie; the whole is then put into the oven and cooked according to the recipe.

Terrine maison (right), terrine of pork and chicken and calves liver pâté (overleaf) are often considered more suitable for serving as a main course.

Simple terrine

1 lb veal, or pork (minced)
8 oz sausage meat
1 small onion (finely chopped)
8 oz pigs, or lambs, liver (minced)
2 hard-boiled eggs (chopped)
1 tablespoon mixed herbs (chopped)
1 teacup of breadcrumbs
salt and pepper
pinch of ground mace
6 oz thin streaky bacon rashers (unsmoked)
1 bayleaf
luting paste

Method

Mix veal or pork, sausage meat and onion together. Add minced liver. Chop eggs and add to the mixture with herbs, breadcrumbs, seasoning and mace. Mix thoroughly.

Use the bacon rashers to line a terrine or ovenproof casserole, then fill with the liver mixture. Put a bayleaf on top, seal with a luting paste of flour and water and cook in a bain marie in the oven at 325°F or Mark 3 for 1–1½ hours.

Press until cold (using about a 4 lb weight), then turn out and slice for serving.

Terrine maison

8 oz thin streaky bacon rashers (unsmoked)
8 oz shredded raw game (hare, rabbit, or pigeon, or lean pork, or raw gammon rasher)
1 small wineglass sherry, or port (optional)
1 bayleaf
¼ pint jellied stock
luting paste

For farce
8 oz pigs liver (minced)
8 oz veal (minced)
8 oz fat pork (minced)
1 small onion (finely chopped)
1 dessertspoon fresh herbs (chopped), or ½ this quantity if using dried herbs
salt and pepper

Method

Remove rind from bacon rashers and line them into a terrine. Work the minced meats and pork fat with the onion and herbs. Season.

Pour the wine over the shredded game and season to taste.

Put a layer (about a third) of the liver farce into the terrine or casserole. Press down well. Scatter half the shredded game on top and repeat these layers, ending with a layer of farce. Smooth the top and press on a bayleaf. Cover with lid and seal with a luting paste.

Cook in a bain marie in the oven at 325°F–350°F or Mark 3–4 for 1½–2 hours, or until firm to the touch. Remove lid, press well (using about a 4 lb weight). When cold, remove any fat round the sides and fill up with the jellied stock. Leave until quite set before turning out.

Luting paste is a flour and water mixture of a consistency similar to that of scone dough. To seal a casserole or terrine, put 3–4 oz flour into a bowl and mix quickly with cold water to a firm dough (4 oz flour will take ⅛ pint water).

First remove the rind from bacon rashers and then line them into a terrine or casserole

After mincing the meats and mixing them with the herbs and onion, shred the game. Pour over the wine and season

Layer the liver stuffing and shredded game in terrine or casserole; start and end with stuffing. Smooth the top and add the bayleaf. Then seal lid with a little of the luting paste

After cooking the terrine in a bain marie, remove the lid and press well (using about a 4 lb weight).

Terrine of pork

1 lb pork fillets
8 oz streaky bacon rashers
  (unsmoked)

For farce
1 small onion (finely chopped)
1 oz butter, or bacon fat
4 oz flat mushrooms (chopped)
1 dessertspoon fresh mixed herbs
  (chopped), or $\frac{1}{2}$ this quantity if
  dried
4 oz calves, or lambs, liver
  (minced)
4 oz pork (minced), or sausage
  meat
1 teacup of fresh white
  breadcrumbs
1 tablespoon brandy, or 2 of
  sherry
about 12 pistachio nuts
  (blanched and halved) –
  optional
salt
pepper (ground from mill)
luting paste

*Rectangular terrine, or medium-size
loaf tin*

Method
Slit pork fillets and then beat
to flatten them out (the butcher
will do this for you). Remove
rind from bacon, spread out on
a board with a palette knife and
use to line base and sides of a
terrine or loaf tin.

To prepare farce : soften onion
in butter or bacon fat and add
chopped mushrooms. Cook
briskly for 3–4 minutes, then add
herbs and turn mixture on to a
plate to cool. Add minced
liver to the minced pork or
sausage meat, the mushroom
mixture and breadcrumbs. Add
brandy or sherry and the pistachio nuts. Season well.

Put a third of the farce in
bottom of lined terrine or loaf
tin, cover with about half the
pork fillets, then add another
layer and the rest of the fillets.
Cover with the remaining
farce. If any bacon rashers
are left, lay these on top of the
farce. Put on the lid and seal
with a luting paste of flour and
water. If using a tin, cover with
a double sheet of greaseproof
paper and a sheet of foil.

Set in a bain marie and cook
in the oven set at 325°F or
Mark 3 for 1–1$\frac{1}{2}$ hours. Then
press lightly (not more than
3–4 lb weight) until cold.

To serve, turn out and cut into
slices about $\frac{1}{4}$-inch thick. Serve
with salad.

Country-style pâté (1) (Pâté de campagne)

1 lb veal, or pork (minced)
8 oz pigs liver (minced)
4 oz pork fat (minced)
1 shallot (finely chopped)
1 large wineglass port wine
about $\frac{1}{4}$ of a small white loaf
  (crusts removed)
3 eggs (beaten)
small pinch of allspice (Jamaican
  pepper)
1 teaspoon marjoram, or thyme
  (chopped)
pinch of salt
6–8 rashers of streaky bacon

Medium-size loaf tin

Method
Put the veal and pigs liver, pork
fat and shallot into a bowl. Pour
the port over the bread and
leave until thoroughly soaked ;
add this to the meats with the
beaten eggs, allspice, herbs and
salt. Work together in electric
blender, or beat thoroughly.
Line the loaf tin with the bacon
rashers, fill with the mixture and
press well down. Smooth the
top, cover with foil or tie on a
double sheet of greaseproof
paper. Cook in a bain marie for
1$\frac{1}{4}$–1$\frac{1}{2}$ hours at 350°F or Mark
4. The pâté is cooked when firm
to the touch. Press the pâté in
the tin with a light weight
(about 2 lb) and leave until
cold. Then turn out and cut into
slices for serving, or store,
covered, with clarified butter.

Country-style pâté (2) (Pâté de campagne)

1 lb veal (minced)
8 oz raw ham (minced)
1 lb pork (minced)
8 oz pigs liver (minced)
6 oz pork fat (minced)
2 cloves of garlic (crushed)
good pinch of allspice (Jamaican
  pepper)
salt and pepper
1 wineglass brandy, or sherry
about 4 oz fat unsmoked bacon
1 bayleaf
clarified butter, or melted lard
luting paste

Method
Put minced meats and pork fat
into a bowl, add the crushed
cloves of garlic, allspice and

seasoning. Moisten with the
brandy or sherry.

Lay the fat bacon in the
bottom of a terrine and put in
the mixture. Press meat well
down, smooth over the top and
place the bayleaf on top. Put
on the lid, seal with a luting
paste and cook in a bain marie
in the oven for about 1$\frac{1}{2}$–1$\frac{3}{4}$
hours at 350°F or Mark 4 until
pâté is firm to the touch.

Take out of oven, remove lid,
press pâté under a moderate
weight (about 2 lb). Leave until
cold, then cover with clarified
butter or melted lard, and keep
in a cool place until wanted.

Chicken and calves liver pâté

8 oz thin streaky bacon rashers
  (unsmoked)
4 oz chicken livers (sliced)
$\frac{1}{2}$ oz butter
1 clove of garlic (crushed)
1 teaspoon thyme (chopped)
2 tablespoons parsley (chopped)

For farce
2 lb calves, or lambs, liver (in the
  piece)
milk
8 oz pork fat (minced)
8 oz lean pork (minced)
2 shallots (finely chopped)
$\frac{1}{4}$ pint double cream
2 eggs
salt
pepper (ground from mill)
1 small wineglass brandy, or
  sherry
luting paste

This rich pâté is also suitable for
serving as a first course.

Method
Remove rind from the bacon,
line a terrine with rashers.
Sprinkle with a little of the
brandy or sherry and grind over
a little pepper from the mill. Set
aside.

Remove any ducts and soak
calves or lambs liver in milk for
2 hours. Then rinse and dry
thoroughly. Cut in pieces and
pass through a mincer. Mix with
the minced fat, pork and the
shallots. If possible work for a
few seconds in an electric
blender for additional smooth-
ness. Mix in the cream, beaten
eggs and rest of brandy or
sherry. Season well.

Remove any ducts or veins

Cutting liver into pieces

Liver pâté is a good first course, served with buttered toast

Pressing the made pâté

from the chicken livers and slice. Sauté in butter for 2–3 minutes, add garlic and herbs and mix well.

Put half the farce into the terrine and scatter the liver mixture on the top. Cover with rest of the farce and put any remaining bacon rashers on the top. Cover with lid and seal with luting paste. Cook in a bain marie in the oven for 1–2 hours at 325°F or Mark 3, until firm to the touch. Remove lid, press, using about a 2 lb weight, and leave to cool. Store in a refrigerator overnight. Turn out and serve cut in slices about $\frac{1}{4}$ inch thick. Serve with salads.

Chicken liver pâté

8 oz chicken liver
1 small onion (finely chopped)
1 clove of garlic (finely chopped)
4 oz butter
salt and pepper
1 tablespoon brandy
pinch of dried thyme, or mixed
  herbs
clarified butter (see page 76)

China pot, or small cocottes

This pâté is not cooked au bain marie.

Method
Cut away any veins from liver

and chop the onion and garlic finely. Melt 1 oz butter in a pan, cook the onion and garlic until soft, then add the liver, increase the heat and sauté briskly for 2–3 minutes, when liver should be firm to the touch.

Cool the mixture and chop finely or pass through a mincer Then rub through a fine sieve or work in an electric blender. Cream the remaining butter and beat into the liver mixture. Season well and add the brandy and herbs.

Put into a china pot or small cocottes. Smooth over the top, cover with a little clarified butter.

Liver pâté

1$\frac{1}{2}$ lb pigs, or calves liver
8 oz very fat bacon (unsmoked),
  or fat from cooked ham
2–3 tablespoons double cream
  (optional)
1 dessertspoon anchovy essence

For béchamel sauce
$\frac{1}{2}$ pint milk (infused with slice of
  onion, 6 peppercorns, 1 bay-
  leaf, 1 blade of mace)
1 oz butter
1 rounded tablespoon flour
salt
pepper (ground from mill)
pinch of ground mace, or nutmeg

*1 lb cake tin, or 6-inch diameter top
  soufflé dish (No. 2 size)*

Pigs liver is excellent for pâtés, being rich and well flavoured.

Calves liver is more expensive but more delicate in flavour.

Method
Remove any ducts and cut liver into small pieces. Take two-thirds of the bacon or ham fat, cut into small pieces and pass all through a mincer and/or work in an electric blender.

To make the béchamel sauce; put milk and flavourings to infuse. Melt butter in a pan, stir in flour and gradually blend in strained milk. Stir over heat until boiling, then boil for 2 minutes. Season to taste, add ground mace or nutmeg. Turn into a dish and leave to cool.

Mix the liver with béchamel sauce, cream and anchovy essence. Slice the rest of the bacon or ham fat and use to line the bottom of the shallow tin or soufflé dish.

If liver mixture is not very smooth, pass it through a sieve or mix in electric blender. Turn into tin or dish, cover with foil, set in a bain marie half-full of hot water. Bring to boil, then put in oven for 45–50 minutes at 350°F or Mark 4, until firm to the touch. Cover with grease-proof paper, a plate or board and put a light weight (about 2 lb) on top and leave until the next day. Turn out and cut in slices for serving.

Watchpoint If pâté is to be kept for several days, cover top with a little clarified butter (see page 76) and keep in a cool place.

25

Soups

Many cooks fight shy of making their own soups because they feel this will be expensive and time-consuming. In fact, it's quite the opposite. Soups are a good standby for everyday meals and are very economical to make because they can usually be varied to include whatever ingredients you have in the house, from the stock in which meat or chicken has been cooked to the leftovers you may have from vegetables or fish dishes.

Canned or packet soups are extravagant and are best kept for an emergency, or when cooking for 1 person. Cooking times for broths are

quite lengthy but the soup can look after itself, so leaving you free to do other things. Purée and cream soups are cooked quite quickly to retain their flavour.

Make fairly large quantities of soup and store in a refrigerator (but without adding cream) for reheating as needed. A thick broth followed by bread and cheese makes a good meal in itself, whereas puree or cream soups, being lighter and more delicate in flavour, are best as a first course, especially in the evening.

Bisques, veloutés and iced soups are dealt with on pages 33–35.

BROTHS, CREAM AND PUREE SOUPS

BLENDERS AND SIEVES
A blender is invaluable if you wish to make a velvety, well-flavoured soup out of unpromising material, such as any leftovers you may have.

To make a purée use a Mouli sieve for soups that should be sieved rather than blended. First set the Mouli sieve over the bowl and pour the liquid through. Then tip in the food to be sieved a half at a time. Work the handle until it is all through before adding the second portion. It is most important that every bit goes through the sieve, otherwise the soup will lack flavour and will be too thin.

If sieving a thick soup, eg, bean or potato, sieve it into a fresh bowl and then dilute it gradually with the liquid to avoid lumps. If you haven't a Mouli sieve, rub through a sieve over a bowl as above.

BROTHS
These are thick, filling soups, made from meat or vegetables, and need long simmering on gentle heat to extract the maximum flavour from ingredients.

CREAM SOUPS
These are made mostly from green vegetables, cooked in milk and thickened with egg yolk and cream.

Sieving or blending gives them a smooth consistency. For a really excellent cream soup, use chicken or veal stock because the liquid together with egg and cream liaison gives a special smooth consistency; this type of soup is called velouté.

PUREE SOUPS
These have a farinaceous or root vegetable, or solid meat, such as game, base. After cooking they are sieved or mixed in an electric blender.

Purée and cream soups have a fairly short cooking time – between 20 and 40 minutes. Once cooked the soup should be puréed or sieved. Prolonged cooking ruins the flavour and may well spoil the consistency.

Dried vegetables, in the same way as vegetables used in broths, need long, slow cooking to make them really soft and almost falling apart before they are sieved or blended.

Gazpacho is the classic cold soup of Spain (see page 35), made of a piquant cucumber and tomato mixture

Mulligatawny

1 lb lean mutton, or lamb (a piece of double scrag is suitable)
2 onions (sliced)
1 carrot (sliced)
1 small cooking apple (sliced)
1 large tablespoon dripping, or butter
1 dessertspoon curry powder
1 rounded teaspoon curry paste
1 rounded tablespoon flour
2½ pints cold water
¼ pint milk
few drops of lemon juice

For liaison (optional)

little arrowroot
1–2 tablespoons water

This soup can be made from any kind of meat or trimmings of meat.

A good stock can be used instead of water in mulligatawny; in this case the meat will not be needed. For a richer soup, add a little cream to the milk.

A curry paste adds to the flavour; it is more spicy and blander than a curry powder and the two mix well together. This mixture, though not essential, is often used in curries.

Method

Soak meat for 1 hour in salted water. Slice vegetables and apple. Wipe and dry meat. Melt the fat in a pan and brown the meat lightly in it. Remove meat, add vegetables and apple; cook for 3–4 minutes. Add curry powder and paste.

Watchpoint The curry powder is first fried for 2–3 seconds to ensure that it is cooked.

After 2 minutes stir in the flour and pour on the water. Bring to the boil and add the meat. Cover and cook gently for 1–1½ hours. Then take out the meat and sieve or blend liquid and vegetables. If using an electric blender, add some of the meat, reserving a little for a garnish, if liked.

Rinse out pan, pour in blended soup, add the milk and bring to the boil. Add lemon juice. If you have sieved the soup, it may be necessary to thicken it with a little arrowroot slaked (mixed) in cold water.

Game soup

1–2 pigeons and/or wings and trimmings of 1 hare
1 oz butter
1 onion (sliced)
1 carrot (sliced)
2 sticks of celery (sliced)
2–3 flat, dark mushrooms (sliced)
bouquet garni
2½ pints brown stock, or water
salt and pepper
1 wineglass red wine, or 1 of brown, or golden, sherry

For liaison

1½ oz butter
1¼ oz flour

A good soup can be made out of a comparatively small quantity of game. If brown stock is not available, add 6–8 oz of lean shin of beef to strengthen the flavour.

Method

Wipe the game and brown in the butter in a pan. Remove from pan and split each pigeon in two. If using beef, brown this also and cut into pieces. Remove from pan.

Prepare the vegetables and cook in the butter (reserving the mushrooms) until brown; add game and meat, bouquet garni and stock or water. Season, cover pan and simmer for 1–1½ hours.

Strain the soup. Cut any game into shreds and set aside for garnish. Measure liquid — there should be about 2 pints. Melt half the butter for thickening in the pan, put in the mushrooms and cook briskly for 2–3 minutes, then add rest of butter and stir in the flour. Add wine, or sherry, and soup and stir until boiling.

Adjust seasoning and simmer for 5 minutes. Add shredded game and serve.

The following two recipes are both Italian. The first one, minestrone, has a meat stock base and can have pieces of bacon or ham in it, whereas minestra is purely a vegetable soup. Both these soups can be made with whatever is at hand or needs to be used from the vegetable rack.

Minestrone

2 large tablespoons white haricot beans (soaked overnight)
2–3 pints stock
2 medium-size carrots (diced)
2–3 sticks of celery (sliced)
1 large onion (sliced)
2–3 tablespoons oil
2 leeks (sliced)
2 rashers of fat bacon (cut in small pieces)
1–2 cloves of garlic (crushed)
¼ of a small cabbage (shredded)
1 small can tomatoes, or
    1 rounded dessertspoon tomato purée
bouquet garni
salt and pepper
Parmesan cheese (grated)

Method

Soak beans overnight then drain, put in a pan with about 1 pint of stock, bring slowly to the boil and simmer for at least 30 minutes. Meanwhile dice the carrots and slice the celery and onion. Heat oil in a stewpan, put in the prepared vegetables and fry gently for about 5 minutes.

Slice the leeks and cut bacon into small pieces. Crush garlic and shred cabbage.

Pour rest of the stock into the pan and bring to the boil; add sliced leeks, tomatoes, or purée, and the bouquet garni. Season and add the beans with their stock. Simmer gently for 30 minutes, then add the shredded cabbage. Cook gently until the vegetables are thoroughly cooked and soup is of a good flavour.

A bowl of grated Parmesan should be served separately.

Minestra

1 carrot
1 onion
2 sticks of celery
2 tablespoons oil
about 2¼ pints water
½ bayleaf
1 small leek
6 French beans, or brussels sprouts
salt and pepper
2 small potatoes
1 clove of garlic
2 tomatoes
1 rounded dessertspoon parsley (chopped)
Parmesan cheese (grated)

Method

Cut the carrot, onion and celery into medium-thick julienne strips. Heat the oil in a stewpan, put in the vegetable strips and fry until just turning colour; shake and stir occasionally.

Pour on water, add bayleaf. Cut leek, beans or brussels

Hearty onion soup is a classic French dish

sprouts into shreds and add to the pan. Season lightly and simmer for 30–40 minutes.

Add potatoes, cut in strips, and simmer for a further 20 minutes. Crush garlic with a little salt. Scald tomatoes and skin, cut in quarters, flick out the seeds and cut flesh into strips or chop roughly. Add to the soup with the garlic and parsley. Simmer for a further 10 minutes, adjust seasoning and serve sprinkled with grated cheese.

More water should be added if necessary during the early stages of cooking if the soup seems over-thick.

Watchpoint To cut an onion into strips, cut in half down from crown to root. Lay onion, cut side downwards, on the board, slice fairly thinly, lengthways. The root, which holds the slices in place, can be trimmed off.

Kidney soup

8 oz kidney
2 pints brown stock
bouquet garni
1 oz butter
1 onion (chopped)
1 rounded tablespoon plain flour
1 rounded teaspoon tomato
  purée
salt and pepper
1 wineglass red wine, or golden

sherry
For liaison (optional)
little arrowroot
1 tablespoon cold water

Method

Skin and core the kidney. Soak in warm, salted water for 1 hour then drain, slice and put into a pan with half the stock and bouquet garni. Cover pan and simmer until kidney is very tender (about 1 hour). Remove bouquet garni and turn soup into a bowl.

Melt butter in the pan, add onion and fry gently until brown, then stir in flour and tomato purée. Add the remaining stock, season and stir until boiling. Add wine and kidney stock, season and simmer for 10 minutes.

Rub soup through a wire sieve or mix in an electric blender. Reheat in pan and thicken, if necessary, with a little arrowroot slaked (mixed) in cold water.

French onion soup

8 oz onions
1½ oz butter
1 tablespoon flour
2 pints stock, or water

salt and pepper
1 bayleaf
1–2 rolls (sliced), or 2 slices of
  stale bread (cut into four)
grated Cheddar, or Gruyère

One of the best and most simple vegetable soups to make.

Method

Chop onions. Heat a pan, drop in the butter and when foaming put in the onions. Lower heat and cook onions slowly for 15–20 minutes until golden-brown, stirring occasionally with a metal spoon. Stir in the flour and cook for a further 2–3 minutes. Heat stock or water to boiling point.

Draw pan aside, pour on boiling liquid, add seasoning and bayleaf. Simmer, uncovered, for 30 minutes.

Have a casserole ready with the sliced rolls laid on the bottom (or the bread slices cut into four). Pour in the boiling soup, first taking out bayleaf.

Scatter grated cheese thickly over the top and cook in the oven at 400°F or Mark 6 for 10 minutes or until brown. Serve in the casserole, or in individual pots.

Watchpoint Take care when browning the onions; any scorching or burning spoils the flavour. This soup is improved by using a good stock but it holds its own even with water.

Cream of carrot soup

1 onion (finely chopped)
8 oz carrots (sliced)
1½ oz butter
1½ pints stock
pinch of sugar
salt and pepper
1 small clove of garlic (chopped, or crushed)
¼ pint creamy milk
1 tablespoon rice (cooked)
1 dessertspoon mint (chopped)

For liaison (optional)

little arrowroot
1 tablespoon water

Method

Chop onion finely, slice carrots and cook both in 1 oz of butter in a pan for 10 minutes to soften. Add the stock. Simmer for 30–40 minutes, then rub through a sieve or mix in an electric blender. Add sugar and seasoning to taste and garlic. Add milk and reheat soup; whisk in the rest of the butter, add rice and mint.

Thicken soup, if necessary, with a little arrowroot slaked in cold water before adding remaining butter. Croûtons may be used instead of rice.

Cream of sweetcorn soup

1 small can creamed sweetcorn
1 small can whole kernel sweetcorn (optional)
2 medium-size potatoes (finely sliced)
1 medium-size onion (finely sliced)
1½ oz butter
1 tablespoon flour
1 pint milk
½ pint water
1 bayleaf
salt and pepper

Whole kernel sweetcorn gives soup body, but can be omitted.

Method

Slice the potatoes and onion finely. Melt the butter in a pan, add the potatoes and onion and cook very gently until the vegetables are soft but not coloured. Stir in the flour, and add the milk, water, bayleaf and seasoning. Bring to the boil, stirring well. Add the creamed sweetcorn, simmer gently for 15–20 minutes.

Sieve soup and return to pan with the whole kernel sweetcorn, drained from the liquid. Reheat and adjust seasoning.

Cream of carrot soup – one of many good vegetable cream soups

Tomato and rice soup

1 lb ripe tomatoes
1 clove of garlic (bruised)
2 bayleaves
2 oz butter
2 onions (finely sliced)
1 dessertspoon flour
1½ pints vegetable stock, or water
1 lump of sugar
salt
black pepper (ground from mill)
1 rounded tablespoon rice
2 slices of bread
½ oz grated cheese
½ teaspoon French mustard

Method

Take three-quarters of the tomatoes, scald, skin, quarter and flick out the seeds. Put into a pan with the bruised clove of garlic, bayleaves and ¾ oz butter. Cover and simmer slowly for about 10 minutes. Rub through a sieve to a purée.

Put the sliced onions in a stewpan with another ¾ oz butter, cover and cook slowly for 15 minutes. Remove from heat, add the flour, stock or water and tomato purée. Add sugar and season. Add the rice and simmer for 20–30 minutes.

Scald and skin the remaining tomatoes. Cut into quarters, discard the seeds, cut flesh into shreds and add to the soup.

Toast the bread on one side only. Mix remaining ½ oz butter, cheese and mustard together, then spread on the untoasted side of the bread. Brown under the grill. Cut into strips and serve hot with the soup.

Cream of potato soup

1 lb medium-size potatoes
1 onion
1½ oz butter
1 bayleaf
1 pint milk
½ pint water
salt and pepper

For liaison

1–2 egg yolks
5 tablespoons double cream

Method

Slice potatoes and onion finely. Melt butter in a pan, add vegetables, cover tightly (with greaseproof paper and lid) and cook very slowly for 5–6 minutes. The vegetables must not change colour.

Add bayleaf, milk, water and seasoning. Bring to the boil, cover and simmer for 20–25 minutes until the vegetables are very soft. Take out bayleaf, rub soup through a wire sieve or work in an electric blender. Rinse out pan, add soup, reheat and adjust seasoning.

Mix the egg yolks and cream together in a bowl, add 2–3 tablespoons hot soup to the mixture, then pour back gradually into the soup, whisking well. Stir over heat until very hot but do not boil.

Watchpoint Since eggs cook below boiling point, the liaison will curdle if this point is reached.

Vegetable bortsch contains beetroot, onions, carrots, celery, parsnip, cabbage and tomatoes.

Vegetable bortsch

beetroot
onions
carrots
celery
1 parsnip
salt and pepper
stock (preferably ham), or water
cabbage (coarsely shredded)
garlic (chopped, or crushed) – to
    taste
tomatoes
sugar
little tomato purée
fresh parsley (chopped)

For liaison

little flour (optional)
sour cream

*5-inch diameter pudding basin
    (sufficient for 3 pints liquid), or
    small mixing bowl*

Quantities of vegetables should be used in the following proportions: half beetroot and of remaining half, one-third onion, one-third carrot and the last third equally divided between celery and parsnip.

Method
Cut beetroot, onions, carrots, celery and parsnip into matchsticks and pack into the basin or bowl to fill it.

Lightly season stock or water and bring to the boil. Turn the bowl of vegetables into the pan, cover and simmer for about 20–30 minutes. Coarsely shred enough cabbage to fill the bowl, add this with the garlic to taste. Continue to simmer gently, uncovered, for a further 20 minutes.

Skin sufficient tomatoes to half-fill the bowl, squeeze to remove seeds, then chop flesh very coarsely. Add to soup, season well with salt and sugar and add a little tomato purée to sharpen the flavour. Simmer for a further 10 minutes, then add a handful of chopped parsley.

The soup can be thickened lightly with a little flour mixed with a small quantity of sour cream. Otherwise serve a bowl of sour cream separately.

Watchpoint Bortsch should be slightly piquant in flavour and not sweet. Add salt and sugar until this is reached. The soup should be a thick broth of vegetables but not too solid. Dilute if necessary with additional stock.

This bortsch is improved if made the previous day.

TO SERVE WITH SOUPS

Croûtons

2–3 rounds of stale bread, crusts removed (makes enough for 4)
mixture of butter and oil (for frying)

Method
Cut the bread in small dice and fry in shallow fat deep enough to cover them (about $\frac{1}{2}-\frac{3}{4}$ inches deep); fat must be frying heat when croûtons are added. Turn them to brown evenly (this will take only a few seconds). Remove croûtons with a draining spoon, drain on absorbent paper, shake off excess fat and sprinkle with salt before serving.

Frying can be done ahead of time and croûtons reheated for 1–2 minutes in a hot oven.

Serve separately with cream or purée soups.

Potato croûtons

These are especially good with spinach, tomato or celery soup.

Parboil 2 potatoes, drain and cut into dice while hot. Fry and serve as for bread croûtons.

Cheese croûtes

Any leftover cream sauce, cheese or onion, makes a good croûte. Toast bread on one side, spread the untoasted side with sauce and sprinkle well with grated cheese. Brown well under the grill. Cut in half and then into strips. Serve hot separately with soup.

Cheese butter

Work grated cheese into a little butter, add plenty of pepper and a little salt and shape into pats. Add to a bland soup (like potato) just before serving. Any savoury butter given in the grilling chapter goes well with purée soups; choose to taste.

Three different soups: lobster bisque (left); crème St. Germain, a velouté soup (right) and iced vichyssoise (above and below)

VELOUTE, ICED AND BISQUE SOUPS

The consistency of velouté soups is described by their name meaning velvety (from the French for velvet – velours). Like velouté sauces, they are made by pouring a well-flavoured fish, veal or chicken stock on to a blond roux. This is blended, returned to the heat and stirred until boiling. Then the soup is seasoned and simmered according to the individual recipe, and completed by the addition of a liaison made of egg yolks and cream with, in some instances, a little arrowroot.

Iced soups, unlike velouté soups, are prepared in a variety of ways. Hot soups (and cold soups of the gazpacho type) may be served from a tureen at the table, but iced soups are usually served direct in individual cups.

Bisques are rich cream soups – served hot or cold – generally made from shellfish, such as prawns or lobster, and finished with a rich liaison.

VELOUTÉ SOUPS

Crème St. Germain

12 spring onions (chopped)
the heart of 1 cabbage lettuce (shredded)
1¾ pints well flavoured veal, or chicken, stock
1 pint shelled peas (preferably old and rather floury)
salt and pepper
1 oz butter
1 oz flour
1–2 egg yolks
2½ fl oz double cream

For garnish
½ pint young peas (shelled)
1 dessertspoon chopped mint

This green pea soup may also be served iced. If you plan to do this, you may omit the egg yolks and increase the quantity of cream to ¼ pint, lightly whipping it before adding it to the soup.

Method
Put onions and lettuce into a pan with the stock and peas. Season and bring to the boil. Simmer until tender (about 20 minutes). Then rub the soup through a Mouli sieve or work in an electric blender. Melt the butter in the rinsed-out pan, add the flour and blend in the liquid. Bring to the boil, cover and simmer for 5–6 minutes.

Cook the young peas in water until just tender, drain. Blend the egg yolks and cream together, add this liaison to the soup and reheat without boiling. Add the peas and sprinkle with the mint just before serving.

Walnut soup

2 oz walnut kernels (preferably fresh); dried ones should be covered with boiling water and soaked for 1 hour before using
½ pint creamy milk
1 oz butter
1 small onion (finely chopped)
1 oz flour
1½ pints strong, well-flavoured chicken stock
salt and pepper
2 egg yolks
2½ fl oz single cream
fried croûtons

This soup can also be served iced without the addition of croûtons.

Method
Remove as much skin as possible from the walnut kernels and grind them through a nut mill (or a Mouli cheese grater), or pound well. Scald the milk and pour it on to the nuts. Leave to infuse for 30 minutes.

Melt the butter, add onion and cook until softened but not coloured. Stir in the flour and, after a few seconds, pour on the stock. Blend and bring to the boil, season and simmer for 7–10 minutes. Add the walnuts and milk. Mix the egg yolks and cream together and add a little of the hot soup to this liaison before blending it into the soup. Reheat without boiling, adjust the seasoning and serve with fried croûtons.

Cream of barley soup

2 oz pearl barley (washed and soaked overnight in ½ pint water)
2 pints strong veal, or chicken, stock (well-seasoned)
1 oz butter
1 rounded tablespoon flour
salt and pepper
¼ pint creamy milk
2½ fl oz single cream

For garnish
1 carrot
1 small turnip
2 rounded tablespoons green peas

Method
Add the barley and water to the stock, cover and simmer until barley is tender, about 50–60 minutes. Then strain, reserving 1–2 tablespoons of the cooked barley. Rinse out the pan, make a roux of the butter and flour, and cook it for 2–3 seconds. Then pour on the stock. Bring to the boil, season and simmer for 5–6 minutes. Add the milk and cream and the reserved barley. Continue to simmer while preparing the garnish.

Cut the carrot and turnip into small dice or, if preferred, make small 'peas' from the outside of the turnip and the carrot using a vegetable scoop. Cook these with the green peas until just tender. Then drain, add to the soup and serve.

ICED SOUPS
Vichyssoise

the white part of 3 large leeks
1 stick of celery
2 potatoes (weighing 4–6 oz in all)
1 oz butter
2 pints jellied chicken stock
salt and pepper
¼ pint double cream
1 tablespoon snipped chives

This is the classic iced soup, of American origin, and must be made with jellied chicken stock and cream. In Britain it is not always possible to find leeks in summer, but a mild-flavoured onion such as a Spanish onion can be used instead.

Method
Slice the leeks, celery and potatoes finely and sweat vegetables in butter until just soft, without allowing them to colour.

Watchpoint While sweating the vegetables, press a piece of damp greaseproof paper right down on top of them under the lid of the pan. Stir occasionally to avoid all danger of browning.

Blend in the stock, bring to the boil, season and simmer for 12–15 minutes. Rub through a Mouli sieve or work in an electric blender. Taste for seasoning and stir in the cream. Leave soup until cold, then whisk for a few seconds and chill.

Sprinkle chives on the top of each serving. The soup should have the consistency of cream, and be smooth and bland.

Scooping out carrot 'peas' with a vegetable scoop before cooking them to garnish cream of barley and Hollandaise soups

Avocado soup

2 avocado pears
¾ pint strong, well-flavoured chicken stock (free from grease)
¼ pint double cream (lightly whipped)
½ pint plain yoghourt
½ teaspoon grated onion
1 bottle of tomato cocktail, or tomato juice (about ¼ pint)
salt and pepper
dash of Tabasco sauce

Method
Peel the avocado pears, remove the stones and mash flesh with a fork until smooth. Whisk in the chicken stock, cream, yoghourt, onion and tomato juice. Season well, adding a dash of Tabasco. If the consistency of the soup is too thick, dilute with a little more stock. Turn soup into a bowl and chill well.

Crème normande

1 large mild onion (chopped)
1 oz butter
1 tablespoon curry powder
2 dessert apples
1 dessertspoon flour
1½ pints chicken stock
1 dessertspoon cornflour
¼ pint double cream
2 egg yolks
salt and pepper
lemon juice
watercress (to garnish)

Method
Soften the onions in the butter without colouring. Add curry powder and one apple, peeled, cored and sliced. After a few minutes stir in the flour. Cook for 1 minute, then pour on the stock and add the cornflour, first slaking it with a little of the stock. Bring to the boil and simmer for 5 minutes, then add cream mixed with the egg yolks. Reheat to thicken without boiling, then put the soup through a fine sieve or blender. Season and chill.

Peel and dice the remaining apple, mix with a little lemon juice and add to the soup just before serving. Garnish with watercress leaves.

Almond and grape soup

2 oz almonds
½ pint milk
1 small onion (finely sliced)
1½ oz butter
2 good tablespoons flour
1½ pints strong chicken stock
salt and pepper
2 sticks of celery (sliced)
2 egg yolks
2–3 tablespoons double cream
1 tablespoon chopped parsley
6 oz white grapes (to garnish)

Method
Blanch and finely chop the almonds. Scald the milk, add the nuts, cover the pan and leave to infuse. Slowly cook the onion in butter until soft but not coloured. Blend in the flour and chicken stock, season and stir until boiling. Add the celery to the pan and simmer gently for 15 minutes.

Emulsify the almonds and milk in an electric blender or pass them through a fine nylon sieve. Strain the chicken broth and add it to the almond mixture. Reheat the soup, adjust the seasoning, thicken with the liaison of egg yolks and cream and chill. Serve sprinkled with parsley, with a few peeled and pipped grapes in each soup cup.

Hollandaise soup

2 pints strong chicken stock
salt and pepper
2 oz butter
2 oz flour
scant 4 fl oz single cream
2 egg yolks

For garnish
2 tablespoons shelled peas
1 rounded tablespoon carrot 'peas' (scooped out from the red part of a carrot with a vegetable scoop)
1 rounded tablespoon turnip 'peas'

This soup can also be served hot.

Method
Season stock and remove any grease. Melt the butter in a large pan, stir in flour and cook

for a few seconds. Pour on stock, blend and stir until boiling. Simmer for 10 minutes.

Meanwhile prepare and cook garnish in boiling salted water. Blend cream and egg yolks together. Skim soup, if necessary, and add liaison. Adjust seasoning and add drained garnish. Thicken the soup over heat without boiling, then chill.

Gazpacho

1 cup (3 oz) breadcrumbs
red wine vinegar (to taste)
2 cloves of garlic
salt
2 small ridge, or greenhouse, cucumbers
1 onion
1 green pepper
¼ pint salad oil
2 lb tomatoes (rubbed through a sieve)
iced water
pepper

For serving
croûtons (made from toast)
bowl of ice cubes

Method
Soak the crumbs in 2 tablespoons vinegar. Pound the garlic to a cream with 1 teaspoon of salt. Roughly chop one cucumber, the onion and half the green pepper and put them, with the crumbs, into a mortar. Pound to a paste, then rub the paste through a fine sieve. Add the oil, a few drops at a time as for mayonnaise. Taste soup and season with a little more vinegar, if necessary, and pour into a tureen.

Add the tomatoes and some iced water. The amount of water depends on the juiciness of the tomatoes, but the soup should have a fairly thin consistency. Season and chill well.

The remaining cucumber and pepper, diced, may be added to the soup after chilling or served separately. Small croûtons and a bowl of ice cubes should be handed separately (in Spain, ice cubes are added to this traditional soup before drinking it).

Cream of mushroom soup

8 oz button mushrooms
1 rounded dessertspoon arrowroot
1¾ pints strong, well-flavoured chicken stock (free from grease)
¼ pint double cream
snipped chives

Method
Wash mushrooms well but do not peel; work them in an electric blender or pass through a Mouli sieve. Slake the arrowroot with 3–4 tablespoons of the stock. Heat remaining stock, add sieved mushrooms, bring to the boil and simmer for 2–3 minutes. Add the slaked arrowroot and reboil. The soup should now have the consistency of cream.
Watchpoint If soup is not thick enough, add a little more slaked arrowroot.

Lightly whip cream and add to the soup before chilling. Garnish each serving with snipped chives.

BISQUES

Chilled prawn bisque (Bisque de crevettes glacée)

6 oz shelled prawns (chopped)
1 onion (finely chopped)
1 oz butter
2 lb tomatoes, or 1 medium-size can (1 lb 14 oz) tomatoes
3 caps of canned pimiento (chopped)
1 dessertspoon tomato purée
2–2½ pints chicken stock
arrowroot
¼ pint double cream

This soup can also be served hot.

Method
Cook the onion in the butter until softened, then add the tomatoes (skinned, cut in half and squeezed to remove the seeds). Cover the pan and slowly cook the vegetables to a pulp. Add the pimiento, tomato purée and stock. Simmer for 10–15 minutes. Then add the prawns and work in an electric blender. Thicken the soup lightly with arrowroot and chill.
Note: if a blender is not used, pass the vegetables and liquid through a fine sieve and add the prawns, finely chopped, after the soup has been thickened.

Whip the cream and stir it into the soup just before serving.

Lobster bisque

1 medium-size live lobster
3 oz butter
2 tablespoons oil
1 small onion (finely chopped)
1 wineglass sherry
2 pints fish stock

For velouté
1½ oz butter
1½ oz flour
salt and pepper
¼ pint double cream

If wished, a can of lobster claw meat may be used for this soup, but to get the very best flavour you should make it with a live lobster.

Method
If you have a live lobster, kill and split it (see page 62); remove the bag from the head (discard this) and the coral.

Make lobster butter by working the coral with 1½ oz of the butter. Set this mixture aside.

Heat the oil and 1½ oz of the butter in a large sauté pan. Put the lobster in the pan, cover and cook for 5 minutes, then add the onion and the sherry. Cover and simmer for 10–15 minutes. Take up, remove all the meat from the body and claws.
Note: if wished, some of the tail meat may be reserved for garnish, in which case cut it in slices and add to the soup just before serving.

Pound the meat or work it in an electric blender with a little of the stock.

Now prepare the velouté: melt the butter, stir in the flour, pour on the stock and any juices from the lobster pan. Bring to the boil, season and simmer for 5–6 minutes; draw aside. Add the pounded lobster and the lobster butter (or 1½ oz plain butter) in small pieces and reheat, adding the cream, but do not allow to boil. Serve at once.

Egg Cookery

Eggs are perhaps the most valuable of all basic cooking ingredients. Being high in protein content they provide an easy and quick, balanced meal and there are so many ways to cook them that you really have no excuse if you serve up nothing but plain boiled, fried or scrambled eggs for your family meals. Eggs should be eaten as fresh as possible; you can tell a new-laid one (up to one week old if kept in a cool place) by breaking the shell; if fresh, the white will cling to the yolk. To test an egg without first having to break it, plunge it into cold salted water (use kitchen salt); if very fresh the egg will sink at once; the staler it is the higher it will float (bad ones floating on top).

As eggshells are porous, a certain amount of liquid evaporates every day, resulting in a lighter egg; fresh ones when shaken should feel heavy and well filled.

An omelet, one of the most useful egg dishes, is quick, quite easy to make and delicious whether plain or stuffed. The secret lies in using really fresh eggs and a good omelet pan, which should be kept for omelets only. If the pan is used for frying other foods, it has to be washed, which can cause food to stick.

A true omelet pan is made either of thick aluminium or cast iron, with or without a non-stick finish. The characteristic of the omelet pan is its curved edge, which makes the omelet easier to turn out and gives it a better shape.

Pans come in different sizes, but a 7–8 inch diameter one is a good size and will take 3–4 eggs, which are usually enough for two people.

When buying an omelet pan, treat it before use as follows: wash it well, dry and cover the bottom with salad oil. Leave for at least 12 hours, then heat oil to frying point; remove from heat, pour off oil and wipe pan thoroughly with absorbent paper. The inside of the pan should not be washed after each use, but wiped with a damp cloth dipped in salt. This will season the pan and prevent an omelet from sticking.

BASIC METHODS

Boiled eggs (oeufs à la coque)

1 Make sure that the shells are perfectly clean. If not, wash or wipe with a damp cloth.
2 Choose an enamel pan for boiling eggs because they will blacken an aluminium one. If an aluminium pan has to be used, a little vinegar added to the water will prevent this. Vinegar will also prevent the white seeping away if the eggs crack, which is especially likely with preserved eggs.
3 Never take the eggs straight from a refrigerator or cold larder. Leave eggs at room temperature for a while, so that they are warm, before putting them into boiling salted water.
4 Boil eggs steadily but gently for 3½–4 minutes according to taste. Allow 3½ minutes for a lightly-boiled egg, and 4 minutes for one that is well set. Take the time from when the water reboils after adding them to pan.

It is generally reckoned that the slower the white cooks, the more digestible the egg. In this case, put the eggs into a pan of cold water and bring them slowly to the boil. Allow a further 30 seconds of gentle simmering, when the eggs will be lightly cooked.

Coddled eggs

Put into a pan of boiling water, cover, take off heat and leave for 5 minutes. Eggs cooked in this way will have a soft, creamy white and are ideal for children and invalids.

To make sure egg is cooked if you have no timer, an old-fashioned trick is to lift the egg from the water and count eight. If the shell becomes dry, the egg is coddled.

The mythical superiority of brown eggs may have arisen as a result of the attractive colour of their shells

Soft-boiled eggs (oeufs mollets)

Many dishes, both hot and cold, can be made from soft-boiled eggs. For these dishes the eggs are cooked a little differently.

1 Put them into a pan of boiling water and allow 5 minutes from time water comes back to the boil. Remember, though, that a small egg will take less time to cook through.

2 Take them out at once and put into cold water for 7–8 minutes. Then peel carefully.

3 The eggs may be used straight away. If you want them hot, they may be put (unpeeled) into hand-hot water for 5 minutes. If you want them cold, peel and leave in cold water for several hours until required.

As these eggs are delicate to peel, first crack the shells gently all over with the back of a spoon. This will soften the shell and make it easier to take off without breaking the egg. Once cracked all over, peel off a band across the middle of the egg, and pull off the shell at each end.

Hard-boiled eggs (oeufs durs)

Always put them in boiling water and allow 10–12 minutes steady boiling, but no longer, because over-boiling discolours the yolks and toughens the whites. Plunge them at once into cold water, which will make the eggs easier to peel, however fresh they are. Peel as for soft-boiled eggs.

To stuff hard-boiled eggs: cut them lengthways after peeling and scoop out the yolks with the handle of a teaspoon. Put the whites at once into a bowl of cold water to keep them tender and white.

When required, carefully lift out whites and lay them, cut side downwards, on a clean cloth to drain. If serving cold stuffed eggs, it is easier if the halved whites are arranged in place on the serving dish before filling with the prepared mixture. This will give a better and neater result. Stick them to the surface of the dish with a little of the filling.

Once the halved whites are filled, an alternative way of dishing them up is to put them together to reshape the egg.

Dish up as for the halved whites. If serving boiled eggs under a sauce, especially if it has to be glazed or browned, the eggs should be slightly softer. Before coating them with a sauce, dry eggs well on absorbent paper or a cloth, otherwise the sauce will slide off. Make sure, too, that the sauce, particularly mayonnaise, is of a good coating consistency.

Buttered or scrambled eggs (oeufs brouillés)

These should be soft, creamy and melting and this depends largely on the amount of butter added. Don't add too much milk as this is inclined to give a curdled, watery effect.

To 4 eggs allow 1 good oz of butter and 3 tablespoons of single cream or creamy milk. Beat eggs well with a fork, adding milk, salt and pepper and half butter in small pieces.

Melt remaining butter in a pan, pour in the egg mixture and cook over moderate heat, stirring and scraping the mixture from the bottom of the pan with a spoon, preferably metal, to get thick, creamy flakes. Take care not to overcook eggs. Turn them on to buttered toast while they are still creamy.

Here's an alternative way for those who do not like too rich a mixture. Put the butter and milk into the pan first (here a little more milk may be used) and, when hot, break in the eggs and allow the white to set lightly before stirring. Then season and stir mixture to break up eggs and continue cooking until the scrambled eggs are thick.

Fried eggs (oeufs frits)

You can fry these eggs in either shallow or deep fat.

Shallow frying: make sure that the fat (not less than $\frac{1}{4}$ inch in the pan) is not too hot. If it is, it will toughen the whites. Break the eggs, one at a time, into a cup and gently slide them into the pan. Cook on moderate heat, basting with the fat, until both white and yolk are set. To speed the process, the pan may be put under a hot

grill for a few seconds.

Deep fat frying: half fill a small deep pan with fat; heat until 400°F (oil to 360°–375°F – see pages 96–98). Gently tip in the eggs and cook for 2–3 minutes until golden-brown. Drain the eggs very carefully. For the best results, do not fry more than two at a time.

Poached eggs (oeufs pochés)

New-laid eggs are best for poaching, otherwise the white will detach itself from the yolk. Poach eggs in a saucepan or deep frying pan filled with boiling water – add about 1 tablespoon vinegar to 1 quart of water. Do not add salt as this tends to toughen the white.

Keep heat low and water gently simmering, then break eggs into pan and poach for about $3\frac{1}{2}$–$4\frac{1}{2}$ minutes until firm. Lift out with a draining spoon or fish slice and drain thoroughly before dishing up.

Egg poachers are available but the above method is satisfactory as the eggs do not stick (which sometimes happens in a poacher) and are less obviously 'moulded' in shape.

French poached eggs are well-shaped, plump and round. The above directions apply except that the eggs should be poached, one at a time, in deep water which has been stirred gently immediately beforehand. The action of the water brings the white up, over and round the yolk. The egg is then lifted out and put into warm water unless it is served immediately.

Poached eggs, like soft-boiled eggs, can be kept several hours in water before use. To reheat the eggs, lift into a bowl of hand-hot water and leave 4–5 minutes before taking them out and draining.

For cold poached eggs the whites must be really firm, the yolks should just give under gentle pressure.

For hot poached eggs to be served under a sauce, especially if it has to be glazed or browned, the eggs should be slightly softer. Dry eggs well on absorbent paper or cloth before dishing and coating with a sauce, otherwise the sauce will slide off.

Baked eggs (shirred eggs— oeufs en cocotte or sur-le-plat)

These are delicious and may be cooked and served in individual buttered cocottes, ramekins or soufflé dishes or in a shallow flameproof dish.

In their simplest form they have a little melted butter and cream, or creamy milk, poured over the yolks after the eggs have been broken into a buttered and seasoned dish. They are then baked in the oven at 350°–375°F or Mark 4–5 for 6–8 minutes.

For a more substantial dish and an excellent way of using up leftovers, just break eggs on to a savoury mixture.

If eggs are cooked in shallow flameproof dishes they can be started on top of the stove and finished in the oven, when the white has begun to set, for 4–5 minutes further cooking.

Watchpoint Do not over-cook as eggs will continue cooking after the dish has been removed from the oven.

EGG DISHES

The following 2 recipes are for cold dishes using poached, and soft-boiled or poached, eggs respectively.

Eggs Mikado

5 eggs
4 oz long grain Patna rice
2 caps of canned pimiento (shredded)
2–3 sticks of celery, or 1 small head (shredded)
2–3 tablespoons French dressing
¼ pint thick mayonnaise
1 egg (hard-boiled)
1 tablespoon parsley (chopped) mixed with pinch of herbs (freshly chopped) – optional
watercress (to garnish) – optional

The leftover white of the hard-boiled egg may be shredded and added to the rice salad with the pimiento and celery.

Left: *Eggs mollets à l'indienne – in a curry mayonnaise, garnished with pimiento and watercress.* Right: *To finish eggs soubise, lay onion rings round the eggs and onion sauce*

Method
Poach the eggs and keep in cold water until wanted.

Cook rice in plenty of boiling, salted water for about 10 minutes until tender; drain, rinse with hot water, then drain and dry thoroughly.

Fork the prepared pimiento and celery into the rice and moisten with French dressing. Spoon this salad down centre of a serving dish. Drain and dry eggs and set them on the rice.

Add 1 dessertspoon of hot water to the mayonnaise to thin it, if necessary, and use a little to coat each egg, yet still allow salad to be seen.

Peel the hard-boiled egg, take out the yolk and press it through a sieve over the dish, then sprinkle with the parsley and herbs. Garnish dish with watercress, if wanted.

Eggs mollets à l'indienne

5 eggs
4 oz long grain Patna rice (cooked, drained and dried)
2–3 tablespoons French dressing
½ pint thick mayonnaise
salt and pepper

To garnish

pimiento (shredded)
watercress

For curry mixture
1 shallot (finely chopped)
1 tablespoon oil
1 dessertspoon curry powder
1 teaspoon paprika pepper
1 teaspoon tomato purée (diluted with ½ cup of water), or ½ cup of tomato juice
2 slices of lemon
1 dessertspoon apricot jam

Method
First prepare the curry mixture: soften the shallot in oil, add curry powder and paprika and after 3–4 seconds the remaining ingredients. Stir well and sim-mer for 4–5 minutes. Strain and set mixture aside.

Softboil or poach the eggs. Moisten the rice with a little French dressing; arrange down the centre of a serving dish.

Add enough of the curry mixture to the mayonnaise to flavour it well. Adjust seasoning and spoon curry mayonnaise over the eggs. Garnish with the pimiento and watercress.

The following 2 recipes call for poached or soft-boiled eggs according to the dish.

Eggs soubise

5–6 eggs
2 Spanish onions
little egg white
seasoned flour
deep fat (for frying)

For soubise sauce
½ lb onions (chopped)
1¾ oz butter
1 rounded tablespoon flour
¾ pint milk

One of the best hot egg dishes. The creamy sauce contrasts well with the crisp brown onions.

Method
First make soubise sauce: blanch chopped onions, drain well and simmer in 1 oz butter until soft but not brown. Mix in an electric blender or rub through a strainer.

Melt remaining butter in a pan; add flour, then milk, and stir until boiling. Then add the onion purée and cook for 4–5 minutes until creamy; keep hot.

Slice Spanish onions and push out into rings, moisten with a little raw egg white and dust well with seasoned flour until they are dry. Fry in deep fat, keep hot.

Poach eggs and drain well. Arrange them in a dish, coat with the sauce and arrange the onion rings around them.

Leftover egg yolks can be used up in custards, rich pastry, mayonnaise, or scrambled eggs – whichever best suits your budget. To keep yolks in good condition work a pinch of salt into them and store in a small covered container in the refrigerator (1-2 days). Egg whites provide an excuse to make meringues. The whites will keep well for up to two weeks in a covered jar in the refrigerator. If left uncovered, they become too thick to use, owing to dehydration.

Eggs Bénédictine

5 eggs
scant 1 oz butter
1 clove of garlic (crushed with
    ½ teaspoon salt)
1 lb cooked fresh haddock
    (flaked), or other white fish
¼ pint white sauce (made with
    ½ oz butter, ½ oz flour, ¼ pint
    milk)
2½ tablespoons single cream, or
    creamy milk

To garnish
1 French roll (sliced) – for
    croûtes
oil, or butter (for frying)

For cream sauce
¾ oz butter
1 tablespoon flour
7½ fl oz milk plus 2½ fl oz single
    cream, or ½ pint milk

These are soft-boiled eggs on creamed fish, coated with cream sauce.

Method
Softboil eggs, peel and put in warm water.

Melt butter in pan, add crushed garlic, cook for 1 minute, then add fish. Work over a low heat, adding the white sauce gradually. Stir in cream. Spread on the bottom of a serving dish, drain eggs and arrange on the fish.

To make cream sauce: melt butter in pan, stir in flour off the heat, stir in milk and bring to the boil. Remove pan from heat and add cream (if using).

To make croûtes: fry slices of French roll in fat until brown and crisp, drain on absorbent paper.

Convent eggs – seasoned, covered with cream and baked in individual dishes until set

Coat eggs with the cream sauce, or use a cheese sauce if preferred, serve immediately, garnished with croûtes.

The following 4 recipes use baked eggs.

Convent eggs

4–5 eggs (new-laid)
salt and pepper
1 small carton of double cream,
    or 1 tablespoon per egg
1 oz butter

4–5 individual cocottes

This simple dish may be cooked in a large ovenproof dish instead of individual cocottes.

Tomato sauce may be used instead of the cream, with shredded ham, chicken, or sauté sliced chicken liver, placed in the cocottes under the eggs.

Method
Butter the dish or cocottes. Break each egg into a cup and slide it carefully into chosen dish. Season eggs and spoon over the cream. Set dish or cocottes on a baking sheet and cook in the oven at 350°F or Mark 4 for 7–8 minutes, until the whites are jellied and the yolks barely set.

Eggs à la crème with mushrooms

5–6 eggs
3 oz mushrooms (sliced)
½ oz butter
squeeze of lemon juice
salt and pepper
¼ pint double cream
pinch of grated nutmeg
3 oz Gruyère cheese (grated)

5–6 ramekins

This makes a very good party dish.

Method
Cook the sliced mushrooms very quickly in the butter with a squeeze of lemon. Pour half the cream into the ramekins, break the eggs carefully on top and then cover with the mushrooms.

Season the remaining cream, add grated nutmeg, and spoon it over the mushrooms. Cover each ramekin with a thick layer of grated Gruyère cheese, stand in a bain marie of very hot water and cook in oven at 350°F or Mark 4 for 10 minutes. Serve hot.

Eggs savoyarde

5 eggs
1 oz butter
1 gammon rasher (about 3 oz)
– cut in strips
1 small head of celeriac, or
½ large one (sliced)
1 small onion (sliced)
2 medium-size potatoes (sliced)
salt and pepper
4 tablespoons double cream
grated cheese (preferably
Gruyère)

This dish is a good way of using root celery (celeriac). The bacon can be omitted but gives a good savoury taste to the dish.

Method
Melt butter in a shallow pan, put in the bacon strips and, after 1–2 minutes, the sliced vegetables. Season and cover with a close-fitting lid. Cook gently until the vegetables are tender but not coloured.

Spread this mixture over the base of an ovenproof dish. Break the eggs on top, spoon over the cream and put the grated cheese on top. Cook in oven at 350°F or Mark 4 for about 8–10 minutes.

Eggs flamenco

4–5 eggs
2 potatoes (cooked and diced)
2 oz butter
2 Frankfurters, or smoked
sausages, or saveloys (sliced)
salt and pepper
2 tablespoons peas (cooked)
2 fresh, or canned, sweet red
peppers (cut into shreds)
8 tomatoes (skinned, quartered
and seeds removed)
chopped parsley
2 tablespoons top of milk, or
single cream
cayenne pepper

Method
Peel potatoes, cover with cold water and bring to boil. Cook for 4 minutes, strain and dice.

Melt the butter in a pan, add the potatoes and sausages. Shake pan over the heat until the potatoes begin to brown; season, add peas and sweet peppers. After 4–5 minutes add the tomatoes and a good sprinkling of parsley.

Turn the mixture into the bottom of a flat ovenproof dish, and break the eggs on top.

Season again, pour milk or cream on top and place in oven at 350°F or Mark 4 for about 6 minutes until set.

Sprinkle each egg with a little cayenne pepper to serve.

The following 3 recipes are for hot dishes using hard-boiled eggs.

Eggs portugaise

4 eggs (hard-boiled)
½–¾ lb tomatoes (skinned and
sliced)
2 oz butter
1 tablespoon mixed herbs (finely
chopped)
salt and pepper
grated cheese

For sauce
½ pint milk (infused with 1 slice
onion, 1 carrot, bouquet garni,
6 peppercorns)
¾ oz butter
1 rounded tablespoon flour
salt

Portugaise usually describes a dish in which tomato is used.

Method
Sauté the prepared tomatoes for 1–2 minutes in ½ oz butter. Cut eggs in half lengthways. Sieve yolks, cream remaining butter and mix with sieved yolks, herbs and seasoning to taste. Fill the egg whites with this mixture and arrange on tomatoes in an ovenproof dish.

To prepare sauce: melt the butter in a pan, draw aside and stir in the flour. Strain on the infused milk, return to the heat and stir until boiling. Season to taste and simmer for 2–3 minutes.

Coat the eggs with the sauce, sprinkle with grated cheese and brown in oven at 425°F or Mark 7.

Hungarian eggs

5 eggs (hard-boiled and sliced)
4 small onions (thinly sliced)
½ lb tomatoes (skinned and
sliced with seeds removed)
paprika pepper
about 1 oz tomato butter (to
garnish)

This is an easy and quick dish to make; and the tomato butter gives it an unusual touch.

Method
Fry the sliced onions until golden-brown. Add the pre-

pared tomatoes and simmer for 4–5 minutes.

Put the sliced eggs in the serving dish, cover with the tomato mixture and dust with paprika. Garnish the top with round flat pats of tomato butter.

Tomato butter

Work together 1 oz or more of butter, 1 teaspoon tomato purée, salt and pepper and 2–3 drops of Worcestershire sauce. Chill and shape into pats each about the size of a ten pence piece.

Eggs à la tripe

4–5 eggs (hard-boiled)
½ lb onions, or preferably spring
onions
1 oz butter
salt and pepper

For béchamel sauce
2 tablespoons plain flour
¾ pint milk (infused with 4–5
parsley stalks, 6 peppercorns, 1
blade of mace and 1 bayleaf)
1 oz butter
salt and pepper
grated cheese

This dish is so called because of the way the egg whites are cut, resembling shreds of tripe.

Method
Cut the eggs in half and push out the yolks. Wash whites and cut into shreds. Rub the yolks through a sieve. Keep whites and yolks in separate small basins, well covered.

Cut spring onions into 2–3 pieces, or thinly slice ordinary ones. Put them into a pan of cold water, bring to the boil and strain. Return to the pan with 1 oz butter; season, cover and simmer gently until just tender (about 7–8 minutes).

Meanwhile prepare the sauce: strain milk and leave to cool. Melt the butter in a pan, remove from heat and stir in flour. Pour on the milk, stir over moderate heat until boiling, then boil until thick and creamy. Season.

Butter an ovenproof dish, put in the egg whites, scatter on the onions and lastly the sieved yolks. Spoon the sauce over the top, sprinkle with grated cheese and brown in oven at 400°F or Mark 6 for 7–10 minutes.

The following 2 recipes are for cold dishes using stuffed hard-boiled eggs.

Eggs mimosa

4 large eggs (hard-boiled)
4–6 oz shrimps, or prawns
  (shelled and coarsely chopped)
½ pint thick mayonnaise
watercress (to garnish)

One of the best and simplest egg dishes for a first course. Serve with brown bread and butter.

Method
Cool eggs and peel. Split them in half lengthways, scoop out yolks and carefully push half of them through a bowl strainer into a basin. Add the shrimps or prawns. Mix and bind with 1–2 tablespoons mayonnaise.

Wash whites, dry and set on a serving dish. Fill with the prawn mixture. Thin the rest of the mayonnaise slightly with 1 tablespoon hot water and coat the eggs with this.

Hold strainer over eggs and push rest of the yolks through. Garnish dish with watercress.

Anchovy eggs

4 eggs (hard-boiled)
6–12 anchovy fillets (soaked in
  2 tablespoons milk)
2 oz butter
black pepper (ground from mill)
½ pint thick mayonnaise
1 dessertspoon mixed herbs
  (freshly chopped) – optional
watercress (to garnish)

This is another good dish for a first course.

Method
Hardboil the eggs, quickly cool them, peel and then cut in half lengthways. Soak the anchovies in milk to remove the excess salt, then drain them, unless they have soaked up all the milk, and pound until smooth. Work butter and egg yolks into anchovies. Season with black pepper.

Fill the egg whites with the anchovy mixture and sandwich the halves together again.

Serve the eggs coated with mayonnaise, which may be lightly flavoured with the herbs. Garnish the eggs with sprays of watercress.

Eggs gascon – a substantial dish of fried eggs with gammon rashers, aubergines, onion and tomatoes, served very hot

The following 2 recipes are for dishes using fried eggs.

Eggs gascon

5 eggs
1 medium-size onion (thinly
  sliced)
4–5 tablespoons oil
1–2 aubergines (according to
  size) – sliced and dégorgé
½ lb tomatoes (skinned and
  thickly sliced)
salt and pepper
dripping, or oil (for frying eggs)
2 gammon rashers (shredded)

Method
Sauté onion slices in the oil until just brown. Take them out. Dry the aubergine slices and place them in the pan. Sauté in the oil until golden-brown. Pour off any surplus fat and add the sliced tomatoes. Season, put back onion and cook for 6–7 minutes until mixture is rich and pulpy. Turn into a hot serving dish and keep warm.

Wipe out pan, heat fat (or oil) and fry the eggs. Then place on top of the aubergine mixture. Shred the gammon and fry for 3–4 minutes in the pan. Scatter over the eggs and serve at once.

Eggs romaine

5 eggs
1–1½ lb spinach
1 oz butter
fat (for frying)
salt and pepper
anchovy fillets, or 1 rasher of
  bacon (to garnish)
cream sauce

This is a good way of serving fried eggs as a main course.

Method
Wash and cook the spinach in plenty of boiling salted water, drain thoroughly and chop finely, or leave 'en branche'.

Put butter in pan and cook gently to a noisette (nut-brown). Add spinach and cook it quickly to drive off any moisture. Fry the eggs in deep fat, drain and sprinkle them with salt and pepper.

Dish up spinach on a serving dish and arrange eggs on top. Garnish with the anchovy fillets, split in two, or a curl of fried bacon.

Serve a light cream sauce separately.

A light cream sauce is easily made by heating a little single cream, seasoning with salt, pepper and a squeeze of lemon juice.

The following recipe uses buttered or scrambled eggs.

Pipérade

5 eggs
¾ lb ripe tomatoes
2 red peppers, or 2–3 caps of
   canned pimiento
2 oz butter
1 shallot (finely chopped)
2 cloves of garlic (finely chopped)
salt and pepper
6–8 rounds of bread for croûtes
   (about 1½ inches in diameter)
little garlic butter

This Basque dish is a mixture of sweet red peppers, tomatoes and eggs, well flavoured with garlic, and can be eaten either hot or cold.

Method
Scald and skin the tomatoes, squeeze to remove seeds and chop flesh roughly. Remove the seeds from peppers and chop, blanch and drain (or chop and drain pimiento).

Melt half the butter in a deep frying pan; put in the tomatoes, peppers, shallot and garlic. Season well, cook slowly, stirring occasionally, until it is a rich pulp.

Break eggs into a bowl and beat up with a fork. Spread the rounds of bread with a little garlic butter on both sides. Toast until crisp.

Add the remaining butter and eggs to the frying pan and stir with a metal spoon until they start to thicken creamily. Turn into a hot serving dish and surround with the croûtes.

For a picnic, take a small French loaf, cut off the top (lid) and scoop out most of the crumb. Spread inside and out with garlic butter (including the top). Bake in oven at 350°F or Mark 4 until slightly crisp. Fill with the pipérade and replace lid. Cut in slices and serve when cold.

OMELETS

There are two types of omelet, the plain or French omelet and the fluffy or soufflé one. First we deal with French omelets which are generally savoury ones, either plain or stuffed; they can be served as a first course or as a supper dish. A home-made jam can also go into this type of omelet, although this filling is more suited to a soufflé one.

Plain omelet

4 eggs
1½ tablespoons cold water
salt
black pepper (ground from mill)
1 oz butter

7-8 inch diameter omelet pan

Method
Break eggs into a basin and beat well with a fork. When well mixed, add water and seasoning (this should be done just before making it). Heat pan on medium heat. Put in butter in two pieces and, when frothing, pour in egg mixture at once. Leave 10–15 seconds before stirring round slowly with the flat of a fork.

Folding over, with the pan tilted

Tipping omelet on to a plate

Do this once or twice round pan, stop and leave for another 5–6 seconds.

Lift up edge of omelet to let any remaining raw egg run on to hot pan. Now tilt pan away from you and fold over omelet to far side. Change your grip on pan so that the handle runs up the palm of your hand. Take the hot dish or plate, in your other hand, tilt it slightly and tip omelet on to it. Serve at once.

Herb omelet (Fines herbes omelet)

This is a delicious omelet, especially in summer when herbs are fresh.

Method
Make as for a plain 4-egg omelet and add 1 rounded tablespoon of mixed chopped herbs (parsley, thyme, marjoram or tarragon, and chives) before pouring mixture into pan.

Snip chives finely with scissors rather than chopping them. The mixture should be quite green with the herbs.

Cheese omelet

Make as for a plain 4-egg omelet and scatter 2–3 tablespoons grated cheese thickly over omelet whilst in pan, just before folding it over. A mature cheddar or Gruyère is best.

STUFFED OMELETS

Make these in the same way as a plain omelet and spread the stuffing mixture quickly over omelet before folding it over. A little of the mixture, such as tomato or mushroom, can be reserved to spoon over centre of omelet when turned out.

The following recipe is for a 4-egg stuffed omelet.

Tomato omelet

2–3 tomatoes (peeled and sliced)
¼ oz butter
salt and pepper
mint (chopped)—to garnish

Method
Sauté tomatoes in butter in a pan for 1–2 minutes. Season well and add a good sprinkling of mint before spooning into omelet. Don't overcook tomatoes.

SOUFFLE OMELETS

These are usually served as a sweet and can have various fillings. The mixture may be cooked in an omelet pan on top of the stove, or in a soufflé or ovenproof dish in the oven.

Jam omelet

4 large eggs (separated)
1 tablespoon caster sugar
2 tablespoons single cream, or creamy milk
apricot, or strawberry, or gooseberry jam (preferably home-made)
½ oz butter
little sifted icing sugar

2–3 metal skewers; 8-inch diameter omelet pan

Other fillings which may be used are fresh sliced strawberries mixed with 1 tablespoon of warm redcurrant jelly, or 2–3 bananas sliced and sautéd in a little butter, and then well dusted with caster sugar and sprinkled with lemon juice.

Method
Mix egg yolks with the sugar and cream. Warm 2–3 tablespoons of the jam in a small saucepan. Whip whites to a firm snow and cut and fold into the yolk mixture, using a metal spoon. Set oven at 400°F or Mark 6 or turn on grill. Heat omelet pan until moderately hot, and put skewers in flame or under grill until red hot.

Drop butter into the pan and, while still foaming, put in the egg mixture. Spread out in the pan and cook on moderate heat for less than 1 minute to allow the bottom to brown. Do not stir during this time.

Then slide pan into pre-set oven or under the grill to set the top. Spread omelet quickly with jam, fold over with a palette knife; turn or slide on to a hot dish, dredge with icing sugar and mark a lattice across the top with red-hot skewers. (Heat several skewers at a time rather than heating them one by one.)

Note: marking soufflé omelets with red-hot skewers gives a traditional finish and a pleasant taste of caramel; otherwise just dust the omelet with caster, instead of icing, sugar.

Rum omelet

Make as for jam omelet, and fill with jam or bananas. Then heat 2–3 tablespoons of rum, set alight and pour round the finished omelet before serving.

Soufflé omelet (oven method)

4 egg yolks
1 rounded tablespoon caster sugar
grated rind and juice of ½ lemon
5 egg whites
½ oz butter
little sifted icing sugar
2–3 tablespoons warm jam, or other filling

Oval ovenproof dish

Method
Set oven at 375°F or Mark 5. Well butter an ovenproof dish and dust with icing sugar.

Work yolks with sugar and lemon rind. Add a squeeze of the juice. Whip whites stiffly, then cut and fold into the mixture, using a metal spoon. Turn mixture into the dish and shape into an omelet with a palette knife by making hollow or trough down the centre. Dust with icing sugar.

Bake in pre-set oven for 7–10 minutes, or until lightly coloured. Spread hollow or trough with warm jam and serve at once.

Spread warm jam over cooked omelet with a palette knife

Slide omelet on to a warm dish or plate; flip over with knife

Dredge with icing sugar; use hot skewers to make lattice pattern

Score omelet for traditional finish and taste of caramel

PANCAKES

In most Latin countries the Tuesday before Lent is carnival time, the reason for this feasting being to use up all the rich foods before the rigours of Lent. Pancake batter was a good way of using butter, eggs and milk, and so variations of this batter became regional specialities, served exclusively before Lent at markets, fairs and carnivals.

In England pancakes or crêpes for Shrove Tuesday are eaten, even though there are mostly no celebrations.

GENERAL RULES

Pancakes don't have to be made and served straight away. Not only the batter, but the pancakes themselves, can be made several hours or even the day before they are wanted. For this, however, the batter must contain a good proportion of eggs and melted butter. If pancakes are kept in an airtight container and reheated properly, they taste as if fresh-cooked from the pan.

The right pan is most important for making pancakes. It should be small, with a base of about 6 inches in diameter and made of cast iron or aluminium. A proper pancake pan is shallow (the sides about $\frac{3}{4}$ inch high) to make the tossing easier. These pans are not easy to come by and you can use an omelet pan (which has a curved edge) instead, but choose a shallow rather than a deep one.

Ideally it is better to keep the pan entirely for making pancakes and omelets, as in either

Take 1 tablespoon of batter for each pancake, tilt the pan while pouring so that batter spreads evenly all over bottom of pan

case it is better not to wash it after use unless really necessary.

The pan should be well wiped with a damp cloth or paper dipped in salt, then rubbed lightly with a few drops of oil. It can then be put away for future use. This treatment helps to prevent sticking.

A good pancake should be wafer-thin with a crisp lacy edge. Butter or oil in the batter gives this effect, so little or no fat is necessary in the pan.

To cook pancakes. Once the batter is made it must be allowed to stand before use. This has the effect of softening the starch cells, making the pancakes thinner without being tough.

To cook the pancakes, wipe out the pan before setting over moderate heat. When thoroughly hot put in a few drops of oil. Take 1 tablespoon of the batter and tip this into the pan, immediately rolling it round clockwise to coat the bottom evenly. (This quantity will be sufficient for a 6-inch diameter pan.)

Cook until the underneath of pancake is a good brown colour. Run a palette knife under the edges to loosen the pancake, then raise it slightly with the fingers and slip the knife underneath. Flip the pancake over and cook for about 10 seconds on the other side. Alternatively toss the pancakes. Then turn them on to a rack. Continue to cook pancakes, stacking them one on top of the other, until you have as many as you want. Cover the stack with a bowl or wrap in a tea towel if not for immediate

Turning the pancake over

use. If they are for use the following day, store in foil or a polythene bag with a sheet of greaseproof or waxed paper between each pancake.

To reheat pancakes. Melt about 1 oz of butter, brush a baking sheet or tray with this, then peel off the pancakes and lay them over-lapping along the sheet. Brush well with more melted butter to exclude the air and protect pancakes during cooking.

Put baking sheet into the oven at 400°F or Mark 6 for 3–4 minutes. Do this for pancakes without a stuffing, otherwise stuff them while cold and bake them with the stuffing in for 7–10 minutes.

If all the batter is not used, keep it covered and use within three days.

To deep-freeze cooked pancakes. Stack them one on top of the other with a piece of greaseproof or waxed paper between each one then wrap in foil or a polythene bag.

For ham pancake place slice of ham on the cooked pancake, then a large tablespoon of filling in the middle. Fold two sides to the centre, then fold in half, place in an ovenproof dish.

Basic pancake batter

4 oz plain flour
pinch of salt
1 egg
1 egg yolk
½ pint milk
1 tablespoon melted butter, or salad oil

Method
Sift the flour with the salt into a bowl, make a well in the centre, add the egg and yolk and begin to add the milk slowly, stirring all the time. When half the milk has been added, stir in the melted butter or oil and beat well until smooth.

Add the remaining milk and leave to stand for 30 minutes before using. The batter should have the consistency of thin cream — if too thick, add a little extra milk.

Allow two pancakes per person.

When the following recipes refer to ½ pint of pancake batter, this means batter made with ½ pint of milk, and other ingredients in proportion, as given in the basic pancake batter recipe above.

SAVOURY PANCAKES

Ham pancakes

½ pint pancake batter

For filling
½ lb flat mushrooms
2½ oz butter
1 shallot (finely chopped)
1 teaspoon flour
2½ fl oz stock, or single cream
salt and pepper
1 tablespoon mixed parsley and thyme (chopped)
8 thin slices of ham
1 tablespoon Parmesan cheese (grated)

Method
Prepare pancake batter, leave in a cool place for 30 minutes.

Wash the mushrooms quickly in salted water, drain and chop finely. Melt 1½ oz butter, add the shallot and cook until soft but not coloured, then add the mushrooms and continue cooking until all the moisture has evaporated. Blend in the flour and stock or cream; season and bring to the boil. Add the herbs.

Fry pancakes and place a slice of ham and a large tablespoon of mushroom filling on each one, fold as shown above. Place in a buttered ovenproof dish, melt remaining butter and brush or pour over the pancakes.

Sprinkle with the cheese. Bake in the oven at 400°F or Mark 6 for 7–10 minutes.

Pancakes Beatrix

For batter
3½ oz flour
pinch of salt
2 eggs
2 tablespoons melted butter, or salad oil
¼–½ pint milk
1 oz Gouda cheese (finely grated)

For filling
2–3 smoked trout
béchamel sauce (made with 1 oz butter, 1 oz flour, ½ pint flavoured milk)
salt and pepper
1 teaspoon horseradish cream
1 tablespoon double cream

For finishing
3 tablespoons double cream
1 tablespoon Parmesan cheese (grated)

Method
Make the batter as in basic recipe, adding the grated cheese when half the milk has been added. Leave to stand for 30 minutes in a cool place.

Remove the skin and bone from the trout and divide into neat fillets. Make béchamel sauce, season, then add the horseradish cream and tablespoon of double cream.

Set the oven at 375°F or Mark 5. Fry paper-thin pancakes, fill each one with the fillets and sauce, roll up like cigars and arrange in a buttered dish. Spoon over the extra cream, dust with Parmesan cheese and bake in the pre-set oven for about 10 minutes. Serve very hot.

SWEET PANCAKES

Apple pancakes

½ pint pancake batter (as basic
recipe) – with 1 teaspoon sugar
added with oil

For filling
1½–2 lb apples (peeled, cored and
    sliced)
½ oz butter
brown sugar
cinnamon
lemon rind

For apricot sauce
4 tablespoons smooth apricot jam
grated rind and juice of 1 lemon
½ pint water
1 teaspoon arrowroot

Method

Make batter and leave in a cool
place for about 30 minutes.

Peel, core and slice the apples,
rub the butter over the bottom
of a thick pan, put in the apples
with sugar to taste, cinnamon
and lemon rind. Cover and cook
slowly until tender but not too
mushy, about 10–15 minutes.

Place the jam, juice and rind
of the lemon and the water in a
pan and dissolve over gentle
heat. Mix the arrowroot with a
little water, add to the pan and
stir until boiling. Cook for 2–3
minutes until clear, then strain.

Fry pancakes wafer-thin.
Stack them on to an ovenproof
dish, one above the other, sand-
wiching them with the apple
mixture (see right). Spoon over
some apricot sauce and bake in
the oven at 375°F or Mark 5,
until lightly brown (about 10
minutes). Cut into wedges,
pour more apricot sauce round,
and serve remainder separately.

Layering apple pancakes

Pancakes Longueville

For batter
4 oz flour
pinch of salt
1 oz caster sugar
1 egg
1 egg yolk
grated rind of 1 orange
2 tablespoons melted butter
scant ½ pint milk
1 oz almonds (freshly blanched
    and finely chopped)

For filling
6 dessert apples (pippin)
grated rind and juice of ½ lemon
    and ½ orange
4 tablespoons smooth apricot jam
1 small carton double cream
¼ teaspoon cinnamon

To finish
1 tablespoon melted butter
2 tablespoons icing sugar (sifted)

Method

Prepare pancake batter as basic
recipe, adding grated orange
rind with the egg. Leave for
30 minutes in a cool place.

Don't add almonds until just
before frying the pancakes.

For filling: peel, quarter and
remove the core of the apples
and then cut in thick slices. Put
in a pan with the lemon and
orange rind and juice and the
jam, cover and cook until thick
and pulpy. Whip the cream and
flavour with the cinnamon.

Set the oven at 425°F or
Mark 7. When the pancakes are
fried fold the cream into the
apple mixture. Spread each
pancake with the apple and
cream mixture, fold in four and
place overlapping in a buttered
ovenproof dish. Brush with the
melted butter, dust with icing
sugar and glaze in the pre-set
oven for 3–5 minutes.

Fish and Shellfish

Many people are unaware of the variety of white-fleshed fish available, even allowing that the choice may be limited according to the area in which you live and sometimes the season of the year. (We indicate seasons for Britain.)

Sea-water fish, which come flat or round, white or oily, are perhaps the best known. In white fish the natural fat or oil is held in the liver, e.g. halibut and cod, which is why it is easy to digest; in the richer, oilier fish such as herring, mackerel and salmon, it is spread throughout the flesh. Ideally fish should be eaten fresh out of the sea but this is seldom possible. However, as a general indication of freshness the fishy smell should not be too strong, the flesh must be firm, and in white fish a creamy-white colour. Eyes should be bright and full, the gills red and the body covered with scales or natural slime. Most white fish are bought ready cleaned and filleted, but it is useful to know how to clean, fillet and skin fish yourself.

White fish lend themselves to various methods of cooking and go particularly well with sauces, either made from the liquor in which the fish was cooked, or served separately to contrast with, and enhance, its flavour. The most common method is boiling (really an incorrect term here for simmering), usually done on top of the stove. This is one of the best ways to cook fish simply, whole or in steaks, and a good contrasting sauce should accompany the fish. Poaching is cooking in a small quantity of liquid in the oven, or on top of the cooker, and the resulting juices can then be turned into a coating sauce. All poached fish should be transferred into a clean serving dish before coating with a sauce. Any fish for cooking in this way, whether whole or as a large steak, should be done in a special stock, called court bouillon, rather than water. This is simple to prepare and once the fish has been cooked in it, the liquid should be strained off and used again for poaching or as liquid for a sauce (see recipe for poached cod on page 52). Cooking fish au gratin, a well known method, is where small whole fish (fillets or steaks) are cooked in the oven in a thick, well-seasoned sauce and finished with a topping of browned crumbs, melted butter and sometimes cheese.

All shellfish make attractive and unusual additions to the table, either on their own or in a sauce with other fish; but they are generally thought of as summertime dishes. In fact some are plentiful and reasonably priced at other times of the year, for example scallops and mussels. Though fresh prawns are not always obtainable, the frozen ones go very well with other shellfish as a garnish, or fried with a spicy sauce. Frozen scampi and canned crabmeat are also excellent for mixing with other shellfish.

A selection of shellfish which includes prawns, mussels, shrimps, oysters, crab, lobster, scallops and cockles

HOW TO CLEAN, GUT AND SKIN FISH

Large cod or haddock fillets are usually sold unskinned, and as the skin is thick and tough, it is best removed. In some parts of Britain, particularly in the North, small whole fish of haddock and whiting are sold skinned and boned, and are known as block fillets.

To clean a round fish, slit skin below head, along belly to vent. Scrape out gut and throw away. Remove head, if wished. Wash fish under a running cold tap

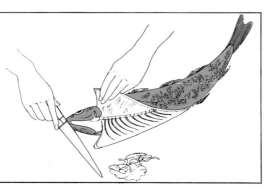

To skin a round fish, lift tail end and slip knife in between flesh and skin. Hold tail firmly, saw flesh away from skin; keep knife at an angle to the board

To skin a flat fish, cut fins off first. Then starting at head end, slip thumb about 1 inch under black skin at cut where fish was cleaned

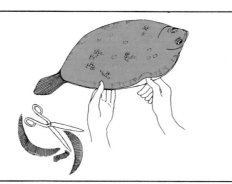

Run thumb round fish, keeping it under the skin. Then grasp tail end firmly and rip skin off. Repeat this on other side of the fish

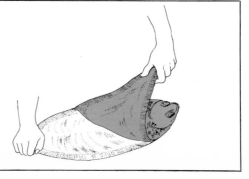

TO CLEAN ROUND FISH

Rinse in cold water, then scrape with the back of a knife from tail to head to remove scales; this applies particularly to scaly fish, such as herrings and salmon.

For large round fish, such as haddock, codling, sea trout, take a sharp knife and slit the skin from just below head, along belly to the vent. Scrape out the gut, discard; the head may then be cut off. Hold fish under a running cold tap to clean it thoroughly. If there is any black skin inside the cavity (sometimes there is, even though the fish has been bought gutted), gently rub it away with a damp cloth dipped in salt.

TO CLEAN FLAT FISH

With fish such as plaice or sole, make a semi-circular cut just below head on the dark side, scrape out the gut and wash fish thoroughly.

TO SKIN LARGE FILLETS OF ROUND FISH

Lay skin side down on the board, lift the tail end and slip a thin, sharp knife in between the flesh and skin. Dip the fingers of your left hand in salt to prevent slipping and, holding the tail skin firmly, saw the flesh away from the skin, keeping the knife at an angle to the board.

TO SKIN FLAT FISH

Sole may be skinned whole and the fishmonger will skin them on both sides if asked.

When doing it yourself, trim away the outside fins with scissors. Lay the fish on the board and, starting at the head end, slip your thumb about 1 inch under the black skin at the cut where the fish was cleaned. Run your thumb right round the fish, then grasp the tail end of the skin firmly and rip it off. Repeat this on the other side of the fish.

Plaice are skinned after filleting, as the skin is thick and would tear the flesh if ripped off. Skin as for large fillets.

HOW TO FILLET FISH

To fillet a round fish, take a sharp knife and cut down back with knife blade on top of the backbone. Lift off the top fillet

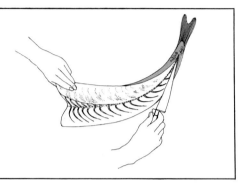

To remove other fillet, slip knife under backbone at head. Keep close to bone, work down to tail with short strokes

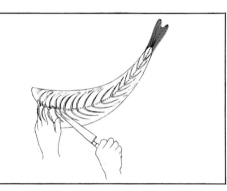

To fillet a flat fish, run knife down backbone; with short, sharp strokes, keep knife on bone and work from head outwards down to tail

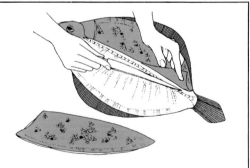

To remove other fillet on same side, turn fish round. Start from tail end and take off fillet in same way. Repeat on the other side

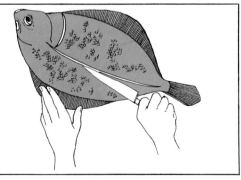

For expert results have fish filleted by your fishmonger; but with a little practice, you can learn to do it successfully.

TO FILLET ROUND FISH

Lay the fish on a piece of wet, rough cloth, or sacking (to prevent slipping) and keep fish steady with one hand. Take a thin sharp knife or filleting knife, and first trim away the fins then cut down the back with the blade on top of the backbone. Lift off the top fillet. Now slip the knife under the bone at the head, and keeping it as close as possible to the back bone, work down to the tail, using short sharp strokes, at the same time keeping a firm hold on the head with the other hand.

TO FILLET FLAT FISH

Plaice and sole (if weighing no more than 1–1½ lb) are usually cut into a double fillet. This means that the flesh on both sides of the backbone, top and underside, is taken off in one piece, ie. two fillets only for each fish. These may be divided into two for cooking. Lemon sole is treated in the same way.

If filleting at home, it is easier to take the flesh off in four fillets. Run the point of the knife down the backbone and with short, sharp strokes keeping the knife on the bone, work from the head outwards until the tail is reached and the fillet is detached. Turn the fish round and starting from the tail take the other half of the fillet off in the same way. Then turn the fish over and repeat the process. Flat fish fillets are larger and thicker on the dark side, which is uppermost when the fish is swimming.

FISH

BASS

These are beautiful, round, silvery fish not often seen on the fishmonger's slab but well worth asking for.

In season from May to July, they weigh from 2–6 lb. Like salmon, bass are 'fighting' fish and so have crisp firm flesh. They may be both fresh- and sea-water fish and are more likely to be found in the south and west parts of the country, the estuaries of south Devon and Cornwall being among the major fishing grounds.

Small bass may be grilled or fried but the larger fish or steaks cut from them are best poached and served with a hollandaise sauce or cooked as for salmon (see page 57).

BRILL

Medium to large flat sea-water fish having a pale brown skin with flesh of a creamy colour, firm and of good flavour. Brill weigh 2–6 lb and they are at their best and most easily obtainable from September to May. Cook filleted or whole and serve with a good sauce and garnishes.

COD

In season all the year round, this deep-sea fish can weigh from $1\frac{1}{4}$–20 lb. It is at its best from May to October. To serve this creamy flaked fish well you should first wash and dry it, rub the skin with a freshly cut lemon and then lightly sprinkle it with salt. After leaving 30–60 minutes in a cool place, tip away any liquid and wipe the fish again.

HADDOCK

This large, round sea-water fish, weighing from $1\frac{1}{2}$–6 lb, with firm white flakes, is in season all the year round. It is distinguishable by the dark line down each side and black 'finger' mark behind each gill, known as St. Peter's mark. Small fillets are sold as block fillets and large ones are often smoked. The most sought after smaller haddock are split open and smoked; these are known as Finnan haddock. Smaller whole fish, well smoked, are called Arbroath smokies.

Cod cutlets bretonne poached in cider and finished in cream sauce

Cod cutlets bretonne

4 large cod steaks (1-inch thick)
squeeze of lemon
$\frac{1}{4}$ pint dry cider
salt and pepper
5 tablespoons water
1 medium-size carrot (shredded)
1 medium-size onion (shredded)
2 sticks of celery (shredded)
1 oz butter
1 tablespoon flour
2–3 tablespoons creamy milk
1 dessertspoon parsley
  (chopped)

Method

Wash and dry fish in absorbent paper. Sprinkle lightly with lemon juice and salt, leave for 30 minutes (cod benefits by this treatment before cooking). Dab away any liquid before lifting into a buttered fireproof dish.

Pour over half the cider, add water. Cover with buttered paper and poach for 10–15 minutes in the oven at 350°F or Mark 4.

Now cut prepared vegetables into thin shreds, put into a small pan with a nut of the butter and 1 tablespoon of remaining cider. Cover tightly, cook 2–3 minutes, then put into oven to finish cooking. Take up fish, carefully pull out centre bone, peel off skin; lift each piece on to a hot serving dish.

When vegetables are cooked, spoon these over fish, keep warm. Strain liquid into the pan, add rest of cider, reduce for 2–3 minutes, then draw aside. Work rest of butter and the flour to a paste (kneaded butter), add to liquid in 2–3 pieces. When dissolved return to heat and stir until boiling, adjust seasoning and add milk and parsley. The sauce should be the consistency of cream; add more kneaded butter to thicken if necessary. Spoon over dish and serve very hot. When food is cooked in a liquid, the exact quantity of which is unknown, adding kneaded butter is quickest way to thicken. Served with creamed potatoes this makes a good main dish. (Haddock fillet cut into portions can be cooked in the same way.)

Poached cod with egg or oyster sauce

2 lb steak of cod (turbot or
  halibut)

For court bouillon

2 pints water
1 large carrot (sliced)
1 onion (sliced)
bouquet garni
6 peppercorns
2 tablespoons vinegar, or juice
  of $\frac{1}{2}$ lemon

Egg or oyster sauce can also be used for turbot or halibut, although the sauce for them is traditionally a shrimp or lobster one (see recipes on page 178).

Method

Put ingredients for court bouillon in a pan, salt lightly, cover and simmer for 8–10 minutes. Cool. Tie fish in a piece of muslin (do this to all fish cooked in a fair amount of liquid), put fish in pan, cover and bring slowly to boil. Lower heat and barely simmer for 35–40 minutes. Take up and drain for 2–3 minutes before unwrapping muslin. Dish up on to a hot dish and serve at once with your own chosen sauce. Traditionally, poached fish is served on a napkin so that no liquid is visible on the dish.

Haddock au gratin

1–1½ lb haddock fillet, or 4–5 block fillets according to size
salt and pepper
mushrooms (cooked and sliced)– optional

For sauce

1 oz butter
1 rounded tablespoon flour
½ pint milk
grated cheese
browned crumbs

Method

Skin fillet and cut into portions; lay flat in a buttered fireproof dish. If using whole fillets, tuck each end under before laying in the dish. The side nearest the bone should be uppermost as this is always the whitest. Season lightly.

To prepare sauce: melt butter, stir in flour off the heat. This mixture is the roux and should be soft and creamy in consistency. When making a roux, the melted butter must be soft and semi-liquid but not too hot; if too much flour is used, it won't blend well with the milk. If lumpy, add a nut of butter. Pour on milk at once, blend well, season and return to the heat. Stir continually until boiling. Taste for seasoning, then spoon over the fish. Grate a little cheese over, scatter with crumbs, then bake in the oven for 20–25 minutes at 350°F or Mark 4.

Sliced mushrooms (cooked) can be put over the fish before the sauce.

Watchpoint The sauce for the fish cooked in this way should be thicker than an ordinary coating sauce to allow for dilution from the juices from the fish. This is why the pieces of fish should be laid flat and completely cover the base of the dish, otherwise the liquid will not blend with the sauce and there will be a watery looking liquid round edge of the dish.

The finished haddock dieppoise, with mussels and shrimps

Haddock dieppoise (with mussels and shrimps)

1–1½ lb haddock fillet (skinned)
butter
lemon juice
3 pints of mussels
1 small onion (quartered)
1 wineglass white wine
½ wineglass water
4 oz shrimps or prawns (shelled)
1 rounded tablespoon cheese (grated)

For sauce

1 oz butter
1 rounded tablespoon flour
½ pint mussel liquor
5 tablespoons creamy milk

Method

Cut fillet into portions, put in a well buttered ovenproof dish, squeeze over a little lemon juice and cover with buttered paper. Poach in the oven at 350°F or Mark 4 for 15 minutes.

To prepare mussels: put well scrubbed mussels into a pan, add the onion, wine and water. Cover and bring to the boil, shaking pan occasionally. When mussels are well opened, remove from shells and take off the beards. Set mussels aside, strain and measure the liquor.

To prepare sauce: make roux, then pour in ½ pint mussel liquor and stir until boiling. Add milk and boil for 2–3 minutes.

Dish up the haddock, scatter the mussels and shrimps over the top, and coat with the

The skinned haddock being cut into portions and placed in a dish for haddock dieppoise

The mussels and shrimps being scattered over cooked haddock before coating it with sauce

sauce. Sprinkle cheese over the top and brown under the grill.

HALIBUT

Generally regarded as a flat fish, halibut range from 2–400 lb and have reached a length of 12 feet; 'chicken' halibut (between 2–5 lb) are considered to have the best flavour.

EELS

These are caught in fresh or salt water and are more often bought ready-cooked as jellied eels or eel pies. The flesh is rich with a delicate flavour and when smoked makes an excellent hors d'oeuvre.

Eels must be skinned before cooking; ask your fishmonger to do this.

HERRINGS

These are of the same family as sprats, whitebait, sardines and pilchards, and are perhaps the most widely known. They are a little smaller than mackerel and must be eaten very fresh.

Herrings can be grilled, rolled in oatmeal (whole or filleted) and fried, or soused in vinegar. They can also be cured, salted and smoked to become bloaters, kippers and buckling.

Sprats, whitebait (see page 59) and fresh sardines are fried; pilchards are treated in the same way as for herrings.

MACKEREL

This is a rich and delicious fish with firm flesh. At its best in late spring and summer, mackerel must be eaten as fresh as possible, otherwise the flesh is too oily and unpalatable.

Good mackerel average 1–1½ lb in weight and are best filleted before cooking. Roll the well dried fillets in seasoned flour and fry in bacon fat or butter; alternatively, they can be grilled. Serve sizzling hot with quarters of lemon. This is one of the best ways to serve fresh caught mackerel.

If you find mackerel on the rich side, try poaching the fillets in the oven at 375°F or Mark 5 for 10–15 minutes in a little salted water with juice of ½ lemon added. Drain and serve with a good sprinkling of freshly chopped parsley accompanied by boiled potatoes.

Stewed eels

2 lb eels (skinned)
1 onion (finely chopped)
salt and pepper
kneaded butter (made with 1 oz
    butter worked with ½ oz flour)
squeeze of lemon juice
2 tablespoons parsley (chopped)

Method

Wash eels thoroughly and cut into 2–3 inch pieces. Put in a pan and just cover with cold water. Add onion and a little salt, cover and simmer for 20–30 minutes. Draw aside, add more salt, if necessary, and season well with pepper.

Add kneaded butter to pan in small pieces. When dissolved, bring slowly to boil, shaking pan gently. When boiling, add a good squeeze of lemon juice and parsley. Liquid should have consistency of gravy and be plentiful. Serve in soup plates.

Soused herrings

6 herrings (split and boned) –
    2 extra for second helpings
salt and pepper
1 tablespoon pickling spice
1 bayleaf
1 onion (thinly sliced)
¾ pint vinegar and water (in equal
    proportions)

Method

Have herrings split and boned. Season cut surface and roll up from head to tail. Pack them in a deep dish or casserole.

Put pickling spice and bayleaf into a pan with onion, vinegar and water. Add salt and bring to the boil. Cool, then pour over the herrings. The liquid should just cover them. Cook in the oven at 325°F or Mark 3 for about 1 hour. Serve the herrings cold.

Pickling spice is a selection of whole spices (pepper corns, allspice and mace, etc.) and is a convenient way of buying spices if you do not use them frequently. If not using pickling spice for soused herrings, you will need 6 peppercorns, 2 blades of mace, 2 allspice berries and 1 clove. For a milder flavoured souse, add 1 tablespoon brown sugar to the vinegar and water. White wine can replace vinegar if preferred.

Mackerel with mushrooms and tomatoes

2–3 mackerel (according to size)
    – filleted
seasoned flour
4 tablespoons dripping, or oil
1 small onion (finely chopped)
¼ lb flat mushrooms (chopped)
1 clove garlic (chopped)
1 dessertspoon mixed herbs
    (chopped), or parsley
2 tablespoons wine vinegar
salt and pepper
¾ lb tomatoes (skinned and
    sliced)

Method

First prepare mackerel fillets: lay the fish on a piece of wet, rough cloth (to prevent slipping) and, keeping the fish steady with one hand, take a thin sharp knife or filleting knife and first trim away the fins; then cut down the back with the blade on top of the backbone.

Lift off the top fillet. Now slip the knife under the bone at the head, and keep it as close as possible to the backbone; work down to the tail, using short sharp strokes, at the same time keeping a firm hold on the head with the other hand. Wash and dry fillets and then roll them in seasoned flour.

Heat the frying pan, put in 2 tablespoons dripping or oil. When smoking, lay in the fillets, cut side downwards, and fry until a good brown; then turn and cook on the other sides.

Lift out fillets and put on a serving dish, overlapping them; keep warm in oven.

Wipe out the pan, reheat and add 1 tablespoon of dripping or oil. Put in the chopped onion and cook slowly to soften it; then add the mushrooms and chopped garlic. Fry briskly for 2–3 minutes, then add herbs, vinegar and season to taste. Reboil and pour over the fish.

Sauté tomatoes in remaining dripping or oil for 1–2 minutes, then put round fish or at either end of the dish. Serve hot.

Mackerel algérienne, with the mushroom and onion mixture down the centre

Mackerel algérienne

4 mackerel
salt and pepper
½ lemon
chopped parsley

For salpicon

1 red, or green, pepper
¾ lb tomatoes
½ oz butter
1 shallot (finely chopped)
1 clove of garlic (crushed with
  ¼ teaspoon salt)
1 teaspoon paprika pepper

Method
Set oven at 350°F or Mark 4.

First split and bone the mackerel, wash and dry well. Place the fish in an ovenproof dish, season and squeeze over a little lemon juice. Bake in pre-set oven for about 20 minutes.

To prepare the salpicon: shred the pepper, blanch and refresh. Skin the tomatoes, re-move seeds and slice flesh. Melt the butter, add the shallot and cook until soft. Then add the tomatoes, garlic and paprika pepper. Stew slowly to a pulp, then add the pepper; continue cooking for 2–3 minutes.

Spoon salpicon over the fish and serve with thin slices of lemon and chopped parsley.

GREY MULLET
In appearance these round sea-water fish bear no rela-tionship to red mullet. The fish are large, weighing from 2–3 lb upwards and are caught off the Cornish coast from spring to late summer. The flesh is beautifully white and firm, the skin silvery-grey. Cook as for salmon (see page 57), sliced and grilled, or poached and served with a sauce such as hollandaise (see page 181), or one made from the poaching liquid, ie. Dugléré (see page 59).

RED MULLET
These much esteemed round sea-water fish have delicate white flesh with a bright pink, fairly thick skin. They average between 6–12 oz in weight and are in season from May to September. The fishmonger, if asked, will clean them through the gills and leave in the liver, which is considered a delicacy to be cooked in the fish. For this reason red mullet is called the 'woodcock of the sea' (this prized game bird being dressed without being drawn or cleaned). Red mullet can also be cleaned as for other fish, if preferred.

A famous method of cooking them is 'en papillote', that is wrapped in an envelope of well-buttered greaseproof paper. In this way all the flavour of the fish is preserved. Red mullet can also be fried or grilled and served with a maître d'hôtel butter.

Red mullet with fennel and lemon

4 red mullet (cleaned)
salt
pepper (ground from mill)
4 tablespoons oil, or melted
  butter
1 shallot (finely chopped)
2 heads of fennel (finocchio)
1 lemon
1 oz butter
chopped parsley

Method
Trim the mullet and make 3–4 diagonal slits on each side of fish. Season and marinate in oil or butter and shallot while preparing fennel.

Cut fennel into thick slices and blanch 2–3 minutes; drain well. Remove peel and pith from lemon and cut flesh into segments. Sauté fennel in butter until just tender, season and add lemon and parsley.

Brush grill rack with oil and pre-heat grill. Remove mullet from marinade and grill for 8–10 minutes, brushing with oil if necessary during cooking. Serve with fennel and lemon on a hot dish.

Red mullet 'en papillote': fish is placed on disc of greased paper and lemon juice is added

Crimping edges of the paper 'envelope' to seal it well so that juices do not escape

Court bouillon

(2 pint quantity)

2 pints water
1 carrot (sliced)
1 onion (stuck with a clove)
bouquet garni
6 peppercorns
2 tablespoons vinegar
salt

Method
Place all ingredients in a pan, salt lightly and bring to boil. Cover the pan with a lid and simmer for 15—20 minutes. Strain before using.

Red mullet 'en papillote'

4 red mullet (cleaned)
2½ oz butter
salt
black pepper (ground from mill)
lemon juice
extra butter (for melting) –
  optional

Method
Cut an oval of greaseproof paper for each fish (large enough to enclose it), spread the centre well with butter, place a fish on each and season well, adding a good squeeze of lemon juice. Wrap up the fish, crimping the edges of the paper together by making small 'pleats' in it (see photographs left).

Slide on to a baking sheet and cook in the oven at 350°F or Mark 4 for 15–18 minutes.

To serve, unwrap the papers carefully and slide fish on to a hot dish or individual plates. Serve a little melted butter separately, if wanted.

Red mullet duxelles

4 red mullet (cleaned)
2 wineglasses red wine, or fish
  stock and squeeze of lemon
  juice
quarters of lemon (to garnish)

For duxelles

6 oz mushrooms, or mushroom
  stalks
1 oz butter
1 tablespoon shallots, or onion
  (finely chopped)
2 tablespoons parsley (chopped)

Method
To make duxelles: wash mushrooms and chop finely. Cook with shallots and parsley in melted butter for 3–5 minutes, until most of the moisture has evaporated. Turn into a buttered ovenproof dish, spreading the mixture evenly. Lay mullet on top and pour over wine or stock (if no wine, add a squeeze of lemon juice). Cook in the oven at 350°F or Mark 4 for 15–20 minutes, basting occasionally. When ready the liquid should be well reduced.

Serve garnished with quarters of lemon and boiled potatoes.

PLAICE

These flat sea-water fish are easily recognised because of their grey-brown skin and orange spots; they weigh up to 5 lb. Being rather tasteless, plaice need to be served with a well-flavoured sauce or savoury butter.

Fillets of plaice Sylvette

1½–2 lb plaice (filleted and
  skinned)
salt
¼ pint water
squeeze of lemon juice
1 slice of onion
1 bayleaf
6 peppercorns

For vegetable mirepoix

4 oz carrots
2 oz onion
2 oz turnip
2 oz French beans, or brussels
  sprouts
1 stick of celery
2 tomatoes
salt and pepper
1 oz butter

For sauce

1 oz butter
1 rounded tablespoon flour
¼ pint creamy milk

Method
To prepare vegetable mirepoix: dice all the vegetables finely, reserving the tomatoes. Melt 1 oz of the butter in a shallow pan and put in the vegetables, season and cover with a paper and lid. Cook gently for 3–4 minutes over heat before adding the tomatoes, skinned, with seeds removed and cut in dice. Cover again and put the pan in the oven at 350°F or Mark 4 for about 20 minutes.

Wash the fish, lay in a buttered ovenproof dish, sprinkle with salt and cover with the water and lemon juice. Add onion, bayleaf and peppercorns and poach in the oven at 325°–350°F or Mark 3–4 for 15 minutes.

To make sauce: melt the butter in a pan, blend in the flour away from the heat and strain on the liquor from the fish. Stir over gentle heat until thick, add the creamy milk and simmer for 1–2 minutes.

Turn mirepoix on to a serving dish, arrange fillets on top and spoon over the sauce.

SALMON

These are fish from 3 years old, weighing from 8 lb, an average weight being 12–16 lb. Under that age they are known as 'grilse' and weigh about 5–6 lb.

The season is from February to August but varies slightly according to area, some rivers having an earlier season than others. As salmon is an expensive fish, buy it when it is most plentiful, ie. from May to the end of July.

Whole fish cost slightly less per lb than fish bought by the piece, and they are suitable for a large party. A salmon is usually served cold, poached, skinned and suitably decorated. Allow 4–6 oz per person but take the head into account (it is about one-fifth of the total weight). Where possible, choose a fish with a small head and broad shoulders.

When buying in portions, the fish is scaled, but for cooking whole it is better left unscaled. This gives protection and makes it easier to skin when cooked.

The fishmonger will clean the salmon for you but, if you are doing it yourself, take care to remove the gills as well as the insides. Run your thumb down the backbone to remove the dark membrane which lies against it. Wash the salmon under cold running water and dry thoroughly before cooking. With scissors, snip away the fins and trim the tail into a 'vandyke' (ie. follow the line of the tail, and trim the centre of tail to a sharp 'V'). Leave on head.

Smaller cuts or steaks taken from the centre of the fish can weigh from 1½–3 lb. Individual portions, such as cutlets, weigh from 4–6 oz and should be poached or grilled.

Poaching. For cooking a whole salmon, especially if it is large, a fish kettle with a lift-out drainer grid is essential because the salmon must be covered with liquid to poach it properly. The grid enables you to remove the fish without it breaking.

A salmon should be cooked in a court bouillon (see opposite). This can be simply salted water or have vegetables, vinegar or wine added to flavour it. Salted water is adequate for a whole fish, but when a steak or cutlets are cooked use a flavoured court bouillon.

A tepid court bouillon, which gives a better colour to fish, is usual for larger pieces, but with smaller cutlets you should use a hot one, which prevents too much seepage from the fish.

If cutlets are to be eaten cold, the flavour is improved by adding wine to the court bouillon. In this case leave fish to cool in the liquid.

To dish up, carefully lift fish out of kettle with the grid. Rest this for a few seconds on a piece of muslin to dry fish as much as possible. Then peel off skin and remove centre bone, if wished.

Serve with mayonnaise (see page 183) or hollandaise sauce (see the butter sauces section, page 181), a cucumber salad and boiled potatoes.

Smaller fish, such as grilse or salmon trout, can be cooked in the oven at 350°F or Mark 4 in an ovenproof dish with a small quantity of liquid; they must be basted frequently. Alternatively, wrap fish in foil.

Cooking times for salmon, grilse and salmon trout are as follows:

Whole fish (over 5 lb): 8 minutes per lb.

Whole fish, or middle cuts (under 5 lb): 10 minutes per lb.

Whole fish (under 2 lb): 10–20 minutes per lb.

Cutlets: 12–15 minutes, according to thickness.

Steaming. For a thick steak or large piece of salmon, first season, then wrap fish in buttered foil. Cook in a steamer or fish kettle, allowing 20 minutes per lb. If serving cold, cool fish before unwrapping.

SALMON TROUT (SEA TROUT)

This is very like salmon but smaller with pale pink, delicate flesh. A fish weighs from 1½–3½ lb and is cooked whole. Salmon trout are in season from May to July.

The simplest way to cook them is poaching. Curl them slightly after washing and trimming and put them into an ovenproof dish or tin. Pour round a little water, add salt and a good squeeze of lemon juice and cover with foil or greaseproof paper. Cook in the oven at 350°F or Mark 4, basting frequently. Cooking times as for salmon (see above).

Leave on the head because this gives a good indication of when the fish is cooked – the eyes become firm and white.

Salmon steaks aux gourmets

3 salmon steaks (each weighing 6–8 oz)
1 wineglass white wine
squeeze of lemon juice
1 slice of onion
6 peppercorns
sprig of parsley

For hollandaise sauce
4 tablespoons tarragon vinegar
1 blade of mace
6 peppercorns
3 egg yolks (beaten)
4–6 oz butter

For garnish
3 tomatoes
3 oz button mushrooms
½ oz butter
salt and pepper
tomato purée
grated rind of ½ orange

This recipe serves 6 for a first course. If serving as a main course for 4, use 2 salmon steaks, each weighing 8–12 oz.

Method
Wash and dry salmon steaks. Set oven at 350°F or Mark 4. Place steaks in an ovenproof dish and poach them in the white wine and lemon juice, with onion and seasonings, in pre-set moderate oven for about 15 minutes.

To prepare hollandaise sauce: reduce tarragon vinegar with the mace and peppercorns. Cream the egg yolk with ¼ oz butter; strain and add the liquid. Thicken sauce in a bain marie, gradually adding remaining butter. Set sauce aside.

To prepare the garnish: scald and skin tomatoes, cut in four, squeeze away the seeds and cut flesh into neat shreds. Slice the mushrooms and sauté in butter, with a squeeze of lemon juice and seasoning.

Strain the liquor from the fish, reduce it to 1 tablespoon and add it to hollandaise sauce with a 'touch' of tomato purée, and the orange rind. Remove the skin and bones from the salmon, divide each steak in two and arrange in a warm serving dish. Add the garnish to the sauce and spoon it over the fish. This may be glazed quickly under a hot grill, if wished, before serving.

SKATE

This flat sea-water fish has become much more popular in recent years and therefore more expensive. At one time it was seldom seen outside fried fish shops; now it is in most fishmongers.

The flesh is creamy white, very digestible and excellent in flavour. Skate is at its best from August to April. As a whole fish it is extremely ugly and the only parts that are sold are the side pieces or 'wings'. Each wing weighs 1½–2½ lb; the underside is white, the upper side mottled brown and black. After cooking, both skins are removed. At first sight the wing may seem full of bones but these are really a gelatinous gristle and are easily removed on the plate.

The best methods of cooking are deep fat frying or poaching in a court bouillon before finishing off in various ways. One of the best recipes for it, skate in black butter (au beurre noir), is given here.

Skate in black butter

This dish is cooked the same way as poached cod. Only the side pieces (wings) of the fish are eaten. The flesh is white, light and easy to digest. Wings of skate weigh from 1½–2½ lb; the best method of cooking them is to poach them in a court bouillon and serve with black butter, or finish with a light cheese sauce.

1–2 wings of skate (weighing about 2 lb in all)

For court bouillon
as for poached cod but with double amount of vinegar

For black butter
2–3 oz butter
1 tablespoon capers
1 dessertspoon parsley (chopped)
5 tablespoons wine vinegar
salt and pepper

Method
Have ready court bouillon. Strain into a comparatively shallow pan such as a deep frying pan with a lid. Well wash the skate and cut into wedges; the bone looks tough but is quite easy to cut through. Put fish into warm stock, cover,

Poached wings of skate in black butter with a garnish of capers

bring slowly to boil and simmer gently for 15–20 minutes. Lift out fish, drain on muslin, or absorbent paper, and gently scrape away any skin. Place on a hot dish, slide into oven to keep hot.

To make black butter: pour off the stock, reheat the pan, drop in the butter and cook to a rich brown (not black) colour. Spoon quickly over the fish, season, if necessary, then scatter over the capers and parsley. Add vinegar to the pan and reduce quickly by half. Pour over the dish and serve very hot with plain, boiled potatoes.

SOLE
Considered the best of white fish, there are two main varieties, Dover (or black) sole, which is the most prized and most expensive, and the lemon sole. Both are flat sea-water fish, the Dover sole with a brownish-black skin and rather narrow shape and the lemon a paler, more sandy brown and a larger oval in shape.

Lemon soles weigh from 1–2 lb and, after skinning on both sides, may be grilled whole, or filleted and served fried meunière (in foaming butter with beurre noisette poured over), or poached and coated with various sauces.

Small Dover or black soles, weighing 8–12 oz are known as 'slip' soles. Skinned on both sides, they may be grilled, fried, or boned and stuffed. Soles are available all year round but at their best from April to January.

Sole véronique

1½ lb sole (filleted)
1 wineglass water
¼ wineglass white wine
6 peppercorns
1 slice of onion
4–6 oz green grapes
lemon juice

For sauce
1 oz butter
1 rounded tablespoon flour
salt and pepper
4 fl oz creamy milk, or single cream
1 egg yolk
parsley (chopped)

Method
Wash and dry fillets. Fold and place in a buttered ovenproof dish. Pour over the water and wine and add the peppercorns and onion. Cover with buttered paper and poach in the oven at 325°–350°F or Mark 3–4 for 10–15 minutes.

Meanwhile peel and pip grapes. Sprinkle with lemon juice and keep covered until wanted.

To make sauce: melt butter in saucepan, stir in flour off heat, strain on the liquor from the fish. Blend and stir until boiling, season and draw aside. Mix cream and yolk together and add to the sauce. Thicken over the heat without boiling, then add grapes. Put sole on serving dish and spoon over the sauce. Sprinkle with chopped parsley.

Fillets of sole Dugléré

1½ lb sole (filleted, with bone)
½ pint fish stock (made from 1 shallot, 6 peppercorns, 1 bay-leaf, salt)

For sauce
2 tomatoes (ripe and firm)
1 oz butter
1 rounded tablespoon flour
stock from fish
4–5 tablespoons single cream, or top of milk
salt and pepper
1 dessertspoon parsley (chopped)

This dish is a classic and best made with Dover or lemon sole. For a main course, allow 2 fillets per person.

Method

First make stock. Break fish bone into 2–3 pieces, put into a pan with shallot, peppercorns and bayleaf. Pour on ½ pint water, add a little salt then simmer, covered, for 20 minutes. Strain and cool.

Skin fillets, if not already done by the fishmonger, then wash and dry. Fold them over, skinned side under and the tail end on top to make the fillet slightly pointed. Lay in a buttered fireproof dish and pour over stock. Cover with buttered paper or foil, poach in oven for 10–12 minutes at 350°F or Mark 4.

To prepare sauce: scald, peel and quarter tomatoes. Cut away stalk from each quarter, flick out seeds. Cut lengthways into three strips. Then melt the butter, blend in the flour and cook for 2–3 seconds, then draw aside. Take up the fish, dish up and keep warm. Strain the stock on to the roux, blend, return to the heat and stir until thickening. Then add cream or milk, season and bring to the boil. Simmer 1–2 minutes, then add tomatoes and parsley. Spoon over fillets at once.

This sauce is known as a velouté, ie. velvety, and is made with a lightly-cooked roux (see page 178). The liquid should always be stock with cream or creamy milk added at end; if fish has been poached in fish stock, this makes for a better sauce, but you can use plain water with sliced shallot and backbone laid on top.

FOLDING

This process is especially important when cooking any advanced recipe using filleted fish. Careful and neat folding makes a vast difference to the appearance of the finished dish.

Fold the fillets once over, skinned side underneath; keep the tail half on the top and tuck the tip under, making sure that all the fillets are the same length. This may mean less of the top part of two fillets being tucked underneath in order to even them out.

Where fish is served as a main course, a double fillet may be either folded over as above, or folded over lengthways.

To fold a fillet in three, tuck under tail and head end

To fold fillet in two, bring the head end to meet the tail

Fillet of sole Dugléré was named after the French chef Dugléré who used to work at the famous Café Anglais in Paris (no longer in existence).

SPRATS

These are very like herrings but much smaller, and the fry (young) is often sold as white-bait. Smoked sprats are used in an hors d'oeuvre.

To fry sprats: first wash and dry in absorbent paper. Roll in seasoned flour, then fry in shallow or deep fat. (See page 96.)

TURBOT

This is one of the finest white fish, with firm white flesh and a gelatinous skin. Turbot can grow to an enormous size, but small fish, known as chicken turbot, weighing about 6 lb, can be bought whole or filleted.

TROUT

This freshwater fish is related to the sea trout and salmon, and there is a wide variation in size and colour. The common brown trout is easily identified by the red spots on the side of its body, and generally weighs up to 10 lb.

WHITEBAIT

These tiny silvery fish are the fry of herring and are held in great esteem. Always deep fat fried, they are served as a first course with quarters of lemon and thinly-sliced brown bread and butter. They should be crisp yet slightly soft inside, and eaten heads, tail and all.

To fry whitebait (allow 4 oz per person): spread out fish and pick over, discarding any broken ones or weed, but do not wash. Roll them in seasoned flour, shake in a bowl strainer to remove surplus flour (or put them in a paper bag containing some of the flour, shake well and tip out on to a strainer).

Heat oil or fat to 350°F or 370°F in deep fat bath. Put just enough whitebait into frying basket to cover bottom, lower into fat and fry for 2–3 minutes only.

Lift out, drain and tip on to absorbent paper. Repeat until all whitebait are fried. Then reheat fat to 400°F, oil to 375°F, put all fish into frying basket and fry until just brown and crisp (3–4 minutes). Drain, sprinkle with salt and pepper, or cayenne pepper. Serve hot.

WHITING

These round, sea-water fish are light and silvery in colour, weighing from ½–1 lb. The delicate flesh is 'friable' (apt to crumble) and easy to digest.

Boning out a trout

There are two ways of boning out, depending on whether or not the trout is raw or cooked.

Raw trout. First snip off the fins and vandyke the tail with scissors. Cut off the head and, with a sharp knife, slit down the back, keeping the knife on top of the backbone. Open up the fish until it lies flat on the working surface.

Slip the knife under the bone at the head end and cut down to just above the tail. Lift out the bone.

Cooked trout. In this case, the head is usually kept on. First carefully remove skin, then slit down the back as above; nick through the backbone at head and tail end with scissors. Gently pull out bone, sideways, starting at the tail end.

Cutting head off raw trout

Removing its cooked skin

Slitting down trout's back

Pulling out its backbone

Stuffed trout

4–5 even-size trout
melted butter

For cream farce
1 lb whiting, or fresh haddock fillet
3 egg whites
7½ fl oz double cream
salt and pepper

To finish
1–2 shallots (finely chopped)
1½ oz butter
1 wineglass white wine
1 teaspoon brandy
1 tablespoon chopped parsley

Method
Bone out trout and set them aside. Set oven at 350°F or Mark 4.

To prepare farce: wash and dry fish, skin, then pass flesh through a mincer or work in a blender. Break egg whites with a fork and beat into the fish gradually, either by hand or in a blender. Pass mixture through a wire sieve, turn it into a bowl and gradually beat in the cream, then season.

Spread farce along the trout, reshape them and lift carefully into a well-buttered ovenproof dish. Pour over a little melted butter and cook them in pre-set oven for 15–20 minutes. Then slide dish under a hot grill for 3–5 minutes to crisp the skins and keep warm.

To finish: soften the shallots in butter and cook until they begin to change colour. Add wine and seasoning and cook rapidly for 1 minute; add the brandy and parsley to the pan, stir, then pour over the trout.

Turbot basquaise

2 lb turbot (cut in 6 even-size steaks)

For court bouillon
¼ pint water
1 wineglass white wine
squeeze of lemon juice
salt and pepper
1 teaspoon tomato purée
1 clove of garlic (crushed with a pinch of salt)
½ pint mayonnaise
2 red peppers
6 oz firm mushrooms
2 tablespoons oil
4 tablespoons French dressing
6 oz prawns (shelled)

Method
Set oven at 350°F or Mark 4. Wash and dry turbot steaks. Place them in a buttered oven-proof dish with the water, white wine, lemon juice and seasoning to flavour. Poach in pre-set moderate oven for 15–20 minutes and leave to cool.

Add the tomato purée, garlic and a little of the strained fish liquor to the mayonnaise. Grill the peppers or pierce them with long skewers and hold in a gas flame until the skin is charred and easy to scrape away; wash them under a cold tap to stop them cooking further, then dry and shred them. Wash the mushrooms quickly in salted water, then cut them in thick slices. Heat 2 tablespoons oil in a pan, add the mushrooms and peppers and sauté briskly for 1 minute. Tip them into a basin and moisten with French dressing.

Drain fish steaks, and remove the bones and black skin, and place them in a serving dish; add enough of the flavoured mayonnaise to bind the prawns and spoon over the fish. Garnish with the salpicon of pepper and mushrooms and serve remaining mayonnaise separately.

The **Basque** country lies both in France and Spain, being divided by the Pyrénées. The people of the region have developed an individual cuisine although much has been borrowed from both cultures. Mushrooms are a popular ingredient, and red peppers suggest a Spanish influence.

SHELLFISH

LANGOUSTE (CRAWFISH)

This is a rock lobster which is very popular on the continent. It is usually very large, weighing 3–4 lb with a rough brown red shell and no large claws. The meat is all in the tail and is cut into 'scallops' for serving. Langoustes are used as a 'pièce montée' (centrepiece) on a cold table. The flavour is similar to a lobster but the texture of the meat is coarser. Prepare and serve as for lobster.

CRAB

Crabs are in season in Britain from May to September and are usually sold ready cooked. If alive, boil them gently in salted water or a court bouillon (allow 15 minutes per lb). Then cool in the liquid before taking out and allowing to get quite cold. The crab is then dressed, whether it is to be served hot or cold. Some fishmongers sell them dressed or will dress them for you at a small extra charge.

Good crabs are heavy for their size. The claws contain most of the white meat, the cock's claw's being larger than the hen's. Frozen crab meat, both white and brown, is available throughout the year, and is excellent for mousses and soufflés, both hot and cold, and for savouries. For 4 people allow a 2 lb crab or 2 smaller ones.

To dress crab: first remove big claws, and set aside, then twist off the small claws, at the same time removing the crab's body or undershell. Set aside. Take out and throw away the following parts:

1 The small sac lying in the top of the big shell
2 Any green matter in the big shell
3 The spongy fingers or lungs lying around the big shell

Using a teaspoon, scrape into a small bowl all the brown creamy part lying round the sides of the big shell. Now take a cloth and, holding the big shell firmly, break down the sides, which are recognisably marked. The shell should now be well washed and dried.

Dressed crab, garnished with sieved boiled egg and chopped parsley, crab claws, lettuce and radishes, cut to form roses; serve with mayonnaise and brown bread and butter separately

Cut the body of the crab into two and extract all the white meat with a skewer and place in a bowl, but take care not to break off any fine pieces of shell. Crack the big claws, extract all the meat and shred it, break it up well, again avoiding breaking off any fine pieces of shell.

Collect all the white meat together; thoroughly cream the brown part and season it well with pepper, salt and mustard. Add about 2 tablespoons of dry breadcrumbs (and 1 tablespoon of cream if the mixture seems stiff). This brown mixture is then arranged across the middle of the shell with the white meat piled on either side. When serving crab cold, you can decorate it with sieved, hard-boiled egg and some chopped parsley. Make a ring of claws by sticking the small ones into one another and lay the shell in the middle of this. Surround with crisp lettuce leaves, radishes, etc. and serve with mayonnaise (see page 183), or tartare sauce (see page 63), or a sharp French dressing, all with brown bread and butter. Alternatively serve with pats of maître d'hôtel butter and toast.

Crab soufflé

¾ lb crab meat (white and
    brown, or all white)
2 shallots (finely chopped)
1 oz butter
1 teaspoon each curry powder,
    and paprika pepper
2 tablespoons single cream
1–2 tablespoons sherry
¼ pint béchamel sauce (made
    with 1 oz butter, 1 tablespoon
    flour, ¼ pint flavoured milk)
dash of Tabasco sauce
salt and pepper
3 egg yolks
4 egg whites
browned crumbs
grated Parmesan cheese

*6-inch diameter top (No. 2 size)
    soufflé dish*

Method

Set oven at 375°F or Mark 5
and prepare the soufflé dish.
Soften shallots in half the butter,
add curry powder and paprika
and cook for 2 seconds. Add to
the crab meat with the cream
and sherry. Have ready the
béchamel sauce, beat it into
the crab meat with the seasonings and egg yolks. Whip whites
to a firm snow, then cut and
fold them into the mixture. Turn
into prepared dish, dust top
with crumbs and cheese. Put
into a pre-set oven and bake
for 20–30 minutes. Serve the
soufflé at once.

LOBSTERS

These are among the best of
shellfish and are delicious
eaten cold (freshly boiled), or
hot with one of the classic
sauces associated with lobster.
The season in Britain is from
March to October, but they are
available at other times of the
year, though very expensive.

When raw, lobsters are a dark
greenish-blue but their shells
change to a brilliant red when
cooked. Avoid buying very
large lobsters and those that
are covered in barnacles – this
usually indicates tough flesh.
Hen lobsters are esteemed for
their coral or spawn which is
used to flavour and colour
lobster butter for sauces and
soups, while a cock lobster is
prized for its fine, slightly
firmer flesh. The average weight
is 1–1¼ lb and one of this size
will serve two people. Smaller
lobsters, averaging ¾ lb each,
are especially suitable for a first
course. Again, serve half per
person. Choose live lobsters
that feel heavy for their size
and lively. If making a hot
lobster dish, it is essential to buy
them alive; in this way double
cooking is avoided so that meat
and sauce will be delicious and
full of flavour. The process of
killing a lobster is not difficult
and for the lobster it is quick and
painless.

To kill a lobster: choose a
sharp chopping knife. Lay the
lobster out flat on a wooden
board, hard shell uppermost.
Have the head toward your
right hand and cover the tail
with a cloth. Hold lobster firmly
behind the head with your left
hand and with the point of the
knife pierce right through the
little cross mark which lies on
the centre of the head. The
lobster is killed at once.

To split a lobster: cut through
the top part of the head, turn
lobster round and continue to
cut through the rear part of the
head and down through the
tail. Open out the two halves on
the board and take out the dark
thread (the intestine) which
runs down the tail, and a small
sac usually containing weed
which lies in the top part of the
head. These are the only parts
to be thrown away. The greenish
part also in the head is the liver
which should be retained as it is
considered a delicacy.

To boil a lobster: rinse
lobster quickly in cold water,
have the court bouillon (or
salted water) ready on the boil.
Put in the live lobster, making
sure there is sufficient liquid to
cover it. Cover pan, reboil and
simmer gently, allowing 20
minutes for a lobster 1 lb in
weight, 30 minutes for 1½ lb,
and over that weight, 45
minutes. Draw pan aside and
cool it in the liquid. Lift out and
allow lobster to get quite cold.
Rub shell and whiskers with a
little oil before splitting.

To dress a lobster: split
lobster in two, remove sac and
intestine, and twist off the big
claws. Crack these and carefully
lift out the meat, removing the
piece of membrane which lies
down the middle of the claw.
Twist (or snip off with the
scissors) the small claws, being
careful to keep the creamy part
in the head. Using the handle
of a wooden spoon, roll the
small claws with this to extract
the meat, then fit one into
another to form a circle. This

makes a good base to set the
half shells on for serving. With
the point of a small knife lift
out the tail meat, cut diagonally
into thick slices or scallops and
replace them, rounded side up,
in the opposite half shell.
Arrange the claw meat on the
head shells, set the lobster
on the claw circle in the
serving dish, garnish with
watercress and serve mayonnaise separately.

Watchpoint If time is short
omit the rolling out of the small
claws, they can be used instead
for garnish.

See page 35 for a recipe for
lobster bisque soup.

Court bouillon
for shellfish

Slice 2 medium-size onions
and a carrot, soften them
slowly in ½ oz butter, using a
pan large enough to hold the
shellfish. Add the juice of ½
lemon, a large bouquet garni, 6
peppercorns, 2 pints water, ¼

Hot lobster thermidor

Splitting the uncooked lobsters

Coating the cooked lobsters

Lobster thermidor

2 live lobsters (about ¾–1 lb each)
2 tablespoons oil
1½ oz butter
béchamel sauce (made with 1 oz
  butter, scant 1 oz flour, 7½ fl oz
  flavoured milk)
2 shallots (finely chopped)
1 wineglass dry white wine
1 teaspoon each tarragon and
  chervil (chopped), or pinch of
  dried herbs
2 tablespoons double cream
½ teaspoon French mustard
2 tablespoons grated Parmesan
  cheese
salt and pepper

To finish

browned crumbs
melted butter
watercress

Method

Kill and split lobsters, remove sac and intestine. Have ready the oil and 1 oz of the butter, heated in a sauté pan. Put in the lobster, cut side downwards, cover pan and cook gently for 12–15 minutes or until the lobster is red. Turn once only.

Make and set aside béchamel sauce in pan. Put shallot in a smaller saucepan with rest of butter, cook for ½ minute then add wine and herbs. Reduce to half quantity then add to the béchamel sauce. Set this mixture on low heat.

Take out the lobsters and strain any juice into the sauce. Stir well, add cream. Simmer for 2–3 minutes, then draw aside and mix in mustard and half the cheese. Season, cover pan and leave off heat.

Take out lobster meat, coarsely chopping claw meat and slicing tail into 'scallops'. Add 1–2 tablespoons of sauce to the claw meat and put into the head shells. Put 1 tablespoon of sauce into the tail shells and replace 'scallops', rounded side up. Place shells on a baking sheet, wedging them with a piece of potato or on circles of claws. Coat lobster with rest of sauce, sprinkle with crumbs, rest of cheese and a little melted butter. Brown in the oven at 400°F or Mark 6 for 7–10 minutes. Garnish with watercress and serve very hot on a napkin.

Watchpoint This dish can be prepared in the morning and left ready for browning before serving in the evening.

Note: if there is coral (spawn) in the lobster, remove after splitting. Work on a plate with a palette knife, adding about ½ oz butter, then rub through a bowl strainer. Lobster thermidor does not have coral added but if you have no other immediate use for it (such as for a soup) add it to the sauce with the cream.

Lobster salad Valencia

2 live lobsters (¾ lb each)
2 pints court bouillon
pinch of saffron
1 cucumber
1 red and 1 green pepper
  (blanched)
1 lb tomatoes (skinned, seeds
  removed)
½ lb long grain rice

Method

Cook the lobsters in court bouillon for 15 minutes and allow to cool in the liquid.

Soak the saffron in a very little water; slice the cucumber and sprinkle with salt, cover and leave for about 30 minutes in a cool place. Shred the peppers and roughly chop the tomatoes.

Cook the rice in boiling water and the saffron liquid, drain, rinse and dry thoroughly.

Cut the lobster meat in neat, even-size pieces and mix with the rice and vegetables.

pint white wine and 1 teaspoon salt. Simmer together for 15–20 minutes.

Tartare sauce

2 eggs (hard-boiled)
1 egg yolk (raw)
salt and pepper
½ pint oil
1 tablespoon vinegar
1 teaspoon chopped parsley
1 teaspoon snipped chives
1 teaspoon chopped capers,
  or gherkins

Method

Cut the hard-boiled eggs in half, remove the yolks and rub them through a strainer into a bowl. Add the raw yolk and seasoning; work well together. Add the oil drop by drop, as for a mayonnaise, and dilute with the vinegar as necessary. Finish off with the herbs and capers. If wished, add the shredded white of one of the hard-boiled eggs.

Moules marinière

2 quarts mussels
1 onion (quartered)
1 carrot (quartered)
1 stick of celery (sliced)
large bouquet garni
1 wineglass white wine
   (optional)
1 wineglass water, or 2 if no
   wine is used
1 oz butter
1 rounded tablespoon flour
1 rounded tablespoon fresh
   parsley (coarsely chopped)
pepper

Piece of butter muslin

Scrub the mussels well with a stiff brush after first rinse

Moules marinière are best eaten with a fork and your fingers; as this dish is quite messy, put out finger bowls and a spoon for juice. Open mussels with your fingers, prise flesh from shells with a fork

MUSSELS

These are small shellfish found round the shores of Britain, Holland and France. They live on rocks and sandbanks and, like all shellfish, they should be eaten as fresh as possible.

They are sold by quart measure rather than weight, and must be tightly closed before cooking. Examine them carefully during the first thorough rinsing in cold water, and sharply tap any that are not tightly closed with the handle of a knife. If they do not respond by closing, discard them.

Scrub the mussels well with a small stiff brush and pull or scrape away any small pieces of weed from the sides. Rinse under a running tap, then soak them in a bowl of fresh water; do not tip this water off the mussels as this might leave sand still in them, but lift them into another bowl or colander and wash again. When thoroughly

clean, lift them out and put into a large pan for cooking.

If mussels have to be kept overnight, store in a bowl without water in a cool place and cover them with a heavy damp cloth.

If storing mussels for a day or two, cover them with cold sea-water (if available) after washing and add a good tablespoon of oatmeal. This will feed them and keep them plump.

Some people eat the beard — the slightly gristly ring round the mussel — but this can be pulled away with a fork, knife or finger before serving. As it is a lengthy process to take off both top shell and beard, it is really best left to each individual at the table.

Moules marinière are eaten from soup plates and may be dished up in these with the sauce poured over them. Have a large bowl in the middle of the table for empty shells.

Method
Put the well-washed mussels into a large pan. Tuck the vegetables down among the mussels with the bouquet garni. Pour over the liquid, cover pan

with a close-fitting lid and put on moderate heat. Leave until the liquid boils right up over mussels. Draw pan aside at once.

Work the butter and flour together and set aside. Strain mussel liquid from pan through a piece of butter muslin into a smaller pan. Then add the kneaded butter, piece by piece, off the heat whisking it in well. Put this pan on heat, bring to the boil and cook gently for 4–5 minutes. Add the parsley and season well with pepper.

To serve, turn the mussels into a deep dish or soup tureen and pour over the sauce.

OYSTERS

In Great Britain oysters are in season from September to April – when there is an 'r' in the month. They are at their best served chilled and raw as a first course, with quartered lemon, tabasco sauce and black pepper handed separately. Freshly cut brown bread and butter should also be served.

Second-grade oysters are smaller in size than the best; use in sauces or, instead of canned ones, as in the following recipe.

Angels on horseback

8 oysters (2 per person)
8 bacon rashers
4 slices of toast
butter (for toast)

Raw oysters are expensive and difficult to open; canned ones are more convenient to use.

Method

Wrap oysters in bacon rashers, fasten each roll with fine skewers and grill for 4–5 minutes, or bake in the oven for 5–6 minutes at 400°F or Mark 6.

Serve on hot buttered toast.

Angels on horseback are oysters wrapped in bacon rashers

PRAWNS

Fresh prawns in season are best but the excellence and value of the frozen variety makes them an all-year-round delicacy.

Quick thawing toughens them and spoils the flavour though, so they are best bought the day before and left overnight in the body of the refrigerator, or a very cool larder. They should then be succulent and tender.

Prawns Frederick

1 lb prawns (shelled)
1 small head of celery (cut in small sticks)
little cornflour
oil (for frying)
6 oz rice (boiled)
3 quarts salted water

For sauce
2 onions (sliced)
3 tablespoons oil
1 teaspoon curry powder
1½ gills tomato juice, or tomato cocktail
1 dessertspoon tomato purée
salt and pepper
2–3 tablespoons tomato and pepper chutney, or a sweet tomato chutney, or pickle

The sauce, which is best made well before frying the prawns so

that it can mellow, is also good with fried or grilled fish.

Method

To prepare sauce: slice onions, cook in hot oil until turning colour, add curry powder and after 1–2 minutes, tip on the tomato juice. Add tomato purée, season to taste, and simmer for 5 minutes. Draw aside and add the chutney.

Cut celery in small sticks, roll these and the prawns in cornflour, fry at once in a pan of hot oil to a golden-brown.

Pour over the sauce and serve at once with boiled rice

SHRIMPS

These can be used as for prawns, but being much smaller they are troublesome to shell. They may be bought frozen or in cans and are especially suitable for shrimp sauce to serve with boiled fish or for savouries. See page 21 for Shrimps Mariette – a party starter.

DUBLIN BAY PRAWNS

If bought raw, in the shell, boil them gently in a court bouillon for 10–15 minutes. Serve them cold as a first course with mayonnaise, or French dressing, and brown bread and butter. The meat is sweet and delicious and is easier to get at if the body and claw shells are lightly cracked before serving. Have finger bowls on the table and a small fork or lobster pick for each guest.

SCALLOPS

Scallops, when alive, have their shells tightly closed, but they are usually bought ready prepared (opened and cleaned).

The easiest way to open them yourself is to put the shells into a hot oven for 4–5 minutes. The heat will cause the shells to gape. You must then carefully scrape away the fringe or beard which surrounds the scallop, attached to the flat shell, and the black thread (the intestine) which lies round it.

Slip a sharp knife under the scallop to detach it and the roe from shell. Scallops must be handled carefully as the roe is delicate.

Scrub each shell thoroughly; these make good dishes to serve scallops in and can be used several times over.

Scallops take only 6–7 minutes to cook and, like all shellfish, should be simmered – not boiled (which makes them tough and tasteless). They can also be baked, fried or grilled.

Scallops with red wine and mushrooms make a very attractive dish. The creamed potato piped round edge is browned in oven just before serving, then sprinkled with a little chopped parsley

Scallops with red wine and mushrooms

4 large scallops
¼ pint water
2–3 drops of lemon juice
1 oz butter
1 medium-size onion (finely chopped)
3 oz button mushrooms (quartered)
1 clove of garlic (crushed with salt)
1 rounded dessertspoon flour
1 wineglass of fish, or vegetable, stock, or liquor from scallops
1 teaspoon tomato purée
salt
black pepper (ground from mill)
1 wineglass red wine
2 tomatoes
4 tablespoons breadcrumbs (browned)
2 oz butter (melted)
creamed potatoes (for piping) – optional
parsley (chopped)

Method

Remove scallops from shells, wash and dry them well.

Put scallops into a shallow pan, pour on the water and add lemon juice. Cover and poach for 5 minutes. Turn into a basin, reserving liquid. Melt butter in the pan, add onion, cover and cook gently for 2 minutes. Put in mushrooms, increase heat and cook briskly for a further 2 minutes, stirring all the time. Draw pan aside, stir in garlic and flour and blend; add the stock or liquor from the scallops, tomato purée and seasoning. Bring to the boil and simmer for 2–3 minutes.

Boil wine in a small pan until reduced by about a third. Add to the sauce and simmer for a further 5 minutes.

Scald and skin tomatoes, quarter and remove the seeds and cut away the little piece of hard stalk. Cut each piece of tomato in half lengthways and add to the sauce with the scallops. Spoon at once into the deep shells. Sprinkle well with the breadcrumbs tossed in melted butter.

If using creamed potato (see right), pipe it round the shells to make a thick border before setting them on a baking sheet.

Put scallops in oven for about 5 minutes at 375°F or Mark 5 until they are brown. Dust with chopped parsley before serving.

Creamed potato for piping

Boil peeled potatoes, drain and dry well. Mash or put through a Mouli sieve.

Gradually beat in boiling milk (½ pint to every 1½ lb potatoes), with about 1 oz butter, and season to taste. This can be kept hot for up to 30 minutes by covering the levelled surface in the pan with 2–3 tablespoons of hot milk and the lid. Beat up before piping (use a vegetable rose nozzle) thickly round shells and browning, preferably in oven or under the grill.

SCAMPI

Frozen scampi must be allowed to thaw out gradually (12 hours or more in a refrigerator). If using fresh Dublin Bay prawns, remove head and claws and cut away the body shell after cooking.

Scampi make an excellent, if somewhat expensive, first course and also mix well with other shellfish.

Serve scampi provençale surrounded by plain boiled rice

Scampi provençale

1 lb scampi
seasoned flour
1 oz butter (to sauté)
3 oz button mushrooms (sliced)
3 tomatoes (skinned, hard stalk and seeds removed)
5 oz boiled rice (for serving)

For sauce
2 shallots (finely chopped)
bouquet garni
1 wineglass white wine
1 oz butter
½ oz flour
1 clove of garlic (crushed with ½ teaspoon salt)
1 teaspoon tomato purée
½ pint good stock

Method
Prepare the sauce. Simmer shallots with bouquet garni and wine until liquor is reduced by half, then remove bouquet garni and set sauce aside.

Melt ½ oz butter, add flour, brown lightly, then add garlic, tomato purée and stock. Simmer for 10–15 minutes, then pour in reduced wine and cook a further 5 minutes. Draw aside and add small shavings of butter. Keep hot.

Roll scampi in seasoned flour and sauté lightly in 1 oz butter for 5–6 minutes. Lift into serving dish. Sauté the mushrooms in the pan and add to the sauce with the tomatoes, roughly chopped. Reboil for 1 minute, then spoon over scampi, serve with rice.

Scampi à la crème

1 lb scampi
1 oz butter
1 teaspoon paprika pepper
1 glass sherry
3 egg yolks
7½ fl oz double cream
4 tomatoes (skinned, quartered, seeds removed and the quarters cut in half)
5 oz rice (boiled)

Method
Heat the scampi gently in the butter, add the paprika and flame with the sherry, boil so as to reduce liquid by half.

Blend the egg yolks with the cream, strain into the pan and cook carefully until the sauce coats the back of a spoon. Add the tomatoes, season to taste, turn into a warm dish to serve.

Serve with boiled rice.

67

Grilling Meat and Fish

As a method of cooking, grilling has certain advantages; it is quick, straightforward and good for a meal which has to be on the table in a hurry; it is ideal for the diet-conscious because grills have little fat and almost no liquid. However, cuts have to be of the best quality, so a grill is not a cheap dish. On the following pages, you will find basic rules for grilling, together with recipes for grills and savoury butters.

Since a grill is a last-minute dish and one that should be served at once, it is not easy for the cook/hostess. Some grills such as cutlets, chops and kebabs can be kept hot for a short time in the grill pan with the juices, and heat turned low. Steaks, however, should be served at once. All grilling calls for a certain amount of attention, especially gammon steaks or white fish such as plaice or sole, which tend to be dry unless brushed with melted butter or oil every 2–3 minutes.

The grill should be turned on at least 5–6 minutes before use to get the maximum heat. While it is heating leave grill pan underneath with grid set at right height. If food is getting overcooked when actually grilling, lower grid rather than grill heat.

Do not salt meat or fish before grilling; this causes juices to run, making food less succulent, but meat may be peppered (ground from mill). Then brush meat or fish with oil, turn over once or twice while grilling, keeping well brushed with oil (or as specified in individual recipe).

Buy the best cooking oil you can afford. Olive oil is the finest, but you can also use groundnut, or corn-based oil instead. It is more economical to buy large tins or bottles. The given times for grilling are approximate, depending on the grill, thickness of food and whether or not meat is to be pink inside or well done. A rule-of-thumb guide for steak is to press with your fingers: if it gives like a sponge, it is rare; if firmer and more resilient – medium rare; or firm with no resilience – well done.

An alternative method of grilling is dry frying. Take a thick, heavy frying pan – iron, ridged or enamelled iron, or cast aluminium. Set on full heat for several minutes, then put in 1 tablespoon of oil or dripping (free from gravy) and after a few seconds, put in meat. Keep on full heat until well browned on one side, pressing the food well down with a palette knife; then turn and brown on the other side.

Time this process and lower heat if necessary to complete cooking. The time will vary, depending on what is being grilled and how well cooked it is to be (see chart overleaf). Grills should be accompanied by savoury butters served separately or in pats on top of steak, cutlets, etc. Grilled meats look best when served plainly garnished with a sprig of watercress and chip/jacket potatoes. A mixed green salad also goes well with a grill.

Brochettes of kidney (see recipe on page 75) are made with lambs kidneys and lambs liver marinated in red wine

MEAT

BEEF

STEAK CUTS	GRILLING TIMES	
Rump (1½ lb slice, 1 inch thick, serves 3–4) This steak has incomparable flavour but to be tender must be well hung. A guide to this is the colour, which should have a purplish tinge with creamy-white fat. It improves if brushed with oil 1–2 hours before grilling. During grilling time brush once or twice with oil to prevent scorching	Rare: Medium rare: Well done:	6–7 minutes 8–10 minutes 14–16 minutes
Sirloin or entrecôte (¾–1 inch thick, serves 1) This steak is cut from the top part of the sirloin	Rare: Medium rare: Well done:	5 minutes 6–7 minutes 9–10 minutes
Minute (½ inch thick, serves 1) Thin slice of entrecôte. This steak should be cooked very rapidly and to get it properly browned without over-cooking, dry fry rather than grill	Rare: Medium rare:	1–1½ minutes 2–3 minutes
T-Bone (1½–2 inches thick, serves 2–3) A whole slice cut from the sirloin with the bone	Rare: Medium rare:	7–8 minutes 8–10 minutes
Porterhouse (1½–2 inches thick, serves 1–2) A slice cut from the wing rib, taken off the bone	Rare: Medium rare:	7–8 minutes 8–10 minutes
Fillet (1–1½ inches thick, serves 1) The most expensive and possibly most tender of steaks. There is a large demand for these slices cut across the fillet, so they are in short supply. The fillet (averaging 6–7 lb) lies under the sirloin and there is a comparatively small proportion of fillet in relation to the weight of the rest of the animal. Dry fry or grill	Rare: Medium rare to well done	6 minutes 7–8 minutes
Tournedos (1–1½ inches thick, serves 1) These are cut from the 'eye' of the fillet, ie. from centre after it has been trimmed (fillet steaks include the side or edges, ie. trimmings). A tournedos is very much a delicacy and may be served plainly grilled or dry fried with a garnish as for a fillet steak, or as a dish such as tournedos chasseur. The crisp dry fat in which fillet is encased (kidney suet) is very special; a small nut of this may be fried or grilled to top each tournedos	Rare: Medium rare to well done:	6 minutes 7–8 minutes
Chateaubriand (3–4 inches thick, serves 2) A thick cut taken from the heart of the fillet. This steak, once grilled or dry fried, is sliced downwards for serving	Rare to medium rare:	16–20 minutes

PORK

CHOPS

Loin chops are really the only cut of pork suitable for grilling. They should be neatly trimmed and any surplus fat removed before brushing with melted butter. Heat grill well before cooking chops thoroughly for 5–7 minutes on each side, brushing with butter to keep them moist.

Garnish with watercress and serve with an apple or barbecue sauce and sauté or fried potatoes. A salad goes better with pork chops than a cooked vegetable. (If using barbecue sauce, spoon a little over base of serving dish, arrange chops down the centre and serve remaining sauce separately.)

GAMMON STEAKS

These are ½-inch slices from the gammon of bacon which may be smoked or green, ie. unsmoked. The latter is milder in flavour. Cut away the rind and brush well with melted butter while grilling. Set the grid lower in the grill pan than for other meats. Allow about 7–8 minutes grilling time.

A slice of fried pineapple (preferably fresh) makes a good garnish. Serve with any of the following vegetables: spinach 'in the leaf' or creamed; runner or French beans; peas; fried or sauté potatoes.

LAMB

CUTLETS

These are taken from the best end of neck and though cutlets may be bought ready-cut and trimmed, it is more economical to buy the neck and prepare them at home.

Ask the butcher to chine the neck for you, that is to saw the half backbone (chine bone) through so that the cutlets can easily be divided. He will also saw through the end bones to shorten them by about 2–3 inches. Cut away this 'flap' which can then be divided into 4–5 pieces and grilled with the cutlets. The chine bone is also detached and used for broth or gravy. A whole best end contains 6–7 cutlet bones with an average weight of $1\frac{3}{4}$–2 lb, depending on the size of the animal.

Cutlets must be plump, otherwise they curl when grilled, or dry fried, and so become dry and tasteless. If the neck is medium-size, allow 5 cutlets from a whole piece of best end. This will give a nut of meat $\frac{3}{4}$–1 inch thick.

Divide the neck into cutlets with a sharp knife, taking two bones if necessary. Cut out the second bone and any excess fat. Leave a rim of fat (about $\frac{1}{4}$ inch) round the meat and the small piece that lies just under it. Scrape the bone clean.

To be attractive cutlets must be well trimmed and fat trimmings can be rendered down for use as dripping.

Brush with fat or oil and cook on grid or base of grilling pan for 7–8 minutes, turning once or twice and keeping well brushed with fat. The cutlets should be well browned with the fat crisp on the outside, and delicately pink when cut. Serve plain or with pats of savoury butters such as tomato, orange or chutney. Vegetables to accompany lamb cutlets are sauté cucumber with spring onions; peas and baby carrots; sauté artichokes.

NOISETTES

These are cutlets without the bone. Butchers will cut them for you, but you can prepare them at home.

Take the best end unchined and start boning at the chine bone end. Use a small sharp knife and with short strokes cut down to, and along, the cutlets' bones. Keep the knife well pressed on to the bones to avoid cutting into meat.

When the bone is out, season the cut surface of the meat and roll up, starting at the chine end. Trim off the end piece if there is more than enough to wrap once round the nut of meat. Tie securely at 1–1¼ inch intervals with fine string, then cut between each tie to make a noisette. Grill 7–8 minutes as for lamb cutlets.

Noisettes look best as a dish with special accompanying vegetables.

CHOPS

Loin chops are bought ready-cut and trimmed, and are 1–1½ inches thick.

Brush with oil and grill 8–9 minutes as for lamb cutlets. They should be well browned but slightly pink when cut. Serve with any of the savoury butters, especially chutney butter. Best vegetables are runner beans; ratatouille (dish from Provence, France, made with aubergines, sweet peppers, courgettes and tomatoes); courgettes in butter; new or creamed potatoes.

KEBABS

The traditional shashlik, ie. skewer, dish consists of square chunks of meat, usually lamb, cut from the shoulder or leg and threaded on to long metal skewers, interspersed with slices of onion and bayleaves. But a mixture can be made from chipolata sausages, bacon rolls and pieces of lamb or fillet steak. Put these on a skewer, brush with melted butter and grill, turning skewer to cook evenly.

Kebabs are generally dished up on boiled rice or a pilaf (rice cooked in seasoned stock until tender and all liquid has been absorbed). Barbecue sauce goes well with kebabs.

Choose lamb cutlets, sausages, mushrooms, and tomatoes for a tasty mixed grill, and garnish with watercress

Mixed grill

For a mixed grill, the following ingredients for one person are a guide. You need 1 cutlet, 1 kidney, 1 sausage, 1 tomato, 2 mushrooms, 1 rasher of bacon, some watercress for garnish and maître d'hôtel butter.

First prepare cutlets and kidneys (as before) and skewer kidneys to flatten. Do not prick the sausage as this makes it more likely to burst when cooking. Halve the tomatoes and season the cut surface. Peel the mushrooms (preferably large, flat ones) and cut stalks level with the caps. De-rind and flatten the bacon. Pick over the watercress. Prepare the maître d'hôtel butter and chill. Then heat the grill.

Grill tomatoes, rounded side uppermost first, and turn after 3–4 minutes. Dust tops with caster sugar, put a knob of butter on each and grill for the same time. Grill mushrooms in the same way, putting a knob of butter on each side. Lift on to a plate and keep hot.

Grill bacon, then the sausages, allowing 7–8 minutes, turning them once. Dish up with tomatoes and mushrooms. Keep hot.

Now grill the cutlets and add to the dish. Top the kidneys with a pat of maître d'hôtel butter, garnish dish with the watercress, serve piping hot. (Chip potatoes may also be served.)

> **Mushroom stalks** and peelings should not be thrown away. Chop them finely, cook in butter until dry and then store in an airtight jar. Use with soups and sauces to add flavour.

Kidneys

Lamb's kidneys, once a popular breakfast dish, are a classic ingredient of a mixed grill. To prepare them, carefully peel off the hard fat which encases them (imported kidneys have this already removed). Keep this suet which, when rendered down, makes an excellent frying fat or dripping.

Skin kidneys by nicking the skin on the rounded side and drawing it back towards the core. Pull gently to get out as much of the core as possible before cutting away the skin. Split open on the rounded side and thread a skewer through to keep flat. Brush with melted butter before grilling on rounded side first. Allow 6–8 minutes grilling time according to size. **Watchpoint** Do brush with melted butter from time to time to prevent kidneys from becoming dry. Don't overcook or they become very leathery.

Serve kidneys with maître d'hôtel or anchovy butter.

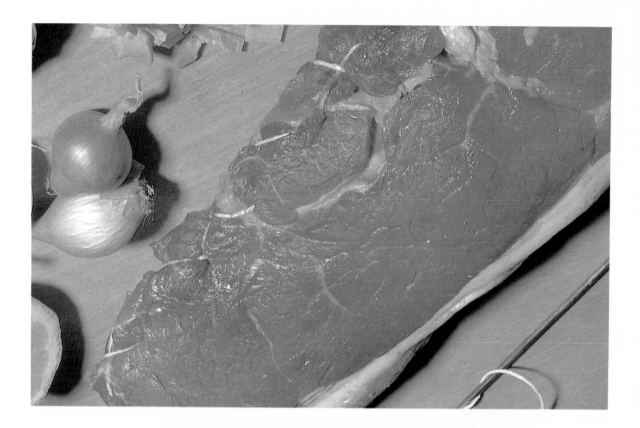

Garrick steak with parsley butter

(serves 3–4)

1½ lb rump steak (piece cut about
   1½ inches thick)
brushing of salad oil

For mushroom filling

1 shallot, or 1 teaspoon onion
   (finely chopped)
½ oz butter
4 oz mushrooms
1 teaspoon each parsley and
   thyme (chopped)
1 rounded tablespoon ham
   (chopped)
1 tablespoon fresh breadcrumbs
salt and pepper

For parsley butter

½ oz butter
1 teaspoon parsley (chopped)
dash of Worcestershire sauce, or
   squeeze of lemon juice

1 *trussing needle and fine string, or
poultry pins/lacers (tiny skewers with
a ring one end)*

*Garrick steak – an original way
to serve tender rump steak.
Meat is slit to form a pocket
and stuffed with a mushroom
and ham filling; then sewn up
and grilled*

Method

First prepare filling : soften the
chopped shallot or onion in the
butter. Wash mushrooms, chop
finely and add to the pan with
the herbs. Cover and cook 5–7
minutes. Draw aside and add
ham, crumbs and seasoning;
Turn out and cool.

Slit the steak on one side to
form a pocket, fill with the purée
and sew up with a trussing
needle and fine string, or secure
with poultry pins/lacers. Brush
steak with a little salad oil and
grill 4–5 minutes on each side.

Before serving remove string
or pins/lacers.

To prepare parsley butter :
Melt butter and when light
brown, add parsley and
Worcestershire sauce (or lemon
juice) and pour over the steak.
Slice downwards in ½-inch
slices.

Soubise denotes a purée of
onions, usually mixed with
rice, seasonings, butter and
cream, or with a béchamel
sauce instead of the rice.

Minute steak soubise

5 – 6 minute steaks
1 oz butter (for frying)
1 lb onions (thinly sliced)

For sauce

1 – 2 oz butter
2 wineglasses red wine
salt
black pepper (ground from mill)
¼ pint single cream
1 teaspoon arrowroot
2–3 tablespoons jellied stock, or
   bouillon cube

Minute steaks are often chosen
to be served plainly grilled, but
this recipe has a delicious sauce
for use on special occasions.

Method

Slice onions very thinly, sauté
(fry) slowly in 1 oz of the butter
until golden-brown. Add 1 glass
of wine, season and cook slowly
for 5–10 minutes. Strain onions
(reserving the liquid) and place
down centre of a serving dish.

Fry steaks quickly in butter,
dish up on bed of onion.

To prepare sauce: tip the
second glass of wine into the
frying pan, boil up well and then
add reserved liquid. Season and
add the cream. Mix the arrowroot with the stock, add to the
sauce and boil well. Spoon a
little of this sauce over the meat
and serve the rest separately.

Sirloin steak provençale has a salpicon of peppers and aubergines

Sirloin steak provençale

4 sirloin steaks
fat, or oil (for frying)

For salpicon

1 large onion (sliced)
2 red and 1 green peppers (shredded and blanched)
2 medium-size aubergines (sliced)
salt
oil (for frying)
12 small black olives (stoned)

For sauce

2 shallots (chopped)
1 dessertspoon tomato purée
1 wineglass white wine
½ wineglass stock

Method

First prepare salpicon: slice onion into rounds, shred peppers and blanch by putting into boiling water and boiling for ½ minute before draining. Slice aubergines and sprinkle with salt. Fry onion in oil until golden-brown, add peppers and shake over the heat for few minutes. Turn out and keep warm. Fry aubergines until brown and tender, add olives. Keep hot with onions and peppers.

Dry fry the steaks over high heat in fat or oil barely covering the base of a thick frying pan. Cook according to taste (see page 70). Dish up and cover each steak with the salpicon.

To make sauce: add shallots, tomato purée, wine and stock to same pan and boil up. Spoon sauce over the steaks and salpicon.

Provençale dishes make use of some of the vegetables characteristic of that region in southern France, such as tomatoes, peppers, aubergines, olives, and usually garlic.

Salpicon is the name given to a mixture of shredded ingredients usually bound with a rich sauce. This may be used as a garnish, a stuffing for pastry cases and other dishes, or be made into croquettes.

Carpet bag steak

This recipe is a speciality from New South Wales, particularly Sydney, where the oysters are really first class. For barbecue parties a thick rump steak sufficient for 4–6 people is usually used, but for a dinner party dry fried fillet steaks are the rule. Rump steak cut 1½ inches thick will require 12–16 oysters. For fillet steak, if the oysters are very small use 2 per steak; if large, 1 oyster would be sufficient.

For rump steak cut a pocket in the steak, fill with the oysters and then sprinkle with a few drops of lemon juice and grind on a little pepper from the mill. Secure with poultry pins or sew up with fine string and a trussing needle. Brush with a little melted butter and cook for 7–10 minutes on each side.

To serve, melt ½–¾ oz butter in a small pan and when it is nut brown pour in the juice of ½ lemon, season with salt and pepper and 1 teaspoon of chopped parsley. Pour foaming over the steak and serve at once.

For fillet steak cut a pocket in the same way and fill with 1–2 oysters. Dry fry these steaks and after cooking wipe out the pan and prepare and serve the butter sauce as described above.

Barbecued lamb chops

2 neck, or loin, lamb chops per person
oil

For barbecue sauce

2 large cooking apples (peeled and cored)
1 medium-size onion
¼ pint tomato ketchup
2 tablespoons brown sugar
½ teaspoon salt
¼ teaspoon black pepper
2 oz butter

Method

Brush chops with oil and leave for 1–2 hours before cooking.

To prepare the sauce: grate or mince the apple and onion into a saucepan, add all the other ingredients and bring to boil; simmer for 2–3 minutes.

Grill or fry lamb chops for 3 minutes on each side, spoon a little of the barbecue sauce over them and continue cooking a further 3 minutes until sauce is brown and sticky. Serve very hot with the remaining barbecue sauce handed separately.

Brush devilled turkey kebabs with oil and grill until the bacon is brown and crisp

Brochettes of kidney

Allow one skewer per person and for each skewer the following ingredients:

2 lambs kidneys
2 or 3 squares of lambs liver
boiled rice (for serving)
chopped parsley (to garnish)

For marinade
2½ fl oz olive oil
2–3 tablespoons red wine
few sprigs of thyme
salt
pepper (ground from mill)

Method

Skin and split kidneys (see page 140), cut the liver into 1–1½ inch squares and remove the ducts. Marinate the liver and kidneys in the mixture of oil and red wine, adding seasoning and the thyme. Leave for 2–3 hours.

Thread the kidneys and liver alternately on to skewers and grill for 6–8 minutes, moistening with the marinade throughout the cooking time.

Serve brochettes on a bed of boiled rice and sprinkle with chopped parsley. Serve with bowl of crisp bacon rolls.

Threading the liver and kidney alternately on to skewers (see photograph of the finished dish on page 69).
The brochettes are served on a bed of boiled rice

Devilled turkey kebabs

16 pieces of dark turkey meat
4½ tablespoons olive oil
½ teaspoon dry mustard
1 tablespoon Worcestershire sauce
2 tablespoons tomato ketchup, or similar bottled, fruity sauce
dash of Tabasco sauce
1 large green pepper
12 small mushrooms
4 bayleaves
1 medium-size onion
8 rashers of streaky bacon

8 'lolly' sticks (sharpened at one end)

Method

Mix 1 teaspoon of the oil with the mustard and sauces, pour over turkey meat, and leave to marinate while preparing the other ingredients.

Core and deseed pepper, cut flesh into squares and blanch in pan of boiling water for 1 minute, then drain and refresh.

Trim the mushroom stalks level with the caps, put into a basin and pour over boiling water, leave for 1 minute, then drain. This preparation of the mushrooms helps to prevent them breaking when they are skewered.

Cut the onion in quarters and divide into segments. Cut each bayleaf in half.

Remove the rind from the bacon and cut each rasher in half, then stretch them by smoothing out with the blade of a heavy knife. Wrap each piece of devilled turkey meat in half a rasher of bacon.

Thread all the ingredients on to the sharpened lolly sticks in the following order: turkey, bayleaf, onion, pepper, mushroom, pepper, turkey.

Brush the finished kebabs with remaining oil and grill until bacon is brown and crisp on all sides.

Cut bacon rashers in half, stretch and wrap round turkey

Thread the prepared kebab items on the sharpened sticks

Bacon rolls

Allow 2 rashers of finely-cut streaky bacon per person. Remove the rind and rust. Stroke out rashers with blunt blade of a heavy knife until really thin. Cut them in half, then spread with French mustard. Roll up and skewer. These rolls can be grilled or baked, but they must be crisp and brown.

ACCOMPANYING BUTTERS AND SAUCES

Clarified butter

As this is an extravagant grilling or frying medium, it is best used for special occasions. For example, from 8 oz butter you only get about 6 oz clarified butter, but the end certainly justifies the means as the colour and taste of the food after cooking are quite excellent. The moisture and salt having been removed, the butter is less apt to burn when heated.

To clarify butter: take 8 oz or more of butter at a time (as it will keep when clarified), cut it up and put into a thick saucepan. Melt over slow heat and once melted continue to cook until it is foaming well. Skim well, strain through a muslin into a basin and leave to settle, then pour into another basin, leaving sediment behind.

The butter will then form a solid cake which can be used at once or melted down to pour into pots which should be covered before storing in the larder or refrigerator.

Noisette butter

1–2 oz butter
juice of ½ lemon

Method
Melt the butter in a pan and, when brown, add the lemon juice. Use while still foaming.

SAVOURY BUTTERS

When these mixtures are made, pat into balls with butter 'hands' (wooden shaping boards), or spread a ¼–½ inch thick on greaseproof paper and chill. Then cut into small round or square pats before using. The quantities given are enough for 4 people.

Anchovy butter

2 oz unsalted butter
4 anchovy fillets (soaked in milk to remove excess salt)
black pepper (ground from mill)
anchovy essence

Method
Soften the butter on a plate with a palette knife and then crush or pound the anchovies, adding these to the butter with ground pepper and enough essence to strengthen the flavour and give a delicate pink colour.

Serve with mutton, chops or cutlets, and fish.

Orange butter

2 oz unsalted butter
grated rind of ½ an orange and 1 teaspoon juice
1 teaspoon tomato purée
salt and pepper

Method
Soften the butter on a plate with a palette knife, and then add other ingredients, seasoning to taste.

Serve chilled, in pats, with lamb cutlets, steaks and fish.

Maître d'hôtel butter

2 oz unsalted butter
1 dessertspoon parsley (chopped)
few drops of lemon juice
salt and pepper

Method
Soften the butter on a plate with a palette knife, then add parsley, lemon juice and seasoning to taste.

Serve chilled, in pats, with steaks, mixed grills and fish.

Parsley butter

½ oz butter
1 teaspoon parsley (chopped)
dash of Worcestershire sauce, or squeeze of lemon juice

Method
Melt the butter in a pan and, when light and brown, add the chopped parsley and Worcestershire sauce or lemon juice. Blend together and then pour sauce over the meat.

Chutney, garlic, mustard or tomato butters

Other savoury butters are made in the same way using 2 oz unsalted butter with either pounded chutney, crushed garlic, 1 dessertspoon French mustard, or tomato purée.

The following is one of the simplest barbecue sauce recipes and can be used with many dishes, including left-overs, that are improved with a sharp sauce.

Barbecue sauce

1 teaspoon flour
⅓ pint potato stock (water in which potatoes have been cooked)
1 tablespoon soy sauce
dash of Worcestershire sauce
salt and pepper
2 tomatoes (skinned, de-seeded and shredded)

Method
Skim off the fat from the grill pan, leaving about 1 dessertspoon and any sediment. Stir in flour and cook very gently for 2–3 minutes. Draw aside and blend in potato stock, sauces and seasoning, then return to heat and stir until boiling. To skin the tomatoes: place them in a bowl, scald by pouring boiling water over them, count 12, then pour off the hot water and replace it with cold. The skin then comes off easily. Cut the flesh into shreds and add to the mixture. Simmer for 1 minute.

This sauce goes well with lamb kebabs or pork chops.

Mackerel are scored three times on each side and brushed with oil or butter before grilling

FISH

Grilling is a good and attractive way of cooking small whole fish (round or flat), particularly the rich and oily variety such as herring and mackerel. The intense heat crisps the skin making the fish especially appetising. Also excellent as straightforward grills are sole and halibut, turbot and salmon steaks.

Like meat, fish should not be salted before grilling but served with various savoury butters, such as maître d'hôtel, anchovy or orange, which give all the seasoning necessary; watercress makes a good garnish.

Unlike oily fish, white fish needs to be well brushed both before and during the cooking, with ordinary melted (or for a better colour – clarified) butter.

When grilling round fish score, ie. make a diagonal cut to slit the skin, in 2–3 places to allow the heat to penetrate more easily and so shorten the cooking time. It is not necessary to do this scoring with flat fish unless they are very large.

Grilling times depend on the thickness of the fish, not on the weight, for the fish should be well done.

HALIBUT OR TURBOT STEAKS

(6 oz steak per person)
Of all the white fish, with the exception of sole, these are best for grilling as they are firm-fleshed and less likely to break up when being turned.

For a good even colour, first dip in a little milk and then roll in seasoned flour before brushing with ordinary melted, or clarified, butter. The steaks must be kept well brushed and basted with the butter while grilling. Allow 8–10 minutes in all for steaks $\frac{3}{4}$–1 inch thick, turning once.

Dish up, top each one with a pat of savoury butter (maître d'hôtel, anchovy or orange).

HERRING

Grill these whole, or split open (in which case the backbone and many of the side bones may be removed). If grilling whole, cut off the heads and score herring twice on each side. Brush with oil or melted butter, then grill on full heat. Allow about 4–5 minutes on each side, 8–10 minutes in all.

For split, or filleted; herring brush with butter and grill on cut side first for 5–6 minutes, then turn and allow a further 2–3 minutes on the skin side.

Dish up and serve piping hot

To 'vandyke' the tail of a fish, accentuate the line by cutting an acute V-shape and making two distinct points. This is aptly named after the style of small, pointed beard made famous by Anthony Van Dyck, the 17th-century Court painter to Charles I.

---

with maître d'hôtel or mustard butter.

MACKEREL

These run larger than herrings and a big one can weigh over a pound. They are excellent grilled whole or filleted. Score fish 3 times on each side. Brush with oil or melted butter. Allow longer grilling time than for herrings: whole fish 10–15 minutes, filleted 8 minutes on the cut side and 3–4 on the skin side.

Serve with maître d'hôtel butter and/or quarters, or slices, of lemon.

SALMON STEAKS

(4–6 oz steak per person)
While grilling salmon steaks keep them succulent by brushing frequently with ordinary melted or clarified butter.

Serve with maître d'hôtel or orange butter.

SOLE AND PLAICE

The best type for grilling is black or Dover sole. These may be in the form of small slip soles (8–10 oz each), or larger, one of which is sufficient for 2 people.

Ask your fishmonger to skin the sole both sides. Grill with the head on, first brushing well with melted or clarified butter. Brush again from time to time and turn after 5–6 minutes. When nicely brown dish up and pour over any juices from the grill pan.

Put a pat or two of maître d'hôtel butter on each sole before serving.

Treat plaice in the same way but fillet before skinning. Serve as for sole.

Roasting

Roasting is the traditional – and certainly most popular – method of cooking, so it is up to every serious student of cookery to master this most important art. Roasting embodies all that is best in English food: first-class meat plainly cooked, with vegetables, sauce and rich gravy served separately.

True roasting was always done on a revolving spit over an open fire. Only recently, however, has this become a practical reality in the home. Gas-fired and electric spits are now combined with the grill on many domestic cookers, or can be bought as separate units.

If you are not lucky enough to own a spit, you can obtain equally good results by roasting the meat in the oven. But, extra care is needed because cooking in the oven is really baking. The best procedure is as follows:

1 Remove the meat from the refrigerator 30 minutes before cooking – all meat for roasting should be at room temperature.

2 Pre-heat the oven to the correct temperature, first checking that the shelf is in position and will take the joint comfortably. The correct position varies with the type of oven, so follow the manufacturer's instructions carefully.

3 Put the roasting tin in the oven with 2–3 tablespoons of dripping, depending on the size of the joint.

4 When the dripping is smoking, set the meat on a grid or simply on the bottom of the tin. Baste well to seal in the juices and return to the oven. If you are not using a grid, place the joint on its edge rather than flat on the outside, since the part in contact with the tin may get hard and overcook. This is especially important with a round joint, eg. sirloin.

5 Cook according to the weight and thickness of the joint (see chart overleaf), basting every 15–20 minutes to keep the meat moist and tender until done.

6 Once the meat is cooked, it should be dished up and placed in the warming drawer of the cooker. Plan the cooking time to allow the meat to stand for 15 minutes while the gravy is prepared and vegetables dished up. This standing time will make the meat much easier to carve.

7 A roast joint needs good gravy: strong and clear for beef, mutton and lamb, and lightly-thickened for pork and veal. Serve gravy separately in a gravy boat.

Gravy

The basis of gravy is, of course, the meat's sediments and juices left in the roasting tin. To increase the amount, add stock. For mutton and lamb, simmer the knuckle bone from the leg or shoulder (or the chine bone from the loin) with water and vegetables to flavour. For a joint of beef when no bone or stock is available, potato water or a bouillon cube can be used, but be sparing with seasoning since both can be salty.

When the meat is dished up, tilt the roasting tin gently to pour off the fat, but keep back the juices and sediment from the meat. Dust in just enough flour to absorb the small quantity of dripping left in the roasting tin (not usually more than 1 dessertspoon of flour for beef or lamb). Allow to colour very slowly, then scrape tin well to take up the sediment round the sides.

Pour on $\frac{1}{2}$–$\frac{3}{4}$ pint stock, bring to the boil and season with salt and pepper. Reduce the quantity to concentrate the flavour. If necessary, you can improve the colour with a little gravy browning. This is better than scorching the flour in a thin roasting tin. Strain into a gravy boat and serve very hot.

Roast lamb served with new potatoes. Mint sauce (see recipe on page 82) is a traditional accompaniment

MEAT

Roasting times for meat

	Oven temperature	Total cooking time (equal for gas and electricity)
Beef	Electric oven 375°F Gas Mark 7 for the first 15 minutes, then reduce to Mark 6	Rare: 15 minutes per lb and 15 minutes over Well done: 20 minutes per lb and 30 minutes over Since the cooking time varies with the thickness of the joint and not always according to the weight, allow: 45 minutes for joints under $1\frac{1}{2}$ lb $1\frac{1}{4}$ hours for joints under 3 lb
Lamb	Electric oven 375°F Gas Mark 6	20 minutes per lb and 20 minutes over
Mutton	Electric oven 375°F Gas Mark 6 for the first 15 minutes, then reduce to Mark 5	20 minutes per lb and 20 minutes over
Pork	Electric oven 375°F Gas Mark 7 for the first 15 minutes, then reduce to Mark 6	25 minutes per lb and 25 minutes over

The electricity settings and gas Marks given here are not always comparable because an electric oven, being entirely enclosed, gives a constant heat all over, whereas a gas oven, with its open flue, has 3 different heat zones.

BEEF

When beef is well hung, as it should be, it is purplish-red in colour. Beef that is too fresh, and bright red, will improve if it is kept in a refrigerator for a few days before being cooked. The fat on the joint should be firm in texture and creamy in colour.

In prime cuts, such as sirloin, there is a light marbling of fat through the lean meat; this helps to keep the joint tender, so make sure that the fat round the joint adheres to the meat, and is not an extra slab that has been tied on by the butcher.

Ideally, roast beef should be a delicate to deep shade of pink inside when cooked, and a crisp, dark brown on the outside. The best roasting cuts are fillet, sirloin and rolled ribs.

If serving cold roast beef with a salad accompaniment, try to allow time for the cooked joint to cool before you carve it, otherwise it tends to lose its flavour and colour and becomes less moist. (This applies to other cold meats like lamb and pork.)

TO SERVE WITH BEEF

Traditional accompaniments to roast beef are Yorkshire pudding, horseradish cream (see recipe on page 179) and vegetables such as roast potatoes, glazed carrots and creamed swedes (see recipes on pages 192 and 194).

Yorkshire pudding

5 oz flour
pinch of salt
1 large egg
$\frac{1}{2}$ pint milk and water mixed ($\frac{3}{4}$ milk to $\frac{1}{4}$ water)
1 tablespoon dripping
1 tablespoon beef suet (finely grated) – optional

Method

Sift the flour with the salt into a mixing bowl. Make a well in the centre and put in the unbeaten egg and half the milk and water. Stir carefully, gradually drawing in the flour. Add half the remaining milk and water and beat well. Stir in the rest of the liquid and leave in a cool place for about 1 hour before cooking.

Heat the dripping in a shallow dish until smoking hot (a tin or enamel dish is most satisfactory). Tilt the dish round to coat sides with the hot dripping. Then pour in the batter. Bake for 30–40 minutes in a hot oven at 400°–450°F or Mark 7 on a shelf well above the meat.

This recipe gives a light, well-risen pudding. If you prefer something more substantial, stir 1 tablespoon beef suet (finely grated) into the mixture before baking.

Chateaubriand with château potatoes, maître d'hôtel butter

The chateaubriand is carved into thick slices when it is served

Chateaubriand

This classic dish is a very thick slice cut from the middle of the beef fillet (or undercut) and is halfway between a steak and a joint for roasting. It is always grilled, so it needs great care in cooking to avoid the outside being overbrowned and hard before it is cooked through.

A chateaubriand will weigh 1–1¼ lb; grill this for 20–24 minutes and baste or brush frequently with melted butter, or oil, during the cooking time.

It is always served with pommes château (an abbreviation of pommes chateaubriand, but written with a circumflex accent). These should be oval-shaped, the size of a large olive, and cooked in butter until golden-brown and tender. Maître d'hôtel butter or béarnaise sauce should accompany the dish.

Fillet of beef in aspic

1½–2 lb fillet of beef
2–3 tablespoons oil (for roasting)
½ pint aspic jelly (this can be made from commercial aspic powder, adding a glass of sherry in place of the same amount of water)

For garnish
4 oz button mushrooms
2 tablespoons olive oil

Method

Roast the fillet at 425°F or Mark 7 for about 35 minutes and allow to cool. Wash and trim the mushrooms and slice, if large, but leave whole if quite small. Sauté them in the hot oil for 1 minute only. Tip them on to a plate and allow to cool, then drain on absorbent paper.

Carve the beef, arrange in overlapping slices around a flat serving dish and garnish with the mushrooms. Brush well with cold but still liquid aspic, covering the beef completely.

Contrefilet Dubarry

2–3 lb top part of sirloin (boned, well-trimmed and tied firmly)
2–3 tablespoons dripping (for roasting)
½ pint strong beef stock
1 large cauliflower and thick mornay sauce (to garnish)

Dubarry is the name given to any recipe in which cauliflower is featured, either as a garnish or as a sauce.

Method

The garnish for this dish can be prepared early in the day and left ready for baking under the meat. Sprig the cauliflower and boil until just tender. Drain and refresh by pouring 1 cup of cold water over. Take about two sprigs at a time and squeeze lightly together in a piece of muslin. Set these bouquets on a greased baking sheet.

Prepare mornay sauce. With this recipe, reserve a little cheese for sprinkling over the cauliflower after coating each sprig with the sauce.

Twenty minutes re-heating in oven is enough to make cauliflower hot and golden-brown.

Spit or oven roast the meat, allowing 15 minutes per lb if you like it rare. Take up the meat and prepare the gravy in the usual way (see page 78). Arrange the small cauliflower sprigs around the meat; serve gravy and potatoes separately.

LAMB

The size of the carcass varies with the breed of lamb, but the best is small with a reasonable covering of firm white fat. The meat is pale to dark red in colour. As with beef, lamb tastes better if it has been hung. It should not be served underdone, but should have just a tinge of pink at the centre. The following joints of lamb are suitable for roasting: best end of neck, loin, leg, crown roast, shoulder and saddle.

Mutton is, technically, the carcass of an animal over 2 years old. It is always served well cooked and the loin or saddle is the best joint for roasting.

TO SERVE WITH LAMB

Traditional accompaniments to roast lamb or mutton are mint sauce, or redcurrant jelly (see recipe on page 185) and onion sauce (see recipe on page 178).

Mint sauce

2 tablespoons fresh mint (chopped)

1–2 tablespoons caster sugar

wine vinegar (to taste)

Method

Mint sauce should be bright green, smooth and pulpy in consistency. Chop the mint and pound with a little of the caster sugar until quite smooth. Add 1–2 tablespoons boiling water, according to the quantity of mint, to improve the colour and melt the sugar. Add a little wine vinegar to taste.

> **Duxelles** is a mince of mushrooms, chopped shallot and herbs, cooked in butter and used to flavour soups, sauces and stuffings. The name may have originated in the 17th century when La Varenne, a famous chef, was an official member of the household of the Marquis d'Uxelles.

One of the more economical cuts of lamb, a best end of neck should be well trimmed and scored

Neck of lamb Conti

2 lb best end of neck of lamb, or mutton (skinned only)
6 fillets of anchovy
1 dessertspoon chopped herbs
little shallot (finely chopped)
dripping, or butter (for roasting)

For garnish
½ pint butter beans (soaked overnight)
1 oz butter
salt
black pepper (ground from mill)
¾–1 lb tomatoes
1 teaspoon caster sugar

Method
Remove chine bone and trim meat. Cut the fillets of anchovy in half lengthways, roll them in some of the chopped herbs and shallot. Lard (sew) the joint with them. Melt the dripping or butter in a roasting tin, put in the meat, baste and roast in the oven at 375°F or Mark 5 for 40–50 minutes.

To prepare garnish: simmer butter beans until tender (about 1–1½ hours), drain and return to the pan with ½ oz butter and seasoning. Keep warm.

Scald and skin tomatoes, cut in thick slices. Melt remaining butter in a frying pan, add sugar and season. When hot put in the sliced tomatoes and cook quickly for 4–5 minutes. Draw aside and sprinkle with the remaining herbs.

Dish up the meat with the beans and tomatoes, garnish with additional anchovy fillets if wished. Serve with gravy.

Ballotine of lamb with mixed herbs

1 small shoulder of lamb (boned)
shoulder bones and bouquet garni (for stock)
1–2 oz butter
1 wineglass white wine
1 tablespoon mixed herbs: parsley, sage, thyme, marjoram
little arrowroot (optional)

For stuffing
2 oz butter
1 small onion (finely chopped)
4 oz mushrooms (chopped)
2 tablespoons fresh breadcrumbs
3 oz cooked ham (minced)
3 oz raw pork (minced)
3 oz raw veal (minced)
salt and pepper

Method
Simmer shoulder bones with bouquet garni, water and seasoning to make a good stock for gravy.

To prepare stuffing: melt the butter in a pan, add onion and cook until soft but not coloured, then add chopped mushrooms and cook for 3 minutes. Turn the mushroom mixture into a bowl, mix in the crumbs and minced meats, and season.

Open out the boned shoulder, dust with the mixed herbs and then spread with the prepared stuffing. Roll up and tie securely with string. Spread the meat with butter. Set in a roasting tin and pour round the wine. Cook for 1½ hours in a moderately hot oven at 400°F or Mark 6.

Take out the meat and keep warm. Tip off the fat in the roasting tin, keeping back any sediment, and add ½ pint of stock made from the bones. Boil up well to reduce the quantity. Adjust the seasoning and thicken with a little arrowroot if wished. Strain. Remove the strings from the meat, carve and arrange slices in the serving dish. Spoon over a little of the gravy and hand the remainder in a gravy boat. Serve with vegetables of your choice.

> A **ballotine** is meat, poultry, fish or game which has been boned, stuffed and rolled up into a 'bundle'.

Leg of lamb duxelles

1 small leg of lamb
2–3 oz butter
garlic slivers
1 wineglass white wine
little arrowroot (optional)
1–2 rounded tablespoons Parmesan cheese (grated)
watercress (to garnish)

For duxelles filling
½–¾ lb mushrooms (finely chopped)
1 oz butter
2 shallots (finely chopped)
1 tablespoon thyme (chopped)
1 tablespoon parsley (chopped)
3 tablespoons white breadcrumbs

Method
Rub the leg well with 1 oz of butter. Insert the garlic slivers, wrap in buttered paper, put in a roasting tin and pour the white wine round, reserving a little. Roast meat in the oven at 350°F or Mark 4, allowing 15–20 minutes per lb. When half done take off the paper; baste meat frequently until cooked. Remove meat from oven and cool slightly. Strain juice from pan, getting rid of excess fat. Deglaze pan with reserved wine and stock. Season, strain into juice. If you wish, thicken with a little arrowroot and set aside.

To prepare filling while lamb is roasting: wash and chop mushrooms finely, melt butter in pan, add shallots and 1 minute later mushrooms, followed by the herbs. Now cook briskly for 5–6 minutes, draw aside from heat before adding crumbs and seasoning.

Slice lamb and insert some of filling between each slice. Reshape leg before putting back into roasting tin. Work 2 oz of the butter with the same amount of cheese and spread all over the surface of the meat. Ten minutes before you serve the leg, put in a hot oven to brown.

Serve on a hot dish with a little of the gravy round and the rest in a gravy boat. Garnish with watercress.

If only the top part of the leg is sliced, there should be enough meat left on the underside to make a good 'rechauffé' (dish made from cooked food) for reheating on following day.

83

Barbecued leg of lamb

3½–4 lb leg of lamb
1 pint water (for stock)
1 teaspoon dehydrated onion flakes, or 1 small onion (chopped) – for stock
1 teaspoon salt
1 teaspoon dry mustard
1 teaspoon sugar
1 teaspoon black pepper (ground from mill)
1 teaspoon ground ginger
2 tablespoons dripping, or 2 tablespoons salad oil
1 large clove of garlic
1 tablespoon flour (for dredging)
1 oz kneaded butter, or 2 teaspoons arrowroot mixed with 1 tablespoon stock (for gravy)

For barbecue sauce mixture (about ¼ pint)
2 tablespoons tomato ketchup
2 tablespoons mushroom ketchup
2 tablespoons Worcestershire sauce
1–2 tablespoons bottled spicy fruit sauce, or 1–2 tablespoons home-made red plum or gooseberry spicy fruit sauce
1–2 oz butter (melted)
1 teaspoon sugar
dash of red wine vinegar
dash of Tabasco sauce

Prepare this dish overnight.

Method
To make stock: cut off the shank end of the leg, put into a pan with the water, add ready-dehydrated and browned onion flakes, or the fresh onion (cooked in a little dripping) and simmer gently for 45 minutes. Strain and keep this stock for the gravy.

Mix all the dry seasonings together, rub over surface of meat, leave overnight.

Heat the dripping or oil in a roasting tin, peel and split the garlic into 4–5 pieces and stick these into the lean of the meat near the bone. Dredge the joint with flour, set in the roasting tin and baste well with hot fat. Cook for 1 hour in oven at 400°F or Mark 6; baste and turn from time to time.

To make the barbecue sauce mixture: add all the sauces to the melted butter, sugar, vinegar and tabasco and mix. Remove meat from the oven, carefully tip off the fat in the roasting tin. Pour half the barbecue sauce mixture over the meat. Reduce the oven heat to 375°F or Mark 5 and continue cooking for 15 minutes. Then baste meat with the remaining sauce. If the pan is dry, add 1 tablespoon of the prepared stock to keep the meat moist. Continue cooking 15–20 minutes. Take up meat, place on the serving dish and keep warm.

To make the gravy: tip the stock into roasting tin, boil up well until it is reduced in quantity to ½ pint. Thicken with kneaded butter (see page 176), or the arrowroot and stock, and serve separately.

Lamb Banyuls

2 lb best end of neck (chined), or 2½ lb loin of lamb (chined)
1 oz butter

For sauce garnish
1 lb onions (very thinly sliced)
1–2 oz butter
2 wineglasses red wine (Burgundy type)
salt and pepper
½ pint jellied stock (made from chine bone and root vegetables) – see Course 3
¼ pint double cream
1 teaspoon arrowroot

Method
If not already chined, remove the chine bone from meat and simmer this with water and vegetables to give a good jellied stock. If using neck, trim bones and score fat. Spread with butter and set meat in a small roasting tin. Roast about 45 minutes at 375°F or Mark 5, basting and turning from time to time.

Meanwhile prepare the sauce garnish. Sauté the onion slices slowly in butter until golden-brown, add 1 glass of the wine, season and cook 5–10 minutes. Drain the onions, place down centre of the serving dish and reserve the liquid.

Take up the meat and keep warm. Tip off all the fat from roasting tin, keeping back the sediment. Pour on half the stock and boil up well. Strain into frying, or sauté, pan, add the second glass of wine, bring to the boil, reduce for 1–2 minutes and then add reserved liquid. Adjust seasoning and add the cream. Mix arrowroot with the remaining stock, add to the sauce and boil well.

Carve the meat, arrange on the onions and spoon over a little of the sauce. Hand the rest separately.

Loin of lamb bretonne

2–3 lb loin of lamb (boned)
2–3 tablespoons dripping

For stuffing
2 tablespoons onion (chopped)
1 oz butter
5 tablespoons fresh white breadcrumbs
2 tablespoons mixed herbs (chopped)
grated rind and little juice of 1 orange
salt and pepper
seasoned flour
beaten egg
browned crumbs

For sauce
1 onion (sliced)
½ pint stock (made with the bones, 1 onion, 1 carrot and bouquet garni to flavour)
1–2 tablespoons redcurrant jelly
orange juice
12 glazed onions and several carrots (to garnish)

Method
Prepare the stuffing: cook the onion in the butter until soft but not coloured. Add it to the white crumbs with the herbs, orange rind and seasoning. Bind with the orange juice and a little beaten egg. Spread this over the inside of the meat, roll up and tie securely with string. Roll in seasoned flour, brush with beaten egg and roll in browned crumbs.

Heat the dripping in a roasting tin and, when smoking, put in the meat, baste and set to roast for 1¼–1½ hours. Prepare a good stock from the bones. When cooked, take up the meat, remove string and keep warm while you prepare the sauce. Tip off fat from the roasting tin, leaving the sediment in the bottom. Add the sliced onion and cook slowly until brown. Dust in a little flour, add the stock and redcurrant jelly, boil up well, season, sharpen with a little orange juice and strain.

Carve the meat, arrange in a serving dish, garnish with glazed onions and carrots (see page 192). Spoon over a little of the sauce and serve the rest separately.

PORK AND HAM

The flesh of pork should be firm, the lean pinkish-white, and the fat white and smooth. The skin of the hindquarter gives the best crackling and both skin and rind should be thin and supple. Pork must always be well cooked to prevent the danger of infection which may be present in the meat. Any juices that run through the meat after cooking should be clear — not pink, which indicates undercooking.

TO SERVE WITH PORK

Traditional accompaniments to roast pork are apple sauce, sage and onion stuffing, and vegetables like braised cabbage or leeks (see recipes on page 194).

Roast leg of pork with a sage and onion stuffing, baked (roast) potatoes, braised leeks and apple sauce. The outside skin has been well scored to give plenty of crisp crackling

Sage and onion stuffing

3 medium-size onions (finely sliced)
2 oz butter, or suet
6 oz breadcrumbs
2 teaspoons dried sage
1 teaspoon parsley (chopped)
salt and pepper
beaten egg, or milk

Method

Slice onions finely and boil 15–20 minutes in salted water.

Drain and stir in the butter or suet. Add remaining ingredients, season well and mix with beaten egg or milk. If the joint is not suitable for stuffing, put the mixture into a small fireproof dish, baste with 1 tablespoon of dripping and cook in the oven for 30–40 minutes at 400°F or Mark 6.

Apple sauce

1 lb cooking apples
rind of ½ lemon (thinly pared)
1 dessertspoon sugar
½ oz butter

Method

Peel and core the apples. Pare the lemon rind thinly. Put apples and rind in a saucepan with 2–3 tablespoons water. Cover tightly and cook until pulpy. Beat with a wooden spoon until smooth, or put through a strainer. Stir in the sugar and butter. Serve hot.

Loin of pork alsacienne

2–2½ lb loin of pork (chined)
½ pint stock (made with chine bone, 1 onion and 1 carrot, both sliced, and bouquet garni)
salt and pepper
2–3 tablespoons dripping
fresh breadcrumbs (optional)
1 tablespoon flour

For cabbage mixture
1 small Dutch cabbage (shredded)
1 oz butter
1 onion (finely sliced)
1 lemon (sliced)
salt and pepper
4 dessert apples
parsley (chopped) – to garnish
2 hard-boiled eggs (to garnish)

Method
To make stock: put the chine bone in a heavy pan with sliced onion and carrot, and brown over steady heat. Cover with cold water, add bouquet garni, season, simmer for 1 hour.

If the pork has rind, score it well and rub with salt before roasting. Baste well with hot dripping and cook for 1¼ hours in the oven at 400°F or Mark 6. If the pork has no rind, cover the fat with fresh breadcrumbs, baste well and return to the oven to brown, 20 minutes before end of cooking time.

Meanwhile, prepare cabbage mixture: cut cabbage in four, remove the hard core and shred leaves finely. Blanch in boiling salted water for 1 minute, then drain, refresh in cold water and tip into a basin.

Melt the butter in a flame-proof casserole, add the onion, cover and cook slowly until soft but not coloured. Turn into the basin of cabbage and mix well together. Peel and slice lemon, mix with the cabbage and season. Peel and quarter the apples and cut away the core. Arrange the quarters, rounded side down, at the bottom of the casserole. Spoon the cabbage mixture on top of the apple, cover with well-buttered paper and put on the casserole lid. Cook gently on top of the stove for 15–20 minutes, then put in the oven on a shelf under the pork and continue cooking for 30–40 minutes.

Take up the meat. Tip off the dripping from the roasting tin, keeping back any sediment, stir in 1 tablespoon flour and cook slowly until brown. Pour on ½ pint stock, season and boil up well. Strain. Slice the meat, lay on a hot serving dish and pour the gravy over.

Run a palette knife round the side of the casserole and turn the cabbage on to a hot dish – it should fall out in a flat cake. Scatter the chopped parsley on the top and surround with quartered hard-boiled eggs.

The term **à l'alsacienne** is often applied to dishes made from sauerkraut, ham and Strasbourg sausage. Pork from the Alsatian region has a firm flesh and delicate flavour, thanks to the Benedictine monks who were among the first to breed pigs specially for eating.

Baked ham

4 lb joint of gammon
1 onion
1 carrot
1 stick of celery
bouquet garni
6 peppercorns

For glaze
4 tablespoons golden syrup
4 oz brown sugar
1 teaspoon English mustard
white wine vinegar (to moisten)
12 cloves

Method
Soak the joint for 4 hours in cold water to cover. Throw away the water, cover the joint again with fresh cold water, bring slowly to the boil and skim well. Add the vegetables, bouquet garni and peppercorns; cover and simmer gently for 2 hours. Take up the joint, remove the skin and score the fat in diamonds with a sharp knife.

Set the oven at 350°F or Mark 4. Place the joint in a baking tin and brush over it with warmed golden syrup. Mix the brown sugar and dry mustard with enough vinegar to moisten and spread over the surface of the ham. Stick with the cloves and bake in the pre-set moderate oven until golden-brown (about 20 minutes). Serve hot with raisin sauce.

Fillet of pork 'en croûte'

3 large pork fillets (about 2½–3 lb in all)
4 oz cooked ham (sliced)
8 oz puff pastry
watercress (to garnish)

For mushroom stuffing
1 medium-size onion (chopped)
1 oz butter
¼ lb mushrooms (finely chopped)
1 teaspoon parsley (chopped)
1 teaspoon sage (chopped)
4 oz cooked ham (chopped)
2–3 tablespoons breadcrumbs
salt and pepper
trimmings of pork fillets (minced)
beaten egg

Method
Trim fillets and carefully split them lengthways.

To prepare the stuffing: soften the onion in the butter. Wash the mushrooms in salted water, chop finely and add to the pan with the herbs. Cover and cook for about 5 minutes.

Draw pan off heat, add the chopped ham, breadcrumbs and seasoning, then turn into a bowl to cool. Work in the minced pork trimmings and enough beaten egg to bind. Fill this stuffing into the fillets, truss or tie neatly, then roast in a hot oven at 400°F or Mark 6 for 1–1¼ hours, until meat is tender. Baste meat frequently.

Leave the meat to go quite cold, then remove the string and roll the meat in the sliced ham.

Roll out the pastry to a large rectangle and trim the sides to give yourself enough pieces to cut fleurons (crescents) for decoration. Turn the pastry over so that the rolled surface, the best side of the pastry, is on the outside when baked.

Set the meat on the pastry, dampen the outside edges and roll meat up in it like a swiss roll; tuck in the ends and press firmly. Brush with beaten egg and decorate with fleurons. Lift on to a dampened baking sheet, cook in oven at 425°F or Mark 7, until well browned (about 30 minutes).

Garnish with watercress and serve a good brown sauce separately.

The gammon joint for baked ham with raisin sauce is first boiled, then skinned and the fat scored in diamond-fashion

Cloves are stuck on to the sugar crust of the ham before the final baking in the oven

Baked ham with raisin sauce is a favourite Canadian main course

POULTRY

Much has been done over the past few years to breed small, plump-breasted birds with specially white flesh. These are frequently marketed frozen and are an excellent buy provided adequate time is allowed to thaw them out properly. Frozen turkeys are sold by dressed weight, ie. plucked and drawn, with feet and legs removed. The weight is clearly indicated on the bird. A 10 lb bird will serve 8–10 people. Allow the turkey to thaw slowly in a cool larder in the polythene bag in which it is wrapped (this will take some 2–3 days).

Fresh turkeys are sold by plucked weight, ie. with the feathers removed but including head and feet, and without being drawn. A 13–14 lb fresh bird is therefore equivalent to a 10 lb frozen one and will serve the same number of people (8–10).

Turkeys for roasting are stuffed to keep them moist and to add flavour. Use pork or veal forcemeat for carcass, celery, apricot and walnut stuffing for the breast or crop. In fact, turkeys are becoming popular alternatives to the traditional weekend joint.

Capons are just right for small families and tight budgets. Smaller than turkeys (they weigh from 5 lb upwards, oven ready), their flesh is particularly white and tender. The stuffing recipes given on pages 89 and 90 for turkey are equally good with roast capon.

Compared with a turkey, a duck or goose does not go as far; as the breast is shallow, it is more difficult to carve, but it is prized for the flavour and richness of its flesh. A goose should be stuffed, but only the carcass as there's little space in the breast or crop. Several kinds of stuffing are suitable, and we give two of them on page 91.

FRENCH ROASTING

French roasting is a good method of cooking chicken, duck or turkey, particularly if the bird is to be served cold, because the flesh remains succulent and full of flavour. The bird is roasted in butter with a little strong stock (as opposed to English roasting, when dripping only is used, which is apt to make the flesh dry).

French roast turkey

1 turkey
pork, or veal, forcemeat (for the carcass)
celery, apricot and walnut stuffing (for the breast)
6–8 oz butter (enough to cover, depending on size of bird)
about 1 pint well-flavoured stock, made from giblets
1 rounded tablespoon flour (to thicken gravy)
salt and pepper

For garnish
8 oz rashers of streaky bacon
watercress
1 lb chipolata sausages

Method
Set oven at 350°F or Mark 4. Prepare the forcemeat and stuffing (see right and page 90). Loosen neck skin and push the stuffing well into breast cavity. Pull skin gently over stuffing and fasten under wing tips. A skewer can be pushed in to hold it firm. Undo trussing string from turkey legs, if necessary, and put the forcemeat into the carcass through the vent end. Re-tie trussing string. Put turkey in the roasting tin.

Spread butter thickly over a double sheet of greaseproof paper or sheet of foil. Lay the buttered sheet over bird and pour round half the stock. Cook for time given in chart (overleaf) according to weight.

Turn and baste bird about every 20 minutes, but keep paper or foil on while cooking. If stock reduces too much during cooking, add a little more. After 1 hour, cut trussing string holding legs.

Just before bird is cooked, prepare the garnish. Remove rind from bacon rashers, and wash and trim watercress. Grill bacon rashers and sausages.

To test if the bird is cooked pierce thigh with a skewer; if clear juice runs out, not pink, the bird is ready. Once cooked, set turkey on serving dish, pull out trussing strings and skewer,

garnish with bacon rashers, sausages and watercress, then keep warm.

If bird is not sufficiently brown towards the end of cooking time, remove paper and leave bird until golden-brown.

To make gravy: strain juices from roasting tin into a saucepan and deglaze tin with remaining stock. Add this stock to juices and skim off some of the fat. Put fat back into tin, stir in flour, then pour in liquid from saucepan. Stir until boiling. Season and strain back into saucepan. When ready to serve, reheat gravy and serve it separately.

Slow-roasted turkey

If more convenient, turkeys can be **slow-roasted**. Do this by rubbing over thoroughly with butter (about 6–8 oz,

First stuff neck end. Fold flap of skin up between wing tips, then tuck them up under bird

Thread a trussing needle with string. Sew up the neck end of bird to keep stuffing in place

Use any stuffing left over for the body cavity; stuffing is usually pork or veal forcemeat

French roast turkey is garnished with crispy bacon rashers, chipolata sausages and watercress. The paper cutlet frills, placed over the ends of the legs, add the finishing touch

according to size), wrapping in foil and placing in a roasting tin. Place in a pre-set oven at 325°F or Mark 3 and cook for 20 minutes per lb, 30 minutes over for birds of 14 lb and under. Cook birds over that weight for 18 minutes per lb, 15 minutes over. Unwrap about 35 minutes before end of cooking time to brown. Increase oven heat to 350°F or Mark 4, if necessary.

STUFFINGS FOR TURKEY

Celery, apricot and walnut stuffing

1 small head of celery (thinly sliced)
2 oz dried apricots (soaked overnight)
4 oz walnuts (chopped)
1½ oz butter
2 onions (chopped)
1½ teacups of fresh breadcrumbs
1 tablespoon parsley (chopped)
salt and pepper

Method
Drain apricots and cut each half into 3–4 pieces.

Melt butter in a pan, add onions, cover and cook until soft. Then add celery, apricots and walnuts. Cook about 4 minutes over brisk heat, stirring continuously, then turn into a bowl. When cool, add crumbs and parsley. Season to taste.

Draw the thighs close to body of the bird, cross legs over the vent and fasten with string

89

Pork or veal forcemeat is a traditional turkey stuffing, but more adventurous cooks may like to try a celery, apricot and walnut one

Pull skin gently over stuffing and fasten edge of skin under the wing tips. A skewer can be pushed in here to hold it firmly in place.

Melt dripping in a roasting tin, put the bird in, baste and cook in the oven for time given in roasting chart (see right), according to weight of bird.

Turn and baste bird about every 20 minutes. Just before the bird is cooked (test as for turkey, page 88), prepare garnish.

Remove rind from bacon rashers and roll up, holding each roll with a cocktail stick. Pierce sausages, grill with bacon rolls.

Remove capon from oven, set on a serving dish, pull out trussing strings and skewer, garnish with bacon rolls and sausages and keep warm.

To make gravy: pour off excess fat from roasting tin. Stir flour into tin, scraping well to mix in the sediment, then pour on stock. Blend, reboil and strain in a saucepan. When ready to serve reheat gravy and serve separately.

PREPARING DUCK AND GOOSE

Though they are available all year round, duck and ducklings are at their best in the early summer, goose around Christmas. They don't serve as many as a chicken of similar weight, as they're shallow-breasted. A 4 lb duck (plucked weight) is only enough for four people.

Roast birds in a hot oven at 375°F or Mark 6, or on a spit. A little butter or dripping may be spread on the breast but, if bird is a good plump one, it can be put in the oven dry.

Once the fat begins to run, baste bird well and turn it over about every 20 minutes so that skin can brown and crisp. The gravy can be lightly thickened.

Roasting times are 15 minutes per lb and 15 minutes over.

Classic accompaniments to roast duck are sage and onion stuffing, apple sauce, peas and new potatoes; for goose, apple or gooseberry sauce.

Pork or veal forcemeat

1½ lb sausage meat, or half sausage meat and minced pork, or veal
1½ oz butter
1 large onion (finely chopped)
1 dessertspoon each dried mixed herbs and parsley (chopped), or fresh thyme, sage and parsley (chopped)
1 teacup fresh breadcrumbs
1 egg (lightly beaten)
stock from amount made for gravy (to moisten)
salt and pepper

Method
Put meat into a bowl. Melt butter in a pan, add onion, cover and cook until soft. Add to meat with herbs, parsley and crumbs. Mix thoroughly with egg and moisten with as much stock as needed. Add 2 good pinches of salt and 1 of pepper. (Keep forcemeat in refrigerator if not using immediately.)

Roast capon

1 capon
pork, or veal, forcemeat (for the carcass)
celery, apricot and walnut stuffing (for the breast)
2–3 tablespoons good dripping
1 rounded tablespoon flour (to thicken gravy)
about ½ pint well-flavoured stock (made from the giblets)
salt and pepper

For garnish

6 oz bacon rashers (for rolls)
½ lb chipolata sausages

Method
Set oven at 375°F or Mark 5. Prepare the forcemeat and stuffing (see recipes, left and previous page). Undo trussing strings from legs, if necessary, and put the forcemeat into the carcass through the vent end. Re-tie trussing string. Loosen neck skin and push second stuffing well into breast cavity.

The body of the goose is filled with potato stuffing before being trussed

Roast goose

1 goose
potato and apple stuffing, or sage
  and onion stuffing with pickled
  walnuts (for the carcass)
salt and pepper
2–3 tablespoons dripping, or
  butter
2–3 tablespoons cold water
1 tablespoon flour (to thicken
  gravy)
½ pint well-flavoured stock
  (made from the giblets)

Method
Set oven at 375°F or Mark 5. Prepare the chosen stuffing. Undo trussing string from legs, if necessary, and rub the inside of the bird with salt and pepper. Put stuffing into carcass through vent end. Re-tie trussing string.

Rub outside of bird with salt and pepper, spread dripping or butter over the breast. Put bird in a roasting tin and cook in the oven for time given in chart (see below), according to weight of bird. Halfway through cooking, lower oven heat to 350°F or Mark 4.

Turn and baste bird about every 20 minutes. Ten minutes before the bird is cooked (test as for turkey, page 88) pour cold water over the breast (this will make the skin crisp).

Remove goose from oven, set on a serving dish, pull out trussing strings and skewer, and keep warm.

To make gravy: pour off excess fat from roasting tin. Stir flour into tin, scraping well to mix in the sediment, then pour on stock. Blend, reboil and strain into a saucepan. When ready to serve, reheat gravy and serve separately.

STUFFINGS FOR GOOSE

Potato and apple stuffing

1 lb potatoes
2 cooking apples
¼ lb onions (finely chopped)
1 dessertspoon fresh or dried
  mixed herbs (chopped)
1 oz butter (melted)
salt and pepper

Method
Peel potatoes and put in a pan. Cover with cold, salted water and boil until cooked. Meanwhile put onions in a pan, cover with cold water and boil gently until tender (about 15 minutes).

Peel, core and chop the apples and put in a bowl with herbs. Drain the potatoes and onions and add to apple mixture with the butter. Mix well and season to taste.

Sage and onion stuffing with pickled walnuts

handful of fresh sage leaves, or
  1 tablespoon dried sage
¼ lb onions (finely chopped)
3–4 tablespoons boiling water
2 cups of fresh breadcrumbs
1 oz butter (melted)
1 large cooking apple (peeled,
  cored and diced)
grated rind and juice of ½ lemon
1 egg (lightly beaten)
4 pickled walnuts (quartered)
salt and pepper
stock from goose giblets (to
  moisten)

Method
Put onions in a pan, cover with cold water and cook until tender (about 15 minutes). Drain, turn into a bowl. Pour boiling water on sage. Leave to stand for 5 minutes, then drain. Chop fresh leaves, if used.

Add sage to onions, with crumbs, butter, apple, lemon rind and juice. Bind with egg, add walnuts and season well. Add a dessertspoon of stock if the mixture is too dry.

ROASTING TIMES FOR POULTRY

BIRD	WEIGHT	SERVES	COOKING TIMES	
Frozen turkey	10 lb Oven ready	8–10	12 lb & under	15 minutes per lb 15 minutes over
Fresh turkey	13–14 lb Plucked	8–10	12 lb & over	10 minutes per lb 10 minutes over
Capon	5–7 lb Oven ready	6–8	5 lb & over	20 minutes per lb
Goose	8–10 lb	6–8	8 lb & over	15 minutes per lb

Note: weigh bird before stuffing

91

Barossa chicken

3½ lb roasting chicken
1½–2 oz butter
1 wineglass white wine
1 lettuce (shredded)
4 oz almonds (blanched and split)
2 tablespoons olive oil
½ lb muscat grapes
squeeze of lemon juice
salt and pepper

For dressing

1 wineglass white wine
juice of ½ lemon
about ¼ pint olive oil
1 tablespoon mixed chopped herbs (parsley, mint and chives)

This recipe was called Barossa after the name of an Australian vineyard.

Method

Set oven at 400°F or Mark 6. Roast the chicken for about 1 hour with the butter and white wine. Reserve any juice from roasting chicken. Leave chicken to get quite cold, then joint it and arrange on the shredded lettuce on a serving dish.

Fry the almonds in the oil until brown, drain and salt them lightly. Peel and pip the grapes, put them in a small basin or tea cup, sprinkle with a little lemon juice to prevent discolouration, cover with greaseproof paper.

To make the dressing : reduce the wine to half quantity, then take it off heat. Mix the wine with the rest of the ingredients, seasoning and juice reserved from roasting the chicken, well skimmed of any fat. Add the grapes, and spoon this dressing over the chicken; then scatter over the almonds.

Roast duckling with mint and lemon

4–5 lb duckling
1 tablespoon chopped mint
1 teaspoon sugar
2 oz butter
grated rind and juice of ½ lemon
salt and pepper
¼ pint stock

To garnish

1½ lemons (sliced)
1 bunch of watercress

Method

Mix half the chopped mint with the sugar, 1 oz butter, the grated rind of ½ lemon and seasoning. Place this mixture inside the duck, rub the remaining butter over the breast of the duck and truss it. Place duck in a roasting tin, pour round half the stock and roast in a moderately hot oven set at 400°F or Mark 6 for 15 minutes per lb and 15 minutes over, basting frequently.

When the duck is cooked remove from the tin and keep hot. Tip off the excess fat from the roasting tin, leaving any sediment behind. Pour in the remaining stock and the juice of ½ lemon, boil up and season carefully to taste. Strain this sauce through a fine nylon strainer or a piece of muslin and add the remaining chopped mint, pour sauce over the duck.

Garnish the dish with slices of lemon and small bouquets of watercress.

Roast duckling is garnished with half slices of lemon and small bouquets of watercress

GAME

Game is a term that covers wild birds and animals that are protected by law. All game needs hanging if the flesh is to be tender and well-flavoured. The length of hanging time allowed depends on personal taste and the weather.

Do not pluck or draw game before hanging. Birds are ready when the tail feathers are easy to pull and, if young ones, the best way to cook them is by roasting. Each kind of game has its classic accompanying dishes.

Grouse, pheasant, partridge and wild duck are the most plentiful; the following recipe for roast game is basic to cooking all these birds.

Roast game

brace of young birds
2 slices of fat bacon
2–3 oz butter, or bacon fat, or good beef dripping
salt and pepper
2 tablespoons flour (for dredging)

For gravy

stock (made from giblets, 1 carrot, 1 onion, bouquet garni)
1 beef bouillon cube (optional)
1 teaspoon flour
watercress (to garnish)

If the birds are bought from the poulterers, they will have a slice of larding fat tied over their breasts; in this case, omit the fat bacon.

Method
Set oven at 400°F or Mark 6.

To make stock: put the giblets in a pan, cover with water and add the vegetables, sliced, and bouquet garni to flavour. Simmer for 30–40 minutes. Since gravy served with all game should be well flavoured, a beef bouillon cube may be added to improve its flavour.

Wipe insides of the birds with a damp cloth, but do not wash. Put a piece of butter (the size of a walnut) mixed with salt and pepper inside each bird and truss them with fine string or thread.

Heat the rest of the butter or bacon fat in a roasting tin, put in the birds and baste well. Turn birds and baste while cooking so that their thighs and undersides are well coloured. Cooking times vary according to type.

Five minutes before dishing up, remove the fat bacon or larding fat, baste the breast well and dredge with flour. Baste again before returning to the oven for the final 5 minutes. This is known as 'frothing the breast' and gives the bird an attractive appearance. Now take birds out of oven, remove trussing strings and keep hot.

To make the gravy: pour off fat from roasting tin, leaving any sediment behind. Dust in a very little flour and blend it into juices in pan. Cook for 2–3 minutes, then tip on stock. Boil up, scrape sides of pan, reduce in quantity by boiling for 1–2 minutes, season and strain.

Serve birds garnished with watercress.

TO SERVE WITH ROAST GAME

Traditional accompaniments to roast game are fried crumbs, game chips (see recipe on page 102) and bread sauce (see recipe on page 179).

Fried crumbs

8 tablespoons fresh breadcrumbs
2 oz butter

Method
Heat the butter gently and skim well. Increase the heat under the pan, add the breadcrumbs and stir until golden-brown. Serve in a sauce boat, or small gratin dish.

Pheasant Viroflay

2 hen pheasants
2 oz butter
1 dessert apple (sliced)
¼ pint stock
1 wineglass white wine, or sherry
2 tablespoons double cream

For farce

1 shallot (finely chopped)
2 oz butter
½ lb green streaky bacon (boiled for about 45 minutes and minced)
1 teacup fresh white breadcrumbs
½ lb leaf spinach (blanched and chopped)
2 egg yolks
1 dessertspoon chopped thyme and sage (mixed)
salt and pepper
Trussing needle and fine string

Method
Cut the pheasant down the back, remove the carcass bones but leave in the leg and wing bones.

To prepare the farce: cook the finely chopped shallot in the butter until soft but not coloured and mix with all the other ingredients, seasoning well.

Set the oven at 400°F or Mark 6. Fill the birds with the farce, sew them up with fine string and truss neatly. Rub the birds with the butter and set in a roasting tin with the apple and stock. Cook for about 45 minutes in the pre-set oven, basting and turning from time to time. Take up the pheasants and deglaze the pan with the wine, boil up and strain. Carve the pheasants and arrange on a serving dish. Add the cream to the gravy and spoon it over the birds. Serve with braised celery.

SLOW ROASTING AND SPIT ROASTING

Through research into providing food at budget cost, it has been discovered that there is much less shrinkage if meat is slow roasted (the oven is set at 350°F or Mark 4 for pork, and at 325°F or Mark 3 for all other meats); and now that beef particularly is so expensive it is worthwhile for the housewife to experiment with this method and to benefit from the information obtained.

When slow roasting, the only way to ensure that the meat is fully cooked in the centre is to use a meat thermometer. The chart (see below) gives an approximate time per lb for the various joints of meat (assuming them to be taken straight out of the refrigerator), and the temperatures your thermometer must register.

Remember the thermometer must be inserted into the thickest part of the meat and must never touch the bone, nor rest on the fat, and that the times given may vary with the size and shape of the joint, and also the amount of fat.

Joints on the bone must always be set on a rack, fat side uppermost, in the roasting tin.

It is not necessary to add extra fat, nor is it necessary to baste. Boned and rolled joints, or those cut from boneless meat, should be spread with a little good dripping and set on a rack in the tin in the same way. There is no need to baste, but they should be turned half way through the cooking.

It is now possible for many more people to spit roast at home, and electrically operated rotating spits do give an almost exact copy of the old spit roast before an open fire. This method is more like slow roasting, the shrinkage is less, and the flavour is particularly fine as the outside fat develops such a good flavour. In fact, we feel that this is the only way to roast a joint of topside, a small lean joint which tends to become hard on the outside when oven-roasted.

It is important that meat to be spit roasted is at room temperature, so remove it from the refrigerator 1–2 hours before cooking.

Joints with a cut surface are cooked on very high heat until the meat just begins to take colour. The heat should then be turned quite low (each cooker will have its own instructions in the handbook), and the meat is cooked at black heat (ie. not radiant heat) until it is tender. Follow the timing given in the chart (see opposite). Brush or baste the joint with dripping from time to time during the cooking.

SPIT ROASTING GUIDE

BEEF

The cut surface of the joint must always be exposed to the heat in order to seal it and retain the juices. In a joint of wing rib or sirloin the spit should be inserted in such a position that it does not touch the bone, so that the fat and both sides of the lean of the meat are exposed in turn as the joint rotates. If the spit touches the bone it upsets the distribution of heat or may stop it altogether.

LAMB

A leg of lamb can be spit roasted but particular care must be taken in inserting the spit because of the position of the bone.

A shoulder of lamb should be fully or partially boned.

PORK

Joints cut from the leg should be boned and stuffed, but remember that the stuffing will

SLOW ROASTING CHART
Set oven at 350°F or Mark 4 for pork, and 325°F or Mark 3 for other meat

Cuts of meat (taken straight from refrigerator)	Approximate time per lb for 3–6 lb joints	Temperature of meat thermometer
Beef on the bone		
sirloin – rare	26	140°F
wing rib – medium	30	160°F
rib roast – well done	35	170°F
Lamb		
leg	35–40	175°F–182°F
neck, best end and loin	45	182°F
shoulder	35	182°F
shoulder, boned and rolled	55	182°F
Pork		
leg	45–50	185°F
loin	35–40	185°F
shoulder, a joint from the blade	40–50	185°F
shoulder, boned and rolled	55	185°F
Veal		
leg	35–40	180°F
loin	35–40	180°F
shoulder, boneless roll	55	180°F

swell, so it is wise to put in only the very minimum amount and secure it well by sewing up with a trussing needle and thread. Extra stuffing can always be made and cooked separately. Shoulder cuts, providing they have been removed from the bone, are suitable for spit roasting, but a whole leg would be too large.

BACON

A joint of boiling bacon is best simmered in the usual way and then finished on the spit at black heat for ½–1 hour with a sugar or syrup glaze.

HARES AND RABBITS

For the best flavour, and to prevent the flesh from drying, wrap in larding bacon. Start them on the spit at black heat, and keep at this for full cooking time.

POULTRY

Start and continue cooking birds at black heat, basting from time to time with melted butter, oil or dripping.

Electrically operated rotating spits give an almost exact copy of the old spit roast before an open fire

Gravy for spit roasted joints

The making of a good gravy is something of a problem when spit roasting because although the drip tray will have collected a certain amount of juice and quite a lot of fat during the cooking time, the tin itself is not suitable for making gravy.

Any juices that fall from the meat, congeal and then brown on the drip tray must be carefully scooped up, added to a little good stock and then boiled up well. If the family likes plenty of gravy, this can be augmented by adding potato water, if there is no stock, and gravy salt for colouring and flavour. It can be thickened too, if liked.

SPIT ROASTING CHART

	Minutes per lb
Beef	
without bone	10–25
with bone	20–25
Lamb	25–35
Pork	30–35
Hares and rabbits	
stuffed	20–25
unstuffed	15
Poultry	
stuffed	20–25
unstuffed	15–20

Frying and Sautéing

After roasting, frying is perhaps the next most important cooking process, and the advantages are that it is quick and simple to do. There are two ways of frying, either in shallow or deep fat. Both methods cover a wide range of basic foods—meat, fish and made-up dishes too, such as fish cakes.

It is important also to know how to prepare food for frying, so overleaf you will learn what coatings to use, with step-by-step photographs on how to egg and crumb, and how to make fritter batters. Properly fried food should look appetising and taste light, leaving you wanting more.

FRYING

SHALLOW FAT FRYING

This is the most commonly used method and, as the name implies, it is done in a frying pan in any of these fats: butter; oil; a mixture of butter and oil; dripping; lard or one of the commercially-prepared shortenings.

The following are foods suited to shallow fat frying: small whole fish; fillets of fish; lamb cutlets and made-up mixtures such as fish cakes. For the best taste and effect use butter, otherwise oil or dripping (do not use the latter with food in an egg and crumb coating because dripping would over-brown the egg).

The amount of fat in the pan is important; it should come half way up the food to be fried so that the sides, say, of the fish cake or cutlet, are completely browned.

Turn the food once only and cook on a moderate to brisk heat; this depends on what is being fried, whether it is raw or cooked, and times are given in the recipes following.

The same pan can be used for all types of food fried in shallow fat, any fat left over being strained off and used again, though fish fat should be kept only for fish frying.

Whole fish need only a roll in seasoned flour or oatmeal just before frying. Sole or plaice fillets may be rolled in seasoned flour and then fried in butter, or dipped into beaten egg after rolling in seasoned flour, then fried until golden-brown.

DEEP FAT FRYING

This method is quicker than shallow fat frying as food is immersed completely. Therefore food usually needs a coating to protect it from the great heat of the fat and also to keep the fat free from taste; in this way, the fat can be used many times for different foods.

When cool, strain used fat through muslin into a bowl till wanted again, covering when it is quite cold, and storing in a cool place.

Choose a deep heavy gauge pan (fat bath or deep fryer) which covers source of heat, complete with a wire basket to fit. Or buy a separate folding wire basket for fitting into any saucepan (which must, however, be of reasonably heavy gauge because fat is heated to high temperatures in deep fat frying). This separate basket is useful when only occasionally deep fat frying because its flexibility means it can be used in an ordinary frying pan for cooking relatively small foods such as croûtons.

When frying foods coated in soft batter mixture, you may find it easier to fry them in a fat bath without using a wire basket since batter tends to stick to the basket.

Suitable fats to use are: vegetable or nut oil; lard; clarified dripping or commercially-prepared fat, but it is better not to mix these. Olive oil and margarine are not suitable for deep frying. Never fill pan with more than one-third fat or oil.

Melt the fat, or put the oil, over moderate heat, then increase heat until right cooking temperature is reached (see chart, overleaf). Oil must never be heated above 375°F, and for sunflower oil, and some commercially prepared fats (eg. Spry, Cookeen), 360°F is the highest recommended temperature. It is important to remember that oil does not 'haze', as solid fats do, until heated to a much higher temperature than is required − or is safe − for frying.

Apart from food cooked on a rising temperature (eg. choux pastry), the fat or oil should

A golden-brown portion of Chicken Kiev, cut to show its butter and herb filling (see recipe on page 102)

never be below 340°F, as it is essential that the surface of the food is sealed immediately. This means that it does not absorb the fat, and is more digestible.

The best way of testing temperature is with a frying thermometer. Before using, it should be stood in a pan of hot water then carefully dried before putting into the fat bath. The hot water warms the glass so that it does not break when plunged into the hot fat.

If you have no thermometer, drop in a small piece of the food to be cooked (eg. a chip). If the fat or oil is at the right temperature, the food will rise immediately to the top and bubbles appear round it. Alternatively drop in a cube of day-old bread, which should turn golden-brown in 20 seconds at 375°F; 60 seconds at 360°F.

COATINGS

There are three types of coatings: seasoned flour with beaten egg and dry white breadcrumbs (for fillets of fish, cutlets and croquettes, etc.); fritter batter (for fillets of fish, sweet and savoury fritters) and pastry.

To get a crisp, golden coating, dry white crumbs are essential, and a jar of these should be kept ready for use in the kitchen.

To make crumbs: take a large loaf (the best type to use is a sandwich loaf) at least two days old. Cut off the crust and keep to one side. Break up bread into crumbs either by rubbing through a wire sieve or a Mouli sieve, or by working in an electric blender.

Spread crumbs on to a sheet of paper laid on a baking tin and cover with another sheet of paper to keep off any dust. Leave to dry in a warm temperature – the plate rack, or warming drawer, or the top of the oven, or even the airing cupboard, is ideal. The crumbs may take a day or two to dry thoroughly, and they must be crisp before storing in a jar. To make them uniformly fine, sift them through a wire bowl strainer.

To make browned crumbs: bake the crusts in a slow oven until golden-brown, then crush or grind through a mincer. Sift and store as for white crumbs. These browned ones are known as raspings and are used for any dish that is coated with a sauce and browned in the oven.

EGGING AND CRUMBING

To make egging and crumbing easy, it is best to follow a certain technique. Whether frying fish or shaping a mixture, the first coating should always be of flour, lightly seasoned with a pinch of salt and half as much pepper.

Start with a board or plate well sprinkled with seasoned flour on the one side, have the beaten egg on a plate in the centre, and the white crumbs on a large piece of paper on the other side. You can then work from left to right, or vice versa, finally placing the coated food on to a large dish.

If using a mixture, first divide this into even-size portions, then shape on the floured board or plate (preferably with palette knives or round-bladed knives to avoid touching with your fingers). With the knives, lift the shaped mixture into the beaten egg (brushing evenly) and on to the paper of crumbs, still not touching with your fingers. Lift each corner of the paper, tipping mixture from side to side, and when well covered, press on the crumbs with a knife. Then lift off on to the large dish already sprinkled with crumbs. The croquettes – the name given to this type of crumbed mixture – are then ready for frying. See page 21 for a recipe for fish croquettes.

In the case of fillets of fish, these must be absolutely dry, so make sure that after washing they are thoroughly dried in absorbent paper or a cloth kept specially for this purpose.

Roll fillets in the seasoned flour and shake gently to remove any surplus. Then draw them through the beaten egg, first on one side, then the other, and gently run down the whole length of the fillet with your finger and thumb to wipe off any surplus egg. Turn on to the paper of crumbs, tip fillets from side to side to cover thoroughly and press on the crumbs with a palette knife until well coated. Lift off on to a dish or rack. When convenient egging and crumbing may be done quite a time ahead.

FRITTER BATTERS

There are two types of fritter batter; the quantities given for both types here are sufficient for fruit fritters for 4 people, but large portions of fish need at least half as much batter mixture again.

Lift the shaped mixtures with palette knives into beaten egg

Brush shapes evenly and then turn with the palette knives

After tipping in the paper of crumbs, press on with knives

Temperature guide to frying

Uncooked doughs — fried on a rising temperature, eg. choux pastry	325°F–375°F
Fish fillets and cooked mixtures, eg. croquettes, fish cakes	350°F–375°F
Meat	350°F–375°F

Chips, game chips and whitebait
   — first frying
   — second frying
	350°F
	360°F–375°F

Fritters — sweet and savoury	350°F–375°F

Fritter batter (1)

4 tablespoons plain flour
pinch of salt
2 egg yolks
1 tablespoon melted butter, or oil
¼ pint milk
1 egg white

Method
Sift flour with salt into a bowl, make a well in centre of flour, add egg yolks, melted butter, or oil, and mix with milk to a smooth batter; beat thoroughly. Stand in a cool place for 30 minutes. Just before frying, whisk egg white stiffly, fold into batter. Fry in deep fat or up to ½-inch depth for shallow frying.

Fritter batter (2)

5 oz plain flour
pinch of salt
small piece of fresh yeast about size of a nut, or 1 teaspoon dried yeast
1 teacup warm water
1 tablespoon oil
1 egg white (optional)

This deep-fry batter is slightly crisper than the first type.

Method
Sift flour and salt into a warm basin. Mix yeast in about half the warm water, stir into flour with oil. Add rest of water to make consistency of thick cream. Beat well and cover, leave in a warm place for 15–20 minutes, by then mixture should be well risen. If using egg white, whisk stiffly and fold into batter just before frying.

Fritters are called beignets in French, and the word is believed to come from the Celtic for 'swelling'.

Soufflé fritters, sometimes known as 'nun's sighs', are made from choux pastry, and after frying are rolled in caster sugar for serving with a sweet jam sauce, or with grated Parmesan cheese for savoury tastes.

Kromeski is the name given to small pieces of cooked, creamed chicken, veal or game mixture which are wrapped in thin bacon rashers before dipping in batter and frying.

Almost anything can be turned into a fritter, from cardoons (edible thistles) and chard (a white sea kale beet) to brains, tongue and truffles, oysters, rice and semolina, crystallised fruit, and even acacia blossoms or violets. But the most common choice is raw fruit, usually apples and bananas.

Fish in batter

When frying fish in fritter batter, choose the second batter recipe and double the quantity for ease in working. For white fish such as haddock or cod fillet, allow 1¼–1½ lb for 4 people, skin and cut into 4-oz portions. Sprinkle lightly with salt and lemon juice, and leave for 30 minutes. Drain off any liquid, dry well and roll in seasoned flour.

Have batter ready in a bowl before heating fat. When fat is smoking hot, drop a piece of the fish into the batter bowl, turn to coat thoroughly, then lift out with a draining spoon and slide carefully into the fat bath. Fry about three pieces at a time, allowing plenty of room to turn them. When well browned and crisp, lift out and drain well on absorbent paper. Take out any scraps of batter before frying the next batch.

Fried onion rings

To make fried onion rings, slice onions and then push the slices out into rings. Moisten with egg white, dust dry with seasoned flour; fry in deep fat, being sure not to crowd the pan. Keep hot. These may be used as a garnish for eggs soubise (see recipe on page 39).

When adding food to oil, like these apple fritters, don't crowd pan

Frying apple and banana fritters in a pan with a clip-on thermometer

Apple and banana fritters

2–3 cooking apples
2 bananas
1 dessertspoon lemon juice
fritter batter
caster sugar
deep fat, or about ½-inch
depth of fat in frying pan

Method
Prepare fritter batter (using either recipe), set aside to stand.

Peel and core the apples; cut across in ½-inch slices. Peel the bananas and cut diagonally in 3–4 pieces. Sprinkle over lemon juice.

Heat fat bath. When fat or oil reaches correct temperature (see page 99), coat half fruit in batter, then lift out with a draining spoon and slide into hot fat. Fry until golden-brown, drain on absorbent paper and arrange on a hot dish. Dust with caster sugar before serving.

FRIED CHOUX

Fried choux pastry, known as fritters or beignets soufflés, may be served as a hot sweet with a jam or fruit sauce, or as a savoury flavoured with cheese. Beignets must be deep fat fried and served at once.

Beignets soufflés

choux pastry for 3–4 people
caster sugar (for dredging)
hot jam sauce

Method
Prepare choux pastry. Carefully add the second egg (beaten), keeping back a little, if necessary. The pastry must be firm enough to keep its shape. Divide it out into heaped teaspoons on a tin or dish. Heat the fat bath to just below hazing point (370°F). Dip a palette knife in the fat and use this to lift each teaspoon of pastry from the tin into the fat. Leave plenty of room for them to swell.

Once the beignets begin to puff out, increase heat gradually and continue cooking for about 8 minutes until they are golden-brown and firm to the touch. Don't put too many beignets into the fat bath or they will not have enough room to turn themselves over.

Lift out beignets with a draining spoon and drain them on absorbent paper. Dust well with caster sugar and serve at once with a hot jam sauce.

Cheese beignets

Make choux pastry as for beignets soufflés but mix in 2 tablespoons finely grated cheese (dry Cheddar or Parmesan) before frying.

Fry as for beignets soufflés. After draining, dust with grated Parmesan cheese and cayenne pepper before serving.

CROQUETTES, RISSOLES AND KROMESKIES

These are a little more difficult to prepare than a straightforward réchauffé but are well worth the additional trouble and care involved.

Croquettes are made with eggs, fish, veal or chicken, finely chopped or minced and bound with a well flavoured thick sauce or panada. The mixture, once cold, is rolled into cork shapes, floured, egged and crumbed ready for frying in deep fat. Shallow fat may be used but it is much easier to use a deep fat pan and frying basket.

A well-made croquette has an even, golden-brown crisp coating on the outside and a soft and creamy inside. To achieve this the mixture should be made several hours before shaping to let it get really set and firm. Sometimes a little gelatine is added while the mixture is still warm, which makes for easier handling of the mixture when cold.

Rissoles are made with minced beef or game, bound with a good gravy or brown sauce. The mixture, firmer than

When frying croquettes make sure that the fat covers them to seal the coating, otherwise they are very likely to burst

Cheese beignets, dusted with cheese and cayenne

that of a croquette, is wrapped in thinly rolled puff, or short-crust, pastry to form small turn-overs. They must be sealed before frying in deep fat. To make an extra crisp coating rissoles wrapped in shortcrust pastry may be brushed with egg, then rolled in crushed vermicelli before frying but this should not be done for rissoles made with puff pastry, because the pastry will puff out or 'move' in the frying and the vermicelli would be lost.

Enclosing rissoles in pastry is the traditional way of making them.

Kromeskies are savoury fritters and may be served as a main course or as a savoury. The mixture is similar to that of a croquette but is put out in dessertspoons on to bacon rashers. Each rasher is rolled up, dipped into fritter batter, and fried. Smoked haddock, devilled prawns and so on can be treated in this way and served as a savoury.

Rissoles

8 oz quantity flaky, or puff, pastry
  trimmings, or 6 oz quantity
  rich shortcrust pastry
½ lb cold cooked beef, or game
  (minced)
1 small onion (finely chopped)
1 dessertspoon dripping
1 tablespoon mushroom ketchup
2–3 tablespoons brown, or
  tomato, sauce
beaten egg

Method
Chill the pastry. Gently fry the onion in the dripping until brown, add to the meat with the mushroom ketchup and stir in enough sauce to bind.

Roll out the pastry thinly, stamp or cut out into rounds about 3–4 inches in diameter. Brush round the edges with the beaten egg and put 1 dessert-spoon of the meat in the centre of each round. Fold over and pinch or crimp pastry edges together. This closed edge will be the top. If using shortcrust, brush the rissoles with beaten egg and roll in vermicelli, crushed well with a rolling pin.

Heat fat bath to approximately 350°F. Immerse the rissoles in the fat and fry steadily, increasing the temperature by degrees to 375°F.

Serve brown, or tomato, sauce separately.

Chicken kromeskies

½ lb (2 cups) cooked chicken, or
  rabbit, or veal (finely diced)
thick béchamel sauce (made with
  1 oz butter, 1 oz flour,
  ¼ pint flavoured milk)
1 egg yolk
16 thin rashers streaky bacon

For fritter batter
5 oz flour
pinch of salt
¼ oz yeast
½ pint warm water

Method
To make batter: sift flour with salt, dissolve yeast in a little of the water and add to flour with more water to make a thick cream. Leave to stand for 30 minutes.

Mix meat with the sauce. Season well, add egg yolk and leave until cold. Cut away rind and rust and flatten bacon on a board with the blade of a knife. Put 2 rashers together so that they slightly overlap, place 1 dessertspoon of mixture at one end, then roll up. Heat the fat bath to 375°F.

Drop the kromeskies, one at a time, into the batter, making sure that they are completely covered before lifting out with a draining spoon and dropping into the fat. Leave enough room for them to expand. Fry until a deep golden-brown; drain and dry on absorbent paper. Serve hot with a tomato sauce.

Prawn kromeskies

6 oz prawns (shelled and chopped), or packet of frozen
  prawns
½ pint thick béchamel sauce
4 oz button mushrooms (sliced)
½ oz butter
2 egg yolks
salt and pepper
½–¾ lb streaky bacon rashers
fritter batter (see above)

Method
Make béchamel sauce: set it aside. Cook mushrooms quickly in butter. Add to the sauce with the prawns (defrost, dry, and chop frozen ones) and the egg yolks; season. Turn out on to a plate and leave until cold.

Prepare as for chicken kro-meskies (above) and fry until golden. Drain well; serve hot.

Chip potatoes (French fried)

1½ lb even-size potatoes
(weighed when peeled)
deep fat, or at least 1-inch
depth of fat in frying pan

Method

Prepare potatoes 1 hour before needed. Square off ends and sides of potatoes, cut in ½-inch thick slices, then into thick fingers. Soak in cold water for 30 minutes, then drain. Wrap in absorbent paper or cloth and leave for 20–30 minutes. Heat fat, dip in basket; when fat reaches right temperature (see chart, page 99), gently lower into fat. If you do not have a thermometer, drop in a finger of potato; if this rises to surface at once and fat starts to bubble gently, fat is ready.

Fry gently until potatoes are just soft but not coloured. Lift out and drain, still in basket, on a plate. Chips can be left like this for a while before the final frying. Reheat fat to frying temperature; carefully lower in basket, fry chips to a deep golden-brown. Drain well on absorbent paper, turn into a hot dish for serving and sprinkle with salt. Potatoes double-fried in this way are crisply tender on the outside and evenly browned. When cooking fish and chips, fry potatoes first so that there is no chance of crumb coating from fish spoiling the fat for the potatoes.

Lamb cutlets Périnette

2 lb best end of neck of lamb
(chined)
seasoned flour
5 tablespoons fresh white
breadcrumbs
2 oz ham (finely chopped)
1 beaten egg
clarified butter (for frying)

For tomato salpicon

1 lb tomatoes
2–3 caps of canned pimiento, or
1–2 fresh red peppers
1–2 leeks
1 oz butter
1 teaspoon tomato purée
1 teaspoon paprika pepper
salt and pepper

Method

Divide the meat into cutlets, trim well and roll them in seasoned flour. Mix breadcrumbs and ham together. Brush cutlets with beaten egg and roll in the crumb mixture, pressing it on well.

To prepare tomato salpicon: scald, skin and slice tomatoes, shred pimiento caps or peppers, set them aside. Cut white part of the leeks into thin rounds, and the green into shreds; blanch the latter and set aside. Soften the white part of leeks in butter, add tomato purée, paprika, tomatoes and pimientos. Season well, cover pan and simmer for 3–4 minutes.

Fry cutlets until golden-brown on both sides (6–7 minutes) and arrange them, overlapping, in a serving dish. Place salpicon in centre, scatter the shredded leeks over dish before serving the cutlets.

Game chips

Choose large potatoes (1½ lb will be sufficient for up to 6 people). Peel and trim off the ends and cut in very thin slices. Soak slices in a large bowl of cold water for 1 hour, separating slices to prevent their sticking together. Drain well and leave wrapped in a clean teacloth for 20 minutes, again separating the slices so that they dry thoroughly.

Fry the slices a few at a time in a basket in deep fat or oil heated to 350°F (see page 99), and remove when bubbling subsides. When all slices have been cooked in this way, reheat the fat or oil to 375°F, put two or three batches of slices together in the basket and fry until they are golden-brown.

As soon as there is no danger of the fat bubbling over, turn potato slices out of basket into pan to finish cooking; keep them separated with a draining spoon. Drain well on crumpled, absorbent paper and then pile on to a hot dish. Sprinkle with salt and serve.

Watchpoint Never cover up game chips or they will lose all their crispness.

Chicken Kiev

3 roasting chickens (2½ lb each)
6 oz unsalted butter
grated rind and juice of 1 lemon
salt
black pepper (ground from mill)
pinch of ground mace, or nutmeg
chopped fresh parsley, or herbs
seasoned flour
1 egg (beaten)
dried white breadcrumbs

Deep fat bath; cutlet frills

This is a specialised and fairly extravagant dish, but basically simple to do even though it calls for a certain amount of deftness in preparation. Once prepared, the chicken can be set aside overnight in the refrigerator to chill. It also deep-freezes well. For this recipe the whole suprême, ie. breast and wing together, is cut from the bird with the wing bone left in to give it shape. If you serve chicken Kiev at home for a party, do warn your guests to cut the chicken carefully or the butter will spurt out all over their clothes.

If making this dish it is wise to choose a recipe to prepare in the next day or so to use up the legs of the chickens.

Method

Cut the suprêmes from the chickens, cover the breasts with a sheet of waxed paper and bat out with a heavy knife or cutlet bat. Work the butter with the lemon rind and juice, seasoning, mace (or nutmeg) and parsley (or herbs) and put in refrigerator until very hard. Cut the hard butter into six finger-length pieces.

Put a piece of butter on each suprême, fold in the sides and roll up. Roll in seasoned flour, brush with beaten egg and roll in the breadcrumbs, pressing these on well. Allow to dry.
Note: at this stage the suprêmes may be refrigerated or deep-frozen. If they are frozen, thaw them in the refrigerator for 6–7 hours before frying.

Heat the fat to 380°F (oil to 375°F) and fry the chicken until golden-brown; allow 4–6 minutes for this. Drain, put a cutlet frill on the wing bone and serve very hot. This quantity allows for two second helpings.

Fritto misto alla milanese uses meat, offal and vegetables

Fritto misto There are several varieties of this delicious dish, from different cities: Rome, Florence, Milan. They differ in the amount and type of ingredients in each dish and the way in which they are fried. Flour, egg - and - crumb, and fritter batter are all used as coatings for the various ingredients: meat and offal, vegetables or fish.

Fritto misto alla fiorentina is similar to the milanese but has not quite so many ingredients. All of the ingredients are egg and crumbed and fried in deep hot oil, as opposed to butter. Typical ingredients are sweetbreads, small lamb cutlets, brains, tiny potato croquettes, sliced courgettes and baby globe artichokes.

Fritto misto alla milanese

2 large escalopes of veal
6 oz calves liver (thinly sliced)
½ lb lambs sweetbreads
¼–½ pint stock
2 sets of calves brains
1–2 veal, or lambs, kidneys
1 small cauliflower
1 small marrow
2 baby globe artichokes
potato croquettes
seasoned flour
2 eggs (beaten)
8–12 oz dried white breadcrumbs
about 6 oz butter (for frying)
1–2 oz butter (for sauce)
juice of ½ lemon

Method
First prepare all the ingredients before frying, then fry in the order given.

Bat the escalopes out thinly and cut each one into 3 pieces. Roll in seasoned flour.

Roll liver in seasoned flour.

Prepare the sweetbreads and simmer them in stock barely to cover until tender, drain and cool. Roll in flour, coat with egg and crumbs.

Prepare the brains, blanch them, drain, cut in half, roll in flour, coat with egg and breadcrumbs.

Skin and split, or slice, the kidneys.

Break the cauliflower into sprigs, boil and drain it and roll in seasoned flour, then dip in beaten egg.

Slice the marrow, blanch and drain it, then roll in flour and dip in egg.

Boil the artichokes and cut them into quarters.

Prepare the potato croquettes.

Now heat a frying pan, put in some butter and begin to fry the ingredients in the order in which they were prepared, ie. begin with the escalopes and end with the potato croquettes, keeping them warm on a rack.

When all are done, pile up in a dish for serving. Wipe out and reheat the frying pan, drop in the 1–2 oz butter, cook to a nut-brown, add the lemon juice and pour this sauce, foaming, over the fritto misto.

HOW TO FRY FISH

For fish such as fillets of sole, or plaice, or small whole sole, an egg and breadcrumb coating is best. More friable (easily crumbled) fish, such as haddock or whiting, are best fried in batter.

Most fried fish should be garnished with sprays of fried parsley and a savoury butter such as maître d'hôtel or anchovy, which should be served separately (see page 76).

Watchpoint Great care should be taken when handling a deep fat bath or fryer. When fat is heating, make sure that the handle of the fat bath or fryer is pushed to one side so that there is no danger of it being caught or knocked over.

Fat is inflammable; if any is spilt, wipe it up at once. Keep the outside of the fat bath clean so that there is no chance of any fat catching alight, which can easily happen if it is overheated, so treat hot fat with the greatest respect.

If fat does catch fire, smother it with a cloth – do not splash water on it or attempt to move the blazing pan. If you have to leave the kitchen at any time while cooking with fat, turn off the heat from under the pan.

Fried fillets of sole or plaice

As a main course, allow 2 fillets per person from a fish weighing about $1\frac{1}{4}$ lb (skinned on both sides). Wash the fillets, dry thoroughly and roll in seasoned flour, beaten egg and white crumbs.

When ready to fry, heat the fat bath and place the basket in it. When the correct temperature is reached (refer to the temperature guide on page 99), take up fillets and holding each end between a finger and thumb, twist them. (This is done to avoid sogginess when deep fat frying. It reduces the flat surface which would normally come in too much contact with the serving dish and the other fillets. The resulting fillets also look more attractive.)

Lower the twisted fillets to the surface of the fat and gently let go; put in about three at a time. When fillets are a deep golden-brown, lift out

Lower twisted fillet to fat surface, let go gently to avoid splashing

basket and stand it on a plate or tray. Leave for 1–2 minutes before lifting out fillets on to a hot dish. Scatter over fried parsley and serve pats of maître d'hôtel butter separately (see page 76).

Fish cakes

This is a good way of using up leftovers. Make with white fish, fresh or canned salmon. The proportion of fish when cooked, skinned and flaked, should be equal that of potato. However, the fish can be more in quantity but never less.

1 lb fresh haddock, or cod fillet, or 12 oz cooked fish
little salt ⎫
butter ⎬ if using fresh fish
lemon juice ⎭ only
3–4 medium-size potatoes
1 tablespoon butter
1 egg
salt and pepper
1 dessertspoon parsley (chopped)

For frying

seasoned flour
beaten egg
dry white crumbs

Method

With fresh fish, wash and dry well, sprinkle with a little salt and if time allows, let it stand for 15–20 minutes. Tip off liquid, place fish in buttered, fireproof dish, with a little lemon juice, cover with buttered paper and cook for 15–20 minutes in the oven at 350°F or Mark 4. Flake fish, remove skin and bones.

Now work prepared fish in a bowl to break up the fibres (if fish is inclined to be wet, eg. cold or canned salmon, this working of fish will thicken the consistency.)

Boil potatoes, drain, dry and mash well. Beat in the butter, egg and fish; season well and add parsley. Put out in tablespoons on to a seasoned, floured board. Shape into cakes, brush with beaten egg, roll in (and press on) the crumbs. Fry in either deep or shallow fat, when fat should be over $\frac{1}{2}$-inch deep in pan. Lift in the fish cakes when the fat is at the right temperature (350–375°F) and after browning on one side turn carefully. Drain when a good colour and serve hot with a tomato sauce or ketchup.

Fried parsley

Choose 6–7 sprigs of fresh parsley. Wash and dry well. Once fish is fried and taken out, put the individual parsley sprigs into the basket.

To avoid fat spluttering, turn off heat, wait until any blue haze has disappeared, then gently lower basket into the fat and fry for 1–2 minutes when parsley will be crisp and bright green. Drain on absorbent paper.

Sauté of chicken with red wine is garnished with croûtes (see recipe on page 106)

SAUTEING

Sautéing is advanced work and is an important method of cooking, calling for care and a certain amount of judgment. This comes with practice. Meat, poultry and game are used for a sauté and must be young, tender and of the best quality. For this reason a sauté is a quick dish to make and good for entertaining as it can be kept waiting without spoiling.

To sauté is also a term used to describe cooking briskly in a small quantity of butter and/or oil and is particularly suitable for vegetables. Freshly boiled potatoes are delicious sautéd in butter until crisp and golden-brown in appearance, with a soft and buttery taste. Cold cooked leftover potatoes, while making a very good 'pan fry', are not the same thing.

Vegetables which can be sautéd raw, with a lid on the pan, include jerusalem artichokes, chicory, marrow, celery and leeks. They should be thickly sliced and cooked in butter with little or no liquid, according to individual recipes. They do not colour, but retain all their flavour and cook comparatively quickly in 7–10 minutes.

To sauté, fry lightly pieces of meat to seal in juices. Add a small quantity of strong stock, with or without wine. It should come barely level with meat or joints in pan and may at this point be lightly thickened.

When cooking is completed the sauce should be rich and concentrated with just enough to allow 2–3 tablespoons per person. To achieve this, a saute pan (similar to a large deep frying pan but with straight sides and a lid) should be used. The wide base allows room for browning and for quick reduction of sauce. The lid helps to slow up this reduction, if necessary, and ensures the cooking of the meat. If you haven't a proper sauté pan, use your deepest frying pan with a pan lid or plate as a cover.

When the meat is arranged in the serving dish you must use your own judgment as to whether the sauce should be further reduced to strengthen the flavour and thicken it a little more.

Watchpoint Care must be taken not to over-reduce, as this will give a harsh taste. If the flavour is right but the sauce is too thin, thicken with a tiny quantity of arrowroot mixed with a little cold water.

In more advanced recipes (see sauté of chicken with red wine, page 106) a previously-made sauce is added towards end of cooking, the sauté taking its name from the sauce or any other ingredient or garnish.

Sauté of chicken Parmesan

2 double poussins
1 oz butter
salt and pepper
little grated rind and juice
    of ½ lemon
3 tablespoons Parmesan cheese
    (grated)
little stock, or water (optional)
1 egg yolk
2 tablespoons cream

For béchamel sauce

1 oz butter
1 rounded tablespoon flour
½ pint milk (infused with 1 slice
    of onion, 1 bayleaf, 1 blade of
    mace, 6 peppercorns)

Method

Split the poussins in half (see pages 149–150). Melt butter in sauté pan, put in birds, skin side down, and cook slowly until golden-brown. Turn the birds, season, strain on lemon juice and add a little grated rind.

Cover pan with a close-fitting lid and cook gently for 20–30 minutes, shaking pan frequently. To keep birds moist, add a little stock or water if the pan gets dry.

Remove birds, trim away backbone, set in serving dish and keep warm. Make béchamel sauce (see page 178) and pour in pan. Boil up well, then strain. Add 2 tablespoons of cheese to sauce, reheat carefully, then taste for seasoning. Work egg yolk and cream together in a bowl, mix with a little hot sauce, then pour slowly back in pan; reheat without boiling and spoon over chicken. Sprinkle with remaining cheese; brown in a hot oven at 400°F or Mark 6, or under grill.

Parmesan cheese, from Parma in Northern Italy, is a hard dry cheese, chosen for its sharp, distinctive flavour. It is always used grated and should be mixed with a mild rich cheese, such as Gruyère or Emmenthal for use in sauces and soufflés. It is often sprinkled over a dish for browning as it takes colour well and quickly. It can be bought ready-grated but it is often cheaper to buy in the piece.

Sauté of chicken with red wine (mâconnaise)

2½–3 lb roasting chicken
1 tablespoon oil
1 oz butter
1 shallot (finely chopped)
2 wineglasses red wine
    (Burgundy)
½ pint demi-glace sauce (see
page 180)

For croûtes

4 slices of a French roll
oil and butter (for frying)

Method

Joint chicken (see pages 148–149). Heat oil in a sauté pan, drop in butter and when foaming put in the joints, the following order:

First, the two legs and thighs which, being the thickest joints, need the longest cooking. When these are beginning to brown, put in two wing joints, then whole breast (watch this tender joint carefully, turning when brown on one side, then remove from pan).

When remaining joints are golden-brown, turn them over, put in breast and shallot, cook gently for 2–3 minutes. Pour in wine, set alight to drive off alcohol and leave to simmer very gently for 10–15 minutes.

Fry the croûtes for garnish.

Pour the prepared demi-glace sauce on to chicken and simmer, uncovered, for about 2–3 minutes. Take up chicken, trim joints and then arrange on a hot serving dish. Spoon over sauce and garnish with croûtes.

Mâconnaise is the name describing various meat or fish dishes which are flavoured with red wine (Burgundy but not necessarily a Mâcon one).

Pork fillet sauté normande

1½ lb pork fillet/tenderloin
1 oz butter
1 medium-size onion (finely
    sliced)
1 dessert apple (peeled, cored
    and sliced)
1 tablespoon flour
1 wineglass dry cider
¼ pint stock
salt and pepper
2 tablespoons double cream

Method

Brown pork fillet on all sides in the butter, remove from the pan, add the onion and cook for 2–3 minutes. Peel, core and slice the apple, add to the pan and continue cooking until both onion and apple are golden-brown. Stir in the flour, cider and stock and bring to the boil. Put the fillet back in the pan, season, cover the pan and simmer gently for 45–50 minutes until meat is tender. This can be done on top of the stove or in the oven at 350°F or Mark 4.

Remove the meat from the sauce, cut in slanting, 1½-inch slices and place on a hot serving dish. Strain the sauce, reheat and then stir in the cream. Taste for seasoning and spoon over the meat.

Dishes à la normande are usually braised fish coated with a cream sauce (normande), but when referring to small cuts of meat or chicken the sauce includes some cider, and sometimes Calvados (the strong eau-de-vie liqueur made from apples).

The most famous eau-de-vie from apples originated in that part of Normandy known as Calvados (named after the Spanish Armada ship which was wrecked on nearby cliffs in 1588). Districts around Calvados are now allowed to use the name for their eau-de-vie.

Veal scaloppine à la crème is served with boiled rice

Veal scaloppine à la crème

3–4 veal escalopes
1 oz butter
1 small onion (finely chopped)
1 small glass sherry
1 dessertspoon flour
¼ pint stock
2 oz button mushrooms (sliced thinly)
salt and pepper
2 tablespoons double cream

Method
Cut escalopes (thin pieces of meat cut from leg or fillet) in half to form scaloppine (small escalopes). Heat a sauté pan, drop in the butter and, while still foaming, put in the pieces of veal. Cook briskly for 3–4 minutes, turning once, remove from the pan, add chopped onion and cook for 1–2 minutes; then pour on sherry.

Boil sherry to reduce a little, then draw aside. Stir in the flour and stock, bring to the boil, add the mushrooms and the veal, and season. Cover the pan and simmer meat gently for 8–10 minutes. Taste for seasoning, add the cream and reheat.

Sauté of veal Marengo

1½ lb fillet or shoulder of veal (weight without bone) – cut in cubes
2 tablespoons oil
2 medium-size onions (finely chopped)
1 tablespoon flour
1 tablespoon tomato purée
1 wineglass white wine
½–¾ pint stock
2 cloves of garlic (crushed with ½ teaspoon salt)
bouquet garni
½ lb tomatoes (roughly chopped)
pepper
4 oz mushrooms

For garnish
1 teaspoon parsley (chopped)
triangular croûtes of fried bread

Method
Cut meat in 2-inch cubes. Heat the oil in a sauté pan and brown the meat a few pieces at a time. Remove from the pan, add the onions and cook slowly until golden, then dust in the flour and continue cooking until a good russet-brown. Remove from heat, stir in tomato purée, wine and ½ pint of stock, and blend until smooth.

Return to stove and stir until boiling, reduce heat, add the meat, crushed garlic, bouquet garni and tomatoes. Season with a little pepper, cover and cook very gently for 45–60 minutes on top of stove, or in oven at 350°F or Mark 4. Stir occasionally, adding reserved stock if there's over-reduction of sauce.

Wash and trim mushrooms, cut in thick slices and add to sauté for last 10 minutes of cooking. Turn into a hot serving dish, sprinkle with parsley and surround with croûtes.

The term **portugaise** means a tomato fondue, made with oil and butter, and flavoured with onion, garlic and parsley. The garlic can be omitted, as with the veal chop recipe here.

Veal chops portugaise

4 veal chops
1 tablespoon oil
½ oz butter
1 small onion (finely chopped)
1 dessertspoon flour
1 teaspoon tomato purée
¼ pint stock
salt and pepper
4 tomatoes
1 bunch of spring onions
1 teaspoon parsley (chopped)

Method
Heat oil in a sauté pan, add butter then brown the chops fairly quickly on both sides, remove from the pan and add chopped onion. Lower heat and, after 2–3 minutes, stir in flour. When lightly-coloured, blend in tomato purée and stock. Season, add chops. Cover pan and cook gently for 10 minutes.

Scald and skin the tomatoes, cut away the small core at the stalk end, remove the seeds and cut flesh into slices. Rub the seeds in a strainer to remove the juice and put this into sauté pan with tomatoes. Cook for a further 10 minutes. Trim and blanch spring onions, add to pan with the parsley. Taste for seasoning.

Boiling and Steaming

Boiling is the most simple and economical form of cooking. The word implies that the food is immersed and cooked in water and for better or worse has become known internationally as the English way of cooking. (You will always find plainly boiled potatoes described on a continental menu as Pommes à l'anglaise.) 'Boiled' custard or fish, however, are inaccurately named as neither is boiled; both must be cooked well under boiling point.

Meat can be boiled in two different ways:

1 A joint such as leg of mutton is plunged into boiling salted water and boiled for 5 minutes to firm the outside and so seal in the juices. The heat is then reduced and the meat simmered until tender. Place the meat in the pan with the side that is to be uppermost when dished up on the bottom. Skim frequently during cooking time and allow 20–25 minutes per pound and 20–25 minutes over.

2 Meat for soups, stocks and beef tea is covered with cold water, salt added, and then allowed to stand for up to 20 minutes before cooking. This is because cold water and salt draw out the juices of the meat. Length of cooking time depends on the weight of meat and only gentle heat should be applied. To get as much flavour into liquid as possible, cut meat into small pieces.

Note: Salted meats – beef, ham, pork and tongue should be put into tepid water to prevent over-saltiness.

Steaming is cooking by moist heat, a comparatively slow method as the food does not come into direct contact with boiling water but only with its vapour. Steaming food takes half as long again as boiling, and twice as long if the texture of the food is particularly dense.

There are two ways of steaming:

1 Using a steamer – a container with perforations at the bottom and a close-fitting lid. This can be bought with graduated ridges at the base rim so that it will fit snugly on to saucepans of varying sizes. For a perfect fit, saucepans can be bought complete with matching steamers. The food is placed directly in the top half – the steamer – and therefore comes in immediate contact with the steam. This method is used for vegetables such as potatoes; puddings; fish and poultry. Different foods wrapped separately in parchment paper can be cooked together in one steamer.

2 Using two plates. The food to be cooked is put between two plates over a pan of boiling water and cooks in its own juice and steam. The result is delicate in flavour and easily digested – an ideal way of cooking for invalids.

Steak and kidney pudding is served with a folded napkin pinned around the basin (see recipe on page 114)

Salt pork with sauerkraut and frankfurters

1½ lb salt belly of pork
2 oz butter
1½ lb sauerkraut (fresh or canned)
1 medium-size onion (stuck with a clove)
1 carrot (peeled)
2–3 tablespoons dry white wine, or stock, or water
salt and pepper
little kneaded butter

For garnish
2 pairs of frankfurter sausages (poached)
boiled potatoes

Salt pork served with sauerkraut, frankfurters and potatoes

Method
Put pork in a large pan, cover with cold water, bring slowly to the boil, simmer gently for about 1 hour, and leave to cool in the liquid. Well grease an ovenproof casserole with half of the butter, arrange the sauerkraut in this with the onion and carrot. Put the pork in the centre, moisten with the wine or stock, or water, season, and cover with buttered paper.

Cover the pan with a tightly-fitting lid and cook in oven at 350°F or Mark 4 for about 1½ hours. At end of cooking time liquid should have evaporated.

Take out the pork, bind the sauerkraut with a little kneaded butter, reheat, stirring constantly, and add remaining butter.

Slice the pork and serve on the sauerkraut, garnished with the cooked frankfurters and boiled potatoes. The onion and carrot may be sliced and mixed with the sauerkraut if wished.

> **Sauerkraut** (choucroute in French) has no true English translation. Literally it means sour or fermented cabbage and can be bought by the pound in some delicatessens, but is also conveniently sold in cans or jars. The white drumhead cabbage is finely sliced and fermented in brine for 4–6 weeks, which makes it digestible. It is usually blanched before being braised or stewed to accompany goose, salt pork, sausages etc.

> **Frankfurter** sausages are made of a mixture of lean beef and pork with salt-petre added to give them a recognisably pink colour. They are smoked in pairs and, before eating, should be poached in boiling water and served hot or cold according to the recipe.

> **Kneaded butter** is made by working to a paste 2 parts of butter to 1 of flour. When added in small pieces this acts as a thickening or binding liaison.

Salt pork and pease pudding

½ leg, or piece of hand, of salt (pickled) pork (4–6 lb)
2 onions (peeled and quartered)
2 carrots (peeled and quartered)
2–3 sticks of celery (cut in half)
6 peppercorns

For pease pudding
1 lb split peas (soaked overnight)
1 oz butter
1 egg
salt and pepper

Method
Place the pork in a large pan, cover with cold water, bring slowly to the boil and skim off fat thoroughly. Add the onions and carrots, the celery sticks and peppercorns. Cover and simmer until the pork is tender and well cooked, allowing 25 minutes per lb.

Meanwhile drain the peas, put them in enough cold salted water to cover well, and simmer until tender (about 1½ hours), adding more water if it reduces too much. Then drain and mash well or, if preferred, sieve or blend in an electric mixer.

Beat in the butter and egg and season well. Turn this mixture into a cloth or muslin, tie up and put into the pan with the pork for the last 35–45 minutes of cooking time. Turn pudding out of the cloth before serving.

Cabbage makes a good accompanying vegetable to pease pudding, or the pork may be served with the vegetables with which it was cooked.

If the pork isn't too salty, the liquid may be kept for pea soup. **Note:** some cooks prefer to simmer the split peas tied in a cloth (leaving room for them to swell). When tender, they are turned out and the butter and egg added. The mixture is then returned to the cloth and cooked as in this recipe.

Boiling is an ideal method of cooking an old chicken; here the bird is ready for carving before serving with parsley sauce

Stuffed breast of mutton Dundee

2–2½ lb breast of mutton
1 onion (stuck with a clove)
1 carrot (peeled)
salt
6 peppercorns
bouquet garni (containing 1 stick of celery)
2 tablespoons wine vinegar
1 lb onions (sliced and blanched)
2 oz butter
1½ oz fresh white breadcrumbs
2 oz dry cheese (grated)

Method

Put meat in a pan of cold water to cover, bring slowly to boil, then skim well. Add whole onion and carrot, seasoning, bouquet garni and wine vinegar and simmer gently for 1½ hours, or until tender. Lift out of pan, remove all bones and then press meat between two plates until cold. Keep cooking liquid.

Cook the onion slices slowly in butter until golden-brown.

Place mutton in a shallow, oven-proof dish, cover with onions and then top with the crumbs and cheese mixed together. Spoon any butter left over from the onions on top and pour round about ¼ pint of the cooking liquid. Bake in oven at 400°F or Mark 6 for about 30 minutes or until brown and crisp.

Serve with a spicy tomato coulis and creamed potatoes.

Spicy tomato coulis

1 medium-size can tomatoes
1 clove of garlic (crushed with ½ teaspoon salt)
1 teaspoon sugar
¼ pint cooking liquid (from the mutton)

Method

Put all the ingredients into a pan and simmer until the mixture is thick and pulpy. Serve with stuffed breast of mutton Dundee.

Boiled chicken with parsley sauce

1 large boiling fowl, or roasting chicken
1 large carrot (quartered)
1 large onion (quartered)
bouquet garni
6 peppercorns
½ teaspoon salt
cold water
streaky bacon rashers

For parsley sauce
2 large handfuls of fresh parsley
¾ pint milk
1 bayleaf
1 blade of mace
6 peppercorns
1½ oz butter
2 rounded tablespoons flour
salt and pepper

The long, slow cooking makes the chicken tender. This is an example of the first method of boiling.

Method

Set the bird on its back in a large saucepan. Surround with the quartered vegetables, add the bouquet garni, peppercorns and salt. For a boiling fowl pour in enough water barely to cover; for a roasting chicken, sufficient just to cover the thighs. Cover saucepan and bring slowly to the boil. Simmer boiling fowl for 2–3 hours until tender; roasting fowl for 50–60 minutes. Turn bird over from time to time. When cooked draw saucepan aside and allow to cool.

To prepare the sauce: pick parsley sprigs from stalks and wash well; reserve some stalks. Boil sprigs for 7 minutes in a saucepan of salted water, drain, press and rub through a bowl strainer to make about 1 dessertspoon of parsley purée.

Meanwhile infuse the milk with the bayleaf, mace, peppercorns, reserved parsley stalks. Strain. Melt the butter, stir in flour, blend in milk and stir until boiling. Season and simmer for 2–3 minutes, then add the parsley purée.

Remove rind from the bacon, and cut rashers in half. Grill or dry fry and keep hot. Take up chicken, remove the skin if using a boiling fowl.

Carve the bird and dish up. Coat with parsley sauce, garnish with bacon, and serve separately any remaining sauce. Serve boiled rice or creamed potato with this dish.

Chicken pilaf

1 small boiling fowl (about
   3½ lb)
1 onion
1 carrot
1 stick of celery
bouquet garni
1 dessertspoon salt
6 peppercorns
4 oz mushrooms

For pilaf

8 oz long grain rice
3 oz butter
1 medium-size onion (finely
   chopped)
1¼–1½ pints chicken liquor
   (see method)
pepper (ground from mill)
1 pinch of saffron (soaked in
   1 egg cup of boiling water)
1 bayleaf
1 oz cheese (finely grated)

Method
Cover the chicken with 3–4 pints cold water, bring slowly to the boil and skim well, add the vegetables, bouquet garni and seasoning and simmer gently for 2–3½ hours until the bird is tender. Leave it to cool in the liquid.

Set the oven at 375°F or Mark 5.

To make pilaf: melt 1½ oz of the butter in a flameproof casserole, add the onion and cook slowly until soft but not coloured, then stir in the rice and cook for 2–3 minutes. Pour on 1¼ pints of the chicken liquor, add a little pepper from the mill, the saffron and liquid and bring to the boil. Put the bayleaf on top, cover the pan and cook in the pre-set oven for about 20 minutes. Look at the rice after 15–18 minutes and, if the liquid has been absorbed but the rice is not quite tender, add the extra liquor and continue cooking.

Meanwhile remove the meat from the chicken and cut in neat shreds. Wash and trim the mushrooms, cut in thick slices and sauté in 1 oz butter for 1 minute only.

Dot the remaining butter over the pilaf, dust with cheese, cover and leave to melt for 2–3 minutes. Stir lightly with a fork, adding the chicken and mushroom.

Serve the pilaf at once with green salad on individual plates.

Pot-au-feu

3 lb rolled rib of beef (with the
   bones)
1 lb knuckle of veal, or a veal
   bone
1 dessertspoon salt
about 5 pints water
2 large carrots (quartered)
2–3 onions (one stuck with a
   clove)
2–3 sticks of celery
1–2 turnips (quartered)
large bouquet garni

When a large quantity of meat is going to be used, ie. up to 6 lb in all, choose two different cuts, eg. 3 lb topside, or top rump, and 2 lb brisket, thus combining lean meat and fat.

This recipe is for making both a classic French soup and the French version of boiled beef at the same time. The beef is unsalted and is gently simmered with root vegetables for 2–3 hours. When the beef is tender it is taken out with the vegetables and served as the main course.

The soup, which is the liquid in which the meat was cooked, can precede the boiled beef or it can be left to simmer for a further hour, or until the broth is full of flavour. For the soup, the fat is skimmed from the liquid and put on slices of French bread, which are then baked in the oven until crisp. Fresh root vegetables can, if wished, be added to the broth while it is reducing and can then be sliced or diced, when cooked, to be served in the soup plate with the bread.

Method
Put the meat into a large pan with the salted water and the washed bones of both the beef and veal. Put on a slow heat without a lid and bring to the boil. As the scum rises to the surface, take it off with a metal spoon and, as the liquid reaches simmering point, add about a coffee cup (2½ fl oz) of cold water. Bring to the boil again, skim once more and add a further coffee cup of cold water. If the liquid is still not clear, this process can be repeated once more. This procedure is not only to help clear the liquid, which will become soup, but also to remove any strong flavour of bone. Simmer for about 30–40 minutes, then add the vegetables

and the bouquet garni. Continue to simmer, skimming again if necessary, and partially cover the pan with the lid. Simmer until the meat is tender (approximately 2½–3 hours), then remove the meat and serve it with the vegetables.

Return the pan to the heat and continue to simmer until liquid is strong and well flavoured. If for use as soup, skim off the fat and spread it on slices of French bread and bake in the oven until crisp.

Boiled beef and dumplings

4–5 lb salted silverside of beef
3–4 onions (peeled)
3–4 carrots (peeled and
   quartered)
1 small cabbage (quartered)
pepper

For dumplings
8 oz self-raising flour
5 oz suet (chopped or shredded)
½ teaspoon salt
about ¾ cup of cold water

The beef should be cooked for 25–30 minutes per lb, so plan the time accordingly. Put in the dumplings 20–30 minutes before end of this cooking time.

Method
Place beef in a large pan, cover completely with cold water and bring slowly to the boil.

Watchpoint Keep liquid well skimmed of fat when coming to the boil. A dash or two of cold water will help to bring the scum to the surface. This, coupled with gentle simmering, will keep the liquor clear (especially important if it is also to be used for soup; see silverside, opposite).

Cover pan and simmer beef for about 50 minutes. Then add the onions and the carrots. Cook gently for a further 15 minutes before adding the cabbage. Then leave the meat cooking while making dumplings.

To prepare dumplings: mix the flour, suet and salt together. Add enough water to make a fairly firm dough. Divide this into walnut-size pieces. Roll lightly in a little flour and drop into the pan with the beef, so that they simmer during the final 20–30 minutes of cooking time. Keep the pan covered and turn the dumplings once during this time.

Dumplings are added to the boiled beef, carrots and cabbage during the last stage of cooking

Watchpoint When adding the dumplings make sure they have plenty of room to swell. If the pan is very full, it is better to cook them separately.

Taste, add pepper if necessary. To serve, take out the dumplings with a draining spoon and arrange round a large dish with the vegetables. Set the beef in the centre and serve some of the liquor in a sauce boat.

Silverside is the classic joint for salt beef, though top side, top rump or aitch-bone can also be used. In Britain boiled beef is usually salted. In France it's bought fresh, then cooked and served in the same way with vegetables. In this case the cooking liquid is returned to the heat, simmered to a good strong broth, to serve as it is with the beef, or to be used as the base for a clear soup or consommé.

Alternatively some of the liquid can be served as a soup before the boiled beef, usually with a slice of baked or toasted bread in the soup cup or plate.

SUET AND SPONGE PUDDINGS

SUET PUDDINGS

Suet puddings should be rich yet light and to get this result, use breadcrumbs to lighten the flour and butcher's suet for flavour (chop finely – membranes are then more easily removed – and dust with flour to prevent sticking).

If you like to ring the changes in your menu, the following basic proportions will be useful. At any time up to half the flour can be replaced with the same weight of fresh breadcrumbs.

Basic recipe

8 oz plain flour
3–5 oz butcher's suet
½ teaspoon salt
2 teaspoons baking powder, or ½ teaspoon bicarbonate of soda if treacle is used in recipe and you like a dark pudding
1–4 oz sugar
1–4 tablespoons treacle, golden syrup, marmalade or jam, or 2–6 oz dried fruit
1 egg
sufficient milk (about ¼ pint if no other liquid is used) to give a dropping consistency, ie. that will just drop from a wooden spoon when shaken

Method
Well grease a pudding basin and have ready a saucepan of boiling water. (If boiling the pudding, there should be enough water to cover the basin completely; if steaming without a steamer, the water should not come more than half-way up basin.)

Sieve the flour with the salt and baking powder (or bicarbonate of soda) into a mixing bowl. If using fresh butcher's suet, remove skin, shred and chop finely, removing membranes. (Use a little of the measured flour to prevent suet sticking.) Add the remaining ingredients to the flour, using enough milk to give a dropping consistency (ie. so that it just drops from a wooden spoon when shaken).

Mix well and turn at once into the prepared basin. Cover with pieces of well-buttered greaseproof paper and foil, both with two 1-inch pleats in the centre, at right-angles to each other, to allow the pudding to rise. Tie down with string. Or for boiling, cover with a scalded cloth, floured on the underside and pleated in the centre.

Tie the cloth round basin rim and knot the four corners back over the top. Make a loop of string after tying to prevent burnt hands when removing basin from the steamer.

Boil for 2½ hours, or steam for 3 hours, ensuring that the water is kept boiling all the time and topped up regularly with boiling water.

Steak and kidney pudding

1½ lb skirt, or sticking, of beef
6 oz ox kidney
1 tablespoon seasoned flour
1 small onion (finely chopped)

For suet crust pastry
8 oz self-raising flour
pinch of salt
5 oz suet
4 fl oz cold water (to mix)

6-inch diameter pudding basin (1½ pints capacity)

For a particularly light crust 1 oz of the flour can be replaced by the same weight of fresh white breadcrumbs.

Method
Cut the steak and kidney into ½-inch cubes.

To prepare the suet crust pastry: sift the flour with salt into a bowl. If using fresh butcher's suet, remove any skin and chop finely, using a little of the measured flour to prevent it sticking to your knife. Stir the suet into the flour and mix to a firm dough with the cold water.

Grease the basin well. Take two-thirds of the pastry and roll out a circle about 1-inch thick.

To make a lining of this crust to fit the basin without creases, first dust centre of pastry with flour, then fold in half and make a large dart in double layer of pastry, tapering to a point on the fold. Then roll out folded end, from point of dart, thus forming a 'pocket' that will fit the bottom of the pudding basin (see photographs, right).

Lift the pastry carefully by putting your fist in the 'pocket' and line into the basin. Work up the thicker part of the pastry with your hands so that it stands about ½–1 inch above the top of the basin. Roll out the remaining third of pastry to a round to fit the top.

Roll the meat in seasoned flour, mix with the onion and fill into the basin; pour in enough cold water to three-parts fill; damp the edge of the pastry, put on the lid and roll and pinch edges well together.

Have ready a piece of clean linen cloth, scald by dipping in boiling water and wring out. Flour the underside, make a 1-inch pleat in the middle to allow for rising and lay over the pudding. Tie round with string and then knot the four corners of the cloth back over the top.

Submerge the basin in a large pan of fast boiling water and boil steadily for 3–4 hours.

To serve, take off the cloth and pin a clean folded napkin round the basin. Serve at the table with a small jug of boiling water. When the first portion of pudding is cut, a little water is poured in to increase and dilute the very rich gravy.

Apple hat

8 oz self-raising flour
pinch of salt
4–5 oz suet
6–8 tablespoons cold water (to mix)
1–1½ lb cooking apples
2 tablespoons demerara sugar
grated rind ½ lemon, or 2–3 cloves
4–5 tablespoons water

6-inch diameter pudding basin

Method
Sift flour with salt into a mixing bowl. If using fresh butcher's suet, remove skin, shred and chop finely using a little of the measured flour to prevent it sticking. Mix suet with flour and work quickly to a light dough with cold water. Knead lightly. Well grease basin and have ready a steamer or saucepan of boiling water.

Roll out pastry to a round 6–7 inches in diameter, dust centre with flour and fold in half. Make

Apple hat turned out and ready to eat. It can also be made with a mixture of apple and blackberries, or gooseberries, or blackcurrants

a large dart in double layer of pastry, tapering to a point on the fold. Then roll out folded end, from point of dart, thus forming a 'pocket' that will fit the bottom of the pudding basin (see photographs, right). Lift pastry carefully and line it into the basin (some of the pastry will overhang the sides); brush away any surplus flour.

Peel, core and slice apples into basin, layering them with the sugar and lemon rind or cloves; spoon over water. Damp pastry edges, draw this thicker, overhanging section up and over fruit and press firmly together. Cover with a piece of well buttered greaseproof paper and foil, both with two 1-inch pleats in the centre, at right-angles to each other, to allow pudding to rise. Tie with string.

If you have no foil, greaseproof paper is sufficient for steaming; but for boiling cover

with a scalded cloth, floured on underside and pleated in centre. Tie down round basin rim and knot four corners of cloth back over the top. Boil for 2–2½ hours, or steam for 2½–3 hours. Then take up pudding, remove cloth or foil and greaseproof and leave for 3–4 minutes before turning out on to a plate. Serve hot with custard or cream and brown sugar.

TO MAKE APPLE HAT

After folding pastry in half, make a large dart in double layer of pastry from open edges, tapering to a point on the fold. Roll out the folded end from point of dart, forming a pocket

Place your fist carefully inside pocket and lift pastry, lining it into the basin (some pastry will overhang sides). Layer apples into the basin, dampen pastry edges and draw up overhanging pastry over fruit. Press edges together

Butter a piece of greaseproof paper, and make two 1-inch pleats in centre, at right-angles to each other, to allow pudding to rise

Cover basin, and tie down securely with string. Repeat process with foil

115

Christmas pudding

8 oz self-raising flour
1 teaspoon salt
½ nutmeg (grated)
1 teaspoon mixed spice
12 oz fresh white breadcrumbs
12 oz beef suet
1 lb demerara sugar
1 lb currants
1 lb sultanas
2 lb raisins (stoned)
4 oz candied peel
2 tablespoons almonds (blanched and shredded)
1 large cooking apple (peeled and grated)
rind and juice of 1 orange
6 eggs
¼ pint milk, or ale, or stout

4 medium-size pudding basins, or 1 large and 2 small ones

Method

Well grease basins; have ready a fish kettle or sufficient large saucepans of boiling water.

Sift flour with salt and spices into a very large mixing bowl, add all dry ingredients and grated apple and mix well together. Beat eggs until frothy, add orange juice and milk, ale, or stout; add to mixture. Stir well. Turn into prepared basins, fill them to the top with mixture.

Butter a large round of grease-proof paper for each basin, cut a piece of foil to same size. Put both rounds together, foil uppermost, fold across centre to form a 1-inch pleat and lay over basins with buttered, grease-proof side next to pudding mixture. Tie down securely with string, leaving a loop for easy removal when cooked. Place basins in fish kettle, or saucepans, with enough fast boiling water to cover. Cook large puddings for 6 hours, small ones for 4 hours. Boil steadily, replenishing with boiling water from time to time.

When cooked, lift basins out carefully, leave foil and grease-proof paper on puddings until cold before retying with freshly-buttered greaseproof paper and foil and storing in dry cupboard.

Watchpoint It's important that puddings do not go off the boil.

When ready to serve at Christmas, boil or steam a further 2 hours, and turn on to hot dish. Hard sauce – brandy or rum butter – should be served separately (see recipes on page 186).

Spotted dick with a syrup sauce

SPONGE PUDDINGS

The following steamed puddings, a little lighter in texture than a suet pudding, are made by the same method as plain cake mixtures. Here the fat is rubbed into the flour and each recipe mentions butter which does, of course, give an excellent flavour but in every case this can be replaced by margarine or a commercially-prepared shortening.

Spotted dick

8 oz self-raising flour
pinch of salt
4 oz butter,
2 rounded tablespoons caster sugar
6 oz currants (washed)
2 eggs
little milk

Method

Sift the flour with the salt into a basin, rub in butter and then stir in the sugar and currants. Whisk the eggs, add to the mixture and stir until smooth with a wooden spoon, adding milk, if necessary, to give a dropping consistency.

Turn into a well-greased basin, cover as before, tie securely and steam for 1½–2 hours. Serve with custard or syrup sauce.

Syrup sauce

Take 1 tablespoon of water to 2 tablespoons of golden syrup; a squeeze of lemon juice may be added. Heat in a saucepan to boiling point, stirring all the time, then dish up.

Marguerite pudding

5 oz self-raising flour
pinch of salt
2½ oz butter
2½ oz caster sugar
1 large egg
6–7 tablespoons milk
3 tablespoons raspberry, or plum, jam
little lemon juice

Method

Grease basin and have ready a saucepan half full of boiling water.

Sieve flour with salt into a bowl, rub in butter, then add sugar. Whisk egg with half of the milk and stir into mixture. Add remaining milk, if necessary, to give a dropping consistency.

Spoon jam into basin, fill with mixture on top. Cover with foil (make a 1-inch pleat to allow pudding to rise), tie foil securely round basin with string, leaving a long loop to facilitate lifting out basin, steam for 1½–2 hours. Turn on to a hot dish, serve with a sauce made from extra jam heated and thinned with a little water and lemon juice.

Note: this pudding can be made with golden syrup or marmalade and served with a matching sauce made as above.

Date pudding

4 oz self-raising flour
½ teaspoon mixed spice
pinch of salt
3 oz butter
4 rounded tablespoons fresh breadcrumbs
2 rounded tablespoons soft brown sugar
4 oz dates (stoned and chopped)
2 eggs
1 tablespoon golden syrup
1–2 tablespoons milk

Method

Sift flour with spice and salt into a bowl. Rub in butter and stir in breadcrumbs, sugar and chopped dates. Whisk eggs with syrup and milk, tip into the dry ingredients and mix with a wooden spoon until smooth, adding extra milk, if necessary.

Turn into a well-greased basin, cover as before, tie securely and steam for 1½–2 hours. Serve with custard or custard sauce (see page 186).

The following steamed sponge puddings are the lightest and are made just like rich, creamed cake mixtures. They make wonderful nursery puddings and are also light enough for a luncheon party.

Canary pudding

4 oz butter
4 oz caster sugar
2 eggs
2–3 drops of vanilla essence
4 oz self-raising flour
pinch of salt
4–5 tablespoons hot jam (preferably home-made)

5-inch diameter pudding basin

Method

Grease the basin well and have ready a steamer on a pan full of boiling water.

Soften the butter in a bowl, add the sugar and work until soft and light. Beat in the eggs a little at a time, add the vanilla essence and then fold in the sifted flour and salt with a metal spoon. (Do not use a wooden spoon because this cannot cut and fold without knocking out air beaten in with the eggs.)

Individual chocolate puddings served with a hot chocolate sauce

Turn the mixture into the basin, cover with pleated buttered greaseproof paper and foil (make a 1-inch pleat to allow pudding to rise) and tie down with string. Steam for 1½ hours. Turn on to a hot dish and spoon round the hot jam.
Watchpoint The basin should be only three-parts full to allow the pudding to rise.

Chocolate puddings

3 oz plain chocolate
¼ pint milk
5 oz stale cake crumbs
2 oz butter
2 rounded tablespoons caster sugar
2 large eggs (separated)
2–3 drops of vanilla essence

8 castle pudding tins (small moulds)

Method

Cut up the chocolate, melt it slowly in the milk in a saucepan, then bring to the boil and pour over the cake crumbs in a basin. Mix well with a fork, cover and leave to stand for 20–30 minutes.

Have ready a steamer over a pan of boiling water.

Soften the butter in a bowl, add the sugar and work until mixture is light. Beat in the egg yolks and then add the soaked crumbs and vanilla. Whisk the egg whites until stiff and use a metal spoon to fold them carefully into the mixture.

Divide mixture into the buttered pudding tins, cover with foil, or with a piece of

buttered greaseproof paper, tie down securely and steam until set (45–50 minutes). Turn on to a hot dish, dust with caster sugar and serve with whipped cream or hot chocolate sauce (see page 186).

Valencia pudding

6 oz raisins (stoned)
6 oz butter
grated rind and juice of ½ lemon
6 oz caster sugar
3 eggs
6 oz self-raising flour
pinch of salt

Charlotte tin (1½ pint capacity), or 5-inch diameter pudding basin

Method

Well grease the charlotte tin or basin and have ready a steamer over a pan of boiling water.

Split and press enough raisins (skin side against the prepared tin or basin) to cover the bottom and to make a pattern up the sides. Cut the remaining raisins into small pieces. Soften the butter with the lemon rind in a bowl, add the sugar and beat well until mixture is light and fluffy.

Beat in the eggs one at a time with 1 teaspoon flour. Sift the remaining flour with salt and use a metal spoon to fold into the mixture with the lemon juice and remaining raisins. Spoon carefully into prepared tin or basin. Cover as for canary pudding and steam for 2 hours. Serve with custard or a mousseline sauce (see page 186).

Casseroles, Stews and Braises

STOCK

As every good cook knows, the best casseroles, stews, braises and sauces owe their fine flavour to the original stock. Poor stock can turn a promising dish into a dull and tasteless mixture.

If you want more, a few beef bones from the butcher will make enough stock for a week for the average family's needs. Bones, on their own, will make a stronger stock than if you use mixed vegetables and bits of meat (mixed stock).

Raw mutton bones and turnips are best left out of stocks unless you are making a Scotch broth; both have a strong flavour and could well spoil the dish for which the stock is intended.

The liquid in a stockpot should be reduced in quantity (by simmering) by about a quarter, or more, before the stock is ready for straining.

Mixed stock

If you want a really clear stock, the only way to make it is to use raw bones. If you are using cooked ones as well, it helps to add these after the stock has come to the boil, although it is better not to mix raw with cooked bones if the stock is to be kept for any length of time.

Any trimmings or leftovers in the way of meat can go into your regular stockpot: chicken carcasses and giblets (but not the liver); bacon rinds; or a ham or bacon bone. This last is often given away and it makes excellent stock for a pea soup.

Add a plateful of cut-up root vegetables, a bouquet garni, 5–6 peppercorns, and pour in enough cold water to cover the ingredients by two-thirds. Salt very lightly, or not at all if there is a bacon bone in the pot. Bring slowly to the boil, skim, half-cover the pan and simmer 1½–2 hours or longer, depending on the quantity of stock being made. The liquid should reduce by about a third. Strain off and, when the stock is cold, skim well to remove any fat. Throw away the ingredients unless a fair amount of raw bones have been used, in which case more water can be added and a second boiling made.

If the stock is to be kept several days, or if there is a fair proportion of chicken in it, bring to the boil every day. If you are keeping it in the refrigerator, save room by storing, covered, in a jug instead of a bowl. Remember that the stronger the stock, the better it will keep.

Watchpoint Long slow simmering is essential for any meat stock. It should never be allowed to boil hard as this will result in a thick muddy-looking jelly instead of a semi-clear one.

Brown bone stock

3 lb beef bones (or mixed beef/veal)
2 onions (quartered)
2 carrots (quartered)
1 stick of celery
large bouquet garni
6 peppercorns
3–4 quarts water
salt

6-quart capacity saucepan, or small fish kettle

Method

Wipe bones but do not wash unless unavoidable. Put into a very large pan. Set on gentle heat and leave bones to fry gently for 15–20 minutes. Enough fat will come out from the marrow so do not add any to pan unless bones are very dry.

After 10 minutes add the vegetables, having sliced the celery into 3–4 pieces.

When bones and vegetables are just coloured, add herbs, peppercorns and the water, which should come up two-thirds above level of ingredients. Bring slowly to the boil, skimming occasionally, then half cover pan to allow reduction to take place and simmer 4–5 hours, or until stock tastes strong and good.

Strain off and use bones again for a second boiling. Although this second stock will not be so strong as the first, it is good for soups and gravies. Use the first stock for brown sauces, sautés, casseroles, or where a jellied stock is required. For a strong beef broth, add 1 lb shin of beef to the pot halfway through the cooking.

White bone stock

This stock forms a basis for cream sauces, white stews, etc. It is made in the same way as brown bone stock, except that bones and vegetables are not browned before the water is added, and veal bones are used. Do not add the vegetables until the bones have come to the boil and the fat has been skimmed off the liquid.

Braised oxtail is an economical and appetising dish with a good flavour (see recipe on page 137)

118

Chicken stock

This should ideally be made from the giblets (neck, gizzard, heart and feet, if available), but never the liver which imparts a bitter flavour. This is better kept for making pâté, or sautéd and used as a savoury. Dry fry the giblets with an onion, washed but not peeled, and cut in half. To dry fry, use a thick pan with a lid, with barely enough fat to cover the bottom. Allow the pan to get very hot before putting in the giblets and onion, cook on full heat until lightly coloured.

Remove pan from heat before covering with 2 pints of cold water. Add a large pinch of salt, a few peppercorns and a bouquet garni (bayleaf, thyme, parsley) and simmer gently for 1–2 hours. Alternatively, make the stock when you cook the chicken by putting the giblets in the roasting tin around the chicken with the onion and herbs, and use the measured quantity of water. This is preferable to bouillon cube stock for, in reducing the liquid with bouillon, there is the danger of the finished sauce being too salty.

CASSEROLES AND POT ROASTING

Casserole cooking is allied to pot roasting. The difference is that the ingredients are cooked in a liquid or sauce, and the meat or poultry is cut up or jointed before the final cooking — not left whole as in pot roasting. Other additions, such as mushrooms and tomatoes, are cooked with the main ingredients.

A casserole is cooked in the dish in which it is served, and as this was usually made of earthenware suited only to cooking in the oven, the food used not to be browned first. Today, there are many types of flameproof casserole on the market so that meat or poultry can conveniently be browned on top of the stove before cooking. The great advantage of casserole cooking is that once in the oven, very little or no last-minute attention to the dish is necessary.

Pot roasting is one of the best and easiest ways of dealing with the cheaper cuts of meat that need slow cooking to prevent them from becoming dry and tasteless. Poultry is also excellent pot roasted, not only the older boiling fowls, but roasting birds and baby chickens too, because they keep all their flavour and succulence.

This method has the great advantage of requiring the minimum of attention once

the meat is cooking. The only proviso is that you must have the right type of pot or casserole. This should be of thick iron, enamelled iron or aluminium with a close-fitting lid, deep and big enough to hold a joint or bird comfortably.

The procedure is simple: meat or bird is browned all over, root vegetables and a bouquet garni are added, but no liquid unless stipulated in the recipe. Even then it should not be more than one-eighth of a pint, ie. a small wineglass of stock or wine. A small quantity of seasoning is also added. Close the lid tightly and set on a low heat; if more convenient, put into a slow oven. Cooking time depends on the size of joint or bird, and is indicated in specific recipes.

Lamb and tomato casserole

1½–2 lb middle neck of lamb
salt and pepper
paprika
1 oz butter
2 onions (thinly sliced)
2 cups tomatoes (14 oz can),
  or 1 lb fresh tomatoes and
  1 teaspoon tomato purée
  (optional)
2–3 tablespoons soured cream,
  or yoghourt
1 tablespoon parsley (chopped)

Method
Divide meat into neat pieces, rub with seasoning. Heat butter on top of stove in flameproof casserole and brown meat on both sides. Take out meat, add onions and allow to brown. Replace meat in casserole, add tomatoes. If using fresh tomatoes, skin, squeeze to remove seeds, slice and cook to a pulp before adding them. A teaspoon of tomato purée can also be added to fresh tomatoes to strengthen flavour.

Cover tightly, cook slowly until meat is very tender (1–1½ hours) in oven at 275°F or Mark 1. (Cooking on top of stove may result in over-reduction of liquid.)

If using an earthenware casserole, first brown meat in a pan, then pack into casserole.

Add a little stock during cooking, if necessary, but gravy should be concentrated and well-reduced. Before serving, add cream to juices in casserole and spoon over meat. Sprinkle with parsley. Serve creamed or boiled potatoes and onion ragoût.

Onion ragoût (stew)

1 lb button onions, or shallots
1 oz butter
1 teaspoon sugar
1 wineglass white wine, cider, or stock

Method
Peel the button onions and blanch in pan of cold water by bringing to coil. Drain and turn into a casserole, add butter, sugar and wine, or cider or stock. Cover tightly, cook until tender (40–45 minutes) in oven at 350°F or Mark 4. Serve in the casserole.

Chicken béarnais

1–2½ lb chicken
1–2 oz butter, or bacon fat
1 large onion
4 oz gammon rasher (in the piece)
6–8 baby carrots
1 wineglass white wine, or stock
3 large tomatoes
2 cloves of garlic
salt and pepper
2 tablespoons double cream (optional)
parsley (chopped) – to garnish

The Béarn province in the French Pyrenees is well known for its good food and local wines.

Method

Joint chicken (ask butcher to do it); when jointing a whole bird for a casserole, put in the back for extra flavour, especially if you have to use water instead of stock. Fry joints slowly until golden-brown in the fat, then take out.

Slice onion thinly, cut bacon into squares, blanch both in cold water (bring to boil and drain). Quarter and blanch carrots, lay them in bottom of casserole. Arrange chicken on top, together with onion and bacon. Moisten with wine, or stock, season lightly, cover and cook gently for 1 hour in oven at 350°F or Mark 4.

Skin and slice tomatoes, flick out seeds, add flesh to casserole with garlic crushed with salt. Cover, replace in oven. Continue to cook for 15 minutes or until chicken and carrots are tender. Take out the back of chicken before serving.

Finish, if wished, with the thick cream poured over top just before serving. Dust with chopped parsley.

Pigeons split in two and cooked in tomato sauce

Rabbit and bacon casserole

1 rabbit
dash of vinegar
2 tablespoons dripping
1 small onion (finely chopped)
1 tablespoon flour
¾–1 pint stock
bouquet garni
1 rounded teaspoon tomato purée
1 clove of garlic (chopped)
salt and pepper
4 oz streaky bacon (in the piece)
12 pickling onions, or shallots

Method

Joint rabbit, trim and soak overnight in salted water with a dash of vinegar. Drain and dry well.

Brown joints slowly in hot dripping in a thick casserole. Add chopped onion, sprinkle in flour. Turn joints over to coat them in mixture and fry for 1 minute. Then draw aside, add enough stock barely to cover, add herbs, purée and garlic. Season lightly, cover pan tightly and cook for 30 minutes in oven at 350°F or Mark 4. Meanwhile, cut bacon into short strips, blanch with pickling onions or shallots (put in cold water, bring to boil). Then drain and add to rabbit. Continue to cook for 1 hour or until all is tender. Remove bouquet garni, serve in casserole.

Pigeons in tomato sauce

4 pigeons
1 oz butter
1 large onion (sliced)
1 dessertspoon flour
4 oz mushrooms, or small can of mushrooms
¾ pint tomato sauce (see method)

Method

Split pigeons in two, first cutting down to breastbone with a knife, then through bone and carcass with scissors. Trim away carcass bone. Slowly brown halves on skin side only in hot butter in a frying pan. Then take out halves and pack into a casserole.

Cook the sliced onion for 4–5 minutes in the pan, adding a little extra butter, if necessary. Take out onion and lay on top of pigeon halves in casserole.

If using fresh mushrooms, sauté briskly in pan of hot butter and set aside.

To prepare a quick tomato sauce: use a small can of Italian tomato sauce (not purée), make it up to ¾ pint with stock and thicken with kneaded butter or with a roux made with 1 dessertspoon flour and ¾ oz butter. Add to mushrooms. (If using canned mushrooms, add them now.)

Pour tomato sauce over pigeons, cover casserole tightly and cook for 1–1½ hours or until pigeons are tender, in oven at 350°F or Mark 4.

Note: for how to make a roux, see page 124.

Fowl-in-the-pot is browned and then cooked slowly with bacon and vegetables

Fowl-in-the-pot

3½–4 lb boiling fowl
½–1 oz butter, or dripping
3 rashers of bacon (streaky)
1 onion (sliced)
1 carrot (sliced)
stick of celery (sliced)
bouquet garni
salt and pepper

For garnish

chipolata sausages and bacon
rolls

Method
Brown the bird carefully all over in the pot with butter or dripping. Then take out, pour off all fat (there is a lot in a boiling fowl). Lay the bacon rashers on the bottom of the pot, set the bird on them and surround with the prepared vegetables. Add herbs and season lightly.

Cover with foil and put on the lid. Set on very low heat for 2½–3 hours, according to the size of the bird, or cook in a slow oven at 300°F or Mark 2. Avoid taking off the lid, particularly for the first 1½ hours. Pierce the thigh meat with a skewer to test for tenderness. Take out of pot and dish up with strained gravy as for the beef pot roast.

To make serving easier, the bird may be carved in the kitchen and dished up in a shallow casserole with a lid on. Spoon gravy over meat and, if you wish, garnish the dish with chipolata sausages and bacon rolls (rolled, skewered and then grilled).

122

Pheasant

1 pheasant
larding, or fat, bacon
1 oz butter
1 onion
1 carrot
bouquet garni
salt and pepper
½ wineglass sherry (optional)

Pot roasting is a good way to cook some game such as pheasant, especially older birds which tend to be rather dry when roasted.

Method
Quarter the vegetables and cover the breast of the bird with larding, or fat, bacon. Heat the pot and drop in the butter. When foaming, put in the bird, surround with the vegetables and add bouquet garni. Season very lightly. Cover and cook for 5–6 minutes on moderate heat until vegetables begin to colour and steam starts to rise. Reduce heat and simmer gently for about 1½ hours.

To serve, take up pheasant and remove the larding bacon, dish up and keep hot. Remove bouquet garni, deglaze pot with ½ cup of stock and then add, if you wish, the sherry. Season, strain and serve separately as gravy.

Alternatively, the pheasant may be carved and arranged in a serving dish. Spoon gravy over the bird and serve chosen vegetables separately. Vegetables that go especially well with pheasant are braised chicory, or braised cabbage.

Baby chickens (poussins)

2 baby chickens
1½ oz butter
salt and pepper
juice of ½ lemon
little stock (made from giblets), or wine
1 oz kneaded butter

Method
Melt butter in the pot and brown birds slowly all over. Sit them on their backs, season and add lemon juice before putting on lid. Cook slowly for 10 minutes, then split birds and dish up.

Deglaze the pot with a little stock, or wine, and gravy thickened with kneaded butter. Pour gravy over birds. Serve with a salad or chosen vegetable.

The giblets (without the liver) should be made into a small quantity of stock for gravy (see page 120).

Beef pot roast

2½ lb joint topside beef
1 tablespoon dripping
1 onion (stuck with a clove)
1 carrot (sliced)
bouquet garni
salt
pepper (ground from mill)
1 wineglass red wine, or stock
1 dessertspoon plain flour (for gravy)

Method
Heat dripping in the pot until smoking. Put the meat in and brown well on all sides. Take out and pour off any surplus fat, leaving 1 tablespoon on the bottom. Replace meat and tuck the prepared vegetables down the sides with the herbs.

Pour over liquid and season very lightly. Lay a piece of buttered paper over the meat so that the cover fits tightly on top and there is no danger of the meat getting hard from contact with the lid while cooking. Set on low heat or, if preferred, in the oven at 325°F or Mark 3. Cook at least 2–3 hours or until the meat is tender, turning it over once or twice if cooking on the top of the stove.

Dish up the meat, skim off the fat, strain off the juice. Mix 1 dessertspoon of this fat with 1 dessertspoon flour. Add to the juice and dilute with a little extra stock or water to taste, and boil for about 5 minutes to cook the flour. This meat juice is concentrated.

Slice meat for serving, spoon over gravy. Garnish with vegetables or serve them separately.

Leg of lamb

Cook a leg of lamb as for beef pot roast, but remember that 2 hours cooking time is usually sufficient for a 4–5 lb leg.

Pot roast shoulder of lamb

1 shoulder of lamb (boned)
2 medium-size onions (sliced)
1 tablespoon dripping
1–2 sticks of celery, or ½ turnip (sliced)
2 carrots (sliced)
1 oz kneaded butter, or little arrowroot

For stuffing
8 oz pork sausage meat
1 medium-size onion (finely chopped)
1 tablespoon dripping
1–2 parsley stalks
1 tablespoon mixed herbs
1 clove of garlic (optional)
salt and pepper

Trussing needle and string or poultry pins/lacers

Method
Bone out the lamb or get the butcher to do it for you. Prepare the stuffing: heat 1 tablespoon of dripping in pan, add chopped onion and cook until soft.

Then add to the sausage meat with herbs, crushed garlic, if used, and seasoning. Put stuffing into lamb; sew up or fasten with poultry pins. Brown the meat in hot dripping in the pot. Take out meat and put in sliced root vegetables. Allow them to colour, then drain off any surplus fat. Replace shoulder of lamb and cover the pot tightly.

Cook slowly for 1½ hours on top of stove or in the oven at 300°F or Mark 2. Then take up meat, remove string or pins, strain off liquid and skim well. Add a little extra stock, if necessary, and thicken lightly with kneaded butter (see page 176), or a little arrowroot. Serve vegetables separately with this pot roast.

123

STEWS

Stewing means cooking food gently in liquid. The food can be meat of any kind, fish, vegetables or fruit.

In general, the meat used is not from the most expensive cuts, but from those that require long, slow cooking to make them tender and to bring out their flavour. Cuts with a slight marbling of fat or gristle are excellent stewed, and this marbling makes meat more succulent.

A stew can be either white or brown. In a white stew, sometimes called a fricassée, the meat is not browned but blanched to whiten and to take away strong flavours before cooking. The liquid is usually thickened after the meat has been cooked, or towards the end, as in Irish stew, when the potatoes break up to thicken the gravy. A white stew is usually cooked on top of the stove.

In a brown stew, sometimes called a ragoût, meat is browned with or without vegetables and a little flour is stirred in just before the stock is added. It may be cooked either on top of the stove, or inside the oven which is easier.

Liquid in both brown and white stews must never be allowed to do more than simmer, since boiling will only toughen meat.

PREPARATION OF STEWS

White stew. Soak meat well, preferably overnight, in plenty of cold salted water. Change the water once or twice during this process to take away any strong flavour. Then rinse and put into the pan ready for cooking; cover with fresh cold water, add salt and – for veal or rabbit – a slice of lemon to whiten meat. Blanch by bringing slowly to the boil, then skim, drain and refresh in cold water to wash away any scum. Return to the pan and add liquid specified in the recipe, usually just enough to cover meat.

Veal or chicken stock, not water, should be used, because it will make a much better sauce. Chicken does not need soaking unless it is jointed raw, and a boiling fowl should be blanched. Keep the pan covered throughout the cooking.

Brown stew. The pan is very important in the making of a brown stew. Choose a thick, enamelled iron pan or flameproof casserole, so that the stew can be cooked and served in it. Failing this, brown the meat in a frying pan and transfer it to a casserole, but make the sauce or gravy in the same frying pan to avoid losing any flavour.

Cut meat (without bone) into 2-inch squares, leaving on a small amount of fat. Gristle appears only in shin or chuck steak and any white streaks may be left on. Cuts with bone should be divided into slightly larger pieces.

Heat pan or casserole well before putting in the dripping or oil. Put in meat just to cover bottom of pan, and leave enough room to turn pieces comfortably. Fry on full heat for beef (not so fierce for veal or lamb) until meat is evenly browned (about $3\frac{1}{2}$ minutes). Turn each piece and brown for the same time on the other side. Do not fry for longer than 7 minutes.

Now take out meat, keep hot and add vegetables as specified in recipe. Lower heat and allow to colour. Pour off all excess fat but for 1–2 tablespoons. Add flour (1 dessertspoon – 1 tablespoon for $\frac{3}{4}$–1 pint stock); use slightly less if stock is jellied. Colour flour slowly for 2–3 minutes, scraping it gently from bottom of pan or casserole with a metal spoon.

Now add stock (1 pint for $1\frac{1}{2}$ lb solid meat). It is better to add two-thirds of the given quantity first, and bring it to the boil. Replace meat. Then add remainder of stock so that it comes just below level of meat. Add specified flavouring, cover pan or casserole tightly and cook as specified in the recipe.

If pre-cooking a stew ready for eating later on, transfer to a cold container so that it cools quickly; when reheating, bring to the boil before keeping warm (the high temperature will kill any bacteria that may be present).

The following cuts are the best for stewing:

Beef: chuck or shoulder steak (cut from the blade bone); clod; sticking; skirt.
Mutton or lamb: middle neck; double scrag or scrag; fillet end of leg.
Veal: breast; knuckle; cuts from the shoulder.
Rabbit: wild rabbit or tame (Ostend) rabbit in joints or whole.

When buying the meat, remember that when a cut contains a fair quantity of bone, as with neck or breast, you must allow a little more than for cuts that are solid meat, such as steak.

A roux is a fat and flour liaison, the basis of all flour sauces. The weight of fat is generally slightly more than that of flour, although individual recipes may vary. As a guide to quantities, use 1 rounded tablespoon plain flour and $\frac{3}{4}$ oz fat to $\frac{1}{2}$ pint liquid.

Roux can be one of three kinds: white, blond or brown. Butter is normally used for white and blond roux, and dripping for brown roux. The other main difference is in the cooking time of the flour.

To make a roux: melt fat slowly in a thick pan, stir in flour off the heat and then pour on liquid (stock or milk or water). Return to gentle heat, stir until roux thickens, season, bring to boil and cook for 1 minute for **a white roux.**

For a blond roux: cook flour until a pale straw colour before adding the liquid (a few seconds).

For a brown roux: brown flour *slowly* in dripping until a good russet colour. Then pour on the meat or vegetable stock.

Paprika goulash

Goulash, or gulyás, is a Hungarian stew, generally of beef flavoured with paprika. If lamb and pork are used, the dish may be called pörkölt. Gulyás means 'herdsmen's stew' and probably originated with the nomadic herdsmen's habit of cooking in a large single pot over the camp fire.

Paprika goulash

1½ lb chuck, or blade bone, steak
2 tablespoons dripping, or oil
8 oz onions (sliced)
1 tablespoon paprika pepper
1 tablespoon flour
1 dessertspoon tomato purée (canned, or in tube)
¾–1 pint stock
1 bouquet garni
1 clove of garlic (crushed)
salt and pepper
1 sweet pepper (red or green), or 1 cap of canned pimiento
2 large tomatoes
4 tablespoons soured cream

Method
Cut meat into large squares, brown quickly in pan of hot dripping or oil and take out. Lower heat and put in sliced onions; after 3–4 minutes, add paprika. Cook slowly for 1 minute, then add flour, tomato purée and stock. Stir until boiling, replace meat, add bouquet garni, garlic and seasoning. Cover and simmer gently for 2 hours, or until meat is very tender, on top of stove or in the oven at 325°F or Mark 3.

Blanch, peel and shred the pepper; scald and peel the tomatoes, remove hard core and seeds, then slice flesh. Now add to goulash together with the pepper. Bring slowly to the boil and dish up.

Spoon over a little sour cream and stir in gently. Serve with boiled potatoes or noodles.

Types of stew

Fricassée. This describes various stews of meat, poultry, fish or vegetables, usually made with a white stock. In France this term refers almost exclusively to a poultry dish in a white sauce.

Ragoût (brown). Pieces of meat, poultry or fish are lightly-browned and then slowly cooked in stock to which vegetables are added.

Salmis. This is a type of ragoût, usually of game or poultry. The meat is first lightly roasted, then jointed and gently simmered for a short time in a rich, brown sauce.

Blanquette. This is a white ragoût of lamb, veal, chicken or rabbit, bound with egg yolks and cream, and sometimes garnished with small onions and mushrooms.

Navarin. This is the French word for a mutton or lamb stew made with root vegetables.

Certain vegetables are good stewed on their own, especially white ones such as onions (see onion ragoût, page 120), celery, artichokes and chicory.

Blanquette of veal

2¼ lb breast of veal
2 medium-size carrots (quartered)
2 medium-size onions (quartered)
1 bouquet garni
pinch of salt
1½ pints stock, or water

For sauce
1½ oz butter
3 tablespoons flour
1–2 egg yolks
¼ pint creamy milk
squeeze of lemon juice

Traditionally, breast of veal is used for this dish to get a rich, jellied stock from bones. But a greater proportion of shoulder meat can be added, ie. twice as much as breast. Breast of lamb can replace the veal.

Method

Cut meat into chunks (ask your butcher to do this if you are using breast of lamb and also trim off excess fat – otherwise cook in the same way). Soak overnight in cold water, blanch, drain and refresh.

Put the meat into a large pan with the quartered carrots and onions. Add bouquet garni, salt and barely cover with the stock or water. Cover and simmer for 1–1¼ hours until very tender and a bone can be pulled from a piece of meat.

Draw pan aside and pour off all liquid, cover pan and keep hot. The stock should measure 1 pint. If it is more, turn into a pan and boil to reduce to 1 pint.

To prepare the sauce: melt the butter in a separate pan, stir in the flour, cook for 1–2 seconds without letting the butter brown, draw aside and allow to cool slightly. Pour on the stock, blend, then stir until boiling. Boil briskly for 3–4 minutes until sauce is creamy in consistency and then draw aside.

Mix yolks with milk in a bowl, add a little of the hot sauce, then pour mixture slowly back into the bulk of the sauce. Taste for seasoning and add the lemon juice. Pour sauce over veal, shake pan gently to mix all together. Cover and keep hot for 15 minutes before serving so that the flavour of the sauce can penetrate the meat. Turn meat and vegetables into a clean hot dish and serve with creamed potatoes or boiled rice.

For a party dish, single cream instead of milk can be used for the sauce, but if you decide to to do this, take out the onions and carrots before serving and replace them with a mixture of previously-cooked peas, baby carrots and button onions.

Ragoût of lamb with savoury rice

½ leg of lamb, shank, or fillet end (about 2 lb)
1½ oz butter
2 onions (thinly sliced)
1 clove of garlic (crushed)
1 tablespoon paprika
1 tablespoon flour
1 teaspoon tomato purée
1 wineglass white wine, or
   1 wineglass dry vermouth (optional)
½ pint stock
salt and pepper
1 bouquet garni, or pinch of mixed dried herbs

For savoury rice
5 oz rice (long-grained)
salt
3 streaky bacon rashers
4 oz mushrooms (sliced)
1 small packet frozen peas, or
   1 cup of cooked peas
4 medium-size tomatoes
1 oz butter

Method

Bone out the meat well before cooking time (or ask butcher to do it) so that a good stock can be made from the bone. Cut meat into 2-inch squares, leaving on a little fat. Heat pan or flameproof casserole. Drop in butter and, when foaming, put in the meat. Fry briskly until meat is just brown, turning occasionally. Keep heat slightly lower for lamb than for beef.

Take out meat and keep hot. Put in onions and garlic. Cook for 4–5 minutes, stirring occasionally, then add paprika and flour. Stir in tomato purée, wine and stock. Bring to boil, season, tip out into bowl and replace meat in pan. Now pour over sauce. Add bouquet garni, cover tightly and cook gently for about 1 hour, or until meat is tender, on top of the stove, or inside the oven at 325°F or Mark 3.

To make savoury rice: boil it

in plenty of salted water until tender (10-12 minutes). Strain into a colander, rinse with hot water and make drainage holes with a spoon handle; leave for 30 minutes. Meanwhile, cut rind and rust from bacon, then cut rashers in short, thick strips. Slice mushrooms and cook peas. Scald, peel and quarter tomatoes; flick out seeds and then cut away the hard stalk: halve the quarters lengthways.

Heat a large frying pan, drop in the butter and, when foaming, put in bacon and mushrooms. Fry gently for 4–5 minutes, then add rice, peas and tomatoes. Season well. Fork up over brisk heat for 2 minutes until thoroughly hot. Then turn into a serving dish.

Dish up lamb after removing the bouquet garni.

If white wine is not available, dry vermouth is a good substitute. If you have neither, use just under ¼ pint extra stock.

Navarin of lamb

2 lb middle neck of lamb, or mutton
2 carrots (cut in strips)
1 small piece of swede, or turnip (cut in strips)
2 onions (quartered)
1 rounded tablespoon dripping
pinch of sugar
1 rounded dessertspoon flour
¾ pint stock, or water
salt and pepper
1 bouquet garni

Method
Cut and trim the cutlets, taking out any superfluous bone. Cut the carrots and swede or turnip into short thick strips; quarter the onions.

Heat a shallow, flameproof casserole or pan, put in the dripping and, when smoking, lay in the meat. Brown cutlets on both sides (do this in two lots, if necessary). Then take out the meat, put in the vegetables and fry more slowly until

Blanched rabbit joints in a pan with stock and sliced onions.

they are just coloured. A good pinch of sugar may be added to help this colouring process.

Now stir in the flour and, 1 minute later, add the stock or water. Bring to boiling point, replace meat in casserole or pan and make sure that the liquid comes just level with the meat. Season, add the bouquet garni, cover the pan and simmer gently for about 1 hour or until the meat is tender. Turn the cutlets from time to time. Serve with creamed potatoes.

Fricassée of rabbit

4–5 pieces of Ostend rabbit, or 1 wild rabbit (jointed)
white stock, or water (to cover meat)
2 onions (sliced)
1 bouquet garni
2 oz button mushrooms
½ oz butter

For sauce
1½ oz butter
3 tablespoons flour
¼ pint creamy milk

Method
Soak rabbit thoroughly in salted water, changing it from time to time. Blanch by putting into cold water, bringing to the boil, draining and refreshing. Trim away any pieces of skin with scissors and neaten the joints. Put rabbit into a shallow pan, barely cover with stock or water and add sliced onions.

For a more delicate flavour, blanch the onions first (by putting into cold water and bringing to the boil). Put in the bouquet garni, cover and simmer for 1–2 hours, or until very tender. Ostend rabbit takes less time than wild rabbit. Then drain off liquid, which should measure about ¾ pint.

Now make a roux in a saucepan with the butter and flour cook for about ½ minute, then let it cool a little and strain on the liquid. Blend and stir until boiling. Boil gently until it is the consistency of thick cream; add the milk and continue cooking. At the same time, sauté the mushrooms in butter in another pan. Add these to the sauce and pour it over the rabbit. Turn the fricassée into a covered dish and leave in a warm oven for 5 minutes before serving. This allows the flavour of the sauce to penetrate through the meat.

Slices of celery and walnuts being tossed in butter over the heat. This garnish goes well with finished ragoût of beef

Ragoût of beef with celery and walnuts

1½ lb chuck steak, or skirt
12 button onions
2 tablespoons dripping, or bacon fat
1 rounded dessertspoon flour
1 wineglass red wine
1 bouquet garni
1 clove of garlic (crushed with salt)
1 pint stock
salt and pepper
1 head of celery
½ oz butter
1 oz walnuts (shelled)
1 dessertspoon orange rind

Method
Cut beef into 2-inch squares and peel onions. Heat thick casserole and put in fat. When smoking, lay in pieces of meat; fry until brown, turning pieces once. Take out meat, add onions and fry slowly until beginning to colour. Draw off heat, drain so that only 1 tablespoon of fat is left in the casserole. Stir in flour, add red wine, meat, bouquet garni and garlic. Barely cover with stock, season, bring slowly to the boil, cover and simmer gently until tender (1½–2 hours).

Meanwhile, cut the trimmed head of celery into slices crossways. Heat the butter in a frying pan, put in walnuts and celery and toss over the heat with a pinch of salt, keeping celery crisp. Then shred and cook orange rind in boiling water until tender, drain and rinse. Dish up ragoût, or leave in casserole for serving, and scatter celery mixture on the top with the orange rind.

Irish stew

2–2½ lb scrag, or middle neck of mutton, or lamb
¾ lb onions
1½ lb potatoes
1½ pints water
1 tablespoon mushroom ketchup (optional)
salt and pepper

The meat can be a mixture of scrag and middle neck; in the days of large households a forequarter of lamb was used. To help tenderize meat and take out some of its red colour, either soak it over night or 2–3 hours before using in a little salty water.

Method
Trim meat after soaking, draining and drying it. Cut into pieces. Slice or quarter onions; wash and slice potatoes thickly, or cut into chunks.

Layer meat and vegetables together in a casserole, starting and finishing with potatoes, and season well. Mix water and ketchup together and pour over. Cover tightly and cook in the oven at 325°F or Mark 3 for at least 2 hours.

Avoid stirring but take the casserole out and shake it occasionally to ensure that the stew is not sticking. Dish up when meat is very tender and gravy thick and rich. Like most stews, it reheats well, but it must be brought to boiling point before keeping hot.

128

BRAISES

Cheaper cuts of meat are often full of flavour but inclined to be tough, so braising is the ideal way of cooking them. The meat is tender and succulent and the rich, strong gravy it was cooked in is a bonus. For a good braise it's essential to use a very small quantity of liquid in a pot with a tight-fitting lid. The meat cooks in the steam from the liquid, thus keeping moist. Most of the cooking is done in the oven so that the braise has both top and bottom heat.

Choosing the right pan is important; it should be of enamelled iron, cast iron or thick aluminium and be deep enough for the joint to fit snugly into it. Glass, or any non-flameproof ovenware, however, is not suitable as part of the cooking is done on top of the stove.

Braising meat and game

Heat the pan and add 2 tablespoons of oil or dripping. When hot, put in the meat and brown well all over. Take out meat and put in a good plateful of sliced or diced vegetables (onion, carrot, a little turnip and celery). This is called a mirepoix.

Cover pan and cook gently (or sweat) for 5–7 minutes. This allows the juice to run from the vegetables and lets them absorb excess fat. Put back the meat on top of the mirepoix, together with a bouquet garni and a little seasoning.

Pour in liquid as required in the recipe. This should cover the bottom of the pan up to a level of 2–3 inches. Cover closely and cook for 1–2 hours (according to the size of the joint) in a slow oven at 325°F or Mark 3.

Baste and turn the meat occasionally; it should be very tender when cooked. If you choose to braise a roasting joint less time can be allowed (20 minutes per lb and 20 minutes over).

When meat is tender, remove it from pan and keep warm. Strain the gravy and skim surface well to take off any fat. A sauce can be added, depending on the recipe, or gravy can be thickened with kneaded butter or arrowroot. The vegetables cooked with the braise are now discarded; they have done their job of flavouring and will be overcooked.

When braising a roasting joint, such as a leg of lamb, the vegetables can be served with the meat as the cooking time is not so long.

Watchpoint For a really successful braise it is essential to have a slightly jellied brown stock. If the stock is not strong, a pig's foot (trotter) tucked in beside the joint gives a beautifully 'sticky' texture to the finished sauce.

Braising fish

Braising is an excellent way of cooking whole fish, such as haddock or carp. The fish may first be stuffed with a herb mixture and then laid on the mirepoix of vegetables. Pour round a glass of cider, white wine or water, add salt and pepper and a bouquet garni (bayleaf, parsley, 2 sprigs of thyme). Cover pot tightly and braise as for meat.

Allow about 15–20 minutes per lb for large fish and about 20–25 minutes total cooking time for small fish such as seabream or red mullet. The fish is served with the juice lightly thickened with arrowroot, and sprinkled with chopped parsley.

Braising vegetables

Good braising vegetables are onions, celery, chicory, cabbage and lettuce. They are first blanched (for root vegetables, put into cold water and bring to the boil; for green vegetables, put into boiling water and re-boil before draining thoroughly), This blanching is done to remove any strong flavour, and to soften the outside and so ensure thorough cooking.

Braised brisket

3 lb piece brisket of beef

For braising

1–2 tablespoons beef dripping, or salad oil
2 onions
2 carrots
2 sticks of celery
salt and pepper
bouquet garni
¼ pint stock

For sauce

1–2 tablespoons dripping, or oil
1 tablespoon flour
¾ pint stock
1 teaspoon tomato purée

Brisket has slightly more fat than most joints, but it makes a succulent dish. If you prefer leaner meat, take a cut from the aitchbone or topside.

Method
Heat the braising pan and put in 1–2 tablespoons dripping or oil. When hot, put in the meat and brown on all sides. Take out meat and lower the heat. Have ready the vegetables, sliced or diced, add them to the pan, cover and cook gently for 5–7 minutes.

Then set the joint on top, season, add bouquet garni and pour round stock. Cover and cook in an oven for 1½–2 hours at 325°F or Mark 3, or until very tender.

Meanwhile prepare the sauce. Melt dripping in a saucepan, stir in the flour. If this roux is too stiff, add more dripping to make it spread nicely over the bottom of the pan. Cook slowly to a russet-brown, then draw aside, cool and pour on the stock. Blend, then add tomato purée, simmer uncovered for 15–20 minutes.

When meat is tender, remove from dish and slice what is needed. The remaining meat can be lightly pressed between two heavy plates (this makes meat easier to cut) and eaten cold. Dish up the sliced meat, cover and keep hot.

Strain gravy and skim well with a spoon to remove fat. Add gravy to the sauce, boil well until thick and syrupy. Spoon enough over the meat to moisten it and serve hot with creamed potatoes and creamed swedes (page 194).

Braised beef provençale, carved in slices, with a garnish of tomatoes and green olives and served with a rich, brown sauce

on each quarter. Add tomatoes to the sauce with the olives 'turned' (cut in spirals) or cut in quarters to remove stones. Slice meat and keep hot in dish.

Bring sauce to the boil again and spoon over the meat. Serve hot with creamed potatoes, or braised chicory.

Watchpoint Bring the sauce quickly to the boil once olives and tomatoes have been added. Any cooking of the olives would make the sauce too salty.

Leg of lamb bretonne

3½–4 lb leg of lamb
8 oz tomatoes
1 clove of garlic
salt and pepper
1 tablespoon dripping
1 wineglass white wine, or stock
1 bayleaf

Method
Scald and skin the tomatoes, remove the seeds and chop flesh finely. Crush the garlic with ½ teaspoon salt.

Brown the meat on all sides in hot dripping in a heavy flame-proof pan. Place the tomatoes and garlic round meat, season with pepper and pour over the white wine or stock. Add the bayleaf, cover the pan and braise for about 2 hours in the oven at 325°F or Mark 3.

Adjust seasoning and add extra wine or stock, if the sauce is too thick.

Serve with haricot beans (these are a good accompaniment to lamb or mutton).

Braised beef provencale

2½ lb aitchbone, or topside, of beef
2 large tablespoons olive, or salad, oil
1 large carrot
1 large onion
1 clove of garlic (peeled)
6 peppercorns
bouquet garni
1 wineglass red wine
¼ pint good stock
salt and pepper

For sauce

I tablespoon oil
1 tablespoon flour
½ pint jellied stock

For garnish

4 ripe tomatoes
6–8 green olives

Method
Brown the beef in oil in the braising pan, then remove. Dice or slice carrot and onion, add to pan and lower the heat. Cook slowly, uncovered, to allow the vegetables to colour a little but keep moist. Put the meat on vegetables, add garlic (whole), peppercorns, bouquet garni, wine and stock. Season very lightly, cover tightly and braise for about 2 hours, or until tender, in oven at 325°F or Mark 3. Turn and baste meat occasionally.

Meanwhile prepare sauce. Heat oil, stir in flour and cook gently. When a rich brown, stir in the stock, bring to the boil and boil gently for 7–10 minutes.

Remove cooked meat from pan, strain off gravy, skim well to remove fat, then add gravy to sauce. Boil until thick and syrupy, and of good flavour. Remove from heat.

To prepare garnish : scald and skin tomatoes, cut in quarters, flick out the seeds and cut away the small piece of stalk

Haricot beans with cream sauce

4 oz dried haricot beans
1 teaspoon bicarbonate of soda
    to 2 quarts boiling water (for
    soaking)
1 head of celery (sliced)
8 oz button onions
1 tablespoon parsley (chopped)

For ¾ pint cream sauce
1½ oz butter
1½ oz flour
¾ pint milk
salt and pepper
2–3 tablespoons single cream

Method

Wash the beans in several changes of water. Pour on the boiling water (with bicarbonate of soda) and leave beans to soak overnight. After soaking, rinse the beans well and place in a pan with celery and whole onions. Cover with cold water and bring very slowly to the boil. Simmer gently for about 1 hour until beans are tender.

To prepare the sauce: make a roux, add liquid off heat, season well and add the cream. Return to heat and boil.

Drain the vegetables and add to the sauce with the chopped parsley. Turn into a casserole for serving.

Fricandeau with spinach purée

2½–3 lb fillet, or oyster, of veal
2 oz larding bacon
3–4 rashers of streaky fat bacon
2 large carrots (cut into rounds)
2 large onions (cut into rounds)

1 wineglass white wine
½–¾ pint jellied stock
salt and pepper
bouquet garni

For spinach purée
2 lb spinach
1–2 tablespoons cream, or cream sauce (see haricot beans, opposite)

Method

Trim the meat, lard with bacon (see photograph, above). Lay bacon rashers in the bottom of a braising pan. Place the vegetables on this, cover and cook gently for 5–7 minutes. Put in veal, add wine, stock, seasoning and bouquet garni. Bring to the boil and braise for about 1–1½ hours in the oven at 325°F or Mark 3, basting frequently. Add extra stock if there's too much reduction.

Remove cooked meat, strain gravy and skim off fat. Return meat and gravy to the pan and cook on top of the stove on a brisk heat, basting well to glaze the meat a little. Remove meat; if necessary boil gravy rapidly to reduce and thicken.

To make spinach purée: first boil spinach in salted water, drain and press well with a spoon to remove as much liquid as possible. Sieve and mix with a little cream or sauce.

Carve meat and serve on a bed of spinach purée. Spoon over the gravy.

To make a purée of sorrel and spinach, add a few handfuls of fresh sorrel with the spinach.

Bacon lardons (¼ inch thick, 1½ inches long) are sewn into surface of veal to keep it from drying out

A Fricandeau is a classic dish in France and a perfect example of a braise. The meat is veal, taken from either the fillet part of the leg or from the shoulder. In France a leg of veal is cut differently, so for the correct cut go to a Continental butcher, or else ask your own butcher to cut you the oyster (a piece that lies on the blade bone), or to bone out a small whole shoulder.

The cut, when trimmed and tied up for cooking, should be about 8–10 inches long and 2–3 inches thick.

Veal is an immature meat and, therefore, has little or no natural fat, so fricandeau is larded (sewn with fat bacon) or barded (piece of fat bacon laid over the top). The meat is not browned but laid on a mirepoix of diced vegetables.

Accompaniments are traditionally a purée of sorrel and spinach, or spinach on its own, either purée or in the leaf (known as 'en branche').

131

MARINATING

Marinating is a process of soaking meat, game or fish in a mixture of wine, oil, vegetables, herbs and spices. The object is to give flavour and, in the case of meat or game, to render it more tender as the presence of the oil in the marinade helps to soften the fibres. Most marinades, that is those for joints and which contain wine, vegetables etc., are first boiled before use. A quick uncooked marinade, however, may be used with foods such as steaks and fish fillets.

For a boiled marinade the ingredients are first brought to the boil and then left to get quite cold before being poured over the joint. As the amount of the marinade is small, the meat must be put into a bowl or deep dish, small enough for it to fit snugly. Turn the joint occasionally and see that the vegetables in the marinade sit on top to keep the joint moist. The marinade is then either added with the stock at the start of the cooking or strained into the liquid just before serving.

With a boiled marinade for beef or lamb, let meat stand in it for 24 hours, and for game up to 3 days. With an uncooked, quick marinade allow steak or fish to stand in the liquid 2–3 hours before cooking.

Marinade for beef

(for a joint of about 2½ lb)

1 large onion
1 large carrot
1 stick of celery (optional)
1 large clove of garlic (peeled)
6–8 peppercorns
2 tablespoons olive oil
bouquet garni
2 wineglasses red wine
(Burgundy or Burgundy-type, or any robust red wine)

Method
Cut the vegetables into thin slices, bruise the peeled clove of garlic but leave whole (chop garlic if a stronger flavour is liked). Put these into a pan with the other ingredients, cover and bring to the boil. Simmer for 2 minutes, then pour off and leave until cold.

Marinade for game, venison and hare

Ingredients as for beef marinade, plus:
2 tablespoons red wine vinegar
2 parings of lemon rind
6 allspice or juniper berries, (crushed)

Method
Prepare as for beef marinade. Rich, dark meat such as venison calls for extra sharpness and seasoning, and spices can be altered to taste (see braised venison, right).
Hare is highly flavoured and excellent to eat. For jugged hare you don't have to marinate the meat before braising, but this soaking will improve the finished dish.

A hare is at its best when young (up to its second year).

Quick marinade (for grilled steaks, fish, and meat for a terrine)

1 dessertspoon onion (finely chopped, or sliced)
2–3 tablespoons olive oil
1 teaspoon of lemon juice, or wine vinegar
black pepper (ground from mill)
2–3 tablespoons Madeira, or golden sherry (for steak marinade)

Method
Lay meat or fish on a dish and sprinkle over the ingredients. Give a good grinding of black pepper to finish. Leave at least 2 hours before cooking.

Braised celery

3 large sticks of celery
1 large onion (diced)
1 large carrot (diced)
1 oz butter
½ pint jellied stock
salt and pepper
bouquet garni

Method
Wash celery, split sticks in two, blanch in boiling, salted water and drain.

Dice the onion and carrot, sweat them in butter in a pan. Then add the celery, stock, seasoning and bouquet garni. Cover and braise for 1–1½ hours, or until tender, in an oven at 325°F or Mark 3. Baste well from time to time.

When cooked, the gravy should be well reduced and the celery glazed. Dish up and strain gravy over the celery.

Braised venison

3 lb venison (from the haunch)
marinade for venison (see left)
pared rinds of 1 orange and 1 lemon

To braise
dripping (for browning)
2 onions (diced)
2 carrots (diced)
2 sticks of celery (diced)
bouquet garni
½ pint good stock
salt and pepper
1 tablespoon redcurrant jelly
kneaded butter (to thicken)
2–3 tablespoons double cream (optional)

Method
Wipe the meat, put into a deep dish and pour over the cold marinade; add rinds. Put prepared vegetables on top and cover. Leave 2–3 days in cool place, turning venison occasionally.

When ready to cook, take meat out of marinade, wipe it with a cloth, then brown all over in a pan in the hot dripping. Remove, and put in the mirepoix of diced vegetables. Cover and cook gently for 7 minutes, then add venison, bouquet garni, strained marinade and stock.

Season, bring to boil, cover meat with a piece of grease-proof paper or foil, then the lid, and braise gently for 2–3 hours or until very tender in oven at 325°F or Mark 3.

Strain off the gravy, skim well to remove fat, add the redcurrant jelly and thicken with the kneaded butter. Reduce by boiling, if necessary, until sauce is the consistency of thin cream. Taste for seasoning. Slice the cooked venison, put in serving dish and spoon over the sauce.

For a special occasion add 2–3 tablespoons cream to the sauce just before serving. Serve with braised celery (see left).

When jugging hare, it is first marinated and then braised; redcurrant jelly and port are added to the gravy before serving it with forcemeat balls

Jugged hare

Legs and wings of hare, or 1
   hare jointed (with the blood)
1 tablespoon dripping
2 onions (diced)
2 carrots (diced)
1 stick of celery (sliced)
bouquet garni
1½ pints stock, or water
1 tablespoon redcurrant jelly,
   preferably home-made
1 small glass port wine
1 teaspoon arrowroot (to
   thicken), or kneaded butter

For forcemeat balls

1 oz butter
1 shallot, or small onion (finely
   chopped)
1 teacup fresh breadcrumbs
1 dessertspoon dried herbs
1 dessertspoon parsley (chopped)
salt and pepper
beaten egg, or milk (to bind)

For frying
seasoned flour
1 egg (beaten)
dried white crumbs
deep fat bath

Method

Marinate hare overnight. Then drain and strain marinade. Braise the hare (see general instructions, page 129), then lift the pieces of cooked hare into a casserole for serving. Strain the gravy into a pan, skim off fat and add redcurrant jelly and the port.

Now make forcemeat balls: melt butter in a pan, add onion, cover and cook until soft but not coloured. Mix breadcrumbs, herbs and seasoning together in a basin, add the onion and enough beaten egg or milk to bind. Shape mixture into small balls, roll in seasoned flour,

then egg and crumb; set aside on a plate.

Boil gravy and reduce a little, if necessary, to give a good strong flavour. Draw aside and stir in the blood mixed with the arrowroot. Stir over heat until it has the consistency of cream but do not boil. Pour sauce over the hare and reheat in the oven for 5 minutes.

Heat fat bath; when at correct frying temperature, lower in forcemeat on draining spoon and fry until golden-brown. Drain on absorbent paper. Then serve with the hare.

Watchpoint If the blood is not available, kneaded butter can be used to thicken the sauce. The blood binds the sauce together while the arrowroot helps to prevent it curdling. Serve with braised celery, red cabbage and creamed potatoes

Offal and Minced Meat Dishes

Offal is the name given to the edible internal parts of an animal, such as the liver, kidneys and heart, together with the head, feet and tail. Good, rich dishes are made from offal; they are often economical as there is very little wastage, and certain parts are cheap.

All offal, especially the liver, heart and kidneys, should be very fresh when cooked, which means it is not hung at all. It is advisable to buy it the day you intend to cook it–if you do need to store it in the refrigerator for a short time, make sure it is completely covered, as some parts, such as kidneys, have rather a strong smell and might taint the other foods you may have in the refrigerator.

There are many excellent meat dishes that do not come into any special category. They are usually economical and in most cases cooked with a vegetable, making them complete dishes in themselves and suitable for serving for lunch or supper. If you choose to use cooked meat, however, reheat it quickly and only to boiling point; further cooking will toughen the meat and render it tasteless and indigestible. In the case of cottage pie, or where deep fat frying is involved, the meat is protected from over-cooking by either a layer of potato or a coating of crumbs, pastry or batter.

OFFAL

PREPARATION OF OFFAL

Liver. The most popular type is calves or lambs liver, the former being more expensive and considered to have the more delicate flavour. Pigs liver is best for stuffings, pâtés and terrines; ox liver is seldom used because it is coarse in texture and over-strong in flavour.

The most usual way of cooking liver is to slice and fry it with bacon but it may also be braised whole (in the piece). It is then sliced for serving with the gravy and garnish with which it was cooked.

Calves livers vary slightly in colour, some being paler than others. This has no significance where cooking is concerned. All liver should be fresh and clean-looking and have little or no smell.

Kidneys are for grills and sautés. The type most often used is lambs kidney, which is usually sold individually, though some shops now sell by weight.

English kidneys are generally enclosed in a casing of fat (kidney suet). This keeps the kidney moist and fresh and is useful for rendering down as dripping, or it may be chopped and used in a suet crust (although beef suet is more popular for this purpose as it has a less pronounced flavour).

Imported kidneys are sold without fat and are cheaper.

Pigs kidneys may also be grilled or sautéd, but as they are strong in flavour they are better treated as for ox kidney.

Pigs and lambs kidneys are bean-shaped and should be skinned before cooking. The skin is slit on the rounded side and drawn back towards the core. It is then pulled gently, in order to draw out as much of the core as possible, before being cut off. Cut open and remove rest of core. For grilling, the kidney may be split open and skewered flat; for a sauté or stew, cut it completely in half. Allow 1–2 per person according to size.

Veal kidney is something of a delicacy and in Britain not

Braised lambs tongues Florentine (see page 142): the tongues are surrounded by spinach creams (see page 192)

always easily come by. It is usually sautéd and served in a rich or piquant sauce. The kidney, bought singly, may weigh from 6–12 oz and should be skinned with as much of the core as possible cut away before cooking. After trimming, cut across in $\frac{1}{4}$–$\frac{1}{2}$ inch slices. This kidney, like ox kidney, has a different formation from that of the lamb or pig.

Ox kidney is used chiefly for pies and puddings, mixed with steak. It can also be braised or stewed, and before skinning may be soaked in warm, salted water for 1 hour to remove any strong taste. Ox kidney is sold by weight.

The heart makes another cheap and nourishing dish. Stuff lambs hearts with a good herb stuffing and braise until very tender.

Calves or pigs hearts may be prepared in the same way, but call for long and careful cooking to make them tender. Allow one lamb's heart per person; one of the other type is sufficient for two people.

Tripe. This makes an easily digested, nourishing dish, but must be carefully prepared and cooked. Tripe, the lining of a bullock's stomach, is sold 'dressed' (already cleaned and blanched). After this it needs long, slow cooking to make it tender. Although the classic dish is a white stew with onions, it also makes a good brown stew. Allow 6–8 oz tripe per person.

The head. Salted pigs head is classic for a brawn. A calf's head may also be salted, or left fresh and used for jellied veal. When boiled it should be served either hot with a parsley sauce or cold with a vinaigrette dressing. Half a head is usually sufficient for four people and should contain a portion of the tongue and brains. The meat is gelatinous and easily digested.

Feet. These are particularly gelatinous and are often used in a dish where additional 'jell' is wanted. Calves feet are especially good for this as the jell is strong, with a delicate flavour, and it is excellent for making sweet and savoury (aspic) jellies.

Pigs feet or trotters may be added to stock for a jelly or to a beef braise to give a rich gravy. They also make a dish on their own; boil them first, then braise or grill

Cow heel also makes a good brown stew and is a cheap and filling dish.

Tail. Oxtail makes an excellent, inexpensive dish, especially in winter. It is usually braised or made into a nourishing soup. When buying, choose one that has an equal amount of meat to bone. It is sold jointed and the fat must be white, the meat bright red. An average-size tail is enough for four people.

Note: for some offal, which needs prolonged cooking, a pressure cooker saves time and fuel. The preparation of tongues, brains and sweetbreads (not strictly offal but included in this chapter) are covered on pages 138–142.

Fried liver with orange

6 good slices of calves liver
2 tablespoons flour
seasoning (salt, pepper, dry
   mustard, cayenne pepper)
2 oz butter
1 onion (finely sliced)
2 cloves of garlic (crushed)
5 tablespoons red wine
5 tablespoons strong stock
1 tablespoon parsley and thyme
   (chopped)
1 orange (cut in thin slices)
extra butter, or oil (for frying)

For pilaf
1 oz butter
1 onion (finely chopped)
5 oz rice (long grained)
$\frac{3}{4}$ pint veal, or chicken, stock
salt and pepper
little cheese (grated)

Method

First prepare pilaf. Melt $\frac{3}{4}$ oz butter in flameproof dish, add onion, cover and cook slowly until soft but not coloured. Add rice and sauté for 3–4 minutes stirring all the time. Pour on the stock, season and bring to the boil.

Cover with a tightly-fitting lid and cook in the oven at 350°F or Mark 4 for 20–30 minutes, or until tender. Mix in the remaining butter with a fork and stir in a little grated cheese.

Dust the slices of liver lightly with seasoned flour. Heat 1 oz butter in a pan and cook liver 3–4 minutes on each side. Put in a serving dish and keep warm.

Melt the remaining butter in the pan, add the onion and garlic and cook until onion is

Fried liver with orange is served with pilaf

soft and golden-brown. Moisten with the wine and stock, add herbs and simmer for 1 minute. Pour the sauce over the liver.

Cut the orange in thin slices (leaving on the skin). Sprinkle well with sugar and brown quickly on both sides in hot butter or oil.

Garnish the liver with the orange slices and serve the pilaf separately.

Liver and bacon

This is a classic English dish, and for perfection calves liver, sliced $\frac{1}{4}$–$\frac{1}{2}$ inch thick, should be used. Just before frying, roll lightly in seasoned flour. Have ready the frying pan and in this fry the bacon rashers (one more than the number of slices of liver) in a little dripping or butter. Take out and keep warm. Add a small quantity of extra fat and when hot put in the liver and fry quickly, about 3 minutes on each side.

Arrange alternate slices of liver and bacon on a serving dish, beginning and ending with bacon. Add a little stock to the frying pan, stir and pour gravy over the dish. Serve at once.

Cooked liver should be slightly pink when cut; over-cooking means that it will be

and roll the slices of liver in this. Melt rest of butter in a frying pan, put in the liver and fry for 3–4 minutes on each side, shaking the pan frequently. Put on a serving dish, add herbs to sauce and pour over the liver.

Braised oxtail

1 oxtail (jointed)
dripping
2 onions (peeled)
2 carrots (peeled and quartered)
3 sticks of celery (cut in 2-inch lengths)
1 tablespoon flour
about 1 pint stock, or water
bouquet garni
salt and pepper

Method

Brown the pieces of tail all over in hot dripping in a flameproof dish. Take out; put in the onions, carrots and celery. Leave to brown lightly, then dust in the flour. Remove from heat, add the liquid, bring to the boil, add bouquet garni and seasoning.

Put in the tail, cover dish tightly and cook in the oven at 350°F or Mark 4 for about 1½–2 hours or until tender (when the meat will come easily off the bone). Remove the bouquet garni and serve meat very hot. **Watchpoint** Sometimes oxtail is inclined to be fatty so it is a good plan to cook it the day before, leave to go cold, then skim off the solidified fat. Reheat for serving.

Tripe Italian style

1½ lb tripe
½ pint milk and 1 pint water (salted)
6 tablespoons olive oil
1 large onion (sliced)
2 oz flat mushrooms (chopped)
1 bayleaf
1 lb tomatoes (skinned and finely chopped), or 2 tablespoons tomato purée
1 clove of garlic (crushed with ½ teaspoon salt)
¼ pint white wine, or dry cider
1 tablespoon parsley (chopped)
pinch of dried rosemary, or oregano
grate of nutmeg
salt and pepper
about ¼–½ pint stock, or water

Method

Cook the tripe in salted milk and water for 1 hour, then drain and cut into fine strips, 3½–4 inches long.

Put the oil in a deep pan, add the onion and when beginning to colour add the mushrooms; after 1 minute add the tripe.

Put in the bayleaf, tomatoes or tomato purée, garlic and wine or cider, herbs and spices. Season, cover pan and simmer very gently for about 1 hour until tripe is very tender.

If stew shows signs of drying, add a little stock or water from time to time. The consistency should be thick and rich.

Serve with boiled potatoes.

Braised lambs hearts

4–5 lambs hearts
1 oz butter, or dripping
2 large onions (thinly sliced)
salt and pepper
¾ pint stock
kneaded butter, or arrowroot, or cornflour (mixed with a little cold water) – to thicken

For herb stuffing

5 tablespoons fresh breadcrumbs
2 tablespoons mixed herbs (chopped), or parsley (chopped) and 1 teaspoon dried herbs
salt and pepper
1 small egg (beaten)

Trussing needle and fine string, or thread

Method

Trim hearts with scissors, cutting away any fat and blood vessels; snip the wall dividing the interior of the heart. Soak them for about 1 hour in salted water. Dry thoroughly.

Mix the ingredients for the stuffing, adding enough egg to moisten. Stuff the hearts and sew up the openings with fine string or thread.

Brown the hearts in butter or dripping, take out of the pan, put in the onions, cook them until brown, then set the hearts on top. Season, add the stock, cover with foil and then put on the lid. Braise in oven at 350°F or Mark 4 for 1½ hours, or until very tender.

Dish up and thicken the liquid slightly with kneaded butter, or arrowroot, or cornflour. Pour over the hearts and serve very hot.

tough and dry. If kept for even a short time after cooking, it tends to harden and dry.

Sauté of liver italienne

6 slices of calves liver
3–4 oz butter
1 medium-size onion (finely chopped)
3 oz mushrooms (finely chopped)
½ wineglass white wine
½ wineglass stock
1 good teaspoon tomato purée
3 oz sliced, cooked ham (diced, or chopped)
1 tablespoon flour
salt and pepper
pinch of ground mace, or nutmeg
1 tablespoon mixed fresh herbs (parsley, tarragon and chervil) – chopped

Method

Heat about 1½ oz of the butter in a saucepan, add the onion and cook gently for 2–3 minutes. Then add the mushrooms, increase heat and cook quickly for 3–4 minutes. Add the wine and boil to reduce a little. Stir in the stock and tomato purée, cover and cook gently for 10 minutes. Then add the ham, and leave to simmer gently.

Put the flour, sifted with salt, pepper and spice, on to a plate

BRAINS
(Cervelles)

Unfortunately there is a slight prejudice against brains, possibly because of their appearance when raw. This is a pity, as they can be delicious if properly cooked and they make a pleasant change on a menu.

Like other offal, brains must be eaten really fresh. This type of offal calls for a little preparation in the way of soaking or blanching before cooking and this is done ahead of time.

Brains may be from the calf or sheep, the former being slightly larger, and are sold by the set (two lobes). Allow 1 set per person or, if large, 1 between two people.

To prepare brains
They must be soaked for some hours in well-salted cold water. Change the water if necessary during this time. After this they are blanched and refreshed and ready for further cooking. Brains are inexpensive and there is little wastage.

Brains bourguignon
(see photographs opposite)
2 sets of calves brains
1½ pints court bouillon
5 rounds of bread for croûtes (about 2½ inches diameter)
butter (for frying)

For sauce
2 wineglasses red Burgundy
1 medium-size onion
½ oz butter
1 dessertspoon flour
1 wineglass good stock

For garnish
¼ lb streaky unsmoked bacon (in the piece)
½ oz butter
4 oz mushrooms (sliced)
6–8 oz button onions (well blanched and simmered until tender)
parsley (chopped)

This dish is suitable for entertaining but find out first if your guests like brains. If in doubt, use this recipe with sweetbreads, which are more widely known and appreciated.

Method
Soak and blanch brains. Drain and put into sufficient court bouillon just to cover. Poach for 15–20 minutes or until firm to the touch. Draw aside and drain them well.

Prepare sauce (this can be done the day before if wished). Reduce wine by about a quarter, pour off and reserve. Chop onion finely, colour lightly in the butter, stir in the flour and after a few seconds add the reduced wine and stock. Simmer until syrupy (5–6 minutes). Draw aside.

Fry croûtes in butter until golden-brown. Wipe out pan.

Cut bacon into lardons, blanch and put into the frying pan with about ½ oz butter. When turning colour, add mushrooms and, after a few minutes, the onions. Shake pan over heat.

Set the croûtes in a serving dish, arrange the brains on top, heat sauce, add a nut of butter and spoon over the dish. Sprinkle well with chopped parsley and garnish with the bacon, mushrooms and onions.

SWEETBREADS

Lambs breads (ris d'agneau) are small and are suitable for filling vol-au-vents and bouchées, and for a ragoût or salpicon. They are less expensive than calves breads and are sold by the pound. The method of preparation is the same. Allow about 4–6 oz per person and 4–6 oz over. Use up leftovers in pancakes or bouchées.

Calves breads (ris de veau) are much larger, weighing about 6 oz each. They are sold by the pair and in some shops by the pound. Calves sweetbreads are very much a delicacy and are comparatively expensive. They are used mostly for entrées, with a special garnish, but can be cooked in several different ways. The texture is lightly firm and the flavour delicate. Allow 2–3 pairs for 4 people.

To prepare sweetbreads
Like brains, sweetbreads must be eaten really fresh and need some preparation before cooking. Soak them for several hours in salted water; 1–2 slices of lemon or a few drops of vinegar may be added to the water. Rinse breads, put into a pan and cover with cold water, add a little salt and a slice of lemon. Bring slowly to the boil, removing any scum as it rises to the surface. Drain, rinse quickly, then remove any ducts or 'pipes' and any skin which will pull off easily. Lay the breads on a flat dish or tray with another tray on top. Set a light weight (approximately 2 lb) on this and leave breads until quite cold. They are then ready for further cooking. There is little wastage with sweetbreads.

Sauté of sweetbreads with white wine sauce

1½ lb (2–3 pairs) calves sweetbreads
1–2 oz butter
2 shallots (finely chopped)
1 wineglass white wine
3 oz mushrooms (thinly sliced)
1 teaspoon flour
7½ fl oz strong veal stock
1–2 tablespoons double cream (optional)
French beans (to garnish)
a little butter

Method
Prepare sweetbreads as directed. Heat a sauté or frying pan. Drop in the butter, add the breads and allow to colour on both sides, then remove, add the shallots to the pan and, after a few minutes, the wine. Reduce to a little more than half, then add the mushrooms. Cook for a few minutes, then draw aside; dust in the flour, add the stock, bring to the boil and put in the sweetbreads. Simmer gently for 20–30 minutes. Stir in the cream just before serving. Slice the sweetbreads, arrange in the serving dish and garnish with the French beans, boiled and tossed in butter. A good purée of potatoes can be served with this quick and simple dish.

Brains bourguignon; poaching the brains in court bouillon, flavoured with onion and carrot

Adding the onions to bacon and mushrooms to make the garnish

The finished dish: the brains are placed on fried croûtes, have red wine sauce poured over them and the garnish added

Kidneys Turbigo surrounded with triangular croûtes of bread

Removing the skin from a lamb's kidney and (below) halving the kidney before cutting out its core

Kidneys Turbigo

5 lambs kidneys
12–18 pickling onions
2 oz butter
¼ lb chipolata sausages
¼ lb button mushrooms
  (quartered)
1 dessertspoon flour
1 teaspoon tomato purée
1 tablespoon sherry
7½ fl oz brown stock
salt and pepper
1 bayleaf
2 slices of stale bread (cut into
  croûtes)
oil (for frying croûtes)
parsley (chopped)

Method

Blanch the onions and drain. Skin the kidneys, cut in half lengthways and core.

Heat a sauté or deep frying pan, drop in the butter and, when it is foaming, put in the kidneys and sauté briskly until evenly browned.

Lift out kidneys and put in chipolata sausages, lower the heat and cook until brown on all sides. Take them out, add the onions and mushrooms, shake over a brisk heat for 2–3 minutes, then draw pan aside.

Stir in the flour, tomato purée, sherry and stock and bring to the boil; add the bayleaf and season. Slice sausages and kidneys and put in the pan. Cover and simmer gently for 20–25 minutes, or until tender.

Serve the kidneys and sausages surrounded with croûtes and sprinkled with parsley. For croûtes, cut bread into triangular pieces and fry in a little hot oil until golden-brown.

140

TONGUES

All tongues are improved by soaking in cold water, fresh tongues for 2–3 hours, salted tongues for a little longer. Then rinse them well, by putting in a roomy pan of cold water, bringing to the boil, draining and returning to the pan. Cover with cold water and add a few root vegetables for flavouring, bouquet garni and 6 peppercorns. Put a lid on the pan and simmer until the tongue is three-parts cooked (or completely cooked for salted tongue). Fresh lambs tongues take 1 hour; calves tongues, 1½ hours; ox tongue, 3 hours; and salted ox tongue, 3½–4½ hours.

To test a salted ox tongue for cooking, pierce the thick part at the side with a knitting needle or thin skewer. If the tongue is cooked, it should go in easily. Also, if the root bone can be pulled out this is another indication that the tongue is cooked.

When tongue or tongues are cooked, remove them from the pan and plunge into a bowl of cold water. Reserve the stock from fresh tongues, but discard it from salt tongues – it would be too salty for further use.

Nick the skin on the underside of the tongues and peel off carefully. For fresh tongues pull out the little bones in the root of the tongues, and trim away some of the fat if necessary. They are then ready for braising. For salted ox tongue just trim away a little root and bones and press in a tongue press (see ox tongues, right).

Watchpoint It is essential that all tongues should be tender and well cooked. In fact it is difficult to overcook a tongue and, if this does happen, it is a fault on the right side.

Lambs tongues These weigh 4–6 oz each; allow at least 1 per person – say 6 tongues of average size for 4 people. Whatever way they are to be served they must first be prepared as described above; after skinning they are then ready for further cooking.

Before serving, split the tongues in two lengthways. It is usual to arrange them on a small quantity of potato or spinach purée to lift them off the surface of the dish.

Calves tongues These are sweet, tender and delicate in flavour, and average 12 oz–1 lb

Remove skin from the cooked tongue after it has been cooled

in weight. For serving hot they are best fresh and must have the preliminary cooking, as described left, before further preparation.

Ox tongues These average 3½–4½ lb in weight and are usually sold salted rather than fresh. Unless they are on display ask your butcher in advance to salt one for you. Cook a tongue as described left, then curl round and put into a tongue press or in a cake tin, preferably with a loose bottom. Curl tongue round as tightly as possible; if using a cake tin it helps to wedge the side of the tongue with a piece of paper to bring the tip towards the root. Apply the pressure if using a press, otherwise set a small plate on top of the tongue with a 2–3 lb weight on the top. Leave in a cool place overnight.

For a 3½ lb tongue use a cake tin between 6–7 inches in diameter. If cooking tongues fairly frequently it is well worth while investing in a tongue press, they do the job well and efficiently. When carving a round of tongue, start slicing on the slant and continue in this way: this enables you to slice right down to the base of the tongue. Cold salted tongue should always be cut in wafer thin slices.

If you want to serve salted tongue hot, cut the slices thickly and warm them through in a suitable sauce, eg. madère or bigarade (see page 181). Serve the tongue immediately it is warmed through, otherwise the flavour of the sauce might be spoilt by salt from the tongue.

Fresh ox tongue (like calves tongue) is cut in ¼-inch diagonal slices. Fresh ox tongue does not spoil when reheated. It is very good to eat and

Press the tongue well down into the tin so that it fits snugly

requires no soaking. Cook, skin (as described left), but press only if the tongue is to be eaten cold.

Pressed tongue

1 ox tongue (4½–6 lb)
cold salted water
1 large carrot
1 large onion (peeled)
6–8 peppercorns
1–2 bayleaves

Tongue press (available in two sizes), or round cake tin, or soufflé dish

Method

Put the tongue into a large pan, cover well with cold salted water. Bring slowly to the boil, then add other ingredients. Cover pan and simmer gently for 4–5 hours, or until the tongue is very tender.

Test by trying to pull out the small bone at the base of the tongue – if it comes away easily the tongue is done. It is also advisable to stick the point of a knife into the thickest part (just above the root). It will slip in easily if the meat is cooked.

Cool in the liquid, then lift out the tongue and put in a bowl of cold water. This will make it easier to handle.

Peel off the skin, cut away a little of the root and remove any bones. Curl the tongue round and push into the tongue press, cake tin or soufflé dish. The tongue must fit closely into the tin or dish. Press down well, using a small plate with a weight on top, if no press is available. Leave in a cool place until the next day before turning out. Cover the tongue and store in larder or refrigerator (can be kept for up to 1 week).

Cumberland sauce (see recipe on page 185) makes a good accompaniment.

Braised lambs tongues florentine

6 lambs tongues
3 rashers of streaky bacon (unsmoked)
2 onions
2 carrots
1 stick of celery
bouquet garni
6 white peppercorns
½ pint jellied stock

For sauce

1 oz butter
1 shallot, or small onion (finely grated)
1 rounded tablespoon flour
¾ pint jellied stock
1 dessertspoon tomato purée
1 glass brown sherry

For serving

spinach creams (see recipe on page 192)
1 lb potatoes (cooked and beaten to a purée with ½ oz butter, 4 tablespoons hot milk, salt and pepper)

Method

Blanch and refresh the tongues, put in pan with enough water to cover, then simmer gently for 1¼–1½ hours. Drain tongues, plunge them into a bowl of cold water and skin them. Trim and cut away the root.

Set oven at 350°F or Mark 4.

Remove the rind from the bacon, stretch each rasher under the blade of a heavy knife and place them at bottom of a flameproof casserole. Slice the onions, carrots and celery, put in the casserole and cover. Cook over gentle heat for 10–12 minutes or until the bacon starts to brown. Place the tongues on top of the vegetables, add bouquet garni, peppercorns and the ½ pint of stock. Cover the tongues with a double thickness of greaseproof paper and lid and braise for 45 minutes in pre-set oven. **Watchpoint** This braising is to give the tongues extra flavour, but they must be quite tender before the process is started, so do not cut the initial stewing time.

To prepare the sauce: melt the butter, add shallot or onion and cook slowly for 2 minutes; stir in the flour and continue cooking until onion and flour are deep brown. Draw pan

off the heat, blend in ½ pint of the stock, the tomato purée and sherry; return to the heat and stir until boiling. Then, with the lid half off the pan, simmer gently for 15–20 minutes. Pour in half the remaining stock, skim sauce and re-boil; simmer for 5 minutes. Pour rest of stock into sauce, skim again and simmer for a further 5 minutes. Strain, cover and set aside.

Take up tongues, strain off the braising liquid, return it to the pan and boil hard until it is reduced by half. Add the sauce to this liquid, taste for seasoning and boil up together. Return tongues to casserole and keep warm while beating the potato purée and taking up the spinach creams.

To serve: place the potato purée in the serving dish, take up the tongues, slice in half and arrange on top. Turn out the spinach creams and place round the dish. Boil up the sauce and spoon over just enough to coat the tongues and the base of the dish; serve the rest separately in a sauce boat.

Trimming away the root of a tongue; the one in the foreground is already trimmed

Placing the trimmed lambs tongues on top of the sliced onions, carrots and celery

Pork brawn

½ pig's head (salted)
1–1½ lb shin of beef
1 large onion (peeled)
1 large bouquet garni
cold water
black pepper (ground from mill)

Two 7-inch diameter basins

It is difficult to cut down on the quantity given above, but brawn will keep in a refrigerator up to 1 week.

Method

Rinse the pig's head in cold water and put into a large pan with the beef, peeled onion (left whole) and bouquet garni. Barely cover with cold water, cover pan closely with a tightly-fitting lid, bring to the boil and then simmer for 2½–3 hours or until both head and shin are very tender.

The head is cooked when the bones can be pulled out easily. Cool slightly. Lift meat on to a large dish, strain stock and return to pan, boil gently.

Meanwhile remove bones and pull the meats into pieces with two forks. Pepper well, put meat into the basins. Ladle in enough of the reduced stock to come level with the meat. Leave overnight in a cold larder or refrigerator. Turn out when required, slicing fairly thinly to serve. A sharp dressing or sauce, like a Cumberland sauce, is good with most rich meats.

MINCED MEAT DISHES

Scotch collops, or mince

1½ lb good quality beef (minced)
2 tablespoons beef dripping
1 medium-size onion (finely chopped)
1½ oz flour
¼ pint stock, or water
salt and pepper
1 tablespoon mushroom ketchup (optional)
2 slices dry toast (for garnish)

Method

Melt dripping in a shallow pan. When hot add the onion and,

after 2–3 minutes, the minced beef. Stir well with a metal spoon over brisk heat to break up the meat (mince is apt to remain in a solid cake). Stir in the flour and add the liquid. Season, bring to the boil and cover. Simmer gently 1½–2 hours, until meat is very tender. Stir occasionally and add a little liquid if necessary. When finished the consistency should be of very thick cream and the colour a rich brown.

Mushroom ketchup can be added if wished. When ready to serve, make the toast. Remove crusts and cut each round into 8 triangular pieces or sippets. Dish up the mince and surround with the sippets or scatter them over the top. Boiled rice makes a good accompaniment.

Moussaka

12 oz cold cooked lamb
1 medium-size onion (finely chopped)
¾ oz butter
3–4 tablespoons tomato sauce, ready-bottled
salt and pepper
1 clove of garlic (crushed with ½ teaspoon salt)
pinch of grated nutmeg, or ground mace
1 aubergine (sliced, dégorgé)
3–4 tablespoons oil
2–3 potatoes (boiled in their skins, peeled and sliced)
½ lb tomatoes (peeled and sliced)

For béchamel sauce
¾ oz butter
1 tablespoon flour
7½ fl oz milk (infused with 1 slice of onion, 2–3 peppercorns, 1 blade of mace and 2–3 parsley stalks)
little mustard
1 egg (separated)
½ oz cheese (grated)

Method
Slice the meat and cut into neat dice. Soften the onion in the butter, add the meat and moisten with tomato sauce. Season and add garlic, nutmeg or mace.

Have ready the aubergine, previously sliced and sprinkled with salt. Drain, dry and fry in oil, then remove the slices. Arrange meat mixture, potatoes, tomatoes and aubergine in layers in a hot ovenproof dish.

Prepare béchamel sauce, then add mustard. Beat in egg yolk, whip white to a firm snow and

fold into mixture with the cheese. Spoon it over moussaka and brown in oven at 400°F or Mark 6 for 10–15 minutes.

Mazagrans

½ lb cooked game, or hare, or venison, or duck (minced)
1 medium-size onion (finely chopped)
1 tablespoon dripping, or butter
½ cup gravy, or brown sauce
1 dessertspoon Worcestershire sauce, or mushroom ketchup
1–1½ lb potatoes (boiled and mashed)
butter
4 gherkins

4 scallop shells

These are also delicious made with left-over jugged hare plus a little cooked ham.

Method
Sauté the onion in 1 tablespoon of dripping or butter until lightly coloured and soft. Add to the game with enough of the gravy or sauce to moisten. Season and add the bottled sauce or ketchup.

Butter scallop shells, spread a thin layer of potato in the bottom of each and fill with about 2 tablespoons of the mixture. Using a palette knife, cover each with the rest of the potato. Smooth over with the knife; mark with the rounded end (in a figure of eight or criss-cross pattern). Brush with a little melted butter and brown in the oven at 400°F or Mark 6 for 7–10 minutes. Slice each gherkin into the shape of a fan, place one on each shell and serve very hot.

Cooked stuffed tomatoes ready to be served on squares of toast

Stuffed tomatoes

4 large even-size tomatoes
4 tablespoons minced cold beef, or lamb, or pork
1½ oz butter
2 small pickling onions (finely chopped)
2 tablespoons breadcrumbs
salt and pepper
1 tablespoon tomato ketchup
pinch of mixed herbs
1 tablespoon gravy
2 slices of bread (for toast)

Method
Set the oven at 375°F or Mark 5. Cut a slice from the top (not stalk end) of each tomato; this means the tomato will sit well on the toast when served and the lid will look neater.

Rest the tomatoes very carefully in the hollow of your hand and scoop out the seeds and core with the point of a teaspoon. Strain the juice from the seeds and set aside. Put the meat in a basin.

Melt 1 oz butter in a small pan, put in the onions, cover and cook slowly until golden-brown. Add the onions and breadcrumbs to the meat, season well with salt and pepper. Mix in the ketchup with the juice from the tomato seeds and work into the meat and crumb mixture with a fork. Add the herbs and gravy.

Fill the tomatoes with mixture and put back the lid on the slant. Toast the bread, remove the crusts and cut out a square for each tomato. Butter the toast, set a tomato on each, cover with buttered paper and bake for 15–20 minutes in preset oven.

Beef olives

about 2 lb topside of beef, or
   buttock steak
1 tablespoon dripping
1 large onion (sliced)
1 large carrot (sliced)
1 stick celery (sliced)
1 tablespoon flour
1 glass sherry
1 dessertspoon tomato purée
$\frac{1}{2}$–$\frac{3}{4}$ pint stock
salt and pepper
bouquet garni
1$\frac{1}{2}$ lb potatoes (creamed)

For stuffing

1 lb minced pork
4 tablespoons breadcrumbs
2 tablespoons sherry
1 teaspoon mixed herbs
1 tablespoon parsley (chopped)
1 small onion (finely chopped and
   cooked in 1 oz butter)
salt and pepper
1 small egg (to bind)

Ask your butcher to cut the
meat into large, thin slices
(allowing 1 per person).

Method

Beat out the slices of beef
between two pieces of waxed
paper, using a rolling pin or
small heavy pan. Trim, and cut
each slice in half.

Mix all the ingredients for the
stuffing together, spread on the
slices of meat and roll up to
form the 'olives'; tie securely
with thread or fine string.

Brown the 'olives' in the hot
dripping in flameproof casserole,
take out, put in vegetables.
Reduce heat, cover casserole
and cook until the vegetables
have absorbed the fat and are a
good russet brown. Dust in
flour, cook for 2–3 minutes, add
sherry, boil up well.

Blend in the tomato purée
and stock, and season to taste.
Put the 'olives' carefully back in
casserole, tuck in bouquet
garni and bring to the boil.
Cover casserole and simmer
gently on top of the stove, or in
the oven at 325°F or Mark 3 for
about 2 hours or until tender.

Meanwhile prepare creamed
potato and when ready to dish
up beef olives arrange potato
first in the serving dish with the
meat on top. Strain the remaining sauce, boil to reduce a little
and then spoon over the dish.

Serve with mixed sprouts and
chestnuts, and carrots in a
poulette sauce (see recipe for
sauce on page 179).

Cottage pie

$\frac{3}{4}$ lb cold roast beef (minced, or
   finely diced)
1 small onion (finely chopped)
1 tablespoon dripping
3–4 tablespoons good gravy
salt and pepper
3–4 medium-size potatoes
$\frac{1}{2}$ oz butter
milk

This can also be made with
cooked lamb, in which case it
is known as shepherd's pie.

Method

Put potatoes to boil.

Fry onion in dripping until just
turning colour, then mix with
the beef, moisten with the
gravy and season very well.
Watchpoint If you have no
leftover gravy, use meat glaze
scraped off the bottom of a cake
of dripping and diluted with 2–3
tablespoons of water.

Turn beef mixture into pie
dish so that it is threequarters
full. Set oven at 375°F or Mark 5.

Drain and dry the potatoes,
crush well with a masher, add
butter and seasoning and beat in
a little milk — keep to a fairly
thick purée. Spread this over
the meat, dome the top slightly
and roughen the surface. Dot
with a few knobs of dripping
and bake in pre-set oven about
40 minutes until the potato has
a good crisp crust.

Potted meat

6 oz cold cooked beef
3 oz butter (clarified)
2 tablespoons sharp fruit sauce
   (O.K., or H.P.)
salt and pepper
pinch of ground nutmeg

Method

After removing skin and gristle
from the meat, pass it twice
through a mincer. Pound the
meat with half the butter, sauce
and seasonings. Press into small
pots and smooth the top with
a palette knife. Pour the remaining butter in a thin layer over the
top of each pot and leave to get
cold.

Steak tartare

(see photographs opposite)

2 lb best beef steak (free from
   fat)
1 teaspoon black pepper (ground
   from mill)
1$\frac{1}{2}$ teaspoons salt
3–4 tablespoons oil
1 tablespoon wine vinegar
1 teaspoon made mustard
dash of Tabasco sauce
4 shallots (chopped)
4 gherkins (chopped)
2 tablespoons chopped capers
4 egg yolks
$\frac{1}{2}$ onion (sliced and pushed out
   into rings)
2 gherkins (sliced)
2 eggs (hard-boiled)
chopped parsley

This quantity serves 6 people.
There are several variations of
this dish, but there is no deviat-
ing from the main ingredients:
raw beef steak and egg yolks.
This is a delicious and easily
digested dish, which calls for
careful seasoning and mixing.

Allow approximately $\frac{1}{4}$ lb
steak per person. This should
be of the best quality — either
fillet, sirloin or topside (some
people consider the latter to
have the best flavour). Buy
it in the piece and mince it
finely or ask the butcher to
mince it for you.

Method

Put the minced steak into a
large bowl with the seasoning.
Work together well with the
oil, vinegar, mustard and Tabasco, then add the shallots,
gherkins and capers. When
thoroughly mixed, put in the
egg yolks and taste for seasoning. Mix again, then mound in a
dish for serving. Garnish with
onion rings, gherkin slices and
chopped hard-boiled egg white,
sieved egg yolk and chopped
parsley. Serve with brown
bread and butter.
To serve individually (as
shown) mound a portion of the
steak on each plate, make a
depression in the centre and
place an egg yolk in this.
Garnish with the chopped
shallots, gherkins, capers and
hard-boiled egg white. The
guest then mixes in the egg
yolk with the other ingredients,
adding seasoning, oil, vinegar
and mustard according to personal taste. The parsley and
sieved egg yolk are sprinkled on
before eating.

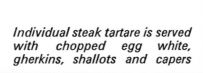
Mincing raw beef steak, ready to make steak tartare

Placing a raw egg yolk in the centre of the steak tartare

Individual steak tartare is served with chopped egg white, gherkins, shallots and capers

Poultry and Game

Chicken, turkey, duck and goose are all classed as poultry but fall into two different categories: either white-fleshed, with little natural fat, or dark-fleshed, with plenty of natural fat.

Chicken and turkey are in the first category and can be cooked in many different ways, such as grilling, roasting and casseroling.

Duck, like goose, has rich, dark flesh, thickly-covered with fat under the skin. They are both, therefore, best roasted or pot roasted to keep the skin crisp. They should be accompanied by a sharp sauce or fresh-tasting salad, such as the traditional orange, to offset their richness and to give a contrasting flavour.

When choosing a fresh bird, it should have a plump breast and be a good creamy colour; avoid those that have a purplish or greenish tinge. A bird's dressed weight is taken after plucking and drawing and includes the giblets, ie. neck, gizzard, heart and liver.

A frozen bird has its weight clearly marked. Thaw it out slowly in the refrigerator or cold larder for 24 hours. Never put it in hot water to thaw; this merely toughens the flesh. If you must thaw a bird quickly, put it into a large bowl and place this under a slowly-running cold tap.

We first mentioned game in the roasting chapter, when a general method for roasting all types, together with traditional accompaniments for roast game, was given. Here we deal with the subject at greater length. As already said, the word game covers wild birds and animals which, in Great Britain, are protected by law and strict regulations ensure that they are shot and sold only within certain periods or seasons of the year. Only people possessing a game licence (usually poulterers and fishmongers) are allowed to sell game over the counter. Rabbits and pigeons are not classed as game, so they may be shot at any time of the year. Rabbits are at their best during the autumn and winter, and pigeons during the spring and summer.

All game must be hung if the flesh is to be tender and well-flavoured; the time varies depending on the type of game and, to a certain extent, the weather: warm, damp conditions will cause the flesh to decompose more rapidly than in colder weather. Ideally all game should be shot in the head leaving the body unmarked; badly shot game should hang for a shorter time and needs careful watching.

POULTRY

Chickens vary considerably in size and flavour according to age.

Poussins are baby chickens (4–6 weeks old) usually sufficient for only one person. Double poussins (6–10 weeks old) are slightly larger and will serve two. Poussins are best roasted, pot roasted or grilled.

Spring chickens (broilers) are birds about 3 months old, weighing 2–2½ lb. They may be roasted or pot roasted and are ideal for a sauté as the joints are not too large. One bird is sufficient for 3–4 people, depending on the method of

Poussins dijonnaise (see page 150): the cooked birds are browned, and then the sauce is poured around them

146

Boning a chicken

Remove the trussing string. With a sharp knife, slit the skin down the underside of the bird. Work skin and flesh from the carcass with the knife until the leg joint is reached

Nick sinew between ball and socket joint joining thigh bone to carcass; hold end of joint in one hand, and working from inside of leg, cut away flesh. Scrape thigh bone clean

Then continue cleaning the drumstick until the whole leg bone is free of flesh. Now remove the leg bone from carcass. Repeat this cleaning process with the other leg

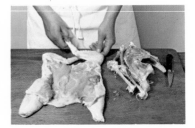

Sever the wing joint from the carcass. Still using the knife, work down towards and on to the breastbone; stop there. Free the other wing in the same way

Now very carefully cut away the skin from the top of the breastbone. Take great care not to split the skin and to keep both sides of the chicken attached so that it remains in one piece for stuffing

Lay the chicken flat ready for stuffing to be spread over cut surfaces. Then sew up or secure with poultry pins/lacers; truss in the usual way

---

cooking.

Roasters average 3–4 lb and are birds about 6–12 months old. This is the most popular size chicken for a family and may be roasted, boiled or pot roasted, and served with an appropriate sauce and garnish.

Boilers are chickens of 12 months and over, weighing about 4–6 lb. They are used for making broths, for cold dishes or mousses, or served with a sauce. They are usually meaty but inclined to fat.

Boilers should be simmered for 2–3 hours in water with root vegetables and a bouquet garni to flavour; add also a little salt and a few peppercorns. Keep the liquid well skimmed of fat and the pan covered. Cool chicken a little in the liquid before taking out for carving. As the skin is inclined to be thick it is best removed just before serving.

Capons are young cockerels treated by injection and then specially fattened for the table.

They usually weigh 5–8 lb and are good for a large family meal. They can be roasted or poached for about 2 hours for use as a cold buffet dish.

JOINTING A FRESH CHICKEN

A sauté, grill or similar dish using chicken joints is much more attractive in appearance if you cut up the bird. If you buy ready-cut joints, they will include all the bone (eg. knuckle) and won't look so neat. When you joint a bird yourself, a proportion of carcass bone must be taken with wing and breast portions, otherwise flesh shrinks during cooking.

In some recipes a chicken is browned whole, then jointed as shown opposite, but legs are divided after cooking as for a roast chicken.

For a sauté, the legs are left whole and the knuckle bone usually cut away after the bird has been cooked.

CARVING A COOKED CHICKEN

It is easier to carve in the kitchen than at the table as the bird can then be dished up with the gravy and kept warm until ready to serve.

1 Set bird on a board with front part of breast towards you. Cut and draw out trussing string. Insert carving fork into bird towards back to hold it firm. With a sharp knife, slit skin round leg and press it gently outwards and down with flat of knife. This will break leg from carcass at the joint; cut through, slip knife point under back to release the oyster (a small nut of choice meat lying on back adjacent to joint) with thigh.

2 With knife at top end of breastbone, opposite where breastbone and wishbone meet, cut parallel to one side to give a good slice of breast attached to the wing. To detach wing on its own (always holding carcass firmly with the fork) make a cut

Jointing a fresh chicken

Hold chicken firmly on board with one hand. With sharp knife, saw away skin between leg and breast. Then, pressing flat of knife against carcass, take leg in other hand and bend it outwards until the oyster bone breaks away from carcass

Slide the knife around the leg joint cutting down towards the 'parson's nose', keeping it between the oyster and backbone. Leg is now severed from the carcass and has the oyster bone attached. Cut off the other leg in exactly the same way

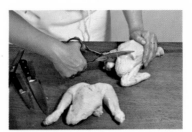

Now make a slantwise cut with knife half-way up the breast across to the top of wishbone from the neck end, to end of the wing joints. With scissors, cut down through wishbone and ribs to detach the wing with a good portion of breast

Twist the wing pinion out and tuck it under this breast meat to hold the joint flat. This makes for even browning of the meat. To get both wings of even size, make the slantwise cuts at the same time. Detach the other wing in the same way

Cut away the breast meat in one piece with the scissors. All that is now left of the carcass are the ribs, the backbone and the 'parson's nose'

The joints are now ready for cooking. The carcass may be cut in half and then sautéd with the chicken joints to give the finished dish additional flavour

---

at the top of wishbone, then turn knife so that it presses against carcass; with a gentle sawing movement, cut down and through to wing joint. This will sever wing and knife will find joint automatically.

3 Detach similar pieces from other side in the same way.

4 Slice off wishbone by carving behind it down front of carcass; keep knife pressed against carcass.

5 Divide breast in two, lengthways or across, using knife and then scissors to cut through bone. If carving at the table, the breast should be carved in slanting slices.

6 Cut off knuckle ends of drumsticks with poultry scissors. With a large chicken, divide legs into two by cutting with scissors, or knife, not at hock (knee) joints, but just above so that a portion of thigh meat is attached to drumstick.

To cut suprêmes from a cooked chicken: cut down from the breastbone, taking care to keep the knife close to the rib cage

BONING A POUSSIN

A bird can be completely boned out and then stuffed, but a better shape is obtained if it is only partially boned, with leg and breastbone left in for a young poussin, but breastbone removed from an older one. This makes trussing easier.

1 Remove trussing strings,

turn bird on to breastbone; with a small, sharp knife, slit skin down underside of bird.

2 With tail of bird towards you, ease flesh and skin away from carcass on left-hand side. Work evenly, with short, sharp strokes (keep knife edge against ribs). Sever leg and wing through the ball and socket joints.

3 Turn bird round, lift skin and flesh off other side, sever the joints as before.

4 Cut away the rib and backbone with the scissors.

5 Bird is now ready to have stuffing spread over cut surfaces. Sew up underside, or secure with poultry pins/lacers, and truss.

SPLITTING A POUSSIN
see photographs on page 150

1 Hold bird firmly on board with one hand, make a cut with a sharp knife through skin and flesh on top of the breast.

2 Split in half with scissors, starting at wishbone end, and cutting through on one side of backbone. When divided, trim away backbone from the other half of the poussin.

3 Trim off the knuckle bones and end wing pinions after grilling.

To split a cooked poussin
Lift bird carefully from pan on to a board. Cut and draw out trussing strings before splitting as above.

Before grilling the birds for poussins dijonnaise, first split them down the undersides (the backs), using a sharp knife

Then trim away the backbones from the halves with a pair of scissors (detailed instructions are given on page 149)

Spatchcock denotes any small bird which is split down the back before grilling. **Spitchcock** refers to the same process with eels.

Poussins dijonnaise

(see photograph on page 147)

2 double poussins
2 oz butter
¾ cup of chicken stock
salt
pepper (ground from mill)
1 dessertspoon plain flour
grated rind and juice of ½ orange
1 dessertspoon Dijon mustard
1 tablespoon double cream (optional)
watercress (to garnish)

Method
Heat a large flameproof casserole, drop in half the butter and when foaming put in the poussins with ¼ cup of the stock and season. Cover the pan at once and cook on a slow to moderate heat or in the oven at 350°F or Mark 4 for 20–30 minutes or until tender.

Take up the birds, split and trim away the backbones; arrange for grilling in a separate ovenproof dish.

Blend the flour into the butter and juices remaining in the casserole, add the remaining stock and stir until boiling. Strain and keep warm.

Sprinkle the birds with the orange juice, dust with a little more salt and pepper. Melt remaining butter, spoon it over the birds and then grill until golden-brown and crisp. Add mustard and orange rind to sauce and taste for seasoning. Stir in cream (if using). Pour sauce round chicken, garnish with watercress.

Dijon mustard is made from white and black powdered mustard seeds. These are mixed with verjuice (the acid juice from large unripened grapes) in place of vinegar, sometimes with the addition of a few herbs.

Chicken parisienne

2½–3 lb roasting chicken
salt and pepper
2 oz butter
¼ pint good stock
⅛ pint sherry

For forcemeat
1 oz butter
1 shallot (finely chopped)
6 oz ham (minced)
6 oz veal (minced)
2–3 tablespoons fresh breadcrumbs
1 dessertspoon mixed herbs and parsley (chopped)
1 egg (lightly beaten)

For velouté sauce and liaison
about 2 tablespoons flour
1¼ oz butter
½ pint chicken stock
1 egg yolk
¾ gill single cream
2 oz mushrooms (thinly sliced and cooked in ½ oz butter and squeeze of lemon juice)

Poultry pins/lacers

Method
First prepare stuffing: melt butter in a saucepan, add chopped shallot, cook until soft and leave to cool. Mix the minced ham with the minced veal, breadcrumbs, herbs and parsley. Add shallot, season and bind with beaten egg.

Bone out chicken, rub inside with salt and pepper and spread with forcemeat. Sew up or secure with poultry pins/lacers, reshape and truss firmly.

Set in a roasting tin, rub bird well with butter and pour round stock and sherry. Cook for about 1½ hours or until tender in the oven at 400°F or Mark 6. Baste and turn every 20 minutes while cooking.

Meanwhile prepare sauce: cook flour in melted butter until lightly coloured, draw pan aside, add stock, stir until thick and boiling and simmer for 3–4 minutes, then set aside.

Make a liaison by beating egg yolk lightly and mixing cream into it. Add this to sauce, reheat carefully without boiling, and add cooked mushrooms.

When chicken is cooked, take up, remove pins and trussing string and carve. Arrange in a serving dish, spoon over a little sauce with mushrooms. Serve remaining sauce separately.

DUCKS

Carving duck/goose

Since these birds are awkward to carve, this is best done in the kitchen.

Small or medium-size bird

1 Remove trussing strings and set the bird on a board.
2 Cut straight down through breastbone and back. Use scissors and cut through bone.
3 Lay each half on board, make a slanting cut between ribs to separate wing and leg, making two good portions of each half. With scissors, trim away any carcass bone. The portions should be two wings and two legs, with a piece of breast attached to all portions.

Large bird

1 Cut off legs. Remember that leg joint is set differently to a chicken, right under back of the bird.
2 Raise fillets (wing and breast) by slipping knife under them and along carcass down to wing bones which can then be severed at joint. Slice off a piece of breast with each wing bone attached.
3 Cut rest of the breast into slanting slices.

To serve: arrange legs at one end of a hot serving dish, wings at other end, pieces of breast in centre. Pour on gravy or sauce.

Duck with cherries

4–5 lb duckling
¼ pint stock
2½ fl oz red wine

For sauce

1 oz butter
mirepoix of 1 tablespoon each
   chopped onion and shallot
¾ oz flour
¾ pint stock
1 tablespoon chopped
   mushroom stalks
1 wineglass red wine
salt and pepper

To serve
cherry compote (see page 268)

Method

Set the duck in a roasting tin with the giblets and stock, but reserve the liver. Roast in a moderately hot oven at 400°F or Mark 6 for 15 minutes per lb and an extra 15 minutes.

Prepare cherry compote (see page 268) and sauce. Brown the mirepoix in the butter, add

Roast duck, here garnished with caramelised turnips and onions

the flour and brown it too, put in all the remaining ingredients and simmer together for 30–40 minutes. Strain the sauce, reserving the vegetables.

Carve the duck and arrange in a serving dish. Pound the carcass and raw liver with the 2½ fl oz wine and reserved vegetables, bring to the boil, strain, and add liquor to sauce.

Spoon the sauce over the duck and serve the cherry compote (either hot or cold) separately.

Duck with turnips (aux navets)

4 lb duckling
1½ oz butter
1 lemon
salt and pepper
¼ pint stock
½ pint demi-glace sauce
1 wineglass white wine

For garnish

1 lb small new turnips
1 oz butter
1 tablespoon caster sugar
½ lb small onions (blanched)

This recipe should only be made with small, new turnips. Do not

attempt it with the large, old variety as they are much too strong in flavour.

Method

Place the thinly-pared rind of the lemon inside the bird with a good nut of butter and seasoning. Smear remaining butter over the breast; truss the bird and place it in a roasting tin with the stock. Roast it in a moderately hot oven at 400°F or Mark 6, basting and turning from time to time.

Meanwhile prepare the demi-glace sauce. Blanch the turnips, melt the butter and place in a shallow pan or casserole with the caster sugar. Cook over a gentle heat, shaking the pan from time to time, until turnips are tender and the sugar has caramelised. Then add the blanched onions and cook for a few more minutes.

Remove the duck from pan and keep hot on a serving dish, skim off fat, add the wine, and the juice of ½ lemon to the roasting tin and boil well. Strain this mixture into the demi-glace sauce, reduce rapidly until syrupy. Spoon a little sauce over the duck (serve the remainder separately), garnish with turnips and onions.

151

Braised duckling with olives — the duck is browned and then casseroled gently until tender

Braised duckling with olives

1 duckling
1 oz butter
1 medium-size onion (sliced)
1 glass port
1 teaspoon paprika pepper
½ pint jellied stock (see page 118)
bouquet garni
salt and pepper
2 tomatoes
12 large green olives, or olives stuffed with pimento
1 dessertspoon flour

Method

Brown the duck in the butter in a deep casserole; when evenly coloured, tip off the fat and add the onion; cover and cook slowly until the onion is soft.

Moisten bird with the port; allow liquid to reduce by half and then stir in the paprika and cook for 2–3 minutes. Pour on the stock, add the bouquet garni and season lightly. Cover casserole and cook very gently for about 45 minutes or until duckling is tender. This cooking can be done on top of the stove, or in the oven at 350°F or Mark 4.

Meanwhile skin and quarter the tomatoes, remove the seeds, then cut the flesh again into neat shreds. Set aside.

If using large olives, cut in strips off the stones; if using stuffed olives, leave them whole, blanch in boiling water for 5 minutes, drain and leave to soak in cold water for 30 minutes, then drain again.

Remove the duckling from the casserole and keep hot; take out the bouquet garni. Skim the fat from the liquid in casserole.

Mix the flour with 1 tablespoon of the liquid, return this to the casserole and stir until it boils. Cook liquid for 5 minutes. Add the tomatoes and olives, reheat and taste for seasoning.

Divide the duckling into four portions, place them in a hot serving dish and spoon over the sauce. Serve with beans, peas and very tiny roast potatoes.

GAME

AGE OF BIRDS

To be sure that your bird is a young one, look first at the legs and feet; these should be smooth and pliable. In the case of a cock bird, the spurs should be rounded and short with supple feet and toe-nails. The feathers on the breast and under the wing should be downy and soft, and the tips of the long wing feathers pointed; rounded points indicate an older bird. End tip of breastbone should give slightly in a young bird.

HANGING

Game should be literally hung (ie. suspended from a hook), to allow the air to circulate freely around it. Hang it in a cool, dry place, such as an outside larder well protected from flies, or in a dry cellar. (A garage, toolshed or potting shed – if rat-free – would be good, but if not available, a well-ventilated larder would do, although it is better not to hang game near other food, which may pick up its strong flavour.) Feathered game is hung from the neck; other game (hares and rabbits) by the hind legs.

To test if birds are ready for cooking, pull out a small tuft of feathers just above the tail; this should come away easily. The bird may then be plucked, drawn and trussed ready for cooking. A green or bluish discolouration of flesh shows the bird has been hung too long.

PLUCKING

The poulterer (or butcher) plucks and draws game he sells, but you will have to do this for 'home-killed' game, although your local poulterer may do it for you for a small charge.

Plucking must be done carefully because the skin becomes soft and tender during hanging and it must not be torn.

For a small bird, spread it on newspaper to catch feathers.

For a large bird, place a board over a bin (or large container) and lay the bird on it. When you start plucking, the feathers will then fall straight into the bin. This is the easiest way to do it, especially with a downy bird.

Hold the bird firmly by the legs. Starting from the tail end and using a small, quick jerk, pull out the feathers, away from you, a few at a time, in the direction opposite to that in which they lie. Take particular care with feathers on the breast where the flesh is most tender.

To pluck the wing feathers, bend wing into a natural position. Grip all of the main feathers in one hand and then give them a sharp pull. This will extend the wing and nearly all the feathers should come out at one go. Then pull out any remaining feathers (you may need to use a pair of pliers).

When all the feathers are removed, singe off the remaining down. The best way to do this is to pour 1–2 tablespoons methylated spirit on to an enamel or fireproof plate and set alight. Then holding the bird by the head and feet, turn it round in the flame.

A gas flame can be used in the same way, but it does not have such a wide area of flame. Hold and turn the bird as above, but don't swing it.

DRAWING

All large game birds, such as pheasant, must be drawn before cooking; some of the smaller birds are not drawn. A chicken is drawn in the same way.

Drawing should be done in one operation, and you'll find it less messy if you wrap your hand in a damp cloth.

After drawing, wipe the bird inside and out with a damp cloth or absorbent paper before trussing it. Usually, the feet and legs are cut off just below the hock joints. Truss game birds as for poultry, tucking the neck skin under the wing pinions.

Gravy for game

In recipes for roast game, it is always stressed that strong, clear gravy should accompany it, but you are rarely told how to prepare it. If roast pheasant or wild duck, for example, is served regularly, it's a good idea to make a quantity of good gravy and have it to hand. Ideally, the brown jelly or glaze found on the bottom of a cake of beef dripping is what you should use, but there is not usually enough of it.

The giblets, neck, gizzard and heart are used for making a little concentrated gravy to serve with a plainly roasted bird. The feet (like those from a chicken) should be blanched and scraped before adding to the giblets. The liver may be pounded and mixed with a little strong stock and wine to form the basis of a sauce for a salmis. When buying game, you should ask for the giblets.

The recipe for gravy given here makes 1 pint, and is one that can be deep frozen and used as needed.

1 lb chicken giblets (mixed necks and gizzards, and any game giblets available)
½ lb shin of beef
1 rounded tablespoon beef dripping
1 medium-size onion (sliced)
1½ pints water
bouquet garni
6 peppercorns
1 small carrot (sliced)
1 teaspoon salt
1 clove

Method

Wash and blanch the giblets, then dry them; cut them and the beef into small pieces. Melt the dripping in a shallow pan, put in the onion, giblets and beef. Set pan on low heat and fry until all are lightly coloured.

Pour in about ½ teacup of the water. Continue cooking gently, stirring occasionally, until the liquid has reduced to a brown glaze. Then add the remaining water and the rest of the ingredients. Bring gravy to the boil, then lower the heat and *simmer*, with pan lid slightly off the pan, for 1 hour. Then strain gravy and leave until cold; skim off any fat and use as required.

Watchpoint Gentle simmering will keep the gravy clear; boiling will make it cloudy. If the ½ teacup of liquid first used can be good stock instead of water, the process of the liquid 'falling' to a glaze will be much quicker. The remaining liquid added may be water rather than stock.

GROUSE

Spit or oven roast young birds, at 400°F or Mark 6, for 35 minutes. Serve with browned crumbs, game chips and strong gravy, and either rowan or redcurrant jelly. Bread sauce is not usually served, but you can offer cranberry sauce, in which case omit the jelly. One plump grouse should serve 2 people.

Marinated, jugged grouse

2 good, old grouse
scant ½ pint stock
¾ lb chuck steak
a little dripping
1 medium-size onion (finely chopped)
bouquet garni
1–1½ wineglasses port, or red wine
1 tablespoon redcurrant jelly
pinch of ground mace
forcemeat balls (see page 133)

Method
Split the grouse, trim away the backbones and add the bones to the measured stock. Put into a pan, cover and simmer for 20–30 minutes and then strain. Cut the steak into ½-inch pieces and brown quickly in a little hot dripping. Take out of the pan, add the grouse and the onion, lower the heat and allow just to colour. Then layer the steak and grouse together in a casserole and season well. Tuck in the bouquet garni and pour over the prepared stock. Add the wine, redcurrant jelly and mace, cover tightly and cook in the oven pre-set at 325°F or Mark 3. Prepare the forcemeat balls and set aside. After 1 hour's cooking, remove the casserole lid and place the forcemeat balls on top of the steak and grouse layers. Cover again and continue to cook for a further hour, when the meat should be very tender. If wished, 10–15 minutes before the dish is ready, remove the lid and allow the forcemeat balls to brown. A small glass more of port can be poured into the casserole just before serving. Serve with braised red cabbage and a purée of potatoes.

PARTRIDGE

There are two varieties: the English, or grey, partridge and the French partridge, also known as the Frenchman, which is slightly larger than the English one and has red legs. The latter kind is Continental in origin and is more common than the English bird, especially in the eastern counties of England.

The English partridge is especially prized for its flavour when it is young, and cannot be bettered when plainly roasted. For perfection, spit or oven roast it for 20–25 minutes and serve with the traditional accompaniments of fried or browned crumbs, strong, clear gravy, game chips and bread sauce (optional). It can also be stuffed with mushrooms before roasting; allow one plump bird per person.

The French partridge is considered at its best when more mature, being particularly suitable for stuffing or for any made-up dish. Allow one French partridge for two people, if it is stuffed with a veal forcemeat and garnished.

Hang an English partridge for 3–4 days, a French one for 5–6 days; older birds of both kinds may need hanging for 1–2 days longer. When trussing, it is usual to tuck the feet inside the body of the bird.

The following recipes are suitable for older birds, and most partridge and pheasant recipes are interchangeable.

Partridge with black olives

3 plump partridges
1½–2 oz butter
4–6 oz green bacon rashers
3 shallots (finely chopped)
1 tablespoon flour
1 teaspoon tomato purée
½ pint well-flavoured, jellied stock
2 wineglasses red wine
salt and pepper
bouquet garni
3 oz black olives (stoned and halved)

Method
Brown the birds slowly and carefully all over in the butter. Meantime cut bacon into strips, blanch and drain. Add these to the pan with the shallots and continue to fry gently for 3–4 minutes, then remove the birds; stir in the flour and add the

tomato purée and the stock. Reduce the wine by about one-third in a small saucepan and add this to the casserole. Bring to the boil. Season, add the bouquet garni and replace the partridges.

Cover with a piece of paper or foil and then the lid. Cook for 50–60 minutes in the oven, pre-set at 325–350°F or Mark 3–4, or until tender. Take up partridges, remove trussing strings, split in half and trim away some backbone. Arrange on a dish, boil the sauce rapidly for 2–3 minutes, or until syrupy, then add the black olives. Reboil sauce and spoon it over the dish at once.

Casserole of partridge with red cabbage. The boned out birds are served on croûtes

Game refers to wild birds and animals which are hunted for food, but which are protected by law at certain seasons. The following are the seasons when the various types of game are at their best in Great Britain:
Grouse: 12 August – 10 December, Partridge: 1 September – 1 February, Pheasant: 1 October – 1 February, Squabs: Available all the year round, Venison: late June – January.
The dates when game is in season may vary from time to time, and the ones given here are the latest available for Great Britain.

Casserole of partridge

3 French partridges
½–¾ pint stock (made with carcasses, root vegetables and bouquet garni)
1–1½ oz butter
¼ lb chipolata sausages
1 onion (sliced)
1 carrot (sliced)
1 rasher of bacon (blanched and diced)
1 dessertspoon flour
bouquet garni
4–6 croûtes of fried bread

For stuffing
1 shallot (finely chopped)
1 oz butter
3 oz breadcrumbs
1½ oz raisins (stoned)
1 oz chopped walnuts
1 teaspoon finely chopped parsley
1 small egg (beaten)
salt and pepper

Trussing needle and fine string, or poultry pins

Method
Bone out the partridges (as for chicken, see page 148), leaving the leg bones in, then spread out birds on your work surface. Clean the carcasses, break them up and use to make the stock, with root vegetables and bouquet garni to flavour. Strain off the required quantity of stock and set aside.

To prepare the stuffing: soften shallot in the butter, then mix with the remaining stuffing ingredients, binding mixture with the beaten egg and seasoning to taste. Spread stuffing on the partridges and sew up with fine string or secure with poultry pins.

Heat butter in a flameproof casserole, put in the sausages to brown slowly. Take them out and brown the partridges; add the onion, carrot and bacon. Cook for 2–3 minutes, then dust with flour, add bouquet garni and reserved stock. Cover casserole tightly and braise slowly for 45–60 minutes in the oven, pre-set at 325°F or Mark 3.

When birds are tender, remove them from the casserole. Split them in half and serve each half on a croûte of fried bread. Cut sausages in half diagonally and add to the casserole. Spoon a little of the sauce and the sausages over each croûte and serve the rest separately.

PHEASANT
This handsome bird was originally a foreigner to Great Britain but for some time past has been a native of its woodlands. It is the only game bird which is bred for shooting. Hen birds are as a rule more tender and succulent than the cocks. Pheasants, like most game, are sold by the brace, ie. a cock and a hen. Young birds may be spit or oven roasted for approximately 45–55 minutes. Cocks and slightly older birds should be pot roasted to keep them as moist as possible. The flavour of a pheasant goes well with a sub-acid such as apple, or sometimes even grapes or raisins. A pheasant lends itself to a variety of dishes, but if served plainly roast it must be well hung otherwise it can be dull and tasteless. Serve with sprouts or braised celery, fried or browned crumbs, bread sauce and game chips. A good size bird serves 4–5 people.

Pheasant forestière

1 pheasant
1 oz butter
¼ lb chipolata sausages (halved diagonally)
1 shallot (finely chopped)
6 oz green bacon rasher (cut into thick strips and blanched)
1 wineglass red wine
bouquet garni
4–6 oz button mushrooms (quartered)
1 wineglass stock
a little kneaded butter

Method
Brown the pheasant all over in the hot butter. Remove from the pan and add the sausages, shallot and bacon. When brown, remove sausages from pan and replace the pheasant, adding the wine and herbs. Cover the pan tightly and simmer for 35–40 minutes, then add the mushrooms and sausages. Cover and cook for a further 7 minutes, then carve and dish up pheasant.

Add stock to the pan, first removing herbs, and thicken with kneaded butter. Boil up and spoon this sauce over pheasant. Garnish with glazed onions.

Squabs St. Hubert

3 squabs (very young pigeons)
1½–2 oz butter
2 wineglasses red wine
1 tablespoon redcurrant jelly
1 oz almonds, or cashew nuts

For pilaf
1 medium-size onion
1–1½ oz butter
8 oz long grain rice
1–1¼ pints veal, or game, stock
salt and pepper
2–3 dried apple rings
2 oz dried apricots (soaked
    overnight with apple rings)
1–1½ oz currants (soaked in hot
    water for 30 minutes)

Method

Set oven at 350–375°F or Mark 4–5. Spread the pigeons with about 1½ oz of butter, put them in a small roasting tin and pour in 1 glass of wine. Roast them in pre-set oven for about 25–35 minutes, increasing the heat to 400°F or Mark 6 during the last 5 minutes of cooking; let them brown thoroughly.

To prepare the pilaf: chop the onion finely and sauté gently in 1 oz of butter in a flameproof casserole until just coloured, then add the rice and stir well. Add about 1 pint of the stock, season and bring to the boil. Cover and put casserole in the oven, under the pigeons, for about 12 minutes or until barely cooked.

Meanwhile prepare the dried fruit; cook the apricots and apples for about 10–15 minutes in the water in which they have been soaked, then drain them and cut into pieces. Drain the currants. Stir the fruit into the rice carefully with a fork. If the rice is dry, moisten it with a little of the stock. Season well and dot with the remainder of the butter. Cover with foil and a lid and put into the oven on the lower shelf. Leave for 15–20 minutes, forking the rice once or twice.

When the rice is dry, remove it from the oven. Take up the pigeons, split them and trim away the backbone. Make a gravy in the pan with the remaining glass of wine and some of the stock, finish with the redcurrant jelly and boil up well. Strain. Have ready the nuts fried in a little butter until brown. The rice can be served separately, otherwise dish up by turning on to the serving

Squabs St. Hubert served on a pilaf with fried almonds

dish and arranging the pigeons around. Spoon a little of the gravy over the pigeons and serve the rest in a sauce boat. Scatter the nuts over the dish and serve very hot.

Layering dried apricots and apple rings on rice for pilaf

VENISON

There are three different varieties of deer – fallow, roe and red – and venison can be the meat of any one.

Fallow are the domestic, or park, deer; the roe or roebuck is found in woodlands; the red deer in the high hills and mountains of Scotland. From time to time deer have to be 'culled' or thinned to keep the herd sound and healthy, so the meat can be bought at various times of the year from a butcher or poulterer.

Buck venison (considered the best) is in season only from late June until late September, but doe meat remains in season throughout November and December. The meat of both roe and fallow deer is good and, as the animals are smaller than the red, makes nice-size joints. The red deer has especially lean meat with a gamey flavour and must be well hung. This is normally done before it reaches the consumer, the usual time of hanging being 8–10 days, according to taste and, of course, the weather. Fallow and roe deer do not need so long.

As there is little natural fat on venison and the meat is inclined to be dry, additional moisture and flavour are given in the form of a marinade, a mixture of wine, oil, herbs, and spices. The meat can be marinated from 24 hours up to 3 days or even longer, again depending on personal taste. The best parts are saddle and haunch. Other pieces, such as cuts from the shoulder, are best jugged, or stewed.

Fillets of venison poivrade

1½ lb boned loin of venison (weighed without bone), or slices from the top of the haunch
a little oil
2½ fl oz red wine, or port
pepper (ground from mill)
2 tablespoons of peanuts, or cashew nuts
2 oz stoned raisins (soaked in hot water for 30 minutes)
6 croûtes of stale bread (cut into heart shapes and fried in a little hot oil)

For sauce poivrade

1 small onion (diced)
1 small carrot (diced)
1 small stick of celery (diced)
2–3 tablespoons oil, or dripping
1 tablespoon flour
1 oz mushroom stalks and/or peelings
1 rounded teaspoon tomato purée
bouquet garni
1 pint jellied stock
1 wineglass of red wine
2 tablespoons red wine vinegar

Fillets of venison poivrade, served en couronne

Method

Slice the venison into strips ¾ inch thick. Lay them on a plate. Sprinkle with the oil and wine (or port) and grind over plenty of pepper. Cover and leave for about 1 hour.

Meanwhile prepare the sauce. Add the vegetables to the hot oil and cook gently until barely coloured. Add the flour and continue to cook slowly to a good brown. Then add the chopped mushroom stalks and/or peelings, tomato purée and bouquet garni, two-thirds of the stock, and the wine. Bring to the boil and simmer, with the pan partly covered, for 20–25 minutes. Then add half the remaining stock, reboil and remove any scum as it rises. Then add the rest of the stock and repeat this process. Strain the sauce, return to a clean pan, add the vinegar and continue to boil gently for a further 6–7 minutes. Draw pan aside.

Heat the nuts and stoned raisins in a little butter. Take out and set aside. To cook the steaks: reheat the pan, wipe the pieces of meat and sauté them briskly in a little hot oil or dripping, allowing about 4 minutes on each side. Then dish them up on a hot dish 'en couronne' with a croûte between each steak.

Note: start with a croûte on the dish, then a steak, then another croûte and so on, ending with a croûte.

Reboil the sauce and add the raisins and the nuts. Put several spoonfuls of the sauce into the centre of the dish and serve the rest separately.

Slicing venison fillet before marinating in red wine and oil

Soufflés and Mousses

Hot soufflés are often considered to be the test of a good cook. They are not difficult to make if you follow the basic rules but, as with all tests of skill, circumstances must be right. Don't serve a savoury soufflé as a first course for a luncheon or dinner party unless you know your guests are going to be punctual. However, for everyday family meals, you can experiment with a variety of soufflés and roulades; in the case of the latter the mixture is cooked on a swiss roll tin, spread with a contrasting filling and then rolled up.

Cold savoury mousses are smooth in texture and do not necessarily contain egg. The main ingredient, which can be fish, meat, cheese or a vegetable, is chopped, minced or flaked and bound with either butter, sauce or mayonnaise. Lightly-whipped cream added to a mousse helps to give it a good spongy texture and, if the mixture is to be moulded and turned out for serving, the mousse is set with a very small quantity of gelatine.

Cold savoury soufflés are made in the same way as mousses, the only difference is that whisked egg whites are folded in to give them a very light texture. A cold soufflé should always be presented in the conventional soufflé dish. This is prepared in the usual way, that is a band of oiled greaseproof paper is tied around the outside of the oiled dish, the soufflé mixture is poured into the prepared dish to come 1–1½ inches above the top and when the soufflé is set the paper is peeled away so that it appears to have risen above the dish.

A cold sweet mousse is made with whole eggs plus extra egg yolks beaten together with sugar until thick, flavouring in the form of purée added, and the whole enriched with cream and lightly set with gelatine.

For a cold sweet soufflé, the eggs are always separated, the yolks are beaten with sugar and flavouring (in the form of juice or purée) until thick, or made into a custard with milk when cream is added. Stiffly whisked egg whites are folded in, and the whole is lightly set with gelatine.

HOT SOUFFLES

MAKING SWEET OR SAVOURY SOUFFLES

1 Choose the right size soufflé dish or case for the quantity of mixture being made. Dishes are generally numbered 1–3, and the equivalent diameters are given in recipes overleaf (except for No. 3 which has a 5½-inch diameter top). Before baking, dish should be two-thirds to three-quarters full of mixture.

2 Prepare the dish by rubbing the inside lightly with butter, and in the case of savoury soufflés dust with browned crumbs as it will then be easier to clean.

3 To allow the soufflé to rise 2–3 inches above the dish when baked, cut a band or strip of doubled greaseproof paper, about 6–7 inches wide, and long enough to overlap some 3 inches round side of dish. Make a 2-inch fold along one long side. Butter the strip above this fold, and wrap the band round the outside of the dish, the folded piece at the base and turned inwards. This will keep the paper upright and firm. The greased section of the paper should stand above dish by some 3 inches.

Tie paper securely with string and set the dish on a baking sheet before filling. The string

There is a test of skill in making a light-as-air cheese soufflé, which forms a good supper dish (see page 160)

should be untied and the paper peeled off just before serving.

4 It is the whipped egg whites that make a soufflé rise, so it is important to whip them well. Ideally you should use a copper bowl and a light wire whisk.

Whisking by hand in a bowl of this shape gives more bulk to whites. If you do not have a copper bowl, use a wire whisk with a china or earthenware bowl. Don't use a rotary whisk or mixer.

HOW TO LINE A SOUFFLE DISH

Having rubbed inside of dish with butter, for savoury soufflé dust with browned crumbs; wrap greaseproof paper band round with a 2-inch fold at base and 3-inch overlap to keep it upright

Tying paper band round to stand 2–3 inches above rim of the dish

A little of the egg white is first folded in to soften the mixture

5 When adding egg whites to the mixture, stir in a small quantity with a metal spoon before the main bulk is added. This first addition softens the mixture so that once the remaining whites are added the whole remains light and fluffy.

6 Pre-heat the oven to 375°F or Mark 5. Arrange the shelves so that the soufflé can be placed in the centre of the oven, with no shelf above it. This will give it plenty of room to rise. To avoid any unnecessary opening of oven door, try not to cook anything else when a soufflé is in.

7 A soufflé should be served immediately from the oven. Better to keep the family waiting than the soufflé. When cooked the top should be evenly-brown and firm to the touch (approximate cooking times are given in individual recipes), and the consistency lightly firm, with the centre soft and creamy.

8 Hot soufflés benefit by the addition of 1 extra white to yolks. Though this is not essential it makes for a lighter and fluffier mixture.

SAVOURY SOUFFLES

A cheese soufflé is the most popular of these; not only does it make an excellent savoury but it is also a good supper dish. The mixture can be layered with cooked fish, vegetables or meat and is one of the best ways of using up leftovers.

Cheese soufflé

4 rounded tablespoons cheese
  (grated)
1½ oz butter
1 rounded tablespoon flour
salt
cayenne pepper
¾ cup of milk
1 teaspoon ready-made mustard
4 egg yolks
5 egg whites
1 tablespoon browned crumbs
  (see page 98)

*7-inch diameter top (size No. 1)
  soufflé dish*

Ideally the cheese used should be a mixture of grated Parmesan and Gruyère. Otherwise use a dry Cheddar.

Method
First prepare soufflé dish. Set

oven at 375°F or Mark 5.

Choose a medium to large saucepan. Make a roux by melting the butter, removing pan from heat and stirring in the flour. Season well, blend in milk. Put pan back on heat, stir until boiling then draw aside. Add mustard and beat in 3 rounded tablespoons cheese and egg yolks one at a time.

Watchpoint The basic sauce must be well flavoured with cheese and well seasoned to compensate for the amount of whites added.

When well mixed whip egg whites to a firm snow, stir 2 tablespoons of the whites into the sauce, using a metal spoon. Then stir in the remainder in two parts, lifting the sauce well over the whites from the bottom of the pan. Turn the bowl round while mixing; do not overmix.

Turn lightly into prepared soufflé dish. Quickly dust top with crumbs and rest of cheese mixed together. Bake for 25–30 minutes in pre-set oven, until evenly-brown and firm to the touch. Serve immediately.

Mushroom soufflé

8 oz flat mushrooms, or mushroom stalks (finely chopped)
1 oz butter
1 tablespoon mixed herbs (parsley, mint, chives) – freshly chopped
salt and pepper
4 egg yolks
5 egg whites
1 tablespoon cheese (grated)
1 tablespoon browned crumbs

For béchamel sauce
1½ oz butter
1 rounded tablespoon flour
½ pint milk (infused with 1 slice onion, ½ bayleaf, 6 peppercorns, 1 blade of mace, a few pieces of carrot)

7-inch diameter top (size No. 1) soufflé dish

Method
Prepare the soufflé dish. Set oven at 375°F or Mark 5.

Wash mushrooms but do not peel, chop them finely. Cook in 1 oz butter in a fairly large pan for 4–5 minutes. Increase heat, if necessary, to drive off any excess liquid. Add herbs and seasoning.

Prepare the béchamel sauce and stir it into the mushroom mixture.

Beat the egg yolks into the béchamel and mushroom sauce mixture, one at a time. Whip whites to a firm snow, cut and stir 1 tablespoon of these into the mixture, using a metal spoon. Then stir in remainder.

Turn into the prepared dish. Sprinkle top with cheese and browned crumbs mixed together and bake for 25–30 minutes in pre-set oven.

SWEET SOUFFLES
The light sauce or cream base of a sweet soufflé gives a smoother texture, especially if arrowroot is mixed with the flour and used for thickening, as in the recipe for chocolate soufflé.

Unlike savoury soufflés, a sweet soufflé base is not made on a roux.

Chocolate soufflé

4 oz plain chocolate (cut in small pieces)
2 tablespoons water
½ pint milk
2 rounded tablespoons caster sugar
2–3 drops of vanilla essence
1 tablespoon flour
1 dessertspoon arrowroot
1 oz butter
3 egg yolks
4 egg whites
little sifted icing sugar

7-inch diameter top (size No. 1) soufflé dish

Method
Prepare the soufflé dish. Set oven at 375°F or Mark 5.

Cut up the chocolate into very small pieces, put into a medium-size pan with the water and stir over slow heat until melted. Add the milk, reserving 4 tablespoons.

Bring milk and chocolate to the boil, add sugar and vanilla, cover pan and draw aside.

Blend the reserved milk with the flour and arrowroot, pour this into the chocolate, return to the heat and bring to the boil, stirring all the time. Boil for 2–3 seconds, then draw aside, dot the surface with small pieces of butter, cover and leave for 5 minutes. Then stir to mix in the butter thoroughly and beat in yolks one at a time.

Whip whites to a firm snow, cut and stir 1 tablespoon into the mixture, using a metal spoon, then stir in the rest.

Turn mixture into the prepared soufflé dish and bake in pre-set oven for 20 minutes.

Pull out oven shelf with soufflé on it, dust the top with sifted icing sugar and put soufflé back for 4–5 minutes to caramelise the top. Serve at once.

Orange soufflé

3 oz loaf sugar (about 18 lumps)
2 oranges
½ pint milk
1 rounded tablespoon flour
1 oz butter
3 egg yolks
4 egg whites
little sifted icing sugar

7-inch diameter top (size No. 1) soufflé dish

Method
Prepare soufflé dish. Set oven at 375°F or Mark 5.

Rub some of the lumps of sugar over the outside rind of the oranges until they are soaked with the oil (zest). Then set aside.

Mix 3 tablespoons of the milk with the flour until smooth. Scald remaining milk, add all the sugar lumps and cover. Leave to infuse for 5–7 minutes off the heat. Then return pan to heat. Add the flour mixture gradually and stir until boiling. Boil 2–3 seconds, then draw aside and dot the surface with the butter. Cover and leave for 5 minutes.

Beat in egg yolks, one at a time. Whip whites to a firm snow, stir in 1 tablespoon, then cut and stir in remainder, using a metal spoon. Turn at once into prepared dish and bake in pre-set oven for about 18–20 minutes or until well risen.

Then draw out oven shelf with soufflé on it, dust top quickly with icing sugar and return shelf. Cook for a further 4–5 minutes to caramelise the top. Serve at once.

Lemon soufflé

Make in the same way as for orange soufflé but you will find it is easier to grate the lemon rind with a fine grater than to rub the sugar lumps over the rind. Infuse the grated rind and sugar with the milk and continue as for previous recipe.

ROULADES

With another type of soufflé, known as a roulade, the mixture is cooked on a baking sheet with a raised edge, or a swiss roll tin. It is then turned out, spread with a contrasting filling and rolled up as for a swiss roll.

HOW TO MAKE A PAPER CASE FOR A ROULADE

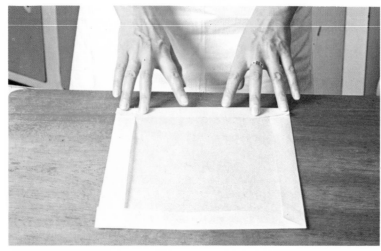

Use thick greaseproof paper or non-stick (silicone) paper. Fold a 1½-inch border on each side, crease into place

Cut a slit at each corner and fold one cut piece over the other to mitre the corners

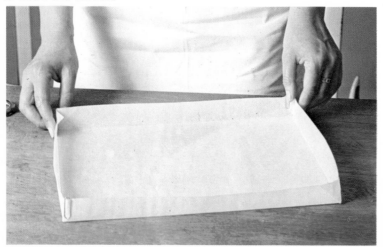

Secure corners with paper clips and slide case on to a baking sheet. Lightly brush greaseproof paper with oil or melted butter before use

Smoked haddock roulade

8 oz (2 cups) smoked haddock (cooked and flaked)
4 eggs
3 rounded tablespoons dry cheese (grated)

For filling

béchamel sauce made with 1½ oz butter, 2½ tablespoons flour, ¾ pint flavoured (see mushroom soufflé, page 161), or plain, milk

salt and pepper
1 dessertspoon anchovy essence
3 eggs (hard-boiled and finely chopped)

Swiss roll tin (12 inches by 8 inches), or baking sheet with a raised edge

Tunny fish, canned or fresh salmon or crab meat may be used in this dish.

Method

First prepare the filling: make béchamel sauce, season and add anchovy essence. The sauce should be creamy and thick enough just to drop from the spoon.

Take 3 tablespoons of sauce and add to the cooked fish. Add the chopped eggs to the remaining sauce; cover and set aside but keep warm.

Grease tin or baking sheet well. Line with greaseproof paper and grease again. Set oven at 400°F or Mark 6.

Separate eggs and beat yolks into the fish with one-third of the cheese. Whip whites to a firm snow and cut and fold into fish mixture, with a metal spoon.

Put on to the tin and spread evenly. Bake on top shelf of pre-set oven for 10–15 minutes or until well risen and firm to the touch.

Have ready a large sheet of greaseproof paper, sprinkled with the remaining cheese. Quickly turn the roulade on to this, strip off the paper it was cooked on and spread roulade with the filling. Trim off sides, then tilt paper and roll up mixture in the same way as for a swiss roll (see photograph, far right). Put on to a hot serving dish and sprinkle with additional cheese, if wished.

Opposite below: finished smoked haddock roulade, sprinkled with cheese

Smoked haddock roulade: prepare fish, filling and sauce, mix a little of the sauce with the fish and then beat in the yolks and the cheese

Having stirred egg whites into fish mixture, spread evenly over the case set on a greased baking sheet. Bake in the oven until firm

Turn cooked roulade on to greaseproof paper sprinkled with cheese; spread filling over roulade, trim sides, tilt paper and roll up

COLD SOUFFLES AND MOUSSES

Cucumber and cheese mousse garnished with watercress

Cucumber and cheese mousse

1 large cucumber
6 oz curd, or cream, cheese
1 teaspoon onion juice (from finely grated onion)
salt and white pepper
¼ pint boiling water, or vegetable, or chicken, stock
½ oz gelatine (soaked in 3 tablespoons cold water)
2 tablespoons white wine vinegar
1 tablespoon caster sugar
pinch of ground mace, or coriander
¼ pint double cream (lightly whipped)

For garnish

1 bunch of watercress
1 large green pepper
¼ pint French dressing

Ring mould (1½–2 pints capacity)

Method

First oil the ring mould. Dice the cucumber very finely, sprinkle with salt and leave it pressed between two plates for 30 minutes. Work the cheese with onion juice and seasoning. Pour boiling water (or stock) on to soaked gelatine, stir until it is dissolved, then add it to cheese.

Drain the diced cucumber thoroughly and mix it with vinegar, sugar and spice. When the cheese mixture is quite cold, fold in the cucumber and the cream. Pour into the prepared mould and leave to set.

Wash and pick over the watercress. Chop the green pepper, blanch in boiling water and refresh it.

Turn out the mousse. Fill the centre with watercress. Add the prepared green pepper to the French dressing and serve this separately with brown bread and butter.

Tongue mousse

½ lb ox tongue (cooked)
2 oz ham (cooked)
½ pint béchamel sauce (made with ¾ oz butter, ¾ oz flour, ½ pint flavoured milk)
¼ pint mayonnaise
½ oz gelatine (dissolved in 5 tablespoons stock)
3 tablespoons double cream (lightly whipped)
1 egg white (stiffly whisked)

For garnish

4 tomatoes
4 oz French beans
½ cucumber
8 black olives
4 tablespoons French dressing

6-inch diameter top (No. 2 size) soufflé dish

Method

Oil the soufflé dish. Mince the tongue and ham. Prepare béchamel sauce in usual way and leave to cool. When sauce is cold, beat it into the meat, add mayonnaise and dissolved gelatine. Fold cream into mixture, then fold in whisked egg white (the latter improves texture of tongue mousse because meat is close-textured).

Turn mousse into oiled dish and leave it to set.

Meanwhile, prepare garnish: scald, skin and quarter tomatoes. Cut the beans into large diamonds and boil until tender; drain and refresh. Peel and shred cucumber and stone the olives. Mix them all together and moisten with French dressing. Turn out mousse, and garnish.

Crab mousse

1 lb crab meat (½ white, ½ dark)
½ pint velouté sauce (made with 1 oz butter, 1 oz flour, ½ pint court bouillon, or light chicken stock)
½ oz gelatine
2½ fl oz white wine
½ pint mayonnaise
¼ pint double cream (lightly whipped)

For garnish

1 cucumber
4 tablespoons French dressing

½ teaspoon paprika pepper
Tabasco sauce

*7-inch diameter top (No. 1 size)
soufflé dish, or cake tin*

Method

Oil the dish or tin. Prepare the velouté sauce, work in the dark crab meat and leave to cool. Soak the gelatine in wine, dissolve it over heat and then stir it into velouté sauce with the mayonnaise. Fold the · flaked white crab meat into the mixture with the cream. Turn mousse into the prepared dish or tin and leave it to set.

Meanwhile, slice the cucumber, and dégorge. Flavour the French dressing with paprika and a good dash of Tabasco and mix with cucumber. Turn mousse on to a serving dish and spoon cucumber over it.

Smoked haddock mousse

8 oz smoked haddock (weighed when cooked and flaked — allow 1 lb on the bone, or ¾ lb fillet)
2 eggs (hard-boiled)
½ pint cold béchamel sauce
¼ pint mayonnaise
½ oz gelatine
2½ fl oz chicken stock, or water
2½ fl oz double cream (lightly whipped)

To finish
2 eggs (hard-boiled)
½–¾ pint aspic jelly

*6-inch diameter top (No. 2 size)
soufflé dish*

Method

Have the haddock ready-cooked and flaked and the eggs chopped. Mix the béchamel sauce and mayonnaise together. Soak the gelatine in the stock (or water), dissolve it over gentle heat and add to the sauce mixture. Stir in the haddock and eggs and, as the mixture begins to thicken, fold in the cream. Turn into the soufflé dish until about three-quarters full, cover mousse and leave it to set in a cool place.

When set, decorate the top with thin slices of hard-boiled

eggs and enough cool aspic to cover; leave to set. Fill the dish with more aspic and leave again to set before serving the mousse.

Salmon mousse Nantua

8 oz cooked salmon (free from skin and bone)
½ pint cold béchamel sauce
¼ pint mayonnaise
salt and pepper
scant ½ oz gelatine (dissolved in 2–3 tablespoons light stock, or water)
1 small carton (about 3 fl oz) double cream (lightly whipped)
2 oz prawns, or shrimps (coarsely chopped)

To finish
2 fl oz thick mayonnaise
tomato juice
Tabasco sauce
1 egg (hard-boiled)
watercress
extra prawns (optional)

6–7 inch diameter top (No. 1 or 2 size) soufflé dish, or cake tin

Method

Lightly oil the dish or tin. Pound or work the salmon until smooth. Add the béchamel sauce and mayonnaise to salmon, a little at a time. Season, fold in the dissolved gelatine, cream and prawns.

Turn mousse at once into the prepared mould and leave to set. Turn out, coat with mayonnaise, lightened with a little tomato juice and seasoned with Tabasco sauce.

To garnish: sieve the yolk and shred the white of the hard-boiled egg and sieve over the mousse; arrange sprigs of watercress and extra prawns round it.

Tongue soufflé

½ lb ox tongue (cooked)
¼ pint béchamel sauce
¼ pint mayonnaise
½ oz gelatine (dissolved in 2½ fl oz aspic jelly)
3 tablespoons double cream (lightly whipped)
2 egg whites (stiffly whisked)

To finish
¼ pint aspic jelly
1 tomato (skinned and cut in very thin slices)
green salad (optional)

6-inch diameter top (No. 2 size) soufflé dish

Method

Prepare dish. Mince the tongue. Prepare the béchamel sauce and leave to cool. When sauce is cold, beat it into the meat, add the mayonnaise and dissolved gelatine in aspic. Fold cream into the mixture. Lastly fold in the whisked egg whites. Turn mixture into the prepared dish and leave to set. Cover with a thin layer of cool aspic, decorate with the slices of tomato. Baste again with more aspic and return to refrigerator to set (about 10–15 minutes). Meanwhile prepare salad. When the soufflé is set, remove paper and serve.

Ham soufflé

8 oz lean ham (cooked)
1 teaspoon tomato purée
1 tablespoon sherry
5 fl oz aspic jelly
½ oz gelatine
¼ pint béchamel sauce
salt and pepper
¼ pint double cream (lightly whipped)
2 egg whites (stiffly whisked)

To finish
¼ pint aspic jelly
1 cucumber (thinly sliced)

5½-inch diameter top (No. 3 size) soufflé dish

Method

Prepare dish. Mince ham twice, pound with tomato purée and sherry and rub it through a wire sieve. Dissolve the gelatine in the aspic jelly and add to the sieved ham with the béchamel sauce, seasoning and cream. As the mixture begins to thicken, fold in the whisked egg whites and pour at once into the prepared dish. When soufflé is set cover with a thin layer of aspic jelly, decorate with the cucumber and cover with more aspic. Remove paper before serving.

> **The cream** added to cold soufflés and mousses is always lightly beaten, so that when a little is lifted on the whisk or fork it leaves a trail across the remaining cream. This gives both soufflés and mousses a spongy texture.

SWEET DISHES

Strawberry mousse

2 eggs
1 egg yolk
3 oz caster sugar
¼ pint double cream
juice of ½ lemon (made up to
  2½ fl oz with water)
½ oz gelatine
good ¼ pint strawberry purée
  (made from ½ lb strawberries)

For decoration

extra cream
pistachio nuts, or browned
  almonds (finely chopped)

*6-inch diameter top (No. 2 size)
souffle dish, or ring mould (1½
pints capacity)*

Method
Oil the dish or mould. Put the eggs, yolk and sugar in a bowl and whisk over gentle heat, at high speed, or until thick and mousse-like. Lightly whip the cream and dissolve the gelatine in the lemon juice and water over gentle heat. Add the strawberry purée, gelatine and cream to the mousse and stir it over a bowl containing ice cubes until it is thickening creamily. Pour mousse into the prepared dish or mould and leave in a cool place to set. Turn out of the dish or mould. Decorate with rosettes of cream and nuts.

Bramble mousse

1 lb blackberries
2 tablespoons caster sugar
3 eggs
3 oz caster sugar
½ oz gelatine
juice of ½ lemon
2 tablespoons water
¼ pint double cream

To decorate

3–4 fl oz double cream
caster sugar (to sweeten)

Method
Pick over the blackberries, put them in a saucepan with the caster sugar and stew gently until soft and pulpy. Rub them through a nylon strainer and leave to cool.

Whisk the eggs and sugar together in a basin over hot water (if using an electric beater, no heat is necessary). Continue beating until the bowl is cold.

Watchpoint The mixture must be so thick that when a little is lifted on the whisk it should remain in a thick ribbon or rope on itself for 1 minute.

Soak the gelatine in the lemon juice and water, then dissolve it over gentle heat.

Lightly whip the cream until it is exactly the same consistency as the egg and sugar mixture. To the egg mixture add 6 fl oz of the blackberry purée, the gelatine and cream and fold together quickly but lightly. Stir the mixture over ice until it begins to thicken, then pour it quickly into a glass bowl; cover and leave for 1–2 hours in a cool place to set. Just before serving, spoon the remaining purée over the top of the mousse.

To decorate: whip and sweeten the extra cream and pipe it in a lattice over the top.

Caramel mousse

6 oz lump, or granulated, sugar
¼ pint water
2 egg yolks
3 eggs
2 oz caster sugar
¼ pint double cream
scant ½ oz gelatine
juice of 1 lemon

Ring mould (1½ pints capacity)

Method
Lightly oil the mould. Put the lump sugar and half the water into a heavy pan and, when dissolved, cook steadily to a rich brown caramel. Use a cloth to cover the hand holding the saucepan (to avoid splashes) and add the rest of the cold water. Stir until caramel is melted, pour into a bowl and leave it to cool. Whisk the egg yolks and whole eggs with caster sugar over gentle heat until very thick and mousse-like (or use an electric mixer without heat). Remove from heat and whisk until quite cold.

Lightly whip half the cream, add to the mousse with the caramel and set the bowl in a second one containing water and ice cubes.

Make the lemon juice up to 2½ fl oz with water, if necessary, dissolve the gelatine in this over heat. Stir gelatine liquid into the mousse until the mixture begins to thicken, then pour into the mould and leave mousse in a cool place to set.

Turn out the mousse and decorate with the remaining cream. The centre may be filled with fresh raspberries or strawberries when in season.

There is another type of mousse, set with egg whites but no gelatine, which is very rich to eat. The following recipe for this kind of mousse comes from the Basque district of France.

Apricot mousse Basque

½ lb dried apricots (soaked
  overnight)
pared rind and juice of ½ lemon
sugar (to taste)
3–4 egg whites
thin squares of chocolate or
  nougat

Method
Stew the apricots in the soaking liquid, with the lemon rind and juice, until very tender (for about 30 minutes), then add sugar to taste and cook for a further 5–10 minutes. Rub apricots through a sieve, or purée them in a blender; leave to cool.

Whip the egg whites until stiff, add to the apricot purée, a little at a time, and continue whisking until stiff. Pile in a serving dish and surround with chocolate (or nougat).

Apricot soufflé

4 eggs (separated)
2 oz caster sugar
½ pint apricot purée (made from
  canned, or cooked fresh, or
  dried, apricots)
½ oz gelatine
5 tablespoons water if using
  fresh, or dried, apricots (or
  juice of ½ lemon and water to
  make 5 tablespoons, if using
  canned apricots)
¼ pint double cream

For decoration

2½ fl oz double cream
pistachio nuts (chopped)

*6-inch diameter top (No. 2 size)
soufflé dish*

Method
Prepare the soufflé dish. Put the egg yolks, sugar and apricot

purée in a basin over a pan of hot water and whisk until the mixture has thickened a little. Remove basin from pan and continue whisking until bowl is cool, and whisk leaves a trail. If using an electric beater, no heat is necessary.

Soak gelatine in lemon juice and water and dissolve it over gentle heat. Whip cream until it just begins to thicken and leaves a trail on itself, then fold this into soufflé mixture; add gelatine liquid. Whisk egg whites until stiff but not dry.

Stand bowl of soufflé mixture in a second bowl of cold water containing a few ice cubes, add egg whites and cut and fold in very carefully. Stir the mixture until it begins to thicken, then pour it at once into the prepared dish. Put soufflé in a cool place to set.

To serve: whip cream until thick, sweeten it very lightly, then continue beating until it is stiff. Put cream in a forcing bag fitted with an 8-cut rose pipe. Remove paper from soufflé and decorate top with rosettes of cream and pistachio nuts.

Soufflé moka praline

For praline
2 oz almonds (unblanched)
2 oz caster sugar

4 eggs (separated)
4 oz caster sugar
2 dessertspoons instant coffee (dissolved in 6 tablespoons boiling water)
½ pint double cream
½ oz gelatine
5 tablespoons cold water

6-inch diameter top (No. 2 size) soufflé dish

Method
First prepare the praline: place the almonds and sugar in a small heavy saucepan and dissolve sugar over gentle heat. As the sugar turns brown, stir the mixture carefully until the almonds are toasted on all sides. Turn mixture on to an oiled tin, slab or plate. When cold, crush praline with a rolling pin or pass through a nut mill or mincer.

Prepare the soufflé dish. Place egg yolks, sugar and dissolved coffee in a basin and whisk over heat until thick and

Soufflé moka praline, decorated with crushed praline and cream

mousse-like (or use electric beater without heat). Remove soufflé mixture from the heat and continue whisking until the bowl is cold.

Lightly whip the cream and fold about two-thirds into the mixture. Soak the gelatine in the water and then dissolve it over heat; add this to the

mixture. Whisk the egg whites until stiff and fold into the soufflé with 2 oz of the praline. Stir it carefully until it begins to thicken, then turn into the prepared dish and leave to set.

When soufflé is set, remove the paper and decorate the top with the remaining whipped cream and the praline.

Whisking egg yolks, sugar and coffee together until thick

Piping whipped cream round the top of soufflé moka praline

Rice and Pasta Dishes

RICE

Rice is the most versatile of cereals and perhaps the most popular. It lends itself to many recipes both sweet and savoury, and is ideal for a quick, nourishing dish. There are several different types, which can be divided into three main categories: long grain, medium grain and short, or thick, grain. Each type of grain carries a name, such as Patna or Carolina, which once used to indicate from where it came. These types, however, are now grown in many countries.

Processed, or partly-cooked, rice is sold under brand names; it can also be bought flavoured. These rices are good but more expensive than the ordinary kinds.

USES OF RICE

Brown rice (long grain type, husked only): has a nutty flavour and more chewy texture than white rice, but has the disadvantage of smelling while cooking.

White rice has less nutritive value because it has been milled, a process removing the hulls, germ and vitamin-filled bran layers. Polished rice is treated with coatings or polishing powders after milling.

Busmatti (thin, short grain): has similar qualities to the Patna type; used in pilafs when a dry, flaky rice is called for.

Carolina (medium grain): for sweet dishes and puddings.

Crème de riz, finer still, is used for thickening soups, sauces or puddings, and for some biscuits, macaroons, etc.

Ground rice is used for puddings.

Italian (white, short grain): used in dishes where the maximum amount of liquid must be absorbed, eg. in rice creams and risottos.

Patna (long grain): for pilafs, curries, salads and wherever boiled rice is called for.

Rice flour, which is fine in texture, is used for cakes, buns and rice creams.

Spanish, Jap or Java (short, or thick, grain): can be used for puddings instead of Carolina rice; also used for risottos.

Wild rice: the seeds of a wild aquatic grass; very expensive and needs long boiling; is often served with game.

TO BOIL RICE

Most people have their own favourite method of boiling rice. That recommended by Asians is to cook the rice in a small quantity of boiling water until this is absorbed, when rice is soft. The amount of water varies according to the quality of the rice. This method is good but can present problems. Really the simplest way is to cook the rice (2 oz washed rice per person) in plenty of boiling, well-salted water (3 quarts per 8 oz rice) for about 12 minutes. You can add a slice of lemon for flavour. Stir with a fork to prevent rice sticking while boiling, and watch that it does not overcook.

To stop rice cooking, either tip it quickly into a colander and drain, or pour ½ cup cold water into the pan and then drain. Pour over a jug of hot water to wash away the remaining starch, making several holes through the rice with the handle of a wooden spoon to help it drain more quickly.

To reheat: spoon into a buttered ovenproof dish, cover with buttered paper, put in oven at 350°F or Mark 4 for 30 minutes.

With a pilaf, the rice is cooked in stock until it has been absorbed and the rice is dry and flaky. Though this can be done over a flame, it is best to put the pan or casserole in the oven to get both top and bottom heat.

Rice pudding

1 pint creamy milk
1 tablespoon (¾ oz) thick grain rice
2 tablespoons cold water
½ oz butter
1 dessertspoon sugar
pinch of nutmeg (optional)

Pie dish (1½ pints capacity)

Barley and sago puddings are cooked the same way.

Method
Wash the rice and put in the bottom of the pie dish. Add the cold water and leave it to soak for 1 hour. Set oven at 300°F or Mark 2. Drain any water off the rice and pour on the milk. Add butter, sugar and nutmeg. Cook in the pre-set slow oven for 2½–3 hours. After the first hour, or when a skin just begins to form, stir with a fork. Then leave without stirring until the skin is golden-brown and the rice and milk thick and creamy. If the pudding is still sloppy 30–40 minutes before it is to be eaten, raise the oven temperature to 325°F or Mark 3. Serve hot or cold.

If you intend to serve the pudding cold, take it out of the oven when it is still lightly creamy, as it will become stiffer on cooling.

Made with ribbon noodles, ham and tomato purée, tagliatelle al prosciutto is a tasty pasta dish (see page 173)

Pilaf (basic recipe)

6 oz long grain rice
2 oz butter
1 onion (thinly sliced, or chopped)
pinch of saffron (soaked in 2 tablespoons hot water for 30 minutes)
¾–1 pint stock
salt and pepper
1–2 oz dry cheese (grated)

Method

Heat a shallow saucepan or flameproof casserole. Add three-quarters of the butter, put in the onion, cook gently for 5 minutes, then add the rice and continue to cook gently for 2–3 minutes. Season well, pour on saffron liquid and about three-quarters of stock. Bring rice to boil, cover pan and put in oven at 350°F or Mark 4 for 15 minutes. Add a little more stock, if necessary, and cook for a further 5–7 minutes, when all stock should be absorbed and the rice tender.

Dot the surface of the rice with the rest of the butter and sprinkle with the cheese. Cover and leave on the top of the stove (not on heat), or in warming drawer, to keep warm. Stir rice lightly with a fork before turning into the serving dish.

Pilafs can be plain, with no additional flavouring other than a little onion, or have various ingredients added. A plain pilaf is best substituted for potatoes for accompanying any meat or chicken dishes, or it can be mixed with any leftovers of chicken, ham or fish.

Shredded ham, cooked chicken, raw chicken livers, etc. can also be added to the pilaf (when rice is added to onion).

A pilaf will keep hot satisfactorily for up to 30 minutes if covered and left on top of stove.

Seafood pilaf

2 pints mussels
1 wineglass white wine
¾ pint water
bouquet garni (containing 1 stick of celery)
6 peppercorns
4 oz mushrooms
4 oz prawns, or shrimps (shelled)
1½ oz butter
pinch of ground mace
½ lb scampi

For pilaf
8 oz long grain rice
2 oz butter
1 medium-size onion (finely sliced)
1 pint chicken stock
salt and pepper

Method

Wash the mussels well, scrub them and remove any weed. Place in a large pan with the wine, water, bouquet garni, and peppercorns. Cover the pan, bring it slowly to the boil, then shake over the heat for 5 minutes. Remove mussels from shells and keep on one side.

Watchpoint Tip the liquid from the pan through a strainer lined with a piece of muslin (or even a coffee filter paper). This is to keep back any sand in the mussel liquor. Mix strained liquor with the chicken stock for the pilaf.

Set the oven at 375°F or Mark 5.

To prepare the pilaf: melt two-thirds of the butter in a flameproof casserole, add the onion and cook slowly until it is soft but not coloured. Add the rice, sauté for 2–3 minutes, then add 1¼ pints of the mixed stock and mussel liquor and bring it to the boil. Taste before adding seasoning as the mussel liquor is sometimes salty enough. Place the casserole, covered, in the pre-set oven for about 20 minutes, adding extra stock, if necessary, after 15 minutes.

Meanwhile wash and trim the mushrooms and sauté quickly in 1 oz butter for 1 minute only. Add the prawns (or shrimps) and a tiny pinch of ground mace to the mushrooms and toss together for a further minute. Put the scampi in the same pan, dot with remaining ½ oz butter, cover the pan and keep warm at the side of the stove until wanted.

When the rice for the pilaf is tender, stir in the remaining butter with a fork, then add the mussels and other shellfish.

Serve pilaf with green salad on individual plates; or with peas or French beans.

Risotto

The difference between a risotto and a pilaf is that where the latter is dry and flaky when cooked, a risotto is creamy and should spread a little on the plate when served.

The secret of a good risotto is to use a thick grain rice (for perfection the Italian rice already mentioned) and well-flavoured chicken or veal stock. Each kind of risotto takes its name from the town or area in Italy from which it originated.

A risotto is best cooked on the top of the stove, with the stock added gradually as the rice thickens. It is this gradual addition as the grain swells, together with the amount of butter used, that gives the soft creamy consistency. Grated Parmesan cheese may either be stirred into the risotto just before serving or sprinkled over it at the table.

Watchpoint Do not wash rice for a risotto, pick it over carefully to remove any unhusked grains. When cooked, the rice grains should be nicely firm, not mushy in any way.

When cooked, risotto keeps hot satisfactorily if kept covered and left on top of the stove (but not on the heat) for up to 30 minutes.

Risotto milanese

8 oz thick grain rice (preferably Italian)
1 marrow bone (optional)
2 oz butter
1 small onion (finely chopped)
1 clove of garlic (chopped, or crushed, with ½ teaspoon salt)
1 pinch of saffron (soaked in 2 tablespoons hot water) – optional
salt and pepper
about 1¼ pints chicken, or veal, stock
2–3 tablespoons Parmesan cheese (grated)

Sliced mushrooms (2–3 oz) are sometimes added to this risotto with the onion. For special occasions, use a glass of white wine in place of the same amount of stock.

The quantity of rice given here is enough for a main course for four people. For a first course, 5–6 oz of rice is sufficient, with the remaining ingredients in proportion.

Method

Scoop out marrow from the bone and cut in small pieces. Melt a good half of the butter in a shallow pan or flameproof casserole, add marrow, onion

and garlic. Fry gently for 4–5 minutes, add rice and continue to fry, stirring continually until all the grains look white – 4–5 minutes.

Then add saffron in its liquid and about a third of the stock. Season and simmer, stirring occasionally until the rice thickens, then add another third of the stock. Continue in this way until the grains are barely tender and the risotto creamy.

Draw pan aside, dot the surface with the remaining butter and sprinkle with 1–2 tablespoons of Parmesan cheese. Cover rice and leave for 5 minutes, or until ready to serve. Stir once or twice with a fork, then turn into a hot dish. Avoid touching with a spoon as this makes it mushy.

Note: bone marrow is characteristic of a risotto milanese but both it and the saffron may be omitted. If more convenient, the marrow bone may be boiled before scooping out the marrow, which is then added to the risotto towards the end of cooking. In either case the bone can be used for stock.

Risotto bolognese (with chicken liver and mushroom)

8 oz thick grain rice
2 oz butter
6 oz chicken livers
1 small onion (chopped)
2 cloves of garlic (chopped)

The finished risotto bolognese garnished with chopped parsley

4 oz flat mushrooms (sliced)
1 tablespoon tomato purée
salt and pepper
1¼ pints chicken stock
1–2 tablespoons Parmesan cheese (grated)

Method
Melt two-thirds of the butter in a shallow pan or flameproof casserole, add the livers and sauté them briskly until just coloured. Take out chicken livers, add the onion and garlic and fry them slowly. Slice the livers and set them aside.

Add mushrooms to the pan and, after a few minutes, the rice; fry for 4–5 minutes, then stir in tomato purée. Season, put in livers and add the stock gradually as for risotto milanese. Continue to cook rice and complete – in the same way as for milanese – with remaining butter and Parmesan cheese.

Paella

6 oz long grain rice
4 tablespoons olive oil
2–3 joints chicken, or rabbit (according to size)
1 onion (sliced)
1 clove of garlic (crushed with salt, or chopped)
4 oz gammon rasher (unsmoked and cut in strips)
½ lb firm white fish (halibut, or rock salmon, or cod) – skinned

and cut in large squares
1 pint mussels
½ pint prawns
2–3 caps of canned pimento (shredded)
1 cup peas (cooked), or small packet of frozen peas
1 large pinch of saffron (soaked in 2–3 tablespoons hot water)
1¼ pints stock, or water
salt and pepper

Anyone who has visited Spain will recognise this dish, and for those who have never sampled it, it is well worth trying. In Spain paella is both cooked and served in a special two-handled iron frying pan (paella) from which the dish gets the name. Here one can improvise with a large, deep frying pan, or sauté pan, or shallow flameproof casserole.

Paella is a colourful dish and the ingredients can be varied at will. For example, cooked chicken can be used or the mussels can be omitted, but the flavour and appearance will not be so good.

Method
Heat oil in a large frying pan, put in the pieces of chicken (or rabbit) and fry gently until they are coloured. Take out meat and add the onion and garlic to pan. Fry for a few minutes, then add the bacon and the rice. Fry rice, stirring continually, until it turns white. Then draw pan aside.

Have the fish ready, the mussels well scrubbed, the pimento and the prawns – leave the heads on a few and set these aside. Arrange all these ingredients (except the reserved prawns) on the rice with the peas and the pieces of chicken (or rabbit) – these can be cut in half if too large.

Tuck the mussels well down in the pan and put the reserved prawns on the top. Add saffron and its liquid to the stock, pour this over the ingredients, season, cover with foil and a lid. Simmer rice gently on top of stove or put into the oven at 350°F or Mark 4 for 20–25 minutes, when all the ingredients should be cooked and the rice tender. Do not lift the lid during the cooking time. Serve very hot.

Watchpoint If your pan is thin, it is advisable to cook the paella in the oven otherwise the rice may stick to the bottom.

PASTA

Pasta is an Italian word meaning literally a paste of flour and water. Spaghetti, macaroni and other different shapes made of semolina, or flour, water and sometimes eggs, are all pasta. Pasta is also made in small shapes, shells, bows, stars and so on. The larger shapes are good with chicken or veal dishes instead of potato. The smaller shapes are used in clear and broth soups. Usually pasta is served with a sauce either mixed in with it, or as an accompaniment. The preliminary cooking is always the same—gentle simmering in salted water or stock until barely tender (10–20 minutes). To test: try a piece between your teeth, it should be just firm (or if you can sever it with your thumb nail it is done). Strain off at once and rinse with 1–2 cups of hot water. Tip back into the saucepan and the pasta is then ready to use. To prevent it becoming sticky if it has to be kept for a little while before finishing off, pour hot water into the pan just to cover the bottom before putting back the pasta; cover pan and leave in a warm place. Just before serving the pasta, toss it with a nut of butter.

Ravioli

This consists of little rounds or squares of pasta filled with a savoury mince or a mixture of spinach and curd cheese. Ravioli can be bought in some Italian provision shops or delicatessens freshly made and ready for cooking. Simmer in stock or water for 15–20 minutes, drain and cover ravioli with a good tomato sauce; continue to simmer gently until golden. Serve well dusted with grated cheese.

To make ravioli at home, use the following recipe.

Ravioli paste

10 oz plain flour
½ teaspoon salt
1½ tablespoons olive oil
2 eggs (beaten)
3–4 tablespoons milk, or water

Method
Sift the flour with salt on to a laminated plastic work top or board, make a well in the centre and put in the oil, eggs and half the milk or water.

Start mixing in the oil, eggs and water gradually, drawing in the flour, add the rest of the liquid as it is needed. Continue to work up the paste until it is smooth and firm, knead well, then cover with a cloth and leave for 20–30 minutes to get rid of any elasticity. Cut in half and roll out one piece, paper thin. Slide to one side, then roll out the second piece as thinly, brush with water and put out the chosen filling in teaspoons at regular intervals on the pastry. Lift the first piece on top and with a small ball of the paste press down the top piece around each mound of filling. Stamp out each one with a small fluted cutter or cut out in squares with a pastry wheel. Leave for 2–3 hours to dry a little, then cook as described.

Spinach and curd cheese filling

1 small packet of frozen spinach purée, or ½–¾ lb fresh spinach
2 oz curd, or cream, cheese
salt and pepper
small pinch of ground mace, or grated nutmeg

Method
If using frozen spinach, put into a pan and cook gently, stirring occasionally until firm. If fresh, boil, drain and dry; sieve to a purée or chop very finely. Sieve cheese and mix in the spinach when cold. Season well and add spice. The mixture should be a firm purée.

Savoury meat filling

1 cup cooked chicken, or ham (minced)
2 tablespoons thick béchamel, or tomato sauce (sufficient to bind the meat)
3 teaspoons mixed herbs, or parsley (chopped)
1 egg yolk

Method
Mix ingredients together and season well. The mixture must be firm and quite stiff.

Cannelloni

1 packet cannelloni (about ½ lb) – allow 3–4 tubes per person
¾ pint thin tomato sauce
grated Parmesan cheese

For filling
½ lb raw veal, or pork (minced), or a mixture of both
¼ pint béchamel sauce (made with 1 oz butter, 1 oz flour, ¼ pint of milk)
1 egg yolk
salt and pepper
pinch of ground mace, or grated nutmeg

These are fat tubes of pasta about 2½ inches long. They are partially cooked then filled with a mince of chicken or veal or spinach and curd cheese as for ravioli (in which case the quantities should be increased).

Method
First prepare filling. Make the béchamel sauce and leave to get quite cold before adding

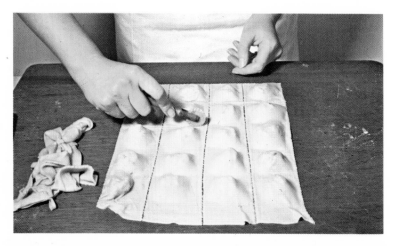

Cutting filled ravioli into squares with a pastry wheel

to the mince. Mix thoroughly, then add yolk and seasoning. The consistency must be quite stiff. Set filling aside.

Simmer the cannelloni in plenty of boiling salted water for about 7 minutes, then lift out carefully, dip into cold water, drain on cloth or absorbent paper.

Put filling into a forcing bag with large, plain pipe, then pipe into the cannelloni. Put them in a well-buttered flameproof casserole and pour over the tomato sauce (this should just cover). Bring to boiling point on top of stove, then cover and cook in the oven at 350°F or Mark 4 for 40–45 minutes. Ten minutes before end of cooking time, take off lid, sprinkle well with the cheese, increase the heat of oven to 375°F or Mark 5 and brown the surface.

If preferred, the cannelloni may be served without browning, just sprinkle well with the cheese before taking to table.

Spaghetti

In Italian shops or in delicatessens spaghetti can be bought in various grades ie., degrees of thickness. Naturally the thicker the spaghetti is the longer it will take to cook. Very thin spaghetti is known as vermicelli. This, though it can make a dish on its own, is really best added to a broth, or crushed and used as a coating for a rissole.

Cook spaghetti in plenty of boiling salted water. Stir once with a wooden fork or spoon. Simmer until tender, allowing 12–15 minutes cooking time, then drain in a colander. Pour over 1–2 cups of hot water, drain again well and then return spaghetti to the pan with 1 tablespoon of oil, or ½ oz butter and seasoned with salt and pepper ground from the mill. It is then ready to be mixed with the chosen sauce or served plain, with the sauce spooned over the top.

Spaghetti al sugo

This is an Italian dish and is entirely different from what we know as spaghetti with tomato sauce. The sauce (see overleaf) is spicy and very thick.

Cook spaghetti and drain well, then add the sauce and mix well with two forks. There should be just enough to coat the spaghetti.

Shake over heat until thoroughly hot, then dish up.

Spaghetti is also good with bolognese, milanese or napolitana sauces (see overleaf).

Tagliatelle

This is the ribbon pasta, also called 'nouilles' or noodles. It can be bought in varying widths though the most usual is about ¼ inch wide. Tagliatelle is also sold flavoured and coloured with spinach or tomato. Cook as for other pastas, allowing 10–12 minutes boiling time until slightly firm, like spaghetti.

Serve with bolognese, milanese or napolitana sauces and grated Parmesan cheese separately.

Home-made tagliatelle

12 oz plain flour
½ teaspoon salt
3 eggs, or 2 eggs and 2½ fl oz milk

Method

Sift flour on to a board, or slab, with the salt, make a well in the centre and break the eggs into this. Start to draw the flour into the centre, working the eggs and flour together with the fingers of one hand, working in the milk by degrees. When you have a firm dough, knead it thoroughly until very smooth. Cover and leave for about 1 hour, when the dough will have lost some of its elasticity.

Divide the dough into 2–3 pieces and roll out as thinly as possible. Lay these on paper over a chair back for 2 hours or longer to dry a little. Then take each piece and roll up. With a sharp knife cut into slices about ½–¾ inch wide. Unroll the strips and put them on a cloth or paper; leave for a further 30 minutes before boiling gently in water or stock, according to the recipe being followed.

For flavoured tagliatelle, add 2–3 rounded tablespoons cooked spinach purée or 2 tablespoons tomato purée.

There should be enough of each to give the dough a good colour. If using milk (instead of the extra egg) cut the amount of milk to less than half to avoid the dough becoming too wet.

Tagliatelle al prosciutto (with ham)

(see photograph on page 169)

8–12 oz tagliatelle
3 oz butter
about ½ lb green gammon bacon (diced)
3–4 sticks of celery (chopped)
1 carrot (chopped)
1–2 cloves of garlic (chopped)
1 rounded tablespoon tomato conserve (concentrated purée)
¼ pint jellied veal bone stock
salt and pepper
2 tablespoons grated Parmesan cheese

Method

Boil tagliatelle gently for 10–12 minutes, then drain and rinse. To keep it warm, pour hot water into the pan just to cover the bottom before putting back the tagliatelle; cover pan and leave in a warm place.

Melt two-thirds of the butter in a shallow pan, put in the bacon and fry gently for 3–4 minutes. Then add the vegetables and garlic, cover and cook for 4–5 minutes. Stir in the tomato conserve and stock. Season and continue to cook, uncovered, a further 5 minutes until syrupy.

Drain the tagliatelle and add the remaining butter, season and shake up over the heat until thoroughly hot, then add the cheese and turn on to a serving dish. Spoon the bacon mixture over the pasta.

Tossing hot tagliatelle in butter and cheese before serving

173

Tomato sauce (For pasta 'al sugo')

1 lb tomatoes, or 1 medium-size
   can
1 small onion (sliced)
1 oz butter, or 2 tablespoons oil
1 clove of garlic (chopped)
good pinch of dried mixed herbs
1 wineglass stock, or water
salt and pepper
tomato purée
½ oz butter

This sauce, which is almost a purée, is made without any thickening, but so reduced that it is red-brown in colour and on the point of 'breaking' (curdling). It is this reduction which gives it its characteristic strong and piquant flavour.

Method
Wipe tomatoes, cut in half and squeeze out seeds. Slice and put into a pan with the onion, butter and garlic. Add herbs and stock or water, season well, cover and cook to a pulp. Rub through a strainer, return to the rinsed out pan and add a little tomato purée to strengthen the flavour. Use your own judgment as to the amount, as this depends on the ripeness of the tomatoes. Add butter and boil until thick, stirring frequently.

When tomatoes are plentiful a double quantity can be made (or more) as it will keep for about a week in a covered container in the refrigerator, or can be deep frozen.

Napolitana sauce

1 oz butter, or 2 tablespoons oil
1 medium-size onion (thinly
   sliced)
1 dessertspoon flour
1 wineglass stock
1 lb ripe tomatoes (skinned, the
   stalk cut out and the tomatoes
   lightly squeezed to remove
   seeds)
1 clove of garlic (crushed with
   salt)
1 teaspoon tomato conserve, or
   purée
1 bayleaf
pinch of sugar
salt
pepper (ground from mill)

This tomato sauce is not reduced as much as that in the al sugo recipe, and is rougher in texture. Serve mixed with, or

Spaghetti with bolognese sauce

over, pasta, or if preferred pasta and sauce can all be turned into a gratin dish and browned in the oven.

Method
Melt butter or oil in a shallow saucepan, add onion, fry gently for 3–4 minutes, then stir in flour and add stock. Bring to the boil. Slice tomatoes and add with the garlic, conserve or purée, bayleaf, sugar, salt and pepper.

Simmer for 25–30 minutes or until well reduced to a thick rich pulp. Remove bayleaf. Have the pasta ready, put in a serving dish and spoon over the sauce.

Serve with either spaghetti, macaroni or tagliatelle.

Bolognese sauce

2 tablespoons oil, or 1 oz butter
4 oz chicken livers (approximately 3)
1 medium-size onion (sliced)
1 clove of garlic (chopped)
1 rounded dessertspoon flour
3 teaspoons tomato purée
¼ pint beef stock (or equivalent
   made from beef bouillon cube)
1 tablespoon Marsala, or brown
   sherry
salt and pepper
chopped parsley
Parmesan cheese (grated)

This sauce is best spooned over rather than mixed in with the

174

spaghetti. Cook spaghetti as basic recipe, finish with oil or butter, turn into serving dish and spoon the sauce in a band over the top. Serve grated Parmesan cheese separately. Bolognese sauce should be made with chicken livers but lamb's liver can be substituted although it does not give the same piquant flavour.

Method

Heat oil in shallow saucepan, put in the livers, sauté for 3–4 minutes until 'seized' and nicely brown. Take out, add the onion and garlic, sauté until turning colour, then stir in the flour, add purée, stock and Marsala or sherry. Stir until boiling. Simmer for 10 minutes, then add liver, coarsely chopped.

Continue to simmer until thick and syrupy for a further 7–10 minutes. Adjust seasoning and spoon sauce over the spaghetti. Sprinkle well with chopped parsley.

Milanese sauce

4 oz mushrooms (sliced)
½ oz butter
½ pint strong, well-flavoured tomato sauce
4 oz lean cooked ham (shredded)
8 oz spaghetti

This sauce is excellent to serve with spaghetti or any type of pasta, especially when served as a main course. In this case extra ham and mushrooms can be added as in this recipe. Otherwise, it is only necessary to use 2 oz each of mushrooms and ham to ½ pint tomato sauce.

Method

Sauté mushrooms in the butter for 3–4 minutes, then add the sauce. Simmer for a few minutes, then add the ham. Have ready the spaghetti cooked, well drained and mixed with ½ oz butter. Add the sauce and toss up over heat. Serve with grated Parmesan cheese.

Finished lasagne, showing the layers of meat, pasta and sauce

Lasagne

½ lb dried lasagne paste
2 oz Parmesan cheese (grated)

For meat sauce
1 lb raw minced beef
2 small onions (finely chopped)
2 oz dripping, or oil
2 tablespoons flour
2 rounded teaspoons tomato purée
2 wineglasses white wine
4 wineglasses stock
salt and pepper

For white sauce
2 oz butter
2 rounded tablespoons flour
1 pint creamy milk
salt and pepper

This paste can be bought at Italian stores and specialist delicatessens, or it can be made at home. The basic paste is the same as that used for ravioli (given on page 172) and it can be flavoured with spinach (lasagne verde) or left plain.

Method

First prepare the meat sauce: lightly brown onion in the fat, add mince and continue to fry, stirring frequently, for 5–6 minutes. Then blend in flour, tomato purée, wine and stock. Season, cover and bring to the boil; simmer for 45 minutes to 1 hour or until the meat is tender and the sauce thick. Add more stock, if necessary, during the cooking.

Meanwhile simmer the lasagne in a large pan of salted water, being careful not to overcrowd the pan. When tender (after about 15 minutes), lift out with a draining spoon into a bowl of cold water, then drain again and spread on a damp cloth.

Prepare the white sauce in the usual way.

Well butter an ovenproof dish, spoon a layer of the meat sauce on the bottom and arrange some squares of lasagne over this to cover completely. Continue with a layer of meat sauce, then white sauce, then lasagne. Repeat this until the dish is full and finish with white sauce. Sprinkle the grated Parmesan cheese thickly over the top and brown in a hot oven, pre-set at 375°F or Mark 5, for about 15–20 minutes.

Layering lasagne squares, meat and white sauce into the dish

175

Sauces and Dressings

WHITE SAUCES

There is no mystique about sauce-making; it's just very important to measure the ingredients exactly because if the proportion of flour to liquid is wrong, no amount of cooking will give the right consistency.

A clever sauce can transform a simple dish into something superlative. From the basic 'mother' (mère) sauces – white, béchamel, or velouté – you can make an infinite variety such as cheese, caper, mustard or mushroom. Although you will have learnt how to make some sauces with dishes from earlier chapters, we are repeating, or giving variations of, recipes here to make this section on white sauces complete in itself. We also deal with liaisons in greater detail as these are mainly used for turning gravies and liquids into white and brown sauces.

Points to remember

1 Weight of fat should be slightly more than that of flour to give a soft, semi-liquid roux, which is the foundation of a flour sauce.
2 If roux is hot, liquid should be warm or cold; if roux is cold, liquid must be warm. This makes blending easier and avoids a granular texture.
3 For a béchamel (or white) sauce, melt fat gently (do not let it sizzle), remove from heat and stir in flour (white roux). For a velouté sauce, cook flour in fat over a low heat for a few seconds until it is a pale straw colour (blond roux) before adding liquid.

4 Fats used may be butter, margarine, dripping or oil, according to the type of sauce being made.

Consistencies
The amount of flour to liquid in sauces can vary their consistencies for different uses:
  Flowing. For serving as an accompanying sauce.
Proportions: $\frac{1}{2}$ oz butter and just under $\frac{1}{2}$ oz flour to $\frac{1}{2}$ pint liquid.
  Coating. Slightly thicker consistency for coating fillets of fish, eggs and vegetables.
Proportions: $\frac{3}{4}$ oz butter and just under $\frac{3}{4}$ oz flour to $\frac{1}{2}$ pint liquid.
  Panada. Thick sauce for binding, used as a base for croquettes, fish or meat creams.
Proportions: $1\frac{1}{2}$–2 oz butter and just under $1\frac{1}{2}$–2 oz flour to $\frac{1}{2}$ pint liquid.

Liaisons
Liaisons play an important part in the making of sauces. The word means a binding together and is a term given to certain ingredients which are used to thicken sauces and soups.
There are various ways in which to bind sauces:
1 Kneaded butter (beurre manié) is a liaison mixture of butter and flour in the proportions of almost twice as much butter to flour, worked together on a plate with a fork to make a paste. It is added in small pieces to thicken liquid in which food has been cooked, eg. fish stews and casserole dishes. This is useful when the quantity of liquid remaining in a dish is unknown, making it difficult to know how much flour alone to use for thickening.
  Kneaded butter should be added to hot (but not boiling)

liquids. Shake pan gently and when the butter has dissolved (indicating flour has been absorbed in liquid) reboil. If the liquid is still not thick enough, the process can be repeated.
2 Fécule, ie. arrowroot or potato flour, should be slaked (mixed) with water or milk and stirred into the nearly boiling liquid off the heat. Once added, reboil and draw aside. Used for ragoûts and casseroles as well as brown sauces.
3 Egg yolks and cream. This mixture may be used to thicken and enrich velouté sauces and some cream soups. The yolk or yolks are worked well together with the cream. 2–3 tablespoons of sauce are blended into the mixture, a little at a time, and when well blended, the whole is returned to the main bulk of the sauce and stirred in gradually. Reheat, stirring continually, but do not boil. This will cook the egg yolks slowly and so give a particularly creamy consistency to the sauce.

Note: 1 rounded tablespoon, ie. as much above as below the rim, is equivalent to $\frac{1}{2}$ oz sifted flour. 1 level tablespoon equals $\frac{1}{4}$ oz sifted flour.

Hollandaise sauce, one of the best known butter sauces (see recipe on page 181), is delicious with fresh asparagus

White sauce

¾ oz butter
1 rounded tablespoon flour
½ pint milk
salt and pepper

A white sauce is quick and easy, made in exactly the same way and with same proportions as béchamel, but the milk is not flavoured. It can be used as the base for cheese, onion or other sauces with pronounced flavour, but béchamel is better for mushroom and egg sauces.

Method

Melt the butter in a small pan, remove from heat and stir in the flour. Blend in half the milk, then stir in the rest. Stir this over moderate heat until boiling, then boil gently for 1–2 minutes. Season to taste.

Béchamel sauce

½ pint milk
1 slice of onion
1 small bayleaf
6 peppercorns
1 blade of mace

For roux
¾ oz butter
1 rounded tablespoon flour
salt and pepper

Made on a white roux with flavoured milk added, béchamel can be used as a base for mornay (cheese), soubise (onion), mushroom or egg sauces. Proportions of ingredients may vary in these derivative sauces according to consistency required.

Method

Pour milk into a saucepan, add the flavourings, cover pan and infuse on gentle heat for 5–7 minutes. Strain milk and set it aside. Rinse and wipe out the pan and melt the butter in it. To give a white roux remove from heat before stirring in the flour. The roux must be soft and semi-liquid.

Pour on half of milk through a strainer and blend until smooth using a wooden spoon, then add rest of milk. Season lightly, return to a slow to moderate heat and stir until boiling. Boil for no longer than 2 minutes.
Watchpoint If a flour sauce shows signs of lumps, these can be smoothed out by vigorous stirring or beating with a sauce whisk, provided sauce has not boiled; draw pan aside and stir vigorously. It can then be put back to boil gently for 1–2 minutes before using. If it has boiled and is still lumpy, the only remedy is to strain it.

Egg sauce

2 eggs (hard-boiled and chopped)

For béchamel sauce
¾ oz butter
1 rounded tablespoon flour
½ pint flavoured milk (see basic recipe)
salt and pepper

Serve with boiled fish.

Method

Make the béchamel sauce, then stir in the well-chopped eggs; season well.

Mushroom sauce

2 oz mushrooms (finely chopped)

For béchamel sauce
1 oz butter
1 rounded tablespoon flour
½ pint flavoured milk (see basic recipe)
salt and pepper

Serve with eggs, fish, chicken.

Method

Wash mushrooms, without peeling, and chop them. Have ready the flavoured milk. Cook mushrooms in half the butter for 2–3 minutes until fairly dry. Draw aside, add rest of butter and when melted stir in flour.

Season and blend in the milk. Stir until boiling and cook for 2 minutes.

Oyster, shrimp or lobster sauce is made in the same way, ie. with a base of béchamel. A small tin of any of these shellfish is sufficient for above amount of sauce.

Use either white or béchamel sauce for following 2 recipes.

Mornay (cheese) sauce

1–1½ oz (2–3 rounded table-spoons) grated cheese
½ teaspoon made mustard (French, or English)
½ pint well-seasoned white, or béchamel, sauce

Serve with eggs, fish, chicken and vegetables.

The cheese can be a mixture of Gruyère and Parmesan or a dry Cheddar. If using Gruyère, which thickens sauce, reduce basic roux to ½ oz each butter and flour (1 tablespoon). If too thick, add a little milk.

Method

Make white or béchamel sauce, remove from heat and gradually stir in grated cheese. When well mixed, add mustard. Reheat but do not boil.

Soubise (onion) sauce

2 large onions (sliced)
1 oz butter
1 tablespoon cream (optional)
salt and pepper
½ pint white, or béchamel, sauce (use 1 oz butter to 2 table-spoons flour for roux)

Serve with eggs and white meat (veal or rabbit).

Method

Blanch onion slices by putting in cold water, bringing to the boil and draining. Then melt butter in pan, add onion and cook, covered, until tender but not coloured (a piece of buttered paper or foil pressed down on to onion slices helps prevent colouring). Remove from pan and rub through a nylon strainer or work to a purée in an electric blender.

Add purée to a hot white or béchamel sauce, stir in the cream (if using) and season sauce well.

Velouté sauce

¾ oz butter
1 rounded tablespoon flour
⅓ - ½ pint stock
2½ fl oz top of milk
salt and pepper
squeeze of lemon juice

For liaison (optional)
1 egg yolk (lightly beaten)
2 tablespoons cream

This sauce is made with a blond roux, at which point liquid is added. This is well-flavoured stock (made from veal, chicken or fish bones, according to dish with which sauce is being served), or liquid in which food was simmered or poached.

Velouté sauces are a base for others, such as caper, mustard, parsley, or poulette.

Method

Melt butter in a saucepan, stir in flour and cook for about 5 seconds (blond roux). When roux is colour of pale straw, draw pan aside and cool slightly before pouring on stock.

Blend, return to heat and stir until thick. Add top of milk, season and bring to boil. Cook 4–5 minutes when sauce should be a syrupy consistency. If using a liaison, prepare by mixing egg yolk and cream together and then stir into sauce. Add lemon juice. Remove pan from heat.
Watchpoint Be careful not to let sauce boil after liaison has been added, otherwise the mixture will curdle.

Caper sauce

1 rounded tablespoon capers
1 dessertspoon parsley (chopped)
½ pint velouté sauce

Serve with boiled mutton or rabbit.

Method

Make velouté sauce. Then stir in the capers and parsley.

Mustard sauce

**1 teaspoon made mustard
   (French, or English)**
½ pint velouté sauce

Serve with boiled fish, grilled herrings and mackerel.

Method

Make velouté sauce. Mix mustard with 1 tablespoon of sauce, then stir into sauce.

Parsley sauce

**1 large handful of fresh parsley
   (picked from stalks)**
½ pint velouté sauce

Serve with eggs, fish or boiled chicken.

Method

Make velouté sauce. Wash parsley sprigs, boil for 7 min-

utes in pan of salted water; drain, press out moisture, then rub through a wire strainer. Beat into hot velouté sauce.

Or add cooked drained parsley to half the sauce without sieving and work in an electric blender.

Poulette sauce

½ pint velouté sauce
**1 rounded teaspoon parsley
   (finely chopped)**
1 teaspoon lemon juice
pinch of savory (chopped)

For liaison
1 egg yolk
2 tablespoons cream

Serve with carrots, broad beans, new potatoes, or boiled veal. Half this quantity is enough for vegetables for 4–6 people.

Method

Add all ingredients, except the liaison, to velouté sauce. Mix thoroughly and boil. Make liaison by working egg yolk and cream together, add 1 table-spoon of hot sauce, then return this slowly to sauce; reheat carefully but do not reboil.

Bread sauce

**4–6 tablespoons fresh bread-
   crumbs**
½ pint milk

**1 small onion (stuck with 2–3
   cloves)**
½ bayleaf
salt and pepper
1 oz butter

Method

Bring the milk to the boil, add onion and bayleaf; cover pan; leave on side of stove for 15 minutes to infuse. Remove the onion, add the breadcrumbs and seasoning and return to heat; stir gently until boiling. Beat in the butter, a small piece at a time and serve hot.

Horseradish cream

**2 tablespoons horseradish
   (freshly grated)**
**1 dessertspoon white wine vine-
   gar**
1 teaspoon dry mustard
1 rounded teaspoon caster sugar
pinch of salt
black pepper (ground from mill)
1 small carton double cream

Method

Mix the vinegar and seasonings together and add the horse-radish. Lightly whip the cream and mix gently into the other ingredients.

When fresh horseradish is unobtainable, use grated horse-radish preserved in vinegar and mix the seasoning with only 1 teaspoon of vinegar.

BROWN SAUCES

A brown sauce for everyday use can be made from stock or even a bouillon cube, and is suitable for serving with cut-lets, rissoles and similar dish-es. But a brown sauce, which is known as a 'sauce mère' (a parent sauce from which others are derived as with a béchamel or velouté sauce), is in the category of advanced cookery.

From the basic parent sauce demi-glace (half-glaze), a number of advanced sauces can be made.

When the famous French chef Carême (who was chief cook to the Prince Regent, later King George IV) made his demi-espagnole sauce — which today would be called demi-glace — he described it as

'gradually taking on that brill-iant glaze which delights the eye when it first appears...'

General points

Every detail must be right for a perfect sauce and as this does call for a little time and trouble, it is sensible to double or treble the quantities and store the excess sauce in a covered con-tainer in the refrigerator, where it will keep for a week.

Much depends on the stock with which the sauce is made. It should be a clear brown bone stock, free of grease and set to a light, but not too firm, jelly. This will give a good flavour and a fine glossy texture to the sauce. (Stocks were covered on pages 118–120).

Do not add more flour than

179

Ingredients for preparing a basic brown sauce

the recipe gives. The consistency of the finished sauce should be that of single cream. This 'half-glaze' is achieved by reduction of the bone stock in the sauce rather than by the addition of extra flour (which is used in the first instance merely to absorb the fat and bind the ingredients together).

Note: all the recipes given here will make ½ pint quantity of sauce. 1 rounded tablespoon, ie. as much above as below the rim, is equivalent to ½ oz sifted flour; 1 level tablespoon equals ¼ oz sifted flour.

Basic brown (demi-glace) sauce

3 tablespoons salad oil
1 small onion (finely diced)
1 small carrot (finely diced)
¼ stick of celery (finely diced)
1 rounded tablespoon flour
1 teaspoon tomato purée

1 tablespoon mushroom peelings (chopped), or 1 mushroom
1 pint well-flavoured brown stock
bouquet garni
salt and pepper

Method

Heat a saucepan, put in the oil and then add diced vegetables (of which there should be no more than 3 tablespoons in all). Lower heat and cook gently until vegetables are on point of changing colour; an indication of this is when they shrink slightly.

Mix in the flour and brown it slowly, stirring occasionally with a metal spoon and scraping the flour well from the bottom of the pan. When it is a good colour draw pan aside, cool a little, add tomato purée and chopped peelings or mushroom, ¾ pint of cold stock, bouquet garni and seasonings.

Bring to the boil, partially cover pan and cook gently for about 35–40 minutes. Skim

off any scum which rises to the surface during this time. Add half the reserved stock, bring again to boil and skim. Simmer for 5 minutes. Add rest of stock, bring to boil and skim again.

Watchpoint Addition of cold stock accelerates rising of scum and so helps to clear the sauce.

Cook for a further 5 minutes, then strain, pressing vegetables gently to extract the juice. Rinse out the pan and return sauce to it. Partially cover and continue to cook gently until syrupy in consistency. It is now ready to be used on its own or as a base for any of the following sauces.

When serving a grill, 1–2 teaspoons of this sauce, added to a gravy or mixed with the juices in the grill pan, makes a great improvement.

Sauce espagnole

2 oz mushrooms (chopped)
1 rounded tablespoon tomato purée
¾ pint demi-glace sauce
½ gill (⅛ pint) jellied stock
½ gill brown sherry
½ oz butter

Serve with dark meats.

Method

Put mushrooms in tomato purée and add both to prepared demi-glace sauce in a pan. Simmer for 5 minutes, then add stock. Continue to simmer, skimming often, until well reduced, then add sherry and beat in butter. Do not boil after this but keep warm in a bain marie or reheat when necessary.

Sauce chasseur

1 shallot (finely chopped)
½ oz butter
2 oz button mushrooms (sliced)
1 large wineglass white wine
1 dessertspoon tomato purée
½ pint demi-glace sauce

Serve with all meats and with chicken, grilled or roasted.

Method

Cook shallot in butter in a pan for 1 minute, add mushrooms and cook for 2 minutes before adding wine. Simmer to reduce by one-third then add, with tomato purée, to prepared demi-glace sauce. Simmer for 3–4 minutes before using.

Sauce bigarade

1 shallot (finely chopped)
½ oz butter
1½ wineglasses red wine (Burgundy)
1 small bayleaf
1 Seville orange
½ pint demi-glace sauce
2 teaspoons redcurrant jelly
squeeze of lemon juice

Serve with duck, venison, pork.

Method
Put the shallot and butter into a small pan, cover and cook gently for 1 minute. Add wine, bayleaf and pared rind of ½ orange. Simmer to reduce by about one-quarter. Strain into prepared demi-glace sauce, add redcurrant jelly and dissolve over a low heat.

Pare and cut rest of orange rind into needle-like shreds. Blanch in boiling water for 5 minutes, then drain. Add to sauce. Cut skin and pith from orange, cut out segments. Squeeze the white membranes to extract any juice for adding to the sauce with the lemon juice. Simmer for 4–5 minutes, then add orange segments. Reheat but do not boil.

Bigarade is the French name for a Seville orange; a sweet orange can replace it with extra lemon juice for sharpness; instead of the segments of sweet orange, juice of ½ an orange can be substituted.

Sauce madère

1 rounded tablespoon tomato purée
¾ pint demi-glace sauce
½ gill (⅛ pint) jellied stock
½ gill Madeira wine
½ oz butter

Serve with roast/braised fillet, cutlets, escalopes, or chicken.

Method
Add tomato purée to the prepared demi-glace sauce and simmer for 5 minutes, then add stock. Continue to simmer, skimming often, until well reduced. Then add wine and beat in butter. Do not boil after this, but keep warm in a bain marie or reheat when necessary.

BUTTER SAUCES

These are basic (mère) sauces from which others are derived. They usually form an accompaniment to fish, vegetables and meat, and should always be served lukewarm.

The best known are hollandaise and béarnaise. A small quantity of hollandaise is often added to a velouté or béchamel sauce for coating fish or delicate meats such as veal or chicken.

It is worth making a good quantity of hollandaise at a time as it can be kept in a screw-top container in the refrigerator. If using hollandaise in another sauce, or making it to keep, omit the cream.

Béarnaise sauce is based on hollandaise but is sharper and finished with herbs. To get the sharpness the vinegar is not reduced as much as for hollandaise sauce. It is the classic accompaniment to fillet steaks and tournedos.

Sauce blanche au beurre (white sauce with butter) is a useful one and may be served with white meats, veal or chicken. It is also an excellent base for a caper or mustard sauce, and with the addition of 1–2 egg yolks becomes 'mock hollandaise' (sauce bâtarde), which is more economical and easier to handle than true hollandaise.

Hollandaise sauce

4 tablespoons white wine vinegar
6 peppercorns
1 blade mace
1 slice of onion
1 small bayleaf
3 egg yolks
5 oz butter (unsalted)
salt and pepper
1–2 tablespoons single cream, or top of milk
squeeze of lemon juice (optional)

Method
Put the vinegar into a small pan with the spices, onion and bayleaf. Boil this until reduced to a scant tablespoon, then set aside.

Cream egg yolks in a bowl with a good nut of butter and a pinch of salt. Strain on the vinegar mixture, set the bowl on a pan of boiling water, turn off heat and add remaining butter in small pieces, stirring vigorously all the time.

Watchpoint When adding butter, it should be slightly soft, not straight from refrigerator.

When all the butter has been added and the sauce is thick, taste for seasoning and add the cream or milk and lemon juice. The sauce should be pleasantly sharp yet bland, and should have consistency of thick cream.

Adding butter to egg mixture for a hollandaise sauce

Béarnaise sauce

3 tablespoons wine vinegar
6 peppercorns
½ bayleaf
1 blade of mace
1 slice of onion
2 egg yolks
salt and pepper
3–4 oz butter (unsalted)
nut of meat glaze, or jelly at base
   of cake of beef dripping
1 teaspoon tarragon, chervil, and
   parsley (chopped)
pinch of snipped chives, or grated
   onion

This quantity is sufficient to put on steaks or cutlets but ingredients should be increased in proportion for a sauce to be served separately.

Method
Put the vinegar, peppercorns, bayleaf, mace and slice of onion into a small pan and boil until reduced to 1 tablespoon. Set pan aside.

Place the yolks in a small basin and beat well with a pinch of salt and a nut of butter. Strain on vinegar mixture and set the bowl on a pan of boiling water, turn off heat and stir until beginning to thicken.

Add the softened butter in small pieces, each about the size of a hazelnut, stirring all the time. Season with pepper. Add the meat glaze, herbs, and chives or grated onion. Keep warm and use as required.

The finished sauce should have consistency of whipped cream.

Mousseline sauce

2 egg yolks
3 oz butter (unsalted)
juice of ½ lemon
salt and pepper
4 tablespoons cream (lightly
   whipped)

Serve separately with asparagus, lamb cutlets and salmon. It is lighter, fluffier and more delicate than a hollandaise.

Method
Put the yolks into a bowl, add a nut of butter and stand bowl in a bain marie. Work until mixture is thick, then add lemon juice and season lightly. Whisk over the bain marie, add the remaining butter (slightly softened) by degrees.

When sauce is thick remove from heat and continue to whisk for 1–2 minutes. Then fold in the cream, adjust seasoning and serve.

Sauce blanche au beurre (white sauce with butter)

2 oz butter
1 tablespoon flour
½ pint water (boiling)
salt and pepper
good squeeze of lemon juice

Method
Melt a good ½ oz of butter in a pan, stir in the flour off the heat and when smooth pour on all the boiling water, stirring or whisking briskly all the time.

Now add remaining butter in small pieces, stirring it well in. Season and add lemon juice.
Watchpoint If the water is really boiling it will cook flour. On no account bring sauce to the boil as this will give it an unpleasant gluey taste.

DERIVATIONS OF SAUCE BLANCHE

Sauce bâtarde (mock hollandaise)

Make the same basic sauce and add 1–2 egg yolks after the boiling water. Then add the remaining butter, seasoning and lemon juice.

Mustard sauce

Make the same basic sauce and then add I dessertspoon French or 1 teaspoon made English mustard per ½ pint sauce. Add an egg yolk, if wished.

Caper sauce

Make the same basic sauce and add 2 tablespoons lightly chopped capers and 1 dessertspoon chopped parsley to the completed sauce.

Caper sauce can have an egg yolk added, if wished.

Ingredients for green salad

Alternative recipes are given on page 179 for mustard and caper sauces on a velouté sauce base.

Ravigote sauce

½ pint sauce bâtarde (mock
   hollandaise)
1 shallot (finely chopped)
2–3 tablespoons wine vinegar
½ oz butter
1 scant teaspoon French mustard
1 tablespoon mixed herbs
   (tarragon, chives and parsley)–
   chopped

Serve with grilled pork chops, salmon and fried fish.

Method
Prepare the mock hollandaise sauce and set aside.

Simmer shallot in a pan in the wine vinegar with a nut of butter until tender (2–3 minutes). Add to the sauce with the mustard and herbs, reheat gently.

This sauce should be slightly sharp and well flavoured with the herbs.

SALAD DRESSINGS

French dressing

1 tablespoon vinegar (red or
    white wine, or tarragon)
½ teaspoon salt
¼ teaspoon black pepper (ground
    from mill)
fresh herbs (chopped — thyme,
    marjoram, basil or parsley) —
    optional
3 tablespoons olive oil, or
    groundnut oil

True French dressing does not
have sugar, but for English
tastes add a good pinch. When
herbs are added to French
dressing it is called vinaigrette.

Method
Mix vinegar with the seasonings, add oil and when the
dressing thickens, taste for correct seasoning. More salt should
be added if the dressing is sharp
yet oily. Quantities should be in
the ratio of 1 part vinegar to 3
parts oil.

Mayonnaise

2 egg yolks
salt and pepper
dry mustard
¾ cup salad oil
2 tablespoons wine vinegar

This recipe will make ½ pint
of mayonnaise.

Method
Work egg yolks and seasonings
with a small whisk or wooden
spoon in a bowl until thick;
then start adding the oil drop
by drop. When 2 tablespoons
of oil have been added this
mixture will be very thick. Now
carefully stir in 1 teaspoon of
the vinegar.

The remaining oil can then be
added a little more quickly,
either 1 tablespoon at a time
and beaten thoroughly between
each addition until it is absorbed, or in a thin steady
stream if you are using an
electric beater.

When all the oil has been
absorbed, add remaining vinegar
to taste, and extra salt and
pepper as necessary.

To thin and lighten mayonnaise add a little hot water. For
a coating consistency, thin with
a little cream or milk.

Eggs should not come straight
from the refrigerator. If oil is
cloudy or chilled, it can be
slightly warmed which will
lessen the chances of eggs
curdling. Put oil bottle in a pan
of hot water for a short time.

Watchpoint Great care must
be taken to prevent mayonnaise
curdling. Add oil drop by drop
at first, and then continue
adding it very slowly.

If mayonnaise curdles, start
with a fresh yolk in another
bowl and work well with
seasoning, then add the curdled
mixture to it very slowly and
carefully. When curdled mixture
is completely incorporated,
more oil can be added if
the mixture is too thin.

Scandinavian dressing

1 dessertspoon caraway, or dill
    seeds (crushed)
¼ pint water (boiling)
1 teaspoon salt
1½ tablespoons vinegar
2 teaspoons sugar

Method
Make caraway liquid by crush-
ing 1 dessertspoon caraway
seeds (or dill) and scald with
¼ pint boiling water. Cool and
strain. Reserve 2½ tablespoons
of caraway liquid and store
remaining liquid in a screw-top
jar for future use. It will keep
up to 2 weeks in a cool place.

Add other ingredients to
caraway liquid and mix all
together. This dressing is good
with a plain beetroot side salad.

Lemon cream dressing

¼ pint mayonnaise
¼ pint cream (lightly whipped)
grated rind and juice of ½ lemon
salt and pepper
made mustard

Method
Stir the cream into the mayonnaise, adding the grated rind
and lemon juice gradually.
Season well; add mustard to
taste. Add 1 tablespoon of
boiling water, if necessary, as
the dressing should be thin. (It
can be made with less cream
and more mayonnaise.)

Tarragon cream dressing

1 egg
2 oz caster sugar
3 tablespoons tarragon vinegar
salt and pepper
¼ pint double cream

Method
Break egg into a bowl and beat
with a fork. Add sugar and
gradually add vinegar. Stand
bowl in a pan of boiling water,
stir mixture until beginning to
thicken, then draw off heat and
continue to stir. When mixture
has the consistency of thick
cream, take basin out of pan,
stir for a few seconds longer,
season lightly and leave till cold.

Partially whip cream and fold
into the dressing.

This dressing can be made up
(without cream) in large quantities and stored, when cold, in
a screw-top jar in the refrigerator. It will keep for 2–3 weeks.
When needed, take out required
amount and add cream.

Boiled dressing

1 tablespoon sugar
1 dessertspoon flour
1 teaspoon salt
1 dessertspoon made mustard
1 tablespoon water
¼ pint each vinegar and water
    (mixed)
1 egg
½ oz butter
cream, or creamy milk

Method
Mix dry ingredients together,
add mustard and about 1 tablespoon of water. Add to vinegar
and water and cook thoroughly
for about 5 minutes. Beat egg,
add butter, pour on the hot
vinegar mixture and beat
thoroughly.

When cold dilute with cream
or milk and mix well. This
dressing keeps well, covered,
in a refrigerator.

SWEET SAUCES

Red jam sauce on steamed pudding, rich orange cream on Eve's (centre), and banana on castle puddings

Unlike savoury sauces, sweet ones are not all made on a standard basic recipe; each is made individually. There are, though, certain recognised categories; we start with fruit and jam sauces, continue with chocolate, and hard, sauces and then those using egg. The last section deals with rich sauces for ice-cream and steamed puddings.

FRUIT AND JAM SAUCES

The following fruit and jam sauces are good served with ice-creams, cold sweets and steamed or baked puddings.

Apricot jam, red jam, or marmalade, sauce

2 rounded tablespoons of home-made apricot, or red, jam, or marmalade

about 7½ fl oz water
2 strips of lemon rind (if using apricot jam, or marmalade)
1 tablespoon sugar
1 tablespoon arrowroot (slaked with 1 tablespoon water) – optional

Serve with sponges and other baked, or steamed, puddings.

Method
Put all the ingredients, except the arrowroot, into a pan and bring slowly to the boil, stirring well. Taste, and if not strong enough in flavour add a little more jam or marmalade. Continue to simmer for 5–6 minutes, then remove the lemon rind and thicken if necessary with the arrowroot. Serve hot.

Pineapple sauce

¼ cut crushed pineapple, or
    1 small can crushed pineapple
3 dessertspoons caster sugar
1 dessertspoon cornflour
pinch of salt
¾ cup unsweetened pineapple

juice
1 teaspoon lemon juice

Method
Mix the sugar, cornflour and salt together. Add the pineapple juice and cook for 5 minutes. Add the lemon juice and then the crushed pineapple.

Banana sauce

1 banana (finely sliced)
juice of ½ lemon (made up to 8 fl oz with water)
1 tablespoon maraschino, or juice from maraschino cherries
1 oz granulated sugar
1 dessertspoon arrowroot

Serve with vanilla ice-cream or castle puddings

Method
Put the lemon juice, water and maraschino or juice into a pan with the sugar and dissolve over

184

SWEET SAUCES

gentle heat. Mix the arrowroot smoothly with 1 tablespoon water, stir into the pan and boil until clear. Add the sliced banana and serve hot.

Orange cream sauce

1 large, or 2 small, oranges
5 lumps of sugar
¼ pint double cream (lightly whipped)

For custard
¼ pint milk
1 teaspoon caster sugar
2 egg yolks (mixed with 1 teaspoon arrowroot)

Method
First make the custard, and leave to get cold. Thinly pare rind from half the orange with a potato peeler, cut into fine shreds and simmer until tender. Drain well and set them aside for decoration.

Rub the lump sugar over the second half of orange to remove all the zest – each lump should be completely saturated with the oil from the skin. Place these lumps in a small basin, strain the juice from the oranges and pour 5 tablespoons of this juice over the sugar lumps, stir until the sugar is dissolved. Stir the orange syrup into the cream and the cold custard, together with fine shreds of orange rind.

Rich orange cream sauce

grated rind and juice of 3 oranges (to give ¼ pint)
juice of 1 lemon
4 oz granulated sugar
2 oz unsalted butter
2 eggs (well beaten)
1 carton double cream (3–4 fl oz) – lightly whipped

Serve with Eve's pudding (see page 266).
This sauce is shown in the photograph opposite.

Method
Put all the ingredients in a pudding basin (except the cream). Stand the basin in a pan of boiling water (or use a double boiler), then stir the mixture gently over a low heat until it is thick.
Watchpoint Do not let the sauce get too hot, otherwise it will curdle.
When the sauce is quite cold fold in the cream.

Melba sauce

½ lb fresh raspberries, or frozen ones without sugar
4 tablespoons icing sugar (sifted)

Method
If using frozen raspberries buy them 2–3 days before wanted and leave them to thaw in refrigerator. Pick over fresh raspberries. Rub the raspberries through a nylon strainer and then beat in the sifted icing sugar, 1 tablespoon at a time.

All the recipes for fruit and jam sauces and for those on pages 186–187 will each make about ½ pint of sauce.

FRUIT SAUCES TO SERVE WITH MEAT

Redcurrant jelly

It is not possible to give a specific quantity of redcurrants as the recipe is governed by the amount of juice made, which is variable.

Method
Wash the fruit and, without removing from the stems, put in a 7 lb jam jar or stone crock. Cover and stand in deep pan of hot water. Simmer on top of the stove or in the oven at 350°F or Mark 4, mashing the fruit a little from time to time, until all the juice is extracted (about 1 hour).
Then turn fruit into a jelly-bag, or double linen strainer, and allow to drain undisturbed overnight over a basin.
Watchpoint To keep the jelly clear and sparkling, do not try to speed up the draining process by forcing juice through; this will only make the jelly cloudy.
Now measure juice. Allowing 1 lb lump or preserving sugar to each pint of juice, mix juice and sugar together, dissolving over slow heat. When dissolved, bring to the boil, boil hard for 3–5 minutes and skim with a wooden spoon. Test a little on a saucer: allow jelly to cool, tilt saucer and, if jelly is set, it will wrinkle. Put into jam jars, place small circles of greaseproof paper over jelly, label and cover with jam pot covers. Store in a dry larder until required.

Raisin sauce

4 oz seeded raisins (cut in small pieces)
8 oz granulated sugar
¼ pint water
1 oz butter
1 tablespoon Worcestershire sauce
3 tablespoons wine vinegar
a few drops of Tabasco sauce
salt and pepper
small pinch of ground mace
4 oz redcurrant jelly

Method
Dissolve the sugar in the water and boil steadily for 5 minutes. Add all the other ingredients and simmer gently until the redcurrant jelly has dissolved. Serve this hot with baked ham.

Cranberry sauce

1 lb cranberries
1 teacup of cold water
4 oz granulated sugar
about 1 tablespoon port (optional)

Method
Wash the cranberries and put them in a saucepan, cover with cold water and bring to the boil. Simmer, bruising the cranberries with a wooden spoon, until reduced to a pulp.
Add sugar and port (if using). Cook very gently until all the sugar is dissolved.

Cumberland sauce

Remove rind from a quarter of 1 orange, with potato peeler. Cut into long fine shreds and cook in boiling water until tender, then drain and rinse well. Dissolve 4 tablespoons of redcurrant jelly over gentle heat, then stir in juice of ½ a lemon, 1 wineglass of port wine and strained orange juice. When cold add orange rind and serve.

185

CHOCOLATE SAUCES

Serve with steamed or baked puddings, choux, profiteroles and ice-creams. If making a rich pudding, use a suchard sauce.

Chocolate sauce 1

1 tablespoon cocoa
2 tablespoons granulated sugar
½ pint water
2–3 drops of vanilla essence

Method
Put the cocoa and sugar in a deep saucepan, mix smoothly with the water and then bring slowly to the boil, stirring from time to time. Simmer gently for 10 minutes, then add the vanilla essence. The sauce is now ready to serve.

Chocolate sauce 2

2 oz plain block chocolate
2 tablespoons sugar
1 teaspoon cocoa
1 teaspoon instant coffee
½ pint water
1 egg yolk (optional)
½ teaspoon vanilla essence

Method
Break up the chocolate and put into a saucepan with the sugar, cocoa, coffee and water. Heat slowly, stirring frequently until dissolved. Then simmer with the lid off the pan until it is the consistency of thin cream.

Draw pan aside, and if using the yolk, blend with 1–2 tablespoons of the hot sauce before adding it to the pan, and then add the vanilla essence. If no yolk is used, continue to simmer the sauce until it is a little thicker before adding vanilla.

Suchard sauce

6 oz plain block chocolate
good ½ pint water
4 oz sugar
1 vanilla pod (split)

Serve this sauce with rich sweets such as ice-cream and chocolate profiteroles.

Method
Put the water and the sugar together into a pan, dissolve over gentle heat and add the vanilla pod. Simmer for 4–5 minutes then remove pod.

Melt the chocolate on a plate over a pan of warm water, discard the water, and put the chocolate into the pan, then beat in the sugar syrup, a little at a time. Simmer until it is a thick rich syrup. Use hot or cold.

HARD SAUCES

Brandy butter (or Senior Wrangler sauce)

4 oz unsalted butter
4 oz caster sugar
2–3 tablespoons brandy (to taste)

This butter is good with plum pudding and mince pies.

Method
Cream the butter thoroughly, beat in the sugar by degrees and continue to beat until white. Then beat in the brandy, a teaspoon at a time. Pile up in a small dish or bowl and chill until firm.

Senior Wrangler is a title dating from 1750, given to Cambridge undergraduates who passed first class in their Mathematics Tripos. The name was given to brandy butter by a forebear of Rosemary Hume, Dr. Whewell, who was a Second Wrangler and Master of Trinity in the mid-19th century.

Rum butter

3 oz unsalted butter
3 oz soft brown sugar
grated rind of ½ lemon and squeeze of juice
2–3 tablespoons of rum

This hard sauce is excellent with plum pudding and mince pies. In Cumberland it is served at christening parties.

Method
Cream the butter thoroughly, add the sugar gradually with the lemon rind and juice. Continue to beat, adding the rum gradu-ally to flavour the butter well. Pile up in a small dish and chill before serving.

Lemon butter

3 oz unsalted butter
grated rind of 1 lemon
2 oz caster, or icing, sugar
juice of ½ lemon

Serve with pancakes.

Method
Soften the butter in a bowl with the grated rind of the lemon, add the caster or icing sugar a little at a time with the juice of half the lemon and beat mixture until light and fluffy. Pile into a small dish and leave until very firm before serving.

EGG SAUCES

Mousseline sauce

1 egg
1 egg yolk
1½ oz caster sugar
2 tablespoons sherry, or fruit juice

Serve with steamed, or baked sponge, puddings.

Method
Put all the ingredients together in a bowl. Whisk over a pan of simmering water until mixture is thick and frothy.
Watchpoint Use as soon as possible, but if it has to be kept a little while, whisk it for a minute before serving.

Custard sauce (Crème à la vanille)

½ pint creamy milk
2 tablespoons caster sugar
2–3 drops of vanilla essence, or ¼ vanilla pod (split)
2 egg yolks

Method
Put the milk in a pan, add the sugar with vanilla essence or, if using a vanilla pod, infuse it in milk for 10 minutes, keeping pan covered. Take out pod, then add sugar.

Cream the yolks in a bowl, bring the milk to scalding point and pour on gradually. Blend mixture together and return to the pan; stir con-tinually over a gentle heat with a wooden spatula or spoon. Stir gently to avoid splashing. When the custard coats the spoon and looks creamy, strain back into the bowl.

Dredge a little caster sugar over the top and leave to cool. This coating of sugar melts and helps prevent a skin forming.

Watchpoint Should the custard get too hot and begin to curdle, turn at once into the basin without straining and whisk briskly for 2–3 seconds. Remember that gentle heat helps to prevent a custard from curdling and makes it creamier.

Hot sabayon sauce

3 egg yolks
1 tablespoon caster sugar
¼ pint sherry
small strip of lemon rind

Serve with fruit puddings.

Method
Put all the ingredients into a small basin and stand it over a small pan, one-quarter filled with simmering water. Whisk the sauce until it becomes very frothy and starts to thicken. Remove the lemon rind and serve at once.

Cold sabayon sauce

2 oz granulated sugar
2½ fl oz water
2 egg yolks
grated rind and juice of ½
**   lemon**
1 tablespoon rum, or brandy, or
**   2 tablespoons golden sherry**
¼ pint double cream

Serve over fresh or sugared fruit and other fruit puddings.

Method
Dissolve the sugar gently in the water, and then boil the sugar until the syrup will form a thread between your finger and thumb. Put the egg yolks into a bowl, beat well and take the syrup off the heat, allow the bubbles to subside and pour on to the yolks, whisking well. Whisk the mixture until thick, add the grated lemon rind and juice.

Flavour with the rum, brandy or sherry and continue to whisk for 1–2 minutes. Whisk the cream until it will just hold its shape, fold it into sauce and chill.

Hot fudge sauce is good poured over coffee ice-cream

SAUCES FOR ICE-CREAM AND STEAMED PUDDINGS

Fudge sauce

3 oz soft light brown sugar
1 tablespoon golden syrup
½ pint milk
2 oz butter
½ vanilla pod (split)
2 teaspoons arrowroot (slaked
**   with 1 tablespoon water)**

Serve hot with vanilla ice-cream.

Method
Put the sugar and syrup in a heavy pan and dissolve over gentle heat. In another saucepan heat the milk with the butter and vanilla, and leave it to infuse.

After about 10 minutes, when milk is well flavoured with vanilla, remove the pod from pan. Boil the sugar mixture until caramelised, then add the milk mixture, stirring until the lumps are dissolved, beat until smooth. Add slaked arrowroot, and boil for 1 minute. Serve at once.

Butterscotch sauce

1 tablespoon golden syrup
½ oz butter
2 tablespoons demerara sugar
½ pint warm water
squeeze of lemon juice
1 dessertspoon custard powder
**   (slaked with 1 tablespoon**
**   water)**

Serve with ice-cream.

Method
Put the syrup, butter and sugar into a pan and cook to a rich brown toffee. Draw aside, add the water carefully and then lemon juice. Boil up sauce and pour on to slaked custard powder – reboil to thicken and cook custard.

Rum sauce

4 oz sugar
½ cup water
dark Jamaica rum (to taste)
1 teaspoon lemon, or fresh lime,
**   juice**

Serve with rich fruit puddings.

Method
Dissolve the sugar in the water, bring to the boil and boil for 5 minutes. Add dark Jamaica rum to taste, with 1 teaspoon lemon juice, but if obtainable fresh lime juice is even better.

Vegetable Dishes and Salads

HOT DISHES

Cauliflower au gratin

1 large cauliflower
1 bayleaf
3 tablespoons cheese (grated)
3 tablespoons fresh white breadcrumbs
½ oz butter

For mornay sauce
1½ oz butter
3 tablespoons flour
¾ pint milk
salt and pepper
3 tablespoons cheese (grated)
French, or English, mustard

When cooking cauliflower, add a bayleaf; this lessens the strong smell and gives a delicate flavour to the vegetable.

Method
Wash cauliflower thoroughly in salted water. Trim stalk but leave some green leaves on. Then break into sprigs (if necessary, use a knife to cut the stalk so that it remains attached to the sprigs and is not wasted) and boil for about 15 minutes, or until tender, in salted water with the bayleaf.

Meanwhile, prepare mornay sauce. Melt butter in a pan and stir in flour off the heat. Blend in milk, then stir until boiling. Cook for 2 minutes, season, draw on one side and cool before beating in the cheese by degrees. Then stir in the mustard to taste.
Watchpoint After French mustard is added, do not boil the sauce because this will spoil the taste.

Now carefully drain cauliflower, butter a basin and arrange sprigs in it with the stalks towards the centre. When the basin is full, spoon in 2–3 tablespoons of sauce. Press down very lightly to bind the sprigs together and then invert the basin on to a fireproof dish. Take off basin, spoon sauce over and around, mix cheese and crumbs together and scatter over the cauliflower. Sprinkle well with melted butter and brown in the oven for about 5 minutes at 400°F or Mark 6.

Aubergines Boston

2 even-size aubergines
olive oil
1 medium-size onion
1 oz butter
salt and pepper
5 oz cooked ham (thinly sliced
   and shredded)
béchamel sauce (made with 1 oz
   butter, 1 rounded tablespoon
   flour, ½ pint flavoured milk)
1 tablespoon cream (optional)
1 oz cheese (grated)

Method
Split aubergines in two length-ways, run the point of a knife round the inside of the skin and score across the flesh. Sprinkle with salt and leave for 30 minutes. Dry the aubergines and fry in hot oil on the cut surface until brown. Put in oven at 375°F or Mark 5 for 5–10 minutes to soften completely.

Meanwhile chop the onion and soften in the butter in a covered pan. Scoop out the aubergine flesh carefully, chop it a little and add to the onion. Season, cook for a few minutes until soft, then add the ham. Put back into the skins and set on a baking tray. Prepare béchamel, adding cream, if wished, and coat aubergines. Sprinkle with cheese and brown in hot oven at 425°F or Mark 7 for 8–10 minutes.

Artichokes au gratin duxelles

2 lb jerusalem artichokes
milk and water (in equal proportions, enough to cover
   artichokes)
6 oz mushrooms (flat)
1 onion
1 oz butter
1 oz flour
salt and pepper
2–3 tablespoons creamy milk
1 tablespoon breadcrumbs
   (browned)
1–2 tablespoons cheese (grated)

Method
Peel artichokes and put them in a pan. Cover with milk and water mixture, simmer for 7–10 minutes, or until just tender, drain and put into a fireproof gratin dish. Retain ½ pint of the artichoke liquid for the sauce.

Wash and chop mushrooms finely. Do not peel or remove the stalks. Chop the onion, melt butter in a pan, add onion and mushrooms, cover and cook slowly for 3–4 minutes. Then take off lid and boil hard to remove some of the moisture.

Draw aside, stir in the flour and pour on the artichoke liquid. Stir over heat until boiling and cook for 2 minutes. Season and finish with creamy milk. Spoon this sauce over the artichokes and scatter over some browned crumbs and then the grated cheese.

Cook for about 10 minutes, or until evenly browned, in an oven at 375°F–400°F or Mark 5–6.

An appetising selection of herbs, fruit and vegetables available during the summer and early autumn months

Dolmas

1 green cabbage

For filling
4 rounded tablespoons rice
   (cooked)
1 medium-size onion (finely
   chopped)
1 oz butter
4 oz mushrooms
2 hard-boiled eggs
1 dessertspoon flour
½ pint vegetable stock
1 dessertspoon tomato purée, or
   1 tablespoon canned tomatoes
kneaded butter
½ lb tomatoes

Method

Boil rice for 10–12 minutes, or until tender in plenty of boiling salted water. Strain, rinse and strain again. Put on one side.

Wash cabbage, trim off stalk. Put into a large pan of boiling salted water and boil gently for 3–4 minutes. Lift out and begin peeling off the leaves. As soon as they become difficult to detach, put cabbage back into the boiling water to make the remainder soft and easy to remove. When all the leaves are detached, apart from the heart, prepare the filling.

To make filling: soften the onion in butter, add mushrooms, washed and finely chopped. Turn into a bowl and mix with the cooked rice and the hard-boiled eggs, finely chopped. Now snip out the cabbage stalk in each leaf with scissors. Place 1 dessertspoon of the mixture on each leaf and roll up like a small parcel. Roll each one lightly in flour, pack into a deep fireproof dish or pan.
Watchpoint Arrange each dolmas at an angle so that it does not come into close contact with the others.

Pour over enough stock just to cover, bring to the boil, put on the lid, or cover with buttered paper, and simmer for about 45 minutes either on top of the stove or inside the oven at 325°F or Mark 3. Then tip stock into a pan, add either canned tomatoes or tomato purée, thicken with a little kneaded butter and boil again. Now peel fresh tomatoes, quarter and flick out seeds, then cut each quarter into three, lengthways. Arrange the dolmas in a serving dish or leave in the pan. Add tomato pieces to sauce and spoon over the dish.

For dolmas, take a softened cabbage leaf and spoon a little of the savoury filling into the centre

Fold leaf corners into the centre and roll up like a small parcel. Repeat this until all leaves are used

Then roll each of the finished leaves in a little flour, and pack in a deep fireproof dish

Cauliflower with mushrooms

1 large cauliflower
1 tablespoon crumbs (browned)
½ oz butter

For mushroom mixture
6–8 mushrooms (flat)
¾ pint milk, or ½ pint milk and
¼ pint water
1½–2 oz butter
2 tablespoons flour
salt and pepper

Method

Peel and stalk the mushrooms; wash the trimmings and simmer these in the milk, or milk and water mixture, in a covered pan for 30 minutes. Strain and reserve the liquid.

Boil cauliflower, head downwards. When the flower is tender, drain carefully and cut off superfluous stalk. Now place the cauliflower in an upright position in a fireproof dish.

To prepare the sauce: slice or quarter mushrooms and cook quickly for 4–5 minutes in ½ oz butter in a pan. Turn out on to a plate. Melt the remaining butter in the pan, stir in the flour and pour on the flavoured milk. Blend and stir until boiling. Season and cook for 2 minutes.

Take some of the sprigs from the centre of the cauliflower and set aside. Fill centre with the mushrooms and replace the sprigs. Carefully spoon the sauce over and round, scatter over the crumbs and add a little melted butter. Bake in the oven for 10–15 minutes at 400°F or Mark 6.

Stuffed peppers

5 red, or green, peppers
¾ pint tomato sauce

For stuffing
1 onion (finely chopped)
1½ oz butter
4 oz rice
2 oz mushrooms (chopped)
4 oz cooked ham, or veal, or
chicken
salt and pepper
¾–1 pint veal, or chicken, stock

Method

Cut tops off peppers and scoop out seeds. Blanch for 2–3 minutes, pushing peppers down well under the water. Then drain, refresh and drain

Turning out the cooked galette

again. Pat them dry with a cloth and set aside.

To prepare stuffing: soften onion in 1 oz of the butter, add rice, stir over heat for 1–2 minutes, then add mushrooms and the meat. Season, pour over stock, bring to the boil, cover and put pan into the oven at 350°F or Mark 4 for 20 minutes, or until rice is tender and stock absorbed. Stir in the remaining butter with a fork.

Put this mixture into the peppers; pack upright in a casserole. Heat the tomato sauce and pour over and round the peppers. Cover dish and put into oven for 25–30 minutes or until peppers are tender.

Galette of aubergines

4–5 aubergines
about 8 tablespoons olive oil
1 clove of garlic (crushed)
1 medium-size onion (finely
chopped)
1 lb ripe tomatoes, or 1 can
Italian tomatoes (about 14 oz)
1 tablespoon tomato purée
salt and pepper
1 carton of natural yoghourt
½ wineglass stock

7-inch diameter cake tin

Make this dish when tomatoes and aubergines are plentiful and inexpensive.

Method

Wipe the aubergines and cut in diagonal slices, sprinkle with salt and leave for 30 minutes. Heat 2 tablespoons of oil in a saucepan, add garlic and onion and fry slowly for 3–4 minutes. Then add tomatoes, skinned, seeds removed, and chopped (or the contents of the can) and the purée. Season and cook to a thick pulp. Set aside.

Wipe aubergine slices, then fry until brown in the remaining oil. Have ready the cake tin, arrange a layer of aubergines on the bottom, spread with a little tomato pulp and a little yoghourt. Continue in this way until all the aubergine slices are in. Do not flavour the top layer of aubergines. Reserve about a third of the tomato pulp and add the stock to this; set aside.

Cover the aubergines with a piece of foil or greaseproof paper, press down lightly, then bake in the oven at 350°F or Mark 4 for 40–45 minutes. Leave tin for a few minutes before turning out galette. Boil up sauce, pour it over the galette and serve.

Spreading yoghourt over layer of tomato pulp and aubergine slices for galette of aubergines

Spinach creams

2 lb spinach
½ oz butter
béchamel sauce (made with 1 oz
    butter, 1 oz flour and ½ pint
    flavoured milk)
2 eggs
salt and pepper
grate of nutmeg

8 dariole moulds

Method

Cook the spinach in a large pan of boiling salted water for 7 minutes; drain, refresh and press between two plates to remove the excess water. In this way the delicate leaves remain whole and unbroken. Carefully lift 8 spinach leaves (16 if they are small) and use to line the buttered moulds; sieve the remaining leaves.

Melt the butter, cook slowly to a nut-brown, add the spinach purée and stir over the heat until dry. Add the béchamel sauce and mix well. Draw aside. Beat in the eggs, season well with salt and pepper and a tiny grate of nutmeg.

Spoon the mixture into the prepared moulds, cover with buttered paper or foil and cook au bain marie in the oven at 350°F or Mark 4 for 15–20 minutes.

Fondant potatoes

2–2½ lb small new potatoes
1½–2 oz butter
salt

Method

Scrape the potatoes, rinse well in cold water and dry in a tea towel. Melt the butter in a sauté pan, add the potatoes, cover and set over a very moderate heat. Shake the pan from time to time to turn the potatoes, but do not lift the lid for the first 10–15 minutes as the steam not only helps the potatoes to cook more quickly, but also prevents sticking. Test to see if the potatoes are tender, season with salt and serve.

Buttered courgettes

7–8 courgettes (according to size)
1–1½ oz butter
1 tablespoon water

Vegetables to go with grills: cucumber, onions, courgettes, spring onions, mushrooms, potatoes

salt and pepper
½ tablespoon parsley
½ tablespoon fresh mixed herbs
    (chopped) – optional

Method

Wipe and trim courgettes; blanch them if large and firm, otherwise put direct into a pan or a flameproof casserole with butter and 1 tablespoon of water.

Add seasoning and press buttered paper on top; cover with a lid (to conserve all juices). Cook slowly on top of stove for 15–20 minutes, or until tender. Garnish with chopped herbs.

Glazed carrots

1–2 lb carrots
1 teaspoon sugar
1 oz butter
salt
mint (chopped)

Method

Peel, leave whole, or quarter if small. If very large, cut in thin slices. Put in a pan with water to cover, sugar, butter and a pinch of salt. Cover and cook steadily until tender, then remove lid and cook until all the water has evaporated when the butter and sugar will form a glaze round the carrots.

Add a little chopped mint just before serving.

Glazed onions

Cover the onions with cold water, add salt and bring to the boil. Tip off the water, add 1–1½ oz butter and a dusting of caster sugar. Cover and cook gently until golden-brown on all sides, and cooked through (about 10 minutes).

To peel onions

First cut off top and root with a sharp knife, then peel off first and second skins, or more (until onion is all white). Do not break the thin underskin —the oil released from here will make you cry.

To skin button onions easily, first scald (plunge into boiling water) for 1–2 minutes, then plunge into cold water.

Sauté potatoes

1½ lb potatoes
2 tablespoons oil
1 oz butter
salt and pepper
1 dessertspoon parsley
 (chopped)

Method

Scrub potatoes and boil in their skins until very tender. Then drain, peel and slice. After heating a frying pan put in oil, and when this is hot add the butter. Slip in all the potatoes at once, add seasoning and cook (sauté) until golden-brown and crisp, yet buttery, occasionally turning the contents of the pan. Draw aside, check seasoning, and add parsley. Serve in a very hot dish.

Lyonnaise potatoes (Sauté potatoes and fried onion)

Method

Slice and fry one onion until brown, then remove from pan and sauté the potatoes as in the previous recipe. When these are brown, add the cooked onion slices.

> **The Lyonnais district** of France is renowned for its potatoes and onions, amongst other excellent foodstuffs and special regional dishes.

Baked (jacket) potatoes

1 large potato per person
salt
pat of butter per person
parsley (optional)

Method

Well scrub large, even-size potatoes and roll them in salt. Bake for 1½ hours (or until they give when pressed) in an oven at 375°F or Mark 4. Make cross-cuts on top of each potato and squeeze to enlarge cuts. Put a pat of butter and sprig of parsley in centre; serve at once.

Baked (roast) potatoes

Choose medium to large potatoes of even size. Peel and blanch by putting into cold salted water and bringing to the boil. Drain thoroughly and lightly scratch the surface with a fork (this will prevent a dry and leathery exterior after cooking). Now put the potatoes into smoking hot fat in the same tin as the meat, 40–45 minutes before the meat is fully cooked, and baste well. Cook until soft (test by piercing with a cooking fork or fine skewer), basting them when you baste the meat and turning after 25 minutes. Drain well on kitchen paper, pile in a vegetable dish and sprinkle with a little salt. Do not cover before serving.

Buttered marrow

1 marrow
1–2 oz butter
salt and pepper
parsley (chopped)

Method

Peel the marrow, remove seeds and cut into 2-inch squares. Melt butter in a large shallow pan and add marrow. Season and cover with buttered paper and a lid. Cook over gentle heat until tender, shaking the pan from time to time. Allow 15–20 minutes cooking time and garnish with chopped parsley.

Sauté cucumber

1 large cucumber
½–1 oz butter
1 bunch spring onions (trimmed),
 or 1 small onion (chopped)
salt and pepper
fresh mint (chopped) – to garnish

Method

Peel cucumber using a stainless steel knife; split in four lengthways. Cut across into 1-inch chunks, blanch in boiling, salted water for 1 minute, then drain well. Melt butter in a pan, add spring onions (or chopped onion). Cover and cook for 1 minute. Add cucumber, season. Cover and cook for 5–6 minutes or until just tender, occasionally shaking pan gently. Garnish with fresh mint.
Watchpoint Do not overcook or cucumber will become watery and tasteless.

Fried onions

1 medium-size onion per person
 (finely sliced)
2–3 tablespoons dripping, or oil
sugar (for dusting)

Method

Peel onion, slice a small piece off the side so that the onion remains firmly on the chopping board while slicing fairly finely across (not lengthways). Push slices out into rings.

To make onions more digestible, blanch after slicing by putting into cold water and bringing to the boil. Refresh by pouring cold water over and draining well on absorbent paper.

Put slices into the frying pan with smoking hot fat or oil and fry fairly quickly, turning occasionally with a fork, dust with sugar to help them brown. When well browned take out and drain on absorbent paper before serving in heaps around, or on top of, steaks.

Stuffed mushrooms

2 mushrooms per person, and 2–3
 over
½ oz butter
1 teaspoon onion (chopped)
1 tablespoon fresh white breadcrumbs, or slice of crust
 soaked in milk
salt and pepper
1 teaspoon parsley
pinch of dried mixed herbs

Method

Cup mushrooms are best for this dish. Wash and peel them, then cut across the stalks level with the caps. Chop the trimmings with the extra mushrooms. Cook for 1–2 minutes in the butter with the chopped onion. Add the crumbs (or soaked crust, squeezed and broken up with a fork). Season and add herbs.

Spread this mixture on to the mushrooms, dot with butter and set them on a baking sheet, or in a fireproof dish. Bake for 12–15 minutes in an oven at 400°F or Mark 7, and serve in a fireproof dish.

Creamed swedes

These should not be dismissed as something nasty remembered from schooldays. Try swedes this way and give them a chance.

1 lb swedes
1 oz butter
black pepper
1 small carton double cream

Method

Peel swedes, cut into even-size wedges and cook in salted water until tender. Drain well and return to the heat to dry. Crush with a potato masher or fork, add the butter and continue cooking over gentle heat until all the water has gone. Season and pour in the cream just before serving the swedes.

Braised cabbage

1 firm white cabbage (finely shredded)
1 large onion (sliced)
1 oz butter
1 cooking apple (peeled and sliced)
salt and pepper
1–2 tablespoons stock

Method

Cut the cabbage in quarters and cut away the core. Shred finely. If you are using hard white Dutch cabbage, blanch by putting into boiling, salted water for 1 minute, draining and refreshing with 1 cup of cold water. This is not necessary for green cabbage. Slice the onion and put in a flameproof casserole with the butter. Cook over gentle heat until soft but not coloured. Add the cabbage to the pan with the peeled and sliced apple. Season, stir well and pour in the stock. Cover with non-stick (silicon) cooking paper and lid, and cook for 45–50 minutes on the bottom shelf of the oven at 325°F or Mark 3.

Braised leeks

6 leeks
1 oz butter

Method

Trim the leeks, make a cross cut in the top and wash thoroughly under running water. Blanch by putting into boiling, salted water for 1 minute. Drain well. Put in a well-buttered casserole, cover tightly and cook for 45–50 minutes on the bottom shelf of the oven at 325°F or Mark 3.

DRIED VEGETABLES

Preparation and cooking

1 Wash the vegetables and pick them over to remove any grit or small stones.
2 Soak them in plenty of tepid water for 8 hours, or leave overnight. If they have to be left longer, change the water or they may start to ferment.
3 Allow 2–3 oz vegetables per person (weight before soaking).
4 Drain them, cover with plenty of fresh warm water and cook in a covered pan. If the water is hard, add a pinch of bicarbonate of soda which will help to soften the outer skins. Salt is never added at this stage as it would harden them. Bring them very slowly to boiling point, allowing 30–40 minutes, then simmer gently for about 1 hour. Drain them again and then use as specified in the recipe.

Cassoulet

1 lb haricot beans (soaked and pre-cooked as directed)
6 oz salt belly pork, or green streaky bacon
4 cloves of garlic (finely chopped)
½ shoulder of mutton, or half a duck
2 tablespoons good beef dripping, or bacon fat, or butter
bouquet garni
salt and black pepper
4 oz garlic, or pork, sausage
¾ lb ripe tomatoes, or 1 medium-size can
1 dessertspoon tomato purée
1 teaspoon sugar
brown breadcrumbs

This is a traditional dish from the Languedoc region of France and it contains many specialities of that region. The following recipe is simplified with mutton to replace the traditional pickled goose. If preferred, half a duck could be used. Garlic sausage can be obtained at most delicatessens, or you can use a pork sausage.

Method

Drain the beans and put into a large flameproof casserole with the pork or bacon and the finely chopped garlic. Pour in water to cover well, put on lid, simmer gently 1–1¼ hours.

Drain, set aside and reserve liquor.

Bone the mutton and cut into large cubes or leave the duck in one piece. Fry until golden-brown in the dripping, add the beans and pork to the casserole with the herbs and a little salt, and a lot of black pepper. Moisten with some of the bean liquor, cover and stew very slowly for 3–4 hours, adding a little more of the cooking liquor from time to time, if necessary. After 2½ hours cooking, add the garlic sausage. When the beans are tender, take out pork, remove skin and slice; also slice the sausage; replace pork (or bacon) and sausage in casserole.

Cook the tomatoes to a pulp in a separate pan, add the tomato purée and season with salt, pepper and sugar. Spoon this mixture over the beans, shake the casserole gently to mix it in, then sprinkle the top of the beans with the browned crumbs. Put in hot oven, pre-set at 375°F or Mark 5, for a further ¾–1 hour to brown.

Chilli con carne

6 oz red beans (soaked and pre-cooked as directed)
1 lb minced steak
2 tablespoons oil, or dripping
2 onions (finely chopped)
2 tablespoons chilli con carne spice, or 1 dessertspoon chilli powder
1 dessertspoon paprika pepper

Method

Choose a large stew pan or deep frying pan, heat the dripping in this, add onion and when it is about to turn colour, add the spices. Add the mince, stirring for 4–5 minutes, then add the drained beans and a little of their cooking liquor.

Cover and simmer until beef and beans are tender (about 1½ hours). During this time the pan should be covered and if the mixture gets too thick add a little of the water. The consistency should be that of a rich stew.

Haricot beans with sausages

½ lb haricot beans (soaked and
    pre-cooked as directed)
1 lb pork sausages
1 oz butter
1 medium-size onion (finely
    chopped)
1 dessertspoon flour
2 tablespoons stock
1 wineglass white wine
salt and pepper
squeeze of lemon juice
½ oz butter

Method

Fry the sausages until cooked
and brown on all sides, then add
the beans and cook until they
are slightly browned and have
absorbed the fat from the
sausages; turn them into a
casserole.

Melt the butter, add the onion
and cook until brown; stir in
the flour, stock and wine,
season and bring to the boil.
Cook for 10 minutes, add a
squeeze of lemon juice and
pour over the beans and sausages. Dot the butter over the
beans and shake well until
absorbed. Serve very hot and
well seasoned.

Butter beans maître d'hôtel

½ lb butter beans (soaked and
    pre-cooked as directed)
¼ lb salt belly pork
1 onion (stuck with a clove)
bouquet garni
1½ oz butter
1 clove of garlic (crushed)
1 tablespoon chopped parsley
juice of ½ lemon
black pepper (ground from mill)

Method

Put beans in a pan with fresh
water to cover, add the pork,
onion and bouquet garni; simmer for 1 hour.

Strain off the liquid, reserving
¼ pint of the cooking liquor,
discard the onion and bouquet
garni. Remove the rind from the
pork, then cut the flesh into

Butter beans ménagère, served in a creamy, white sauce

strips. Return the beans and
pork to the pan, add the reserved cooking liquor and heat
it gently.

Cream the butter with the
crushed garlic, parsley, lemon
juice and black pepper, and
drop it into the pan in pieces.
Turn off the heat under the pan
and shake it gently until the
butter has melted and mixed
with the beans, then serve.

Butter beans ménagère

½ lb butter beans (soaked and
    pre-cooked as directed)
2 sticks of celery (sliced)
1 onion (sliced)
1 bayleaf
salt and pepper
1 tablespoon chopped parsley
2 tablespoons double cream
1 large tomato (skinned and
    sliced)
1 tablespoon caster sugar
¼ oz butter

For white sauce
1½ oz butter
1 oz flour
½ pint milk

Method

Put prepared beans in a pan with
celery, onion and bayleaf; cover
with boiling water, season and
cook for 30–40 minutes until
tender.

Meanwhile prepare a white
sauce with the butter, flour,
milk and seasoning.

Drain the vegetables, remove
the bayleaf and reserve about
¼ pint of the cooking liquor. Add
the vegetables to the white
sauce, shake the pan gently to
mix together, add the parsley
and cream and the reserved
cooking liquor. Taste for
seasoning and tip the mixture
into a hot gratin dish.

Dust the tomato slices with
salt, pepper and caster sugar,
dot with ¼ oz butter and grill.
Arrange them on top of the
beans and serve.

*Adding butter beans, celery
and onion to the white sauce*

SALADS

ACCOMPANYING OR SIDE SALADS

Coleslaw and fruit salad

½ white drumhead cabbage
olive oil (to moisten)
salt
black pepper (ground from mill)
½ lb white grapes
½ lb Colmar grapes
2 Cox's apples
2 oranges
2 clementine oranges
little caster sugar (for dusting)
lemon juice or white wine
  vinegar

The Colmar grape is a sweet variety of black grape. Serve with cold beef and ham, and galantines.

Method

Trim the cabbage and wipe well but keep dry. Shred very finely and then dress with enough olive oil to moisten, season with salt and pepper, cover and put in the refrigerator.

Prepare the fruit: peel grapes and remove pips. Peel and core apples and cut into dice. Peel oranges and clementines and cut into segments, removing membranes. Dust fruits with caster sugar and sprinkle with the lemon juice or vinegar; cover dish and keep in the refrigerator. Just before serving, mix the cabbage and fruits together and pile into a large salad bowl.

Salad composé

4 oz rice
½ lb tomatoes
4 oz small white button
  mushrooms
1 tablespoon olive oil
3 oz black olives
French dressing (made with
  white wine in place of vinegar)

Method

Boil and drain the rice. Scald and skin tomatoes, quarter them and remove seeds; halve each quarter.

Leave mushrooms whole and sauté them in oil. Halve and stone the olives. Combine all the ingredients in a salad bowl and moisten with French dressing.

Serve with grilled steak or pork chops.

Grape, melon and mint salad

1 honeydew, or cantaloup, melon
½–¾ lb green grapes
about 6 sprigs of young mint

For French dressing

2 tablespoons white wine
  vinegar
4 tablespoons olive oil
squeeze of lemon juice
salt and pepper
sugar (to taste)

To serve with roast chicken.

Method

Cut the melon in half, scrape away the seeds carefully, then scoop out the flesh into balls with a round vegetable cutter (potato scoop), or a teaspoon. Peel and pip the grapes.

Watchpoint Peel the grapes before flicking out the seeds with the point of a knife or potato peeler.

Mix ingredients together for the dressing and season well to taste. Cut the scraped out melon rind into slices or leave in 2 halves and arrange on individual plates or in a dish. Mix the melon balls, grapes and mint together with the dressing, then spoon into the melon shells or on to individual slices. Chill a little before serving.

Grapes can be peeled easily if the whole bunch is first dipped into boiling water for a few seconds. The seeds should be flicked out afterwards with the point of a knife or potato peeler.

Spanish salad

¾ lb tomatoes
1 large Spanish onion
1 green pepper
salt and pepper
French dressing (made with 2
  tablespoons white wine and
  6 tablespoons olive oil)
1 tablespoon mixed chopped
  herbs (parsley, lemon thyme)

Method

Scald, skin and slice the tomatoes. Cut the onion and pepper in rings, removing the latter's centre core and seeds.

Put the onion into pan of cold water, bring to the boil, then add the green pepper and boil for 1 minute; drain and refresh.

Mix the tomatoes, onion and pepper together in a salad bowl, season, spoon over the French dressing and dust with herbs.

Serve with cold roast chicken.

Fennel and lemon salad

2–3 heads of fennel (according
  to size)
2 ripe thin-skinned lemons

For dressing

juice of extra ½ lemon (see
  method)
3 tablespoons oil
salt and pepper
sugar (to taste)
1 tablespoon roughly chopped
  parsley

Florence fennel (finocchio) makes an excellent salad, clean and fresh tasting, if somewhat pungent. If the aniseed flavour is a little strong for some tastes, qualify it with other salad vegetables, such as celery and chicory. This salad goes well with rich meat.

Method

Slice the fennel finely and put into a bowl. Pare 2–3 strips of rind from 1 lemon and cut this rind into shreds, then blanch, drain and refresh it and set aside. Slice away the peel and white pith from both lemons and cut out the flesh from between the membranes with a sharp knife, holding the lemon in one hand so that eventually only the membranes are left in your hand. Add the lemon segments to the fennel.

To make dressing: squeeze the membranes left from the two lemons to get out any juice and, if necessary, make up to a good tablespoon with some of the juice from the extra ½ lemon. Beat in the oil and season well. Make the dressing rather sweet, especially if the lemons are not really ripe. Add it to the fennel and lemon with 1 tablespoon of the chopped parsley. Toss well and serve scattered with the blanched lemon rind.

Provençal salad

½ lb courgettes
½ lb tomatoes
1 red pepper
1 green pepper
3 tablespoons olive oil
1 shallot (finely chopped)
1 clove of garlic (crushed with
    ½ teaspoon salt)
bouquet garni
pepper (ground from the mill)

Method

Trim and slice the courgettes. Cut the tomatoes into quarters; scoop out the seeds. Slice the peppers, removing core and seeds. Set oven at 350°F or Mark 4.

Heat oil in a flameproof casserole, add shallot and cook slowly until it is soft but not coloured. Add all the other ingredients, season with pepper and cover the casserole. Cook in pre-set moderate oven for about 30–40 minutes, until courgettes are tender. Remove bouquet garni and allow to cool.

Serve cold with grilled steak, or cold roast beef.

Celery, potato and black olive salad

½ lb new potatoes
1 head of celery (cut in short
    lengths)
2 oz black olives (halved and
    stoned)
1 dessert apple (diced)

For dressing

2 tablespoons tomato sauce, or
    ketchup
2–3 tablespoons double cream
1 tablespoon olive oil
lemon juice (to taste)
salt and pepper (to taste)
sugar (to taste)

Method

Boil the potatoes in their skins until just tender, remove skins, slice potatoes and put them into a bowl with the celery, the olives and the apple.

To prepare dressing: mix all the ingredients together. Spoon over the salad.

Serve with cold ham or tongue.

Breton salad

2 medium-size carrots (diced)
1 turnip (diced)
4 oz French beans (cut in
    diamonds)
2 tablespoons French dressing
3 potatoes (about 6–8 oz)

For mock mayonnaise

½ teaspoon dry mustard
½ teaspoon caster sugar
¼ teaspoon salt
¼ teaspoon pepper
5 tablespoons evaporated milk
5 tablespoons salad oil
2 dessertspoons vinegar

To garnish

1 egg (hard-boiled)
1 tablespoon mixed chopped
    herbs

Method

To prepare mock mayonnaise: place the mustard, sugar and seasoning in a small basin and mix smoothly with the milk. Add the oil gradually, whisking briskly all the time. Whisk in the vinegar, which forms an emulsion with the oil and thickens the dressing.

Cook the carrot, turnip and beans separately until tender, then mix them, while still hot,

A garnish of hard-boiled eggs and herbs gives an attractive finish to Breton salad

with the French dressing. Boil the potatoes in their skins, skin and dice them and add to the other vegetables. Add sufficient mock mayonnaise dressing to bind vegetables together.

Pile the mixture in a salad bowl, garnish with quarters of hard-boiled egg and sprinkle over the herbs.

Serve with cold ham, chicken or veal.

Vichy salad

1 bunch of new carrots
¼ pint mayonnaise
1 large teaspoon Dijon mustard
1 tablespoon double cream
1 tablespoon coarsely chopped
    parsley

Method

Scrape and quarter the carrots. Mix the mayonnaise with the mustard and cream, then stir it into the carrots. Turn them into an hors d'oeuvre dish and sprinkle well with parsley.

Serve with cold roast pork, cold beef, or cold chicken.

Corn salad with beetroot and apple is delicious tossed in French dressing

Corn salad, with beetroot and apple

large bunch of corn salad (lamb's lettuce)
2 medium-size beetroots (cooked and sliced)
1 large tart apple (peeled, cored and sliced)
French dressing

Or substitute for corn salad

1 head of celery (washed)
1 Spanish onion (peeled)
parsley or walnuts (chopped) for garnish

Corn salad (or lamb's lettuce) is rarely seen in the shops. However, it is easy to grow and is unharmed by frost. Though dull eaten alone, it is excellent in a mixed salad (see photograph above).

Method
Wash corn salad well and dry thoroughly. Put corn salad, sliced beetroot and apple in a large bowl, and toss in the French dressing.

As corn salad may be unobtainable we suggest using celery and onion rings instead. Cut washed celery into short sticks, slice onion and push out into rings. Blanch rings by plunging into boiling water for 2–3 minutes, then drain and refresh (rinse in cold water and drain again). Dress as above, and leave covered for 2–3 hours after adding beetroot. Scatter chopped parsley or walnuts over this salad before serving.

Celery, apple and walnut salad

1 large head of celery
2 Cox's apples
handful of walnut kernels (preferably fresh ones)
French dressing
parsley (chopped) – to garnish

Method
Trim and wash celery. Cut into 2-inch lengths, then cut downwards into sticks. Leave in ice-cold water to crisp for 30 minutes, then drain and dry thoroughly. Put into a bowl with apples (cored and sliced but not peeled) and the walnut kernels (slightly broken). Mix with enough French dressing to moisten well. Leave covered for 30–60 minutes and scatter with parsley before serving.

Beetroot, celeriac and walnut salad

1 large beetroot (cooked and sliced)
1 large celeriac root
2 tablespoons walnut kernels (coarsely chopped)
¼ pint thick mayonnaise

Fluted cutter

Method
Slice beetroot and cut into crescents with fluted cutter. Wash, peel and slice celeriac, cut across into julienne strips (about 1½–2 inches long). Blanch by plunging into pan of boiling water until barely tender (4–5 minutes), then drain strips thoroughly.

Lightly brown chopped walnuts in the oven for a few minutes or under the grill. Put celeriac into a bowl and mix in 2 tablespoons of mayonnaise with a little boiling water. Put celeriac in the salad bowl, spoon over rest of mayonnaise and surround with crescents of beetroot. Scatter walnuts over the top. Serve at once.

To boil beetroot: scrub well but be careful not to break skin or it will 'bleed' and lose colour. Boil for about 1½ hours. To test if done, take out and rub off a small piece of skin. If it comes away easily beetroot is cooked. Cool in liquid then peel.

To bake beetroot: wrap it in foil or greaseproof paper and bake in moderate oven for 2–3 hours at 350°F or Mark 4. This takes longer than boiling but gives a good flavour. Test as for boiling, and leave to cool before peeling.

To make a side salad: slice beetroot paper-thin, arrange in a serving dish and pour over a suitable dressing – plain or slightly spiced vinegar, Scandinavian dressing or French dressing. Leave for several hours before serving.

Fresh ingredients for coleslaw, and chicory and orange salads

Coleslaw salad

1 small hard white, or Dutch, cabbage
¼ pint boiled dressing, or less of French dressing (page 183)
salt and pepper
1 dessert apple, Cox's or Jonathan
grated carrot (optional)
paprika pepper, or parsley (chopped)

Method
Cut cabbage into four, trim away hard stalk, then slice into thin strips. Put in a mixing bowl, add the boiled or French dressing and extra seasoning to taste. Thoroughly coat every piece of cabbage, then add apple (cored and sliced but not peeled), and grated carrot. Mix well, cover and leave for 2–3 hours before serving. Pile in a dish and sprinkle with paprika or parsley.

Coleslaw, although originally an American dish, owes its name to the Dutch from the time they took over Manhattan Island. In Dutch, kool (cabbage) and sla (salad).

Chicory and orange salad

1 lb chicory
3 oranges
2 large carrots
French dressing

Method
Wash chicory, trim away stalk, separate leaves or cut into pieces. Remove peel and skin from oranges with a sharp knife, then cut into segments and discard any pips. Shred the carrot into fine julienne strips (about 1½–2 inches long). Mix ingredients together and toss in French dressing.

Potato salad

1–1½ lb medium-size potatoes
3–4 tablespoons French dressing
salt and pepper
¼ pint thick mayonnaise
little top of milk
paprika pepper
slices of pickled walnuts (to garnish) – optional

Method
Scrub potatoes well, boil in their skins for about 15 minutes. Do not overcook them or they will break up when sliced and tossed in dressing. Peel while still hot and cut into slices. Put straight into a bowl; add French dressing at once so it is absorbed. Season, cover bowl and leave until cold.

When ready to serve, mix in 1 tablespoon of mayonnaise and turn potatoes into serving dish. Dilute remaining mayonnaise to a coating consistency with top of milk and spoon over salad. Dust with paprika.

Slices of pickled walnuts make a pleasant garnish for potato salad with cold meats.

199

MAIN COURSE SALADS

Salmon salad en gelée

1 lb salmon steak
1½ pints water
juice ¼ lemon
1 teaspoon salt
6 white peppercorns
bouquet garni

For wine jelly

2 pints jellied chicken stock (this must be the cooking-liquor from a boiled chicken, flavoured with onion, carrot and celery)
salt and pepper
scant ½ oz gelatine
7½ fl oz dry white wine
1 dessertspoon tarragon vinegar
2 egg whites
3 tablespoons chopped parsley
¼ pint mayonnaise
2 tablespoons double cream (whipped)

Method

Wash the fish and dry well. Bring the water and flavourings to the boil, draw aside and leave for 5 minutes. Put the salmon into the hot liquid, cover and bring slowly to the boil again. Reduce the heat, cover the pan and simmer for 15 minutes.

Watchpoint The water must just tremble during this cooking time, not boil, or it will toughen the flesh of the salmon.

Allow the fish to cool a little before draining off the liquid and removing the skin and bones.

To make wine jelly: make sure that the chicken stock is free of fat, season it very well, put it into a large scalded pan and add the gelatine (previously soaked in the wine) and vinegar. Clarify with the egg whites (see Couronne of shrimps recipe, page 18), strain through a scalded cloth and leave to cool.

Flake the salmon carefully and turn it into a glass bowl, cover with the cold but still liquid chicken jelly and leave to set. Add the parsley to the remaining jelly and, when on the point of setting, pour carefully into the bowl. Leave the salad for 2 hours in a cool place before serving.

Serve with the mayonnaise lightened with the cream.

'French roast' chicken and cherries in tarragon cream dressing

Chicken and cherry salad

3 lb roasting chicken
salt and pepper
2 oz butter
½ pint stock (made from the giblets)
1 tablespoon wine vinegar
4 tablespoons oil
1 tablespoon mixed chopped fresh herbs (parsley, mint and thyme)
1 lb red cherries (stoned)
tarragon cream dressing (see page 183)
2 lettuce hearts

Method

Set oven at 400°F or Mark 6. Season and rub ½ oz butter inside chicken, rub the remaining butter over it and then 'French roast', using half the stock, in the pre-set oven for about 1 hour; turn and baste from time to time. When cooked and evenly browned, remove from pan, pour in the remaining stock, boil it up well, strain and reserve.

Carve chicken and place meat in a serving dish. Mix vinegar with salt and pepper and whisk in oil. Remove fat from the chicken juices and add these with the herbs to the oil and vinegar. Taste this dressing for seasoning and spoon it over the chicken.

Mix the cherries with the tarragon dressing. Arrange the chicken on the serving dish. Split the lettuce hearts and fill with the cherry mixture. Place around the chicken.

Prawn salad

½ lb prawns (shelled)
1 Cantaloupe, or Honeydew, melon
1 lb tomatoes
little caster sugar
6 tablespoons French dressing
1 Webb's, or Cos, lettuce
1 tablespoon mixed chopped herbs (parsley, thyme, chives and mint)

For sauce

½ pint mayonnaise
1 teaspoon dry mustard

Method

Cut melon in half and discard the seeds; cut the flesh in cubes, mix with the prawns and set aside. Scald and skin the tomatoes, cut in thin slices and arrange, overlapping, around a serving dish or salad bowl. Dust tomatoes lightly with caster sugar and spoon over a little of the French dressing. Shred the lettuce very finely and place in the middle of the dish.

Add mixed herbs to the

Two finished salads: egg and beetroot, and salt beef, salad

remaining French dressing and pour it over the prawns and melon; pile mixture on top of the lettuce.

Mix the mustard to a paste with a little water, add the mayonnaise and then about 1 tablespoon of boiling water. Serve in a sauce boat.

Egg and beetroot salad

6 eggs (hard-boiled)
4 small, round cooked beetroot, or 1 lb jar of pickled baby beetroot
½ lb small new potatoes
3 spring onions
2 teaspoons caster sugar
1 teaspoon dry mustard
¼ teaspoon salt
black pepper (ground from mill)
1 tablespoon wine vinegar
1 tablespoon grated horseradish
3 tablespoons double cream
¼ pint boiled dressing (see page 183) or mayonnaise

Method
Peel and slice the beetroot, scrape and cook the potatoes and chop the spring onions. Mix the sugar, mustard, salt and pepper with the vinegar, then stir in the horseradish and the cream.

If the potatoes are very small, leave them whole; otherwise quarter or slice them, mix while still warm with the horseradish cream and the chopped onion. Mix in the sliced beetroot and turn on to a serving dish; arrange the halved eggs on top and coat with the boiled dressing (or mayonnaise).

Mixing beetroot with potatoes, horseradish cream and onions

Salt beef salad

8–12 oz salted brisket of beef (sliced)
4 large old potatoes
1 dessertspoon dry mustard
1 tablespoon demerara sugar
1 tablespoon malt vinegar
¼ pint mayonnaise
1 dili cucumber (chopped)
1 lettuce heart (quartered)
2 eggs (hard-boiled)

Method
Shred the salt beef and boil the potatoes in their jackets. Mix the mustard and sugar with the vinegar and stir until dissolved. Peel the potatoes while hot and slice a layer into the serving dish, spread with a thin coating of mayonnaise and sprinkle with a little of the cucumber. Cover with a layer of salt beef and moisten with some of the mustard dressing; continue in this way until all the ingredients are used.

Garnish the dish with the lettuce heart and the halved hard-boiled eggs.

Chopping dill cucumber to add to shredded salt beef salad

Pastry

So many puddings are made with pastry that it is important to be able to make it well. Good pastry is not difficult if certain rules—which are often forgotten—are followed. The main points are:

1 Work in a cool, airy room. Plan to make the pastry before the kitchen becomes warm from other cooking because a damp, warm atmosphere is disastrous.

2 Use fresh, fine-sifted plain flour (self-raising flour or baking powder produces spongy-textured pastry), firm but not hard fat (which would not blend properly with the flour) and ice-cold water for mixing. Baking powder is sometimes used to lighten a rich pastry that has a lot of fat.

3 Handle flour and fat lightly but firmly. When rubbing fat into the flour, keep lifting it up and crumbling the mixture between your fingers. This movement helps to aerate the pastry. Shake the bowl after 1–2 minutes to bring the larger lumps of fat to the surface and to show you how much more rubbing-in is necessary. This is especially helpful when making rich shortcrust where over-rubbing makes the pastry greasy.

4 Make sure that the correct amount of water is added. This may vary a little with the quality of the flour. Too dry a mixture makes the pastry difficult to handle; it will crack when rolled out and crumble after baking and will be dry to eat. Too wet a dough will shrink and lose shape while baking, and also makes for tough, hard pastry. The amount of water is usually indicated in a recipe and it is important that at least two-thirds of the given quantity are added to the dry ingredients before mixing begins. This avoids over-working and brings the ingredients quickly to a firm, smooth pastry, especially when making the foundation dough for puff pastry.

5 A marble slab or slate shelf is ideal for rolling out pastry because it is smooth, solid and cool; otherwise, keep a board especially for this purpose (a laminated plastic surface is cool). Once pastry is rolled out, always scrape slab or board thoroughly before rolling out new pastry to remove any dough that may have stuck and which might cause further sticking. (This applies particularly to flaky or puff pastry when rolling out is of paramount importance.) Use a minimum amount of flour for dusting when rolling, otherwise too much will go into the pastry and spoil it. A heavy, plain wooden rolling pin without handles is best, especially for puff pastry.

6 Chill made pastry for about 30 minutes or leave it aside in a cool place for the same amount of time. This gives pastry a chance to relax and removes any elasticity which may cause shrinkage round edge of dish.

7 It is essential when baking pastry to preset the oven to the required temperature. The immediate heat sets the pastry in its correct shape and makes it possible to control the exact amount of cooking time.

The traditional beefsteak, pigeon and mushroom pie is made here with puff pastry (see recipe on page 213)

SHORTCRUST PASTRY

Basic proportions

For shortcrust pastry the basic proportions of ingredients are half the amount of fat to the weight of flour, and $\frac{1}{4}$ oz salt to each lb flour. For rich shortcrust, allow 2 egg yolks to every lb flour. When more fat is added, as in many recipes using rich shortcrust, the pastry is shorter (ie. lighter and more crisp), and is best for pies and tarts to be eaten cold. A mixture of fats gives the best results, eg. butter and lard, as the former gives a good flavour and the latter a good texture.

When terms such as 8 oz pastry or an 8 oz quantity of pastry are used, this means the amount obtained by using 8 oz flour, not 8 oz prepared dough. As a guide, 8 oz shortcrust pastry will cover a 9-inch long pie dish holding $1\frac{1}{2}$ lb fruit, or line an 8-inch flan ring. For a covered plate pie (8–9 inches diameter), use 10 oz shortcrust pastry.

Shortcrust pastry

8 oz plain flour
pinch of salt
4–6 oz butter, margarine, lard or shortening (one of the commercially-prepared fats), or a mixture of any two
3–4 tablespoons cold water

Method

Sift the flour with a pinch of salt into a mixing bowl. Cut the fat into the flour with a round-bladed knife and, as soon as the pieces are well coated with flour, rub in with the fingertips until the mixture looks like fine breadcrumbs.

Make a well in the centre, add the water (reserving about 1 tablespoon) and mix quickly with a knife. Press together with the fingers, adding the extra water, if necessary, to give a firm dough.

Turn on to a floured board, knead pastry lightly until smooth. Chill in refrigerator (wrapped in greaseproof paper, a polythene bag or foil) for 30 minutes before using.

Rich shortcrust pastry

8 oz plain flour
pinch of salt
6 oz butter
1 rounded dessertspoon caster sugar (for sweet pastry)
1 egg yolk
2–3 tablespoons cold water

Method

Sift the flour with a pinch of salt into a mixing bowl. Drop in the butter and cut it into the flour until the small pieces are well coated. Then rub them in with the fingertips until the mixture looks like fine breadcrumbs. Stir in the sugar, mix egg yolk with water, tip into the fat and flour and mix quickly with a palette knife to a firm dough.

Turn on to a floured board and knead lightly until smooth. If possible, chill in refrigerator (wrapped in greaseproof paper, a polythene bag or foil) for 30 minutes before using.

For even richer shortcrust pastry, see recipes for treacle tart (on page 206) or Bavarian apple tart opposite.

PIES AND TARTS

The word tart is often used instead of pie, but correctly a tart is open, with pastry underneath and fruit or other mixture on top. An English pie is made in a pie dish with a lid of pastry on top. Traditionally, a fruit pie is not decorated but left plain, this custom dating from the days when both meat and fruit pies were baked in the same oven, the meat pies being highly ornamented to distinguish them from the others. Another type of pie is a plate pie, with pastry both on top and underneath. Apples are best used in these, or firm fruit such as gooseberries or blackcurrants.

All plate pies should be stood on a hot baking sheet in the oven in order to cook the pastry underneath. These are not to be confused with covered pies made in a deep pie plate, such as the American pie recipes given on page 206.

Apple pie

8 oz shortcrust pastry
caster sugar (for dusting)

For filling
$1\frac{1}{2}$ lb cooking or mildly acid dessert apples
1 strip of lemon rind
2–3 rounded tablespoons sugar (brown or white)
little grated lemon rind, or 1–2 cloves (optional)

8-inch diameter pie dish

This is one of the oldest of English dishes and delicious when properly made. Use a fair-sized dish that holds plenty of fruit. Apples may be cookers, preferably a variety that will retain shape when cooked, or a mildly acid dessert apple such as Cox's orange pippin. A Blenheim orange apple, though not easy to find these days, makes an excellent pie, and combines both the qualities of dessert and cooking apples.

Method

To get the most flavour, peel, quarter and core the apples, keeping them in a covered bowl (not in water) while making juice from the cores and peel. Put these last in a pan with a strip of lemon rind, barely cover with water and simmer for 15–20 minutes. Then strain. (Water can, of course, be used in place of the juice made from the peel.)

While the juice is simmering, prepare a good shortcrust pastry. Put in the refrigerator to chill, or set aside in a cool place for about 30 minutes.

Cut apple quarters into 2–3 pieces, pack into pie dish.

Watchpoint Do not slice the apples too thinly or the juice will run too quickly and may render the slices tough and tasteless.

Layer these slices with 2–3 tablespoons of sugar, according to the acidity of the fruit. Add, too, a little grated lemon rind or 1–2 cloves. Dome the fruit slightly above the edge of the dish (this is sufficient to prevent

Shown in this selection of shortcrust pastry tarts are, from left, Bavarian apple tart, Bakewell tart, and treacle tart (see recipe on page 206)

the pastry top from falling in, so there is no need to use a pie funnel). Pour in enough of the strained apple juice (or water) to fill it half full.

Take up the pastry and roll out to about $\frac{1}{4}$-inch thick, cut a strip or two from the sides and lay these on dampened edge of the pie dish. Press down and brush them with water. Take up the rest of the pastry on the rolling pin and lay it over the pie. Press down the edge, then lift the dish up on one hand and cut the excess pastry away, holding the knife slantwise towards the bottom of the dish to get a slightly overhanging edge. Pinch or scallop round the edge with your fingers, brush the pastry lightly with water, dust with caster sugar (a dry glaze), or leave plain and dust with caster sugar after baking.

Set the pie on a baking sheet for ease of putting in and taking out of the oven, and to catch any juice that may spill over. Bake for about 25 minutes on the centre shelf of the oven at 375°–400°F or Mark 5–6, when the pastry should be brown. Now lower the oven temperature to 350°F or Mark 4 for a further 10–15 minutes to complete cooking.

Bavarian apple tart

For rich shortcrust

6 oz plain flour
pinch of salt
4 oz butter
1½ rounded tablespoons caster

sugar
1 egg yolk
3–4 tablespoons milk
icing sugar (for dusting)

For apple mixture

1–1½ lb cooking apples
1 rounded tablespoon currants
1 rounded tablespoon sultanas
2 tablespoons fresh breadcrumbs
1–2 tablespoons sugar
(brown, or white)
1 teaspoon ground cinnamon

Method
Rub butter lightly into sifted flour and salt in a bowl, add sugar, mix the egg yolk with the milk and stir in to bind the rich shortcrust pastry together. Set aside to chill.

Now peel, core and slice the apples. Put them into a bowl with the cleaned, dried fruit, crumbs, sugar and cinnamon, and mix well.

Knead pastry lightly to work out any cracks, and roll out thinly to a rectangle about 9 inches by 6 inches. Slide on to a baking sheet (preferably one without edges which makes it easier to remove the tart after cooking). Trim the pastry edges, then place the apple mixture down the middle, leaving about 1½–2 inches of pastry on each side. Lift these sides up and over with a palette knife, so that they rest on the mixture, but leave a gap in the middle to show the filling. Press the pastry down lightly with the knife so that the sides remain in place while baking.

Bake for 35–40 minutes in an oven at 375°F or Mark 5. Slide

on to a rack to cool, then dust thickly with icing sugar before cutting into slices for serving.

Serve with cream or custard separately, or a mixture of thick custard and yoghourt whisked together. Do this when the custard is cold and well sweetened, adding the yoghourt to taste.

Bakewell tart

6 oz rich shortcrust pastry

For filling

1 tablespoon strawberry jam
1 tablespoon lemon curd
1 oz butter
2 oz caster sugar
grated rind and juice of ½ lemon
1 egg
2 oz ground almonds
2 rounded tablespoons cake crumbs

7-inch diameter sandwich tin

Method
Make the rich shortcrust pastry and set aside to chill. When chilled, roll it out and line on to the sandwich tin, knock up pastry edges and scallop with the thumb. Spread the pastry first with jam and then with lemon curd.

Cream the butter in a bowl until soft, add the sugar and lemon rind and continue beating until light. Beat egg, add a little at a time, and then stir in the almonds, cake crumbs and lemon juice. Spread the almond mixture over the lemon curd and bake for 35–45 minutes until set and golden-brown in an oven at 375°F or Mark 5.

Treacle tart

For very rich shortcrust

6 oz plain flour
pinch of salt
1 teaspoon baking powder
3 oz butter
2 oz lard, or shortening

For filling

3 rounded tablespoons fresh breadcrumbs
1 teacup golden syrup
grated rind and juice of ½ lemon

large fireproof plate

Rich shortcrust can be used for this tart but Bavarian apple tart has an even richer pastry (which should only be used for a plate pie). Baking powder is added to lighten the pastry somewhat, as there is a heavy quantity of fat.

Method

Sift the flour, salt and baking powder together. Rub in the fats lightly and quickly, then press the dough firmly together. Knead, roll out, line on to fireproof plate. Trim round the edge and set aside to chill.

Mix the crumbs, syrup, lemon rind and juice together. Turn on to the plate, roll out the trimmings and cut into strips. Twist these and lay over the syrup mixture, lattice-fashion. Press a strip of pastry round the edge of the plate to neaten. Bake for 35–45 minutes in an oven at 375°F or Mark 5. Lower heat slightly once pastry has begun to colour, and continue cooking until well browned. Serve on the plate in which it is cooked.

Mince pies

(makes about 18 pies)

about 1½ lb mincemeat
1–2 tablespoons brandy, or rum, or sherry
caster sugar (for dusting)

For rich shortcrust pastry

8 oz flour
pinch of salt
5 oz butter
1 oz shortening, or lard
1 egg yolk
2–3 tablespoons cold water

Pastry cutters, patty tins

Method

Make the pastry and chill well. Set the oven at 400°F or Mark 6. On a lightly floured surface, roll out half the pastry fairly thinly, and stamp into rounds (size to fit patty tins) with a cutter. Put rounds to one side.

Add trimmings to second half of the pastry and roll out a little thinner than first half. Stamp in rounds, a little larger than first.

Mix brandy, rum or sherry with mincemeat. Put larger pastry rounds into patty tins, with a good spoonful of mincemeat to fill well. Place smaller rounds on top, pinch pastry edges together, brush lightly with cold water, dust with sugar.

Cook for 15–20 minutes until nicely brown. Cool slightly before taking from tins.

AMERICAN PIE PASTRY

Pastry for the American covered pie is slightly different from shortcrust both in ingredients and method. Most recipes for American shortcrust have a high proportion of fat to flour, and usually need more liquid for binding. This is because American and Canadian flour is milled from hard wheat which is very high in gluten (the major part of the protein content of wheat flour, which gives it its elasticity), and consequently absorbs more liquid.

The following recipe is an anglicised version, but has the same short, melt-in-the-mouth texture. As the texture is very short, the pastry is not easy to handle once cooked, so serve the pie in the dish in which it is baked (a round, shallow tin or dish—pie plate—about 2–2½ inches deep). The pastry is lined into the pie plate, fruit or other mixture is poured on top, and the pie is then covered with a lid of pastry.

Basic recipe

8 oz self-raising flour
5 oz lard, or shortening
pinch of salt
2 tablespoons cold water

Method

Place the lard or shortening in a bowl, add a good pinch of salt and the water, and cream ingredients together. Sift the flour over the softened fat and, using a round-bladed knife, cut the fat into the flour and mix to a rough dough. Chill for 30 minutes.

Turn the dough on to a floured board, knead lightly and then use for covered fruit pies.

Cherry pie

8 oz American pie pastry

For filling

2½ cups cherries (fresh or canned, stewed and stoned)
8 fl oz cherry juice
2 rounded tablespoons caster sugar
1 tablespoon melted butter
1 tablespoon fine tapioca, or sago
2 drops of almond essence
1 egg white (for glazing)
cream (optional)

7–8 inch diameter pie plate about 2½ inches deep

Method

Make American pie pastry and set aside to chill. Either fresh or canned Morello or red cherries (ie. not too sweet) are best for this pie. If fresh cherries are used, stone and cook in a little sugar syrup, and drain well.

Mix all the ingredients for the filling together and allow to stand for 15 minutes. Line the pastry on to the pie plate, pour in the fruit mixture and cover with the remaining pastry. Bake for 30–40 minutes in an oven at 400°F or Mark 6.

Take pie out of the oven, brush with lightly whisked egg white and dust with caster sugar. Put back into the oven, bake for a further 5–7 minutes. Serve hot or cold, with cream.

> **Sealing pastry edges:** Lightly flour the back of your forefinger, hold it firmly on pastry rim and, using the back of a knife, make indentations in double edges all round. The pressure from your finger is enough to seal pastry together and cutting with the back of the knife helps the pastry to rise and have an attractive flaky appearance.

FLANS

Flans are open tarts where the pastry (shortcrust, or French flan pastry known as pâte sucrée) is rolled out and lined on to a flan ring laid on a baking sheet. The flan is filled with a cake or savoury mixture, pastry cream, or more usually with fruit.

There are two types of flan ring, the 1-inch deep British one and the true French kind which is barely $\frac{3}{4}$ inch deep. This latter ring is the correct one for all fruit flans and can be found in specialist shops. The deeper ring is good for savoury flans, where a generous amount of filling is used. A flan can be made in a loose-bottomed sandwich tin, but to avoid breaking pastry, or a burn, leave it to cool before removing from the tin.

Apples, gooseberries and stone fruit may be cooked in the raw pastry flan. Other fruits, such as raspberries or poached fruit, are arranged in the pre-cooked flan (this is known as baking blind).

Once filled all fruit flans are glazed, either with a thickened fruit juice (particularly if cooked or canned fruit is used), or a jam or jelly glaze. For serving use a flat plate or board, not a shallow dish.

LINING A FLAN RING

1   Have ready the pastry, well chilled. Set the flan ring on a baking sheet, preferably without edges, for easy removal of the flan. Roll out the pastry to a thickness of $\frac{1}{4}-\frac{1}{2}$ inch, according to the recipe, and to a diameter about $1\frac{1}{2}$ inches bigger than the flan ring. Lift the pastry up on the rolling pin and lay over the flan ring, quickly easing it down into the ring.

2   Take a small ball of the dough, dip in flour and press the pastry into the ring, especially round the bottom edge.

3   Now bend back the top edge and roll off excess pastry with the rolling pin.

4   Pinch round the edge with the side of the forefinger and thumb, then push the dough (with the fingers) up the side from the bottom of the ring to increase the height of the edge. Prick the pastry base of the flan several times with a fork. Then fill with raw fruit.

BAKING BLIND

1   A flan case should be pre-cooked before filling with soft or cooked fruit. Once the flan ring is lined with pastry, chill for about 30 minutes to ensure the dough is well set.

2   Now line the pastry with crumpled greaseproof paper, pressing it well into the dough at the bottom edge and sides.

3   Three-parts fill the flan with uncooked rice or beans (to hold the shape) and put into the oven to bake. An 8-inch diameter flan ring holding a 6–8 oz quantity of pastry should cook for about 26 minutes in an oven at 400°F or Mark 6.

4   After about 20 minutes of the cooking time take flan out of the oven and carefully remove the paper and rice, or beans. (Beans may be used many times over for baking blind.) Replace the flan in the oven to complete cooking. The ring itself can either be taken off with the paper and rice, or removed after cooking. Once cooked, slide the flan on to a wire rack and then leave to cool.

GLAZES

Thickened fruit juice glaze

This is made from the juice of the cooked or canned fruit. To $\frac{1}{2}$ pint of juice take 1 heaped teaspoon of arrowroot and slake (mix) it with 1 tablespoon of

Lift pastry up on rolling pin, lay over the flan ring, quickly easing it down into the ring

Press pastry into ring with ball of floured dough. Bend back top edge, roll off any excess pastry

Pinch round edge with forefinger and thumb; push up sides from bottom of ring to raise edge

Before baking blind, line with greaseproof paper, then three-parts fill with beans or rice

the juice. Dissolve 1 tablespoon of red or yellow jam in the rest of the juice and bring to the boil in a saucepan. Then draw aside and add the moistened arrow-root, stir well, return to the heat and bring to the boil. Strain this mixture and, when cool, brush lavishly over the flan.

Apricot jam glaze

For use with all yellow fruit. Make a pound or so at a time as it keeps well and can be used as wanted. Store in a covered jar.

Turn the apricot jam into a saucepan, add the juice of $\frac{1}{2}$ lemon and 4 tablespoons water per lb. Bring slowly to the boil and simmer for 5 minutes. Strain and return to the pan. Boil for a further 5 minutes and turn into a jam jar for keeping. If for immediate use, continue boiling until thick, then brush amply over the fruit. If using a smooth jam (with no lumps of fruit), water is not needed.

Redcurrant jelly glaze

For use with all red fruit. Home-made redcurrant jelly (see page 185) is best as it gives the right sharpness of flavour to the fresh fruit. Beat the jelly with a fork or small whisk until it liquefies, then rub through a strainer into a small saucepan. Heat gently without stirring until quite clear (boiling will spoil both colour and flavour). When brushing this glaze over the fruit use a very soft brush. Always work from the centre outwards, drawing the brush, well laden with the glaze, towards the edge.

Gâteau basque

For rich shortcrust pastry
6 oz plain flour
pinch of salt
1 oz shortening
3 oz butter
3 rounded dessertspoons ground almonds
6 dessertspoons caster sugar
1 egg yolk
2–3 drops of vanilla essence
2–3 tablespoons cold water
4–5 heaped tablespoons jam (preferably plum, gooseberry, damson, etc.)
1 egg white (lightly beaten)
caster sugar (for dusting)

6-7 inch diameter flan ring

Method

Rub the fats into the flour and salt, in a bowl, add ground almonds and sugar. Mix egg yolk with vanilla and water in a basin and add to dry ingredients. Work up lightly to a firm paste and chill slightly.

Roll out two-thirds of the dough to $\frac{1}{4}$–$\frac{1}{2}$ inch thickness and line on to the flan ring. Fill with the jam, roll out the rest of the dough to a round and lay over the top. Press down the edges, mark the surface, cart-wheel-fashion, with the point of a knife. Bake for 30–35 minutes in an oven at 400°F or Mark 6. Lower oven temperature to 375°F or Mark 5 after the first 15 minutes.

Just before the gâteau is ready, brush the top with a little lightly beaten egg white, dust immediately with caster sugar and return to the oven for about 2 minutes to frost the top. Serve hot or cold.

Watchpoint The sugar must be dusted on to the egg white quickly, before the heat of the pastry has a chance to set the egg white, so that the sugar and egg white combine to make a meringue-like topping of frost.

Beauceronne tart

For rich shortcrust pastry
6 oz plain flour
pinch of salt
4½ oz butter
1 egg yolk
1 rounded dessertspoon sugar
2 tablespoons cold water
whipped cream (optional)

For filling
8 oz curd cheese
2 oz butter
2 rounded tablespoons caster sugar
2 rounded tablespoons raisins
2 tablespoons double cream
3 eggs (separated)
2 level tablespoons plain flour

8-inch diameter flan ring, or sandwich tin

Method

Make the rich shortcrust pastry and set aside to chill. Line the pastry on to the flan ring.

Now sieve the cheese and work well in a warm bowl. This

Strawberry tartlets

Lemon meringue pie

Apricot flan

will help the cheese to absorb the butter, sugar, cream and yolks without curdling, and allow the whisked egg whites to be folded in easily.

Cream the butter with the sugar in a bowl and beat well. Stir in the raisins, cream and egg yolks. When well mixed, whip egg whites stiffly and, using a metal spoon, fold into the mixture with the flour.

Turn into the pastry case and bake for 35–40 minutes in an oven at 375°–400°F or Mark 5–6. When cooked leave to cool as the filling rises a lot during cooking and must be left to subside before attempting to remove the flan ring or turn the tart out of the tin.

Serve cold and, for a special occasion, with lightly whipped cream.

Strawberry tartlets

For rich shortcrust pastry
5 oz plain flour
pinch of salt
3 oz butter
1 teaspoon caster sugar
1 egg yolk
1½–2 tablespoons cold water

For filling
8 oz strawberries
redcurrant jelly glaze

small tartlet tins

Method
Make the rich shortcrust pastry and set aside to chill. Line the pastry on to the small tartlet tins and bake blind (for about 8 minutes in an oven at 375°F or Mark 5). Allow to cool.

Hull (remove stalks from) the strawberries and keep on one side. Warm the redcurrant jelly glaze but do not boil. Brush the cases with the jelly, arrange strawberries in the cases and brush again with the glaze. The amount of glaze should be generous – sufficient to fill the pastry cases and so hold strawberries firmly in place.

> The recipe for apricot flan (right) describes the poaching of fruit and the method of glazing which applies to all fruit.

Lemon meringue pie

For rich shortcrust pastry
6 oz plain flour
pinch of salt
3½ oz butter
1 egg yolk
1–2 tablespoons cold water

For filling
1 rounded tablespoon cornflour
½ pint milk
1 rounded tablespoon sugar
2 egg yolks
grated rind and juice of 1 lemon

For meringue
2 egg whites
4 oz caster sugar

7-inch diameter flan ring

Method
Make the rich shortcrust pastry and set aside to chill. Then line on to the flan ring and bake blind.

Mix the cornflour with a little of the milk in a bowl and heat the rest of the milk in a saucepan. Pour on to the mixed cornflour, return to the pan and boil for 3–4 minutes, stirring continuously to make it smooth. Add the sugar, allow to cool a little, beat in the egg yolks, the grated lemon rind and juice. Pour this mixture into the pastry case; bake for about 10 minutes at 325°F or Mark 3 to set.

To make meringue: whisk the egg whites with a fork or wire whisk until stiff and dry. Whisk in 2 teaspoons of the sugar and then carefully fold in the remainder with a metal spoon.
Watchpoint Whisking in this small quantity of sugar helps set the whites and folding in the bulk is important to avoid knocking out the air beaten into the whites. If you overstir, the sugar starts to liquefy and the egg whites collapse, resulting in a rather thin layer of meringue which is also tough on the top.

Pile the meringue on the top to cover the filling completely, dredge with caster sugar. To set meringue, place in a cool oven for 10–15 minutes at 275°F or Mark 1. The consistency of a meringue topping should be that of a marshmallow, firm to cut, yet soft and with a crisp coating.

Apricot flan

For rich shortcrust pastry
6 oz plain flour
pinch of salt
4½ oz butter
1 rounded dessertspoon sugar
1 egg yolk
2 tablespoons water

For filling
1 lb fresh apricots
½ pint water
3 oz granulated sugar
apricot glaze

7-8 inch diameter flan ring

Method
Make the rich shortcrust pastry and set aside to chill.

Put the water and sugar into a shallow pan, dissolve on a slow heat, then boil rapidly for 2 minutes; draw syrup aside.

Wash the apricots and cut in half with a serrated-edge, stainless steel knife, or fruit knife, by cutting down to, and round, the stone from the stalk end, following the slight groove on the side of the apricot. Give the fruit a twist to halve it. If the stones do not come away easily, poach the apricots whole. Once cooked the stones can be taken out without breaking the fruit. Some of the stones can be cracked, the kernels skinned and added to the fruit for special flavour.

Place the halved apricots in a pan, cut side uppermost, cover in syrup and heat gently to boiling point. This will draw out the juice and so increase the quantity of syrup, although this will not in the first instance cover the fruit. Simmer for about 15 minutes, or until the apricots are tender. Cool in the syrup.

Roll out the pastry, line on to the flan ring and bake blind. Cool on a pastry rack.

The prepared apricot (jam) glaze should be hot and well reduced. If too thin, reduce to a thicker consistency by boiling the liquid quickly in an uncovered pan. Brush a light coating of glaze over the bottom and sides of the flan. Lift the apricots from the syrup with a spoon and arrange in the flan. Brush well with the hot glaze.

Alternatively, the apricot syrup can be thickened (see page 207) and used in place of jam glaze. Jam is better, however, if the flan has to be kept for a while before serving.

Flans with savoury fillings make meals in themselves or snacks; shown above are quiche lorraine (left) and smoked haddock flan

Quiche lorraine

For rich shortcrust pastry
6 oz plain flour
pinch of salt
3 oz butter, or margarine
1 oz shortening
2 tablespoons cold water

For filling
1 egg
1 egg yolk
1 rounded tablespoon cheese (grated)
salt and pepper
¼ pint single cream, or milk
½ oz butter
2-3 rashers of streaky bacon (diced)
1 small onion (thinly sliced), or 12 spring onions

7-inch diameter flan ring

Hot or cold, this bacon tart is the most typical of dishes from the Lorraine region of France.

Method
Make the rich shortcrust pastry and set aside to chill.

When chilled, line the pastry on to the flan ring. Beat the egg and extra yolk in a bowl, add the cheese, seasoning and cream or milk. Melt the butter in a small pan, add the bacon and sliced onion, or whole spring onions, and cook slowly until just golden in colour. Then turn contents of the pan into the egg mixture, mix well and pour into the pastry case.

Bake for about 25-30 minutes in an oven at 375°F or Mark 5.

Smoked haddock flan

For rich shortcrust pastry
6 oz plain flour
pinch of salt
1 oz shortening
3 oz butter
2 tablespoons cold water

For filling
1½ lb smoked haddock (cooked and flaked)
1½-2 lb potatoes (boiled and creamed)
1 egg yolk
2 tablespoons cheese (grated)
1 small bunch of spring onions, or green part of 1 leek (shredded, well blanched)
2 hard-boiled eggs (quartered)

For béchamel sauce
½ pint milk (infused with slice of onion, 6 peppercorns, 1 blade of mace, 1 bayleaf)
¾ oz butter
1 rounded tablespoon plain flour
salt and pepper

8-inch diameter flan ring

Method
Make the rich shortcrust pastry and set aside to chill. When chilled, line pastry on to flan ring and bake blind for 20 minutes in the oven at 400°F or Mark 6.

Add the yolk to the creamed potato with 1 rounded tablespoon of grated cheese. Arrange flaked haddock on the pastry with onions on top and quartered eggs round the edge. Spoon the béchamel sauce over all and decorate with creamed potato round the edge and across the centre (preferably using a forcing bag and an 8-cut rose pipe). Sprinkle with the rest of the grated cheese and brown in oven at 400°-475°F or Mark 7 if filling is already hot. If filling is cold, heat flan for about 20-30 minutes at 350°F or Mark 4.

Salé (Swiss cheese dish)

For rich shortcrust pastry
6 oz plain flour
pinch of salt
3 oz butter
1 oz shortening
1 egg yolk
2 tablespoons cold water

For filling
½ pint béchamel sauce
little double cream
3 eggs
4½ oz Gruyère cheese (grated)
salt and pepper
grated nutmeg

7-inch diameter flan ring

Method
Make the rich shortcrust pastry and set aside to chill. When chilled, line the pastry on to the flan ring. Make the béchamel sauce (but add a little cream to it) and when cool beat in the eggs and grated cheese; add plenty of seasoning and a grating of nutmeg. Pour the mixture into the pastry case and bake for about 25 minutes in an oven at 375°-400°F or Mark 5-6.

Mushroom flan

For rich shortcrust pastry
6 oz plain flour
pinch of salt
2 oz butter
2 oz shortening
2 tablespoons cold water

For filling

½ pint milk
1 blade mace
1 bayleaf
6 peppercorns
1½ oz butter
1 medium-size onion (thinly sliced)
6 oz mushrooms (sliced)
3 tablespoons plain flour
salt and pepper
2 tablespoons double cream (optional)
1 egg yolk
1 small egg

7-inch diameter flan ring

Method

Make the rich shortcrust pastry and line on to the flan ring, reserving about one-third to cut into strips for the top. Set aside to chill.

Infuse the milk with the mace, bayleaf and peppercorns until well flavoured; then strain off into a jug. Scrape (using a plastic scraper) or rinse out the pan, melt half the butter in the same pan and add the onion. Cook slowly until soft but without browning, then add the mushrooms and increase the heat. Cook briskly for 2–3 minutes, stirring occasionally. Then draw off the heat, add the rest of the butter and stir in the flour. Add the milk by degrees, blend thoroughly, and stir over heat until boiling. Draw aside again, to add the cream, yolk and seasoning. Turn on to a plate to cool.

Fill the flan with this mixture. Roll out the remaining pastry and cut into thin strips. Lay a diagonal lattice over the top of the flan, pressing the ends of the strips well down on to the edge. Cover this with a strip of pastry to neaten. Beat the small egg with salt and brush over the flan. Bake for 25–35 minutes in an oven at 400°F or Mark 6.

FLAKY AND ROUGH PUFF PASTRY

Both these traditional pastries originated in farmhouse kitchens where lard from home-killed pigs and home-produced butter were always available. These pastries form the basis of many regional specialities, such as Eccles and Banbury cakes, and are popular crusts for both sweet and savoury pies. When terms such as '8 oz of pastry' or 'an 8 oz quantity of pastry' are used, this means the amount obtained by using 8 oz of flour, not 8 oz of prepared pastry dough. As a quantity guide, 8 oz of flaky or rough puff pastry will cover a 9-inch long pie dish, or an 8-inch diameter pie plate. For recipes, see overleaf.

Flaky pastry

8 oz plain flour
pinch of salt
3 oz butter
3 oz lard
¼ pint ice-cold water (to mix)

Method

Sift the flour with salt into a bowl. Divide the fats into four portions (two of butter, two of lard); rub one portion – either lard or butter – into the flour and mix to a firm dough with cold water. The amount of water varies with different flour but an average quantity for 8 oz flour is 4–5 fluid oz (about ¼ pint or 8–10 tablespoons); the finer the flour the more water it will absorb.

Knead the dough lightly until smooth, then roll out to an oblong. Put a second portion of fat (not the same kind as first portion rubbed in) in small pieces on to two-thirds of the dough. Fold in three, half turn the dough to bring the open edge towards you and roll out again to an oblong. Put on a third portion of fat in pieces, fold dough in three, wrap in a cloth or polythene bag and leave in a cool place for 15 minutes.

Roll out dough again, put on remaining fat in pieces, fold and roll as before. If pastry looks at all streaky, give one more turn and roll again.

Rough puff pastry (1)

8 oz plain flour
pinch of salt
6 oz firm butter, or margarine
¼ pint ice-cold water (to mix)

The first of the two types of rough puff pastry is a quicker and less fussy one, although the same ingredients are used in both types. You can use either type in recipes but the second is likely to be a little lighter.

Method

Sift the flour with salt into a mixing bowl. Cut the fat in even-size pieces about the size of walnuts and drop into the flour. Mix quickly with the water (to prevent overworking dough so that it becomes starchy) and turn on to a lightly-floured board.

Complete the following action three times; roll to an oblong, fold in three and make a half-turn to bring the open edges in front of you so that the pastry has three turns in all. Chill for 10 minutes and give an extra roll and fold if it looks at all streaky, then use as required.

Rough puff pastry (2)

8 oz plain flour
pinch salt
6 oz firm butter, or margarine
¼ pint ice-cold water (to mix)

Method

Sift the flour with salt into a mixing bowl. Take 1 oz of fat and rub it into the flour. Mix to a firm but pliable dough with the water, knead lightly until smooth, then set in a cool place for 10–15 minutes.

Place the remaining fat between two pieces of grease-proof paper and beat to a flat cake with the rolling pin. This fat should be the same consistency as the dough.

Roll out this dough to a rectangle, place the flattened fat in the middle, fold like a parcel and turn over.

Complete the following action three times: roll out dough to an oblong, fold in three and make a half-turn to bring the open edge towards you so that the pastry has three turns in all. Chill for 10 minutes, then roll out and use as required.

Cream horns

8 oz rough puff pastry (well chilled)
1 egg white (beaten)
strawberry, or raspberry, jam
¼ pint Chantilly cream
pistachio nuts (finely chopped) – for decoration

12 cream horn moulds

Method
Lightly grease the moulds and a baking sheet. Set the oven at 425°F or Mark 7.

Roll out the pastry ⅛-inch thick, cut into long, 1-inch-wide strips and brush these with a very little beaten egg white. Wind the pastry round the cream horn moulds, starting at the point and overlapping each round. Trim the tops, brush again with egg white, set on a lightly-greased baking tray and cook in pre-set oven for 7–8 minutes until crisp and pale golden-brown.

Remove the horns from the tins. When cold, put a ½ teaspoon of jam at the bottom of each horn and fill with Chantilly cream. Decorate the top of each one with a small pinch of pistachio nuts.

Cream horns are made with rough puff pastry; they are filled with a little jam and then Chantilly cream

The following recipes all use flaky pastry made with 3 oz butter and 3 oz lard, except where otherwise specified

Banbury cakes

8 oz flaky pastry (well chilled)

For filling
2 oz butter
1 tablespoon flour
4 oz currants
2 tablespoons mixed peel (finely chopped)
½ teaspoon ground allspice, or grated nutmeg
4 dessertspoons sugar
1 tablespoon rum (optional)
1 egg white (beaten)
caster sugar (for dusting)

Method
Melt the butter, blend in the flour and cook gently for 2 minutes. Add the well-washed currants, the peel, spice or grated nutmeg, sugar and rum, if used, and simmer for 2–3 minutes. Allow to cool.

Set oven at 425°F or Mark 7. Roll out the pastry ⅛-inch thick, turn it over and cut large rounds about the size of a saucer, damp top edges and put a good tablespoon of prepared filling on each. Draw the edges into the centre and seal them together; turn the cakes over and roll each round to an oblong, pinching each end to a point to give the traditional Banbury cake shape.

Make three slashes on the top, place the cakes on a baking sheet and bake in the pre-set oven for 15 minutes. Then brush them with beaten egg, dust them with the caster sugar and continue cooking for 5 minutes longer. Dust again with sugar before serving.

Eccles cakes

8 oz flaky pastry (well chilled)

For filling
1 oz butter
1 rounded tablespoon soft brown sugar
4 oz currants
little grated nutmeg, or mixed spice
1 rounded tablespoon candied peel (finely chopped)
1 egg white (beaten)
caster sugar

Method
Set oven at 425°F or Mark 7.

Melt the butter and stir in the sugar; add the currants, well washed and still wet, the nutmeg, or spice, and finely chopped peel.

Roll out the pastry very thinly, turn over and cut into 6-inch diameter rounds (use a saucer to cut round). Put a good tablespoon of filling in the centre of each round and damp pastry edges, draw to the centre and pinch well together. Turn pastry over, flatten gently with the rolling pin so the currants just show through, but still keep the cakes round. Make three small cuts on the top, brush with egg white, dust with caster sugar, place on a baking sheet and bake in preset oven for 10–15 minutes, or until golden.

Veal and ham pie

8 oz flaky pastry (well chilled)
1½ lb veal pie meat, or a piece of oyster (shoulder cut)
1 dessertspoon onion (finely chopped)
1 dessertspoon parsley (finely chopped)
grated rind of ¼ lemon
4 oz lean cooked ham, or gammon rasher
3 hard-boiled eggs (quartered)
salt and pepper
¾ pint jellied stock (well seasoned)
1 egg (beaten)

9-inch diameter pie dish

Method
Cut the veal in pieces 1–1½ inches square. Mix chopped onion, parsley and lemon rind together and roll meat in this mixture. Shred the ham or if a gammon rasher is used, cut off the rind and rust, cut in strips and blanch by putting into boiling water and boiling for ½ minute before draining.

Arrange the meat, ham and quartered eggs in layers till the pie dish is full, doming the top slightly. Pour in stock and three-quarters fill the dish.

Roll out the pastry, cut a strip to cover the edge of the pie dish, press it down well and then brush with water. Lift the rest of the pastry on to the rolling pin and lay it carefully over the dish. Trim round the edge and seal pastry edges with the back of a knife. This separates the layers so that the pastry puffs up during cooking.

Roll out pastry trimmings and cut leaves for decoration. Make a hole in the centre of the pie with the point of a knife and arrange a decoration around this. The hole will allow steam to escape.

Brush with beaten egg mixed with a large pinch of salt (adding salt to egg gives pastry a very shiny brown glaze). Bake for 1–1½ hours in pre-set oven at 425°F or Mark 7.

To cover a veal and ham pie: arrange meat in the pie dish so that it is slightly domed; this will prevent pastry from falling in while cooking. Roll out pastry to shape of dish, then cut off a strip to cover its edge; press down well, then brush with cold water

Beefsteak, pigeon and mushroom pie

2 pigeons
1 oz butter
1½ lb shin of beef (cut into 1-inch squares)
2 pints chicken stock
salt and pepper
½ pint aspic jelly (commercially prepared)
¼ lb flat mushrooms
8 oz quantity of rough puff, or flaky, or puff, pastry
1 egg (beaten)
pinch of salt

9-inch long pie dish

Method
Melt the butter in a large stew-pan, add the pigeons and brown slowly. Remove from the dish, split in half and return to the dish with the squares of beef and the stock. Season with salt and pepper, cover and cook slowly on top of the stove for 2–2½ hours. Then cut the breast meat from the pigeons and discard the carcass; add the aspic to the

pan, turn out into a bowl and leave to get cold. Wash and trim the mushrooms, cut in quarters and put in a pie dish with the cooked meats and liquid. Place a pie funnel in the middle of the dish. Roll out the pastry to an oblong just under ¼-inch thick and about 3 inches wider and 4 inches longer than your pie dish. Cut off extra pastry; roll these trimmings to ⅛-inch thick. From this thinner pastry, cut strips to fit on the rim of the pie dish, and make leaves and a thistle, or rose, from the pastry, for decoration. Dampen the rim of the pie dish and cover with a strip of pastry, pressing it firmly in position, then brush the pastry with cold water. Lift the thicker piece of pastry on your rolling pin and lay it carefully over the top of the pie, taking care not to stretch it.

Trim it and press the two layers of pastry on the rim very firmly together; seal and flute the edges.

Add a large pinch of salt to the beaten egg and beat lightly with a fork until the salt dissolves and the egg darkens in colour; this will give the pastry a rich brown and shiny glaze. Brush pie with egg wash, decorate with pastry leaves, make a hole in the pastry in the centre of the leaves (above pie funnel) to let steam escape during cooking. Brush again with egg wash. Cook the rose or thistle on a baking sheet and put on pie when cooked.

Bake in a hot oven pre-set at 425°F or Mark 7 for about 20–25 minutes, until pastry is cooked. While the pie is still warm add a little more liquid aspic through hole in centre, if necessary. Serve cold.

HOT WATER CRUST

Raised pork pie

1 lb pork (lean and fat mixed)
salt and pepper
1 rounded teaspoon mixed dried herbs
¼ pint jellied stock (made from pork bones)

For hot water crust
1 lb plain flour
1 teaspoon salt
7 oz lard
7½ fl oz milk and water (mixed in equal proportions)
milk (for glaze) – optional

1 jar (eg. kilner jar)

Method
Dice pork for filling, season well and add herbs.

For hot water crust: warm a mixing bowl and sift in flour and salt, make a well in the centre of the flour.

Heat lard in milk and water. When just boiling, pour into the well in the flour, stir quickly with a wooden spoon until thick, then work with the hand to a dough. Turn on to a board or table, cut off a quarter of the dough, put it back in the warm bowl and cover with a cloth.

Pat out the rest of dough with the fist to a thick round, set a large jar in the centre and work dough up sides. Let dough cool

then gently lift out jar. Fill dough case with meat mixture. Roll or pat out remaining dough to form a lid, leave a small hole in it, then put on top of pie, seal edges. Glaze with milk if wished.

Slide pie on to a baking sheet and bake in pre-set oven for 1–1½ hours at 350°F or Mark 4. If pie is getting too brown, cover with damp greaseproof paper towards end of cooking time. Leave till cool before placing a funnel in hole in lid and filling up with jellied stock.

Watchpoint You must work quickly and mould pastry while it is still warm, otherwise lard sets and pastry becomes brittle.

To make a raised pork pie case: work dough up sides of jar while it is still warm

213

PUFF PASTRY

There are three basic points to remember about puff pastry. First, the conditions in which you make it: everything must be cool—ingredients, mixing bowl, pastry board, rolling pin, and, most important, your hands. Second, the first mixing of the dough is all-important. If the foundation dough is not right, it's better to start again rather than waste your fat. Finally, be absolutely sure of the way you roll out the pastry because this stage is vital. The pressure on the rolling pin must always be firm and downwards, and roll one way only to make sure pressure is even at all times.

Puff pastry can be used for making bouchées, vol-au-vents and pastries; recipes are given on the following pages.

Forming the dough

To have perfect results when making puff pastry, you must use the right kind of flour and fat, and always use ice-cold water for mixing.

It is also important to work in a very cool atmosphere. Never attempt to make puff pastry in very hot weather; it will become sticky and difficult to handle. Make it early in the morning (if possible before you have done any cooking), as a kitchen soon becomes warm and steamy.

Fat should be cool and firm. The best puff pastry for flavour and texture is made from butter; this should be of a firm con-

> **Note:** when terms such as 8 oz pastry or an 8 oz quantity of pastry are used, this means the amount obtained by using 8 oz flour, not 8 oz prepared dough. As a quantity guide, 12 oz puff pastry makes 12 bouchées (entrée-size as given here), or 1 vol-au-vent and 6 bouchées.
>
> Also, it is essential when baking pastry to pre-set the oven to the required temperature.

sistency and slightly salted — such as English, Australian or New Zealand. Continental butters are too creamy in texture and result in a sticky pastry, difficult to handle.

If margarine has to be used, again use a firm variety (one that does not spread easily). The cheapest varieties of butter and margarine are the best for this purpose.

Flour should be 'strong', ie. a bread flour which has a high gluten content. It should also be well sifted and quite cool.

The flour is made into a firm dough with a little butter and the water. This preliminary mixing is most important as it is on this that the success of the pastry depends.

Add the lemon juice to approximately two-thirds of the given amount of water. Stir until a dough begins to form, then add remaining water. If water is added a little at a time, it will dry in the flour and the resulting dough will be tough. The finished dough should be firm yet pliable and have the consistency of butter, taking into account the different textures.

Knead the dough firmly — this and the presence of the lemon juice develops the gluten in the flour and means that the dough will stand the frequent rolling and folding necessary in the preparation of puff pastry.

The butter should be cool and firm, but not used straight from the refrigerator. If it is overhard (or not taken from the refrigerator early enough), put it between two pieces of damp greaseproof paper and beat it 2–3 times with the rolling pin. It is then ready to be rolled into the dough.

Rolling out the dough

The method of rolling is also important and differs slightly from the usual way. You roll shortcrust pastry to shape the dough; in puff pastry it is the rolling that actually makes it.

Always roll the dough away from you, keeping the pressure as even as possible. Many people are inclined to put more weight on the right or left hand, which pulls the dough to one side; keep it straight by applying

even pressure all round.

Bring the rolling pin down smartly on to the dough and roll it forward with a strong, firm pressure in one direction only. Continue until just before the edge of the dough.

Watchpoint Never let the rolling pin run off the edge as the object is to keep the dough strictly rectangular in shape.

Lift the rolling pin and continue rolling forward in one direction, bringing it down at the point to which it was last rolled. In this way the whole area of the dough is rolled in even layers, $\frac{1}{2}$–$\frac{3}{4}$ inch thick.

Once rolled to an even rectangle, the dough is folded in three round the butter (see method opposite). Graduate the thickness of the following rollings, so that these subsequent ones are progressively thinner. You must avoid pushing butter through the dough, which might happen if it was rolled thinly in the beginning.

Watchpoint Do not turn the dough over; it should only be rolled on one side.

Each rolling is called a 'turn' and puff pastry usually has six turns with a 15-minute rest between every two. Before each turn the dough is folded in three (ends to middle) and the edges sealed with the side of the hand or the rolling pin to prevent the folds shifting when dough is rolled. The short period of rest is to remove any elasticity from the dough. If at the end of the rollings the dough is at all streaky (showing that the butter has not been rolled in completely), a seventh turn can be given.

Should fat begin to break through dough, stop at once. Dust dough with flour, brush off the surplus, and chill it for 10 minutes before continuing.

Once made, the pastry may be finally rolled out, cut to shape and stored, wrapped in greaseproof paper and a cloth. It need not be stored in a strip. It will keep for 24–48 hours in a cool place.

Save all trimmings and fold them in three. Place all trimmings on top of each other. Roll out and use for making

Left: *After first rolling out of the pastry, butter is laid on the centre and sides turned in over it.* Right: *The pastry is folded into three, ends to middle, like a parcel*

Left: *Rolling pin is brought down lightly on to the pastry to flatten it before rolling out.* Right: *After each rolling, pastry is always folded into three, the ends pulled to keep them rectangular*

mille feuilles, jalousies and sacristans (see recipes given on pages 217–218).

Baking pastry

If the uncooked pastry seems a little soft, place it on a baking sheet in refrigerator for about 15 minutes (no longer) for it to firm up before baking.

Place pastry on a thick baking sheet well dampened with cold water. This helps to prevent pastry from sliding and shrinking too much while baking. A thick baking sheet will not buckle in the hot oven.

Puff pastry is cooked in a hot oven at 425°F or Mark 7. A large case, such as a vol-au-vent or flan, is baked in the centre of the oven. Small pieces such as bouchées and so on, are baked on the top shelf about 5 inches from the roof of the oven. The above applies to gas ovens, as electric ovens vary according to where the elements are placed. Follow your electric cooker's instruction book.

Basic puff pastry

8 oz plain flour
pinch of salt
8 oz butter
1 teaspoon lemon juice
scant ¼ pint water (ice cold)

This quantity will make a vol-au-vent for 4 people or 6–8 medium-size bouchées. Use up trimmings as recipes on pages 217–218.

Method
Sift flour and salt into a bowl. Rub in a piece of butter the size of a walnut. Add lemon juice to water, make a well in centre of flour and pour in about two-thirds of the liquid. Mix with a palette, or round-bladed, knife. When the dough is beginning to form, add remaining water.

Turn out the dough on to a marble slab, a laminated-plastic work top, or a board, dusted with flour. Knead dough for 2–3 minutes, then roll out to a square about ½–¾ inch thick.

Beat butter, if necessary, to make it pliable and place in centre of dough. Fold this up over butter to enclose it completely (sides and ends over centre like a parcel). Wrap in a cloth or piece of greaseproof paper and put in the refrigerator for 10–15 minutes.

Flour slab or work top, put on dough, the join facing upwards, and bring rolling pin down on to dough 3–4 times to flatten it slightly.

Now roll out to a rectangle about ½–¾ inch thick. Fold into three, ends to middle, as accurately as possible, if necessary pulling the ends to keep them rectangular. Seal the edges with your hand or rolling pin and turn pastry half round to bring the edge towards you. Roll out again and fold in three. Set pastry aside in refrigerator for 15 minutes.

Repeat this process, giving a total of 6 turns with three 15-minute rests after each two turns. Then leave in the refrigerator until wanted.

> **A puff pastry flan case** differs from a vol-au-vent in that it is shallow, larger in diameter and made with two pieces of pastry. When baked it may be filled with a savoury mixture (as for vol-au-vent) or with fresh fruit, covered with a glaze.

215

Beef en croûte

2 lb fillet of beef
8 oz quantity of puff pastry
pepper
butter (to sauté and roast)
4 oz button mushrooms
1 dessertspoon chopped mixed
    herbs and parsley
egg (for glazing)
watercress, or parsley (to
    garnish)

These quantities serve 4–6 people. If it is to be served cold it can be made the day before. If hot, do the preliminary cooking the day before, wrap meat in the pastry and keep in refrigerator. Bake it on the day.

Method

First prepare the pastry and keep well chilled in the refrigerator overnight. Set oven at 425°F or Mark 7.

Trim and tie up the fillet; pepper it and brown it quickly all over in hot butter, then roast in oven for 10 minutes. Take out and allow to get cold; remove string or thread. In the meantime slice mushrooms and sauté them in butter for a few minutes; draw pan aside, add the herbs, and cool.

Roll out the puff pastry to a rectangle. Divide it in two, one piece two-thirds larger than the other. Put the mushroom mixture on the larger piece, lay the beef on top and press up the pastry round it. Lay the other piece of pastry over the top, pressing the edges together well, brush with egg glaze and decorate with 'fleurons' of pastry. Bake in pre-set oven for 35–40 minutes or until well browned.

Serve beef hot or cold, garnished with watercress or parsley. If hot, serve a demi-glace, or madère, sauce separately and vegetables of choice. If cold, serve with a selection of salads.

Vol-au-vent

8 oz puff pastry (well chilled)
egg wash

Pan lid (6–7 inch diameter), 3–4 inch
    diameter plain cutter

Method

Set oven at 425°F or Mark 7.
Roll out the made puff pastry on a floured slab or work top to a square, $\frac{1}{2}$–$\frac{3}{4}$ inches thick.

To cut vol-au-vent shape: place pan lid on pastry and cut round it with a knife; hold the knife slantwise to form a bevelled edge, wider at the base. Turn this round upside down on to a dampened baking sheet, so that the widest part is on top. Brush lightly with the egg wash.

Watchpoint Egg wash acts as a seal, so don't let it touch the cut edge or it will stop the pastry from rising.

With the cutter (or a small pan lid), mark a circle in the centre of round with the back of a knife and mark lines for decoration. Chill pastry 10–15 minutes if it seems a little soft, then bake in pre-set oven for 25–30 minutes.

When well risen and a good colour, slide on to a rack to cool. While still warm cut round the circular mark with the point of a small knife to remove the top. Set this aside and carefully scoop out some of the soft centre. Place vol-au-vent case on serving dish before filling. (It can be baked beforehand but do not add filling until just before serving.)

Vol-au-vents can be filled with shellfish, veal, chicken, sweetbreads and mushrooms, bound with a white or velouté sauce.

Make a vol-au-vent shape by placing a pan lid on the rolled out pastry and cutting round it Place pastry underside up on baking sheet; mark out centre circle and lines for decoration. When cooked, cut out the centre circle and scoop out some of soft vol-au-vent centre. The case is then ready for filling

An egg wash is made by beating 1 egg with $\frac{1}{2}$ teaspoon of salt. This liquefies the egg, which makes it easier to brush a thin film on pastry, and also increases the shine when baked.

Bouchées

12 oz puff pastry (well chilled)
egg wash

2$\frac{1}{2}$-inch diameter fluted cutter, 1$\frac{1}{2}$-
    inch diameter cutter (fluted or
    plain)

Method

Set oven at 425°F or Mark 7.
Roll out made puff pastry, not more than $\frac{1}{2}$ inch thick.

To cut bouchées: stamp out rounds with larger fluted cutter, keeping them close together so that no pastry is wasted. As rounds are cut, lift on to a dampened baking sheet.

Lightly brush rounds with egg wash and with smaller cutter make a circular cut (for lid) in centre of each one. To save time, brush whole sheet of pastry with egg wash before cutting out bouchées.

Chill bouchées for a few minutes, then bake in pre-set oven for 15–20 minutes or until golden-brown. Lift on to a rack to cool. With the point of a small knife lift out centre lid and scoop out any soft centre. Insert a good tablespoon of filling and replace top.

If bouchées are very small, they can be split without cutting out centre 'lid', and a good tablespoon of filling put in.

Watchpoint The larger the case, the thicker the pastry must be rolled. A vol-au-vent of 6–7 inch diameter calls for a $\frac{1}{2}$–$\frac{3}{4}$ inch thickness of pastry, whereas a bouchée of 1$\frac{1}{2}$–2 inch diameter needs a $\frac{1}{4}$-inch thickness of pastry. If pastry is too thick for the size of bouchée, it will topple over in oven when it has risen to a certain height.

However good pastry is, some shrinkage in baking has to be allowed for. When choosing a cutter take one a size larger than you want for your bouchée: a 2$\frac{1}{2}$-inch round of uncooked pastry will make a 2$\frac{1}{4}$-inch bouchée.

A **bouchée** (mouthful) is similar to a vol-au-vent but smaller. Individual bouchées served as an entrée are about $2\frac{1}{4}$ inches in diameter, and for cocktail savouries $1-1\frac{1}{2}$ inches in diameter. The fillings are savoury and can be the same as for a vol-au-vent.

Flan case

8 oz puff pastry
egg wash

Two pan lids, or rings (8-inch and 6-inch diameter)

Method
Set oven at 425°F or Mark 7.

Roll out made puff pastry, a scant $\frac{1}{2}$-inch thick.

To cut flan case: cut out a round with larger lid, keeping a straight edge. With smaller lid cut out a centre circle. You will then have one outer ring (1 inch wide) and one large round (6 inches in diameter).

Slide this outer ring to one side and re-roll 6-inch round with any trimmings to make a larger but thinner round (about $\frac{1}{4}$-inch thick and 8 inches in diameter) to form flan base.

Lift this round of pastry on to the damp baking sheet, brush very lightly with egg wash, then lift the ring on to it. Neaten both layers into a perfect round and cut away any surplus pastry. Brush top of the ring with egg wash and mark with the back of a knife in diagonal lines to decorate.

Prick the centre with a fork, chill 10–15 minutes in refrigerator, then bake in pre-set oven for 25–30 minutes. Cool slightly before sliding off baking sheet. The flan case is now ready for a savoury or sweet filling (see shortcrust pastry flans, pages 207–211).

Jalousie

6 oz puff pastry, or trimmings
4 tablespoons home-made jam (gooseberry, apricot or plum), or apple marmelade (see page 266)
1 egg white (beaten)
caster sugar (for dusting)

Method
Set oven at 425°F or Mark 7.

Roll out made pastry to a large rectangle, $\frac{1}{4}$-inch thick.

A fresh fruit flan, a jalousie, and a mille feuilles (see recipe on page 218) are just a few of the mouth-watering puff pastries to be made

Trim and cut out a piece approximately 8 inches by 4 inches. Fold this piece over lengthways and, with a sharp knife, cut across fold at $\frac{1}{4}$-inch intervals, but not right to outer edges (see pages 207–211), leaving a border of about $1-1\frac{1}{2}$ inches.

Fold up trimmings and roll out thinly to a rectangle twice the size of folded pastry; lift on to dampened baking sheet.

Spoon the jam or marmelade down the centre, spreading it a little. Brush the edges with cold water, then lift the first on to the second rectangle of pastry, with the folded edge on the centre. Open out the folded pastry and press the border down on to the lower piece. Cut round edges to neaten, chill for 10 minutes, if necessary, then bake in pre-set oven for 25–30 minutes.

From 5–10 minutes before it's cooked take out of the oven and brush with egg white, beaten to a froth, and dust well with caster sugar. Replace in the

oven and remove jalousie when a golden-brown.

Slide on to a rack to cool. Serve hot or cold.

Sacristans

6 oz puff pastry, or trimmings
1 egg (beaten)
chopped almonds
icing sugar (for dusting)

Method
Set oven at 425°F or Mark 7.

Roll out made pastry to a thin strip, 5 inches wide. Brush with beaten egg, leaving a border of about $\frac{1}{2}$ inch at each side. Sprinkle with almonds and dust with sifted icing sugar.

Cut into strips about $\frac{3}{4}$ inch wide; take up these strips and twist several times before laying them on dampened baking sheet. Press down each end firmly. Bake in pre-set oven for 8–10 minutes. Carefully lift biscuits off baking sheet and leave to cool on a wire rack.

Mille feuilles

6 oz puff pastry, or trimmings
½ pint double cream (whipped)
3 tablespoons raspberry jam

For icing
4–6 oz icing sugar
1½ tablespoons water, or 2 of
  sugar syrup (made with
  2 tablespoons granulated sugar
  dissolved in 4 tablespoons
  water, then boiled for
  10 minutes)
2–3 drops of vanilla essence

Method
Set oven at 425°F or Mark 7.

Roll out prepared pastry as thinly as possible to a large rectangle. Lay this over dampened baking sheet, allowing pastry to come slightly over the edge. Prick pastry well all over with a fork and chill for 5–10 minutes. Then bake in pre-set oven for 10–15 minutes.

When brown in colour, slip a palette knife under pastry and turn it over. Cook in oven for a further 5 minutes, then transfer to a rack to cool. When cold, trim round edges and cut into 3 strips about 3 inches wide. Crush trimmings lightly.

Whip cream but not too stiffly. Spread one strip with half the jam, then half the cream. Lay a second strip on top and press down lightly. Spread with rest of jam and cream, top with last strip, press down again.

To make icing: mix icing sugar to a cream with water or sugar syrup, add vanilla essence. Warm icing slightly and use to coat the top. Press trimmings round edges to decorate.

Watchpoint Mille feuilles pastry must be well-baked, almost nut-brown in colour. You press layers together to prevent them moving when sliced.

Spreading the well-baked layers of puff pastry for mille feuilles first with jam and then whipped cream

CHOUX PASTRY

Although a quick and easy pastry to make, choux does call for care in measuring ingredients, otherwise results may be uneven and unsuccessful. You will find that it is better to weigh dry ingredients on scales rather than use a tablespoon for measuring them.

Most people are familiar with sweet choux pastries such as éclairs and profiteroles, but there are savoury ones too. These can either be baked or fried (beignets soufflés) and make excellent supper dishes.

General points
Choux pastry is not made like other types of pastry. The fat is put into a pan with water and, when this has boiled, the flour is poured in and beaten. It is important, however, that you only beat the flour until the pastry is smooth; this takes a few seconds only. Continued beating at this stage will mean that the pastry will not rise.

Use plain flour, or, for a particularly crisp result, a 'strong' flour (one with a good gluten content). This type of flour is now available in good stores.

Once the eggs have been added, the pastry should then be beaten thoroughly. An electric mixer can be used at this stage with the paddle or dough hook on slow speed.

Choux pastry should be baked in a hot oven on a rising temperature, ie. cooked for 10 minutes at 400°F or Mark 6, then the cooking completed at 425°F or Mark 7 for the length of time given in the recipe. This will ensure that the choux is brown and crisp. If it is still pale in colour, it will collapse when taken out of the oven.

Choux is usually baked on a dampened baking sheet (hold sheet under the cold tap for a few seconds). Once baked and taken off the sheet to cool, make a hole in the side of the choux pastry with a skewer or the point of knife to release any steam and so keep it crisp.

Do not make more choux pastry than you need. Once baked it does not keep well and should be used within 2–3 hours. For frying instructions, see page 100.

Basic choux pastry

Quantity for 3–4 people
¼ pint (5 fl oz) water
2 oz butter, or margarine
2½ oz plain flour
2 eggs

Quantity for 4–6 people
7½ fl oz water
3 oz butter, or margarine
3¾ oz plain flour
3 eggs

Method
Put water and fat into a fairly large pan. Sift flour on to a piece of paper. Bring contents of the pan to the boil and when bubbling draw pan aside, allow bubbles to subside and pour in all the flour at once. Stir vigorously until it is smooth (a few seconds).

Cool mixture for about 5 minutes, then beat in the eggs one at a time. If eggs are large, break the last one into a bowl and beat with a fork. Add this slowly to ensure that the mixture remains firm and keeps its shape (you may not need to use all of this last egg).

Beat pastry for about 3 minutes until it looks glossy. It is then ready to be piped out, using a plain éclair nozzle, or shaped with a spoon for baking or frying.

SWEET CHOUX
Chocolate profiteroles

choux pastry for 4–6 people
½ pint chocolate pastry cream
  (see page 240)

For rich chocolate sauce
  (sauce Suchard)
6 oz dessert, or bitter, chocolate
½ pint water
4 oz granulated sugar

Forcing bag; plain éclair nozzle

Method
Set oven at 400°F or Mark 6. Prepare choux pastry (see basic recipe). Pipe out into small balls or put out with a teaspoon on a dampened baking sheet. Bake for 20–30 minutes on a rising temperature until crisp. Lift profiteroles off sheets, prick sides

Chocolate profiteroles: an eye-catching dinner party sweet

to release steam. Leave to cool.

Prepare chocolate pastry cream and set aside.

Meanwhile make chocolate sauce: break up the chocolate and melt in a pan with the water over a slow heat; when smooth add the sugar. When sugar is dissolved, bring to the boil and simmer with lid off pan for about 10–15 minutes until sauce is rich, syrupy and of a coating consistency. Allow to cool.

Make a slit in the profiteroles and fill with chocolate cream. Pile them up in a pyramid in a serving dish, spoon over sauce.

Eclairs

choux pastry for 4–6 people
½ pint chocolate, or coffee, pastry cream (see page 240), or ½ pint double cream (sweetened and flavoured with vanilla essence)

For glacé icing
2–3 tablespoons water
2–3 oz block chocolate, or 1–2 tablespoons coffee essence
½–¾ lb icing sugar (sifted)
1–2 tablespoons sugar syrup, or water (to mix)

Forcing bag; ½-inch diameter plain éclair nozzle

Method
Set oven at 400°F or Mark 6. Prepare choux pastry and pipe on to dampened baking sheets

in 3-inch lengths. Bake in oven on a rising temperature for about 25 minutes until firm and crisp. Lift off éclairs and prick to release steam. Leave to cool, then slit along one side.

To prepare glacé icing: melt chocolate in the water in a pan until it is a smooth cream. Add sifted icing sugar and stir in

Beating the flour mixture until choux paste is very smooth

Piping out choux with an éclair nozzle on to the baking sheet

enough sugar syrup or water to make a thick cream. Have ready chocolate pastry cream or whipped cream and pipe into the éclairs, making sure that the whole length is filled. Heat the icing to just over blood heat, draw aside, then dip in the top of éclairs. Put on a rack to set.

For coffee éclairs omit the chocolate from the pastry cream and add about 1 tablespoon coffee essence when the cream has cooled. Omit chocolate from glacé icing and add instead coffee essence.

SAVOURY CHOUX
Marjolaine tartlets

For choux pastry
¼ pint water
2 oz butter
2½ oz plain flour
2 eggs
2 oz Cheddar cheese (grated)
salt and pepper

Rich shortcrust pastry
(made with 4 oz flour)

For cheese sauce
½ oz butter
1 tablespoon plain flour
½ pint milk (infused with 1 bayleaf, 1 slice of onion, 1 blade of mace, 6 peppercorns)
1½ oz cheese (grated)
salt and pepper

6–8 tartlet tins; forcing bag and small round nozzle

Method
Line the tins with rich shortcrust pastry. Prick bottom of pastry, line with greaseproof paper and beans or rice and bake blind (see page 207) for 10–15 minutes in oven at 375°F or Mark 5.

Prepare choux pastry. Pipe choux into shortcrust pastry tartlets, leaving a hollow in the middle of each one. Set oven at 400°F or Mark 6.

To prepare cheese sauce: melt butter in a pan, stir in flour and cook to a pale-straw colour. Strain milk, stir it on to the roux and simmer for 2 minutes. Season and add cheese to taste.

Pour sauce into tartlets and bake in pre-set oven for 15–20 minutes to cook choux pastry gently, while browning the cheese in the middle of the tartlets. Serve them immediately.

Cake Making

There are a great variety of ways to make cakes, but which ever recipe you choose, one of the most important aspects is the initial preparation. The success and impact of a home-baked cake in flavour, texture and appearance hinge on this factor. Flavour and texture are dependent on the choice and preparation of the right ingredients. Don't gaily substitute plain for self-raising flour and then complain when you get a sad cake, and it really is important to mix ingredients thoroughly in the early stages.

Appearance depends largely on neat and expert preparation of the cake tin. Cut lining paper to fit exactly; if it has lumps and bumps the finished cake will be bumpy to match.

INGREDIENTS AND METHODS

PREPARATION OF INGREDIENTS

Flour should always be sifted with a good pinch of salt before use. Sifting aerates the flour and removes any small lumps; the salt improves the flavour.

Keep both plain and self-raising flour in your cupboard so that you can use whichever is indicated in a recipe.

Fats play a large part in the success of each cake, and different kinds are suitable for different recipes. Butter is the perfect fat for cake-making because it gives a wonderful flavour and improves the keeping properties of the cake. Margarine, which is easier to cream, can be used in place of butter in nearly every recipe.

Shortening, or a cooking compound, gives very good results, particularly where the proportion of sugar and liquid in the recipe is high. These lard or vegetable fats contain no curd, and if stored properly will keep for many months.

A good beef dripping gives excellent results for plain luncheon cakes, but before use it must be clarified in the following way: turn the dripping into a bowl and pour on an equal amount of boiling water. Stir well, then leave it to set. Remove the solidified fat, scrape away any impurities from the underneath and then heat it gently until it no longer bubbles. Pour into an enamel basin and leave to set.

Sugars are very important. Using the wrong type will completely spoil a cake. Fine caster sugar must be used for all creamed cake mixtures. A coarse sugar results in cakes with spotted tops. Granulated sugar can be used for all mixtures which are 'rubbed in'. Demerara sugar should only be used in recipes where the sugar is dissolved and added to the cake mixture in liquid form, eg. gingerbread made by using the 'warming' method.

Soft brown sugar is good for luncheon and fruit cakes. Barbados sugar (dark brown, rich and moist) is used for rich fruit, wedding, birthday and Christmas cakes to improve the flavour. Some recipes may replace Barbados sugar with caster sugar and black treacle mixed together.

Eggs are essential to make cakes light. They expand and coagulate on heating and so trap any air which is beaten into the mixture.

Fruit, nuts and candied peel. All dried fruit, unless clearly marked as washed and ready for use, should be cleaned. Gritty fruit can spoil the texture and the flavour of the cake.

When using nuts, check the recipe to see whether they should be shredded, flaked or chopped. This seemingly small variation has a decided effect on flavour, texture and appearance, particularly when the nuts are used to finish the cake.

Choose candied peel in caps; as a rule it is softer and fuller in flavour than the chopped variety. Scoop out the sugar from the centre and then shred the peel on a grater. This way you obtain the very best flavour and the fine slivers look attractive in the finished cake.

Raising agents. Baking powder is a commercial preparation made up of two parts cream of tartar and one part bicarbonate of soda. It should be sifted with plain flour in the proportion given in the recipe.

Bicarbonate of soda can be used instead, combined with soured milk, buttermilk, vinegar or black treacle. The proportions to replace 2 teaspoons of baking powder are $\frac{1}{2}$ teaspoon bicarbonate of soda to $\frac{1}{3}$ pint soured milk or buttermilk. This is only suitable for scones or very plain cake mixtures as the proportion of liquid is so high. Use $\frac{1}{2}$ teaspoon bicarbonate of soda plus 1 tablespoon vinegar or black treacle for everyday fruit cakes.

Sifting 8 oz plain flour with 2 level teaspoons of baking powder gives the same result as using self-raising flour.

These two decorative finishes for Christmas cake (see page 226) show really accomplished icing

PREPARATION OF TINS

Brush sides and base of shallow tins with melted fat, line base with circle of buttered greaseproof paper and dust with flour. With tins over 2 inches in depth, sides should also be lined with buttered greaseproof paper as shown in the photographs, below

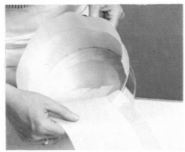

1 *Cut a strip about 1 inch longer than the circumference of tin and 1 inch wider than the depth, fold down $\frac{1}{2}$ inch on the long edge and cut slits in the fold (about $\frac{1}{2}$ inch deep and 1 inch apart). This folded end of the side strip will then overlap at the base*

2 *The circular base lining will then hold this overlap in place*

WAYS OF MIXING

Rubbing-in method. This is used for small cakes and luncheon cakes. These are always meant to be eaten fresh, or at least within 2–3 days of baking. The fat is cut in small pieces, added to sifted flour, then rubbed lightly with the fingertips until it resembles fine breadcrumbs.

Warming (or boiled) method. This is suited to gingerbread and some fruit cakes. A variety of raising agents is used with this method and as a general rule the texture is damp and close and so will improve with keeping.

Fat, sugar and liquids are melted in a saucepan before being added to flour. The mixture before baking (called cake batter) is much thinner than ordinary mixtures and is easily poured into prepared tin.

Creaming method. This is suited to all rich cakes and gives a light, even-textured cake with a soft, slightly moist top which should be smooth and perfectly flat.

For the very best results, follow these rules. First have the butter or margarine and eggs at room temperature (about 70°F). At this temperature the mixture is easier to beat and is less likely to curdle.

Beat the sugar a little at a time into the well-creamed butter, scraping the sides of the bowl once or twice during this process. If you leave any sugar crystals on the sides of the bowl, this will give the finished cake a speckled top.

When the butter and sugar look like whipped cream the eggs may be added. If the amount of sugar is **under** 8 oz, the eggs should be whisked together and added a little at a time. If using **more than** 8 oz sugar, the eggs may be added one at a time. After each addition of egg the mixture must be well beaten.

Watchpoint It is at this stage that curdling is most likely to happen. It is caused either because the butter and sugar have not been thoroughly creamed, or because the eggs are very cold. This curdling can be corrected by standing the mixing bowl in a little hot water and beating vigorously. If, however, you still have more egg to add, stir in 1 tablespoon of the sifted flour with each further addition of egg.

Then, using a metal spoon, gently fold in the flour and any liquid given in the recipe. Do not beat or stir; this will remove air beaten in and make the cake rise and crack.

BAKING

First prepare the cake tins (see above), then turn on the oven, set the temperature and arrange the shelves before mixing the cake. There must be room for the heat to circulate in the oven round baking sheets and cake tins, otherwise the underneath of the cakes will burn.

If you are baking more than one cake in an oven that has back burners or elements, arrange the cakes side by side. If you have an oven with side burners, arrange the cakes back and front. A centre shelf is the best position for baking a cake.

Do not move the cake until the mixture is set and avoid opening the oven door until the minimum time given in the recipe is reached. This is a guide to cooking time but you should always test a cake before removing it from the oven. Creamed cake mixtures should spring back when pressed lightly with the fingertips. Fruit cakes are tested by piercing with a trussing needle or fine skewer which should come away clean.

Gingerbread

4 oz butter
8 oz golden syrup
3 oz granulated sugar
1 tablespoon orange marmalade
$\frac{1}{4}$ pint milk
4 oz self-raising flour
pinch of salt
1 teaspoon ground ginger
1 teaspoon mixed spice
$\frac{1}{2}$ teaspoon bicarbonate of soda
4 oz wholemeal flour
2 small eggs (well beaten)

8-inch square cake tin

Method
Prepare tin and set the oven at 325°F or Mark 3.

Heat the butter, syrup, sugar, marmalade and milk together in a saucepan and stir gently until the sugar dissolves. Allow the mixture to cool a little. Meanwhile sift the self-raising flour with the salt, spices and soda into a mixing bowl, add the wholemeal flour and then mix together.

Add the butter and syrup mixture to the beaten eggs and then pour into the dry ingredients. Stir with a wooden spoon until a smooth batter is formed, then pour into the prepared tin and bake in pre-set oven for about 1$\frac{1}{2}$ hours. Gingerbread is ready when pressed with fingertips and it springs back into place.

Victoria sandwich

about 6 oz butter
about 6 oz caster sugar
3 large eggs
about 6 oz self-raising flour
pinch of salt
1–2 tablespoons milk

To finish
3 tablespoons warm jam, or
    lemon curd
caster sugar (for dredging)

Deep 8-inch diameter sandwich tin

To make a good Victoria sandwich, weigh eggs in their shells and use exact equivalent of butter, sugar and flour.

Method

Grease and line sandwich tin; set the oven at 350°F or Mark 4.

Using the creaming method, soften the butter in a bowl, add the sugar and cream them together until soft and light. Whisk the eggs, add a little at a time and then beat thoroughly. Sift the flour with the salt and fold into the mixture a third at a time, adding enough milk to make the mixture drop easily from the spoon. Spread the mixture in the prepared tin and bake in pre-set oven for about 40–45 minutes.

To test if cake is ready press lightly with fingertips and it should spring back. The colour should be golden-brown, and

Victoria sandwich – spread bottom half with jam and dust top with some caster sugar

the cake shrink from sides of the tin. Have two wire cooling racks ready, and put a folded clean tea towel or double thickness of absorbent paper on one of them. Loosen the sides of the cake with a round-bladed knife, place the rack with the towel or paper on top of the cake (towel next to it) and turn over; remove the tin and disc of paper from the base. Place second rack on top of cake base and carefully and quickly turn it over again. This prevents the cake having the marks of cake rack on its top.

When the cake is cool split in half, fill with jam or lemon curd; dust top with caster sugar.

English madeleines

Victoria sandwich mixture with about 2 eggs and equivalent weights of butter, caster sugar and self-raising flour (about 4 oz of each)
2–3 drops of vanilla essence
4 tablespoons apricot, or red-currant glaze
6 tablespoons desiccated coconut
8 glacé cherries

14–16 dariole moulds, or castle tins

Method
Grease moulds or tins well, and dust with flour. Set the oven at 375°F or Mark 5.

Prepare sponge mixture as for Victoria sandwich (see page 223), flavour with vanilla essence and half fill the moulds or tins. Bake for 8–10 minutes until golden-brown.

When the cakes are cool, trim the tops to give them a flat surface when inverted. Turn them upside down and spear each separately on a fork. Then brush with warm glaze, roll at once in the desiccated coconut, decorate with half a glacé cherry.

Walnut bread

4 oz granulated sugar
6 oz golden syrup
small teacup milk (scant ⅓ pint)
2 oz sultanas
8 oz flour
pinch of salt
3 teaspoons baking powder
2 oz walnuts (roughly chopped)
1 egg (beaten)

Loaf tin, 8½ inches by 4½ inches by 2½ inches deep

Method
Grease and flour loaf tin, set oven at 350°F or Mark 3½.

Heat the sugar, syrup, milk and sultanas in a saucepan and stir gently until the sugar is dissolved; allow to cool.

Sift the flour, salt and baking powder into bowl and add the roughly chopped walnuts. Tip the sugar and syrup mixture on to the beaten egg and then pour into the middle of the dry ingredients and stir until smooth. Pour into the prepared tin and bake in pre-set oven for about 1½ hours. Test as for Victoria sandwich.

Welsh cheese cakes, or tartlets

4 oz quantity rich shortcrust pastry (page 204)

For filling
Victoria sandwich mixture with about 1 egg and equivalent weights of butter, caster sugar and self-raising flour (about 2 oz each)
1–2 tablespoons jam
1–2 drops of vanilla essence
caster sugar (for dredging)

12 tartlet tins

Method
Prepare the pastry, roll thinly and line tartlet tins. Set oven at 400°F or Mark 6.

Put a little jam in each tartlet and prepare the sponge mixture, flavouring it with vanilla essence. Fill each pastry case with 1 teaspoon of the mixture, put in pre-set oven and bake for about 20 minutes until golden-brown.

Dust with caster sugar and eat hot or cold.

Sultana and cherry cake

1½ lb sultanas
12 oz glacé cherries
8 oz plain flour
pinch of salt
6 oz butter
grated rind of ½ lemon
6 oz caster sugar
4 eggs

8-inch diameter cake tin

Method
Prepare cake tin, set oven at 350°F or Mark 4.

Clean sultanas; if cherries are very sticky put in a strainer and wash quickly with hot water. When dry, cut cherries in half, mix with sultanas and one-third of the flour, sifted with a pinch of salt.

Soften butter with lemon rind, add sugar and beat until soft and light. Whisk eggs, add a little at a time, then stir in half of remaining flour. Fold in fruit, then last portion of flour. Turn into prepared tin and bake in pre-set oven for 1 hour, then reduce heat to 325°F or Mark 3; continue cooking about 1 hour and test as for fruitcakes (see page 222).

Coconut buns

8 oz self-raising flour
pinch of salt
3 oz butter
3 oz caster sugar
3 tablespoons desiccated coconut
1 egg
2–3 tablespoons milk
½ teaspoon vanilla essence

9-bun tin

Method
Grease tin and set the oven at 400°F or Mark 6.

Sift the flour with the salt into a bowl and rub in the fat very finely. Add the sugar and coconut and mix well together. Beat the egg with the milk and vanilla essence, add to the dry ingredients and mix with a wooden spoon until smooth.

Spoon mixture into the prepared tin, a tablespoon for each bun, and bake in the pre-set oven for 20–25 minutes, until a fine skewer pressed into a bun comes away cleanly.

Madeira cake

8 oz butter
grated rind of ½ lemon
10 oz caster sugar
5 eggs
13 oz plain flour
pinch of salt
1 rounded teaspoon baking powder
1 teacup milk
slice of candied citron peel

8-inch diameter cake tin

Method
Prepare the cake tin and set the oven at 350°F or Mark 4.

Cream the butter with the grated lemon rind in a bowl, add the sugar gradually and continue beating until the mixture is light and soft. Beat in the eggs one at a time, each with 1 dessertspoon of flour, and then sift the remaining flour with the salt and baking powder and fold into the mixture with the milk. Turn into the prepared tin and bake in pre-set oven for about 1½ hours.

After the first 30 minutes place the slice of citron peel on top of the cake, and after 1 hour reduce the heat to 325°F or Mark 3. Test as for Victoria sandwich.

Battenburg cake

3 egg Victoria sandwich
  mixture
few drops of carmine colouring
2 tablespoons apricot jam glaze
  (see page 208)
1½ lb almond paste (overleaf)

*2 tins, or paper cases, each 10 inches
  by 3 inches by 1½ inches deep*

Method
Place greaseproof paper in
bottom of tins. Grease tins, or
paper cases, and dust with flour.
Set the oven at 350°F or Mark 4.

Prepare the Victoria sandwich
mixture and, before filling into
tins, divide it in two and colour
one portion pale pink with
carmine. Bake each colour in a
separate tin in the pre-set
moderate oven for 15–20
minutes. When cool, trim each
cake and cut in two lengthways.
Brush the strips of cake with
some of the warm apricot glaze
and join them together again
with one pink strip above a
natural colour one (and vice-
versa) to make a square of
alternate colours.

Roll the almond paste into an
oblong the length of the reshaped cake and wide enough
to wrap right round it, leaving
the square ends exposed. First
brush the top of the cake with
apricot glaze and place cake,
inverted, on the almond paste;
then brush the remaining three
sides with glaze and press the
almond paste round, arranging
the join neatly down one side.

Using your fingers or pastry
pincers, crimp the edges of the
cake and decorate the top with
criss-cross scoring.

*Battenburg cake, a traditional
teatime favourite, is an attractive variation on the Victoria
sandwich mixture*

*Joining the four strips of Victoria
sandwich cake together to give
the chequered effect, characteristic of a Battenburg*

225

Coconut cake

7½ oz flour
2 teaspoons baking powder
½ teaspoon salt
4 oz shortening
9 oz caster sugar
2 large eggs (well beaten)
¼ pint milk
4 drops of vanilla essence
American frosting
4 oz desiccated coconut

Two 8-inch diameter sandwich tins

Method
Set the oven at 350°F or Mark 4.

Sift the flour with the baking powder and salt. Cream the shortening with the sugar until light and fluffy, add the well-beaten eggs, a little at a time, and beat them in very thoroughly. Stir in the sifted flour alternately with the milk and flavouring.

Pour the cake mixture into the prepared tins and bake for 25–30 minutes until cooked. Test cake with a fine skewer or trussing needle.

When cool, first sandwich with American frosting and then cover the top and sides. Before the icing sets, cover the cake thickly with the coconut.

Christmas cake

8 oz plain flour
pinch of salt
½ teaspoon ground cinnamon
½ nutmeg (grated)
1 lb sultanas
12 oz seeded raisins
8 oz glacé cherries
4 oz almonds (blanched and shredded)
2 oz candied peel (shredded)
6 oz butter
grated rind of ½ lemon, or orange
6 oz dark brown sugar (Barbados)
4 eggs (beaten)
2 tablespoons brandy, or rum, or sherry, or 1 tablespoon orange juice

8-inch diameter cake tin; Nos. 1 and 2 plain pipes; rosette pipe; scroll pipe

Method
Prepare cake tin with a double thickness of greaseproof paper; set oven at 350°F or Mark 4.

Sift the flour with the salt and spices into bowl, then divide mixture into three portions. Mix one portion with the prepared fruit, almonds and peel.

Beat the butter until soft, add the lemon or orange rind and sugar and continue beating until the mixture is very soft. Add the eggs one at a time, beating well between each one, then use a metal spoon to fold in a second portion of flour. Mix in the fruit and then the remaining flour, spirit, sherry or fruit juice.

Turn the mixture into the prepared tin and smooth the top of the cake. Dip your fingers in warm water and moisten the surface very slightly.

Watchpoint This can be done with a pastry brush but great care must be taken as there should be only a film of water on the mixture. In baking, the small quantity of steam from the water prevents the crust of the cake getting hard during the long cooking.

Put the cake in the middle of the pre-set oven and bake for about 2¼ hours. After 1 hour reduce the heat of the oven to 325°F or Mark 3 and cover the top with a double thickness of greaseproof paper.

Test the cake after 2 hours cooking by sticking a trussing needle or fine skewer in the centre. If it comes out quite clean the cake is done. Allow the cake to cool for about 30 minutes in the tin and then turn it on to a rack and leave until quite cold.

Wrap the cake in greaseproof paper or foil and store it in an airtight container for up to three weeks before covering with almond paste and then glacé icing (see page 229).

To decorate with royal icing (see cake in foreground, page 221), cut a 5- or 6-pointed star from greaseproof paper and place on cake, holding it in position with pins. Using a No. 2 plain pipe, cover rest of top with straight lines ¼ inch apart; let these dry. Using a No. 1 plain pipe, pipe lines diagonally over the first ones to make a lattice. Let these dry before removing paper star.

With a rosette pipe outline the star and round edges of cake. When dry, top rosettes with small silver balls.

Alternatively, 'rough ice' top of cake (see page 221, cake in background), making peaks with a palette knife. With a scroll pipe outline edges with shell shapes.

Finish both cakes with a ribbon and small centrepiece.

Almond paste

10 oz ground almonds
5 oz caster sugar
5 oz icing sugar (finely sifted)
1 egg
1 tablespoon lemon juice
1 tablespoon brandy, or sherry, or extra lemon juice
½ teaspoon vanilla essence
2 drops of almond essence
2 teaspoons orange flower water, or little extra sherry, or lemon juice
apricot glaze (see page 208)

These quantities make 1¼ lb almond paste. To vary this amount, see Quantity guide for icing, opposite.

Method
Place the almonds, caster sugar and icing sugar in a bowl and mix them together. Whisk the egg with the lemon juice and other flavourings and add this to the mixture of almonds and sugar, pounding lightly to release a little of the almond oil. Knead with your hands until the paste is smooth.

Brush or spread the cake thinly with hot apricot glaze. This coating makes sure that the almond paste will stick to the cake. Now place the almond paste on top of the cake; roll it over the top so that it falls down the sides (see photographs right).

Dust your hands with icing sugar and smooth the paste firmly and evenly on to the sides of the cake. Turn it upside down, press to flatten the paste on the the top and roll the rolling pin round the sides. This gives a clean, sharp edge to the paste. Leave the cake in a tin for 2–3 days before icing.

Almond paste is laid on top of the previously-glazed cake, and rolled with a rolling pin so that it falls over the edges and down sides of the cake

Having smoothed the almond paste firmly and evenly on the sides, turn the cake upside down and roll round sides to give a clean, sharp edge

ICINGS

The best icings to use for cakes are glacé, fondant and royal icings. The first two are soft ones which make for more enjoyable eating, but do not give quite the professional finish of the hard, royal icing. For a rich fruit or special occasion cake, therefore, it is better to use a soft icing for coating and the royal icing if you are piping on decorations.

Finally, remember to keep your basin covered with a damp cloth because icing hardens when exposed to air.

Quantity guide for icing

When recipes specify an amount of icing such as '2 lb fondant, or royal, icing', this means the amount of sugar used in the icing. Where the basic recipe, given overleaf, uses 1 lb icing sugar, you will need simply to double the quantities of all ingredients. Similarly, for 8 oz fondant icing, you should halve all the specified ingredients.

To calculate the weight of almond paste, add up the weight of the dry ingredients, ie. the ground almonds and sugar. The proportion of sugar to almonds can vary, but a general guide is to use equal amounts, the term 'sugar' usually meaning half icing sugar and half caster sugar. If wished, however, you can increase the proportion of sugar, and for economy twice as much sugar as almonds can be used, although you will then need more egg to bind the mixture.

Colouring and flavouring icing

You should use edible colouring for icing. Take great care when adding a colour because one drop too many can change a subtle shading into a gaudy one. A skewer dipped in the bottle of colouring is the best method of adding a colour. From one bowl of icing, you can have five colour changes: from white to yellow, to pink or green, to coffee, to chocolate.

Flavourings are varied but are not meant to overpower and spoil the taste of the cake. You can buy several flavouring essences but you can also make them: strained orange or lemon fruit juice; coffee powder dissolved in a little water; melted chocolate, or cocoa blended with water.

To improve the whiteness of royal icing, add a tiny spot of blue colouring on the point of a skewer and beat it in very thoroughly; too much blue gives icing a greyish tint. Also, 1–2 teaspoons of glycerine added to royal icing will prevent it from becoming excessively hard, and a squeeze of lemon juice added helps to counteract its sweetness.

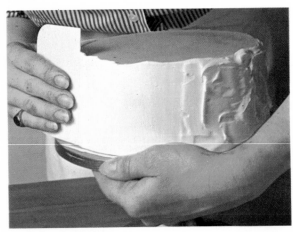

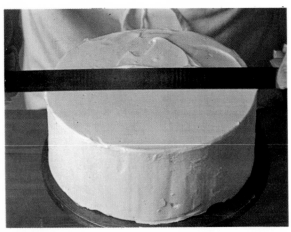

Icing is made less difficult if a cake-stand with a revolving turntable is used. Cover sides of the cake with icing using a palette knife. Hold a plastic spatula with your right hand at an angle of 45° to cake. With your left hand at front of turntable, pull the cake round until the icing is quite smooth, then lift off the spatula. If the finish to the icing is not smooth enough, work again with the palette knife and spatula

Allow sides of the cake to dry before roughly spreading icing over top of the cake. Place a plastic or metal 'straight-edge' ruler (or palette knife) on edge of cake furthest away from you at an angle of 45°. Pull ruler across the top in one continuous movement to prevent bumps forming. If top isn't smooth, work again with a palette knife and ruler. Trim excess icing from the sides with a palette knife. Leave it to dry before decorating

Fondant icing

1 lb lump sugar
8 tablespoons water
pinch of cream of tartar

A sugar thermometer is essential for this recipe.

You can now buy blocks or packets of powder of fondant icing. Simply follow the manufacturer's instructions.

Method
Place the sugar and water in a saucepan and dissolve without stirring over a low heat. Using a brush dipped in cold water, wipe round pan at level of the syrup to prevent a crust forming. Add the cream of tartar (dissolved in 1 teaspoon of water), place the lid on the pan, increase the heat and bring to the boil.

Remove the lid after 2 minutes, put a sugar thermometer in and boil the syrup steadily to 240°F. When it has reached this temperature take the pan off the heat at once, wait for the bubbles to subside then pour the mixture very slowly on to a damp marble or laminated plastic slab. Work with a wooden spatula until it becomes a firm and white fondant. Take a small piece of fondant at a time and knead with the fingertips until smooth.

For storing, pack fondant icing in an airtight jar or tin. When you want to use it, gently warm the fondant with a little stock syrup to make a smooth cream. The icing should then flow easily. Flavour and colour it just before use with vanilla, lemon, etc. Spread over cake with a palette knife.

Stock syrup

Dissolve 1 lb loaf, or granulated, sugar in $\frac{1}{2}$ pint water and boil steadily, without stirring, until sugar thermometer reads 220°F. Allow syrup to cool, then store by pouring it into a large, clean and dry screwtop jar.

Royal icing

1 lb icing sugar
2 egg whites

This icing is not suitable for flat icing on sponge cakes because it would be too hard.

Method
Finely sift the icing sugar. Whisk the egg whites until frothy and add the icing sugar 1 tablespoon at a time, beating thoroughly between each addition. Continue this beating until the mixture will stand in peaks. Add flavouring and colour if wished. Keep the bowl covered with a damp cloth when piping.

American frosting

1 lb lump sugar
8 tablespoons water
pinch of cream of tartar
2 egg whites
flavouring essence

A sugar thermometer is essential for this recipe.

Method
Place the sugar and water in a saucepan over a low heat, and dissolve slowly without stirring.
Watchpoint On no account must it boil at this stage or the sugar will crystallise.

Add the cream of tartar (dissolved in 1 teaspoon of water; this breaks the grains and helps to prevent sugar crystallising); place the lid on the pan, increase the heat and bring to the boil. Remove the lid after 2 minutes, put in a sugar thermometer and boil steadily to 240°F. Meanwhile whisk the egg whites until stiff. Stop the boiling of the sugar syrup by dipping the bottom of the saucepan in cold water, then, holding the pan well above the bowl, pour syrup in a steady stream on to egg whites, whisking all the time. Continue to whisk until icing holds its shape and satiny appearance is lost, then add the flavouring.

Pour the icing on to the cake and spread it over immediately with a palette knife (or metal ruler) in bold strokes. At this stage the icing sets quickly.

Glacé icing

4–5 tablespoons granulated sugar
¼ pint water
8–12 oz icing sugar (finely sifted)
flavouring essence and colouring
(as required)

Method
Make sugar syrup by dissolving sugar in ¼ pint of water in a small saucepan. Bring to the boil, and boil steadily for 10 minutes. Remove pan from the heat and when quite cold, add the icing sugar, 1 tablespoon at a time, and beat thoroughly with a wooden spatula. The icing should coat back of spoon and look very glossy. Warm the pan gently on a very low heat.
Watchpoint The pan must not get too hot. You should be able to touch the bottom with the palm of your hand.
Flavour and colour icing ; spread over cake with palette knife.

Chocolate fudge icing

1 lb granulated sugar
½ pint water
1 tablespoon golden syrup
2 oz unsalted butter
2 oz cocoa

Sugar thermometer

Method
Place all the ingredients in a large saucepan, blend together and dissolve the sugar over gentle heat. Bring to the boil and cook to 238°F on the sugar boiling thermometer – this is known as the soft-ball stage.
Watchpoint To prevent possible sticking, draw a wooden spoon through the mixture from time to time, but never stir continually as this can cause the icing to 'grain' (go sugary).

Remove the pan from the heat, leave the mixture until cool, then beat with a wooden spoon until thick enough to hold its shape.

MAKING A PIPING CONE

In previous chapters, several recipes have called for piping cream or soft fillings, which is usually done with a nylon forcing bag and large vegetable nozzles (with 6, 8 or 12 cuts).

The most practical type of forcing bag is of nylon as it can be easily washed and dried and used time and time again; it is also very flexible which makes it easy to control and to give a good finish.

Piping fancy decoration and names on biscuits and cakes needs more control and generally uses less filling; it is therefore best to use a cone of greaseproof paper as a forcing bag. This is simple to make and inexpensive.

When holding a forcing bag (either nylon or homemade), the pressure must come from the top with your right hand. The other hand, which is held in a lower position near the nozzle, is to guide only.

First take a 10-inch square of greaseproof paper, fold and cut into two triangles. Holding one of these with the right-angled (centre) point uppermost, fold the right-hand acute point over to meet the right-angled point

Next take the left-hand acute point and bring it right over and round to the back until all the points of the paper meet at the back to form cone or bag

Tuck over the flap formed where all the points meet the top of the cone. Crease this firmly to prevent cone from unfolding

Cut a little bit off the point of the cone, drop in the piping nozzle to see if it fits, and cut off a further amount if necessary

PIPING DECORATIONS

Before starting any decoration, practise the shapes. If you want to decorate a cake with flowers, first practise making the centres of the flowers by building up a number of small circles, one on top of the other

Make a new piping cone and cut a small 'V' at the point. Practise making petals by pushing icing through the cone on to a firm surface and then drawing cone away quickly to make a sharp point

For finished flowers, use (non-stick) silicone-treated paper as a base. (Black paper is only used for demonstrating the method.) Pipe on petals for outside of flowers, then pipe inside a second row of petals. Pipe centres, leave completed flowers on paper until dry. Then carefully lever flowers off with point of knife; secure on cake with blob of icing. With experience, flowers can be piped straight on to cake

Angel cake

2 oz flour
6½ oz caster sugar
6 egg whites
pinch of salt
¾ teaspoon cream of tartar
3 drops of vanilla essence
2 drops of almond essence

8–9 inch diameter angel cake tin (with funnelled base)

This should be made with the finest flour available and it is possible to buy flour prepared and packed for just this purpose. But it can, of course, be made with any good plain white flour if first sifted 3–4 times through a fine nylon strainer.

Method
Set oven at 375°F or Mark 5. Sift the flour and 3½ oz caster sugar three times and set on one side. Place the egg whites, salt and cream of tartar in a large, dry basin and whisk with a rotary beater until foamy.

Add the remaining sugar, 2 tablespoons at a time, and the essences and continue beating until the mixture will stand in peaks. Carefully fold in the sifted flour and sugar. Turn the mixture into the clean, dry tin, level the surface and draw a knife through to break any air bubbles. Bake the cake in the pre-set oven for 30–35 minutes or until no imprint remains when your finger lightly touches the top.

When cake is ready, turn it upside down on a wire rack and leave until quite cold, when the cake will fall easily from the tin.

This cake, if served quite plain for tea or perhaps with fruit for a lunch party, is best pulled into pieces with two forks rather than cut with a knife as the texture is very delicate.

A slice of devil's food cake,

Devil's food cake

6 oz flour
¼ teaspoon baking powder
1 teaspoon bicarbonate of soda
pinch of salt
2 oz cocoa
7½ fl oz cold water
4 oz shortening
10 oz caster sugar
2 eggs

Two 8-inch diameter sandwich tins

Method
Set oven at 350°F or Mark 4.

Sift the flour with the baking powder, bicarbonate of soda and salt. Blend the cocoa with the water and set aside. Soften the shortening with a wooden spoon, add the sugar and beat until light and very soft.

Whisk the eggs until frothy, add to the shortening and sugar mixture a little at a time and beat well. Stir in the sifted flour alternately with the cocoa and water, divide the mixture between the two tins and bake in the pre-set oven for 30–35 minutes. Cake is ready when a fine skewer or trussing needle comes away cleanly. Leave to cool, then sandwich the halves, and cover the cake, with chocolate fudge icing (page 229).

Banana cake

8 oz flour
1 teaspoon baking powder
¼ teaspoon bicarbonate of soda
pinch of salt
4 oz shortening
12 oz caster sugar
2 large eggs (well beaten)
3 medium-size bananas (mashed)
4 tablespoons milk

To finish
½ pint double cream (whipped
  and sweetened)
2 bananas (sliced)
2 tablespoons icing sugar

Two 9-inch diameter sandwich tins

Method
Set oven at 350°F or Mark 4.

Sift the flour with the baking powder, bicarbonate of soda and salt; set on one side.

Cream the shortening and sugar together until light and fluffy; add the eggs gradually and beat thoroughly. Stir in the sifted flour alternately with the mashed bananas and milk; pour into the prepared tins and bake in pre-set oven for about 30 minutes or until cake is cooked.

When cool, sandwich cake with the cream and sliced bananas and dust top with sifted icing sugar.

LUNCHTIME PUDDING CAKES

Cocoa and water is stirred into devil's food cake mixture alternately with flour. Below: mixing ingredients for chocolate fudge icing while the cake is cooling

Upside-down cake

2½ oz butter
2½ oz brown sugar

9 oz flour
4 teaspoons baking powder
½ teaspoon salt
2 oz butter, or margarine, or
  shortening
5 oz caster sugar
1 egg (well whisked)
¼ pint milk

To decorate
cooked, or canned, fruit (slices
  of pineapple and cherries, or
  prunes – drained)
glacé cherries, or walnuts

*8½–9 inch diameter layer cake tin
(with sloping sides)*

Method
Cream the 2½ oz butter with the brown sugar and spread mixture over the bottom and sides of the prepared tin.

Arrange the drained fruit over the butter-sugar coating and decorate with the glacé cherries or walnuts.

Set the oven at 350°F or Mark 4. Sift the flour with the baking powder and salt and set aside. Soften the 2 oz butter, or fat, with a wooden spoon; add the sugar and well whisked egg and beat thoroughly until light and fluffy. Stir in the flour alternately with the milk.

Spoon cake mixture into the prepared tin and bake in the pre-set oven for 50–60 minutes. When the cake is ready (test with fine skewer or trussing needle), invert it immediately on to the serving plate. Leave for a few minutes for the brown sugar mixture to run down over the cake, then remove cake tin.

Apple sauce cake

8 oz flour
1 teaspoon baking powder
¼ teaspoon ground cinnamon
¼ teaspoon ground nutmeg
¼ teaspoon mixed spice
1 teaspoon salt
3 oz shortening
11 oz caster sugar
1 egg
¾ cup canned apple sauce
1½ oz walnuts (roughly chopped)
4 oz seeded raisins
icing sugar (for dusting)

8–9 inch square cake tin

Method
Set oven at 350°F or Mark 4 and grease the cake tin.

Sift the flour with the baking powder, spices and salt and set on one side. Cream the shortening and sugar together, add the egg and beat well. Stir in the apple sauce and then fold in the flour, walnuts and raisins. Turn the mixture into the prepared tin and bake in pre-set oven for about 45 minutes.

When cool, dust the top with icing sugar.

WHISKED SPONGES

Whisked sponges are the lightest of all cakes. They contain only a small proportion of flour and their texture depends almost entirely on the amount of air beaten in with the eggs. The mixture is delicate and it is important that there should be no delays in mixing and baking, so remember that preparation plays a big part in the success of the finished cake.

General preparation

Choice of ingredients. Sponge cakes should be made with the finest ingredients to help their keeping qualities.

Eggs are best used when about three days old and give more volume if beaten when at room temperature.

Use caster sugar which is quite free of lumps. Granulated sugar is too coarse and does not dissolve completely when beaten with the eggs. If sugar is not dissolved, the finished cakes will have a speckly surface.

Flour should be plain and as fine as possible. It helps to dry the flour gently in the oven and sift it at least three times.

Finally, check your recipe and weigh ingredients for even results.

Mixing. Make sure that your mixing bowl, or pudding basin, and whisk are free from grease.

If mixing with a balloon whisk, use a mixing bowl. Gentle heat is needed to get the greatest volume from the eggs and at the same time to dissolve the sugar.

If using an electric or rotary beater, use a large pudding basin. In this case heat is not necessary. Whichever method you use, it is essential to get as much air as possible beaten into the mixture.

The cake batter is ready when a little lifted on the whisk falls in a thick ribbon on the mixture in the bowl and holds its shape.

Having beaten the sponge mixture so well, take care not to lose any of the air in it when adding the flour. Remove the whisk, sift the flour over the surface of the batter and cut and fold it in with a metal spoon. Mix in only enough to give a smooth mixture. Pour at once into the prepared tins and bake immediately.

Preparation of cake tins. Sponge cakes should have a firm, sugary casing, so brush or wipe the tins with a little melted or creamed shortening, taking particular care to reach the corners. Pour a little caster sugar in the tin, shake it well to coat the sides, then tip it out. Tap the tin to remove any surplus and then repeat the process with a little sifted flour.

Preparing the oven. Set the oven at the correct temperature according to the recipe and arrange the shelves so that the cake will be in the centre of the oven. This will ensure that the cake has constant heat so that it bakes evenly.

Crusty top sponge cake, sponge drops and sponge fingers

Crusty top sponge

5 oz plain flour
pinch of salt
4 eggs (separated)
8 oz caster sugar
1 dessertspoon orange flower
   water

8-inch diameter cake tin

Method

Set the oven at 350°F or Mark 4 and prepare tin.

Sift the flour and salt well. Place the yolks with half the sugar and the orange flower water in a bowl and beat with a heavy whisk or wooden spatula until thick and mousse-like.

Whip the egg whites until

Baking temperatures		
Type of whisked sponge	Electric and solid fuel	Gas mark
Sponge cake, fingers and drops	350°F–375°F	4–5
Swiss roll	325°F–375°F	3–5

itself. Remove bowl from pan of hot water and continue whisking until mixture is cold (a further 3–4 minutes).

Using a metal spoon, cut and fold the flour into the mixture. Put the mixture into the tin and bake in pre-set oven for 20–25 minutes until risen and brown. Turn out and cool on a rack.

Sponge cake (2)

3 oz plain flour
pinch of salt
2 eggs
4 oz caster sugar

7½-inch diameter savarin mould, or 7-inch diameter cake tin

A firm, dry sponge, suitable for soaking with fruit juice or serving with butter cream.

Method
Set the oven at 375°F or Mark 5 and prepare the savarin mould or cake tin.

Prepare the batter as for sponge cake (1). Bake in pre-set oven for 20–30 minutes until risen and brown. Turn out and cool on a rack.

Sponge fingers

3½ oz plain flour
pinch of salt
3 eggs (separated)
3½ oz caster sugar
icing sugar (for dusting)

Baking sheet, or about 18 sponge finger tins; forcing bag and ½-inch plain éclair nozzle

Method
Line a baking sheet with grease-proof paper, brush with melted lard or oil and dust it with flour (sponge finger tins may be used if preferred). Set the oven at 350°F or Mark 4.

Sift the flour and salt well. Cream the egg yolks and sugar together with a wooden spoon until thick and pale in colour. Whisk the egg whites until stiff. Fold a third of the flour into the egg yolks very carefully and then add the egg whites and remaining flour. Do not stir more than is necessary.

Put mixture into forcing bag and shape into fingers 3½ inches long or fill tins. Dust them well with icing sugar and tilt the sheet to remove any surplus sugar. Bake in the pre-set oven for about 12 minutes. Then leave to cool.

stiff; add the remaining sugar, 1 tablespoon at a time, and continue whisking until the mixture stands in peaks. Then, using a metal spoon, fold egg whites carefully into the yolk mixture with the flour.

Pour the batter into the prepared tin and bake in the pre-set oven for about 45 minutes. Turn out and cool on a rack.

Sponge cake (1)

3 oz plain flour
pinch of salt
3 eggs
4½ oz caster sugar

8-inch diameter cake tin

A soft sponge which keeps well and is suitable for filling with cream and serving with fruit.

Method
Set oven at 375°F or Mark 5 and prepare cake tin.

Have ready a large pan, half full of boiling water, over which the mixing bowl will rest comfortably without touching the water.

Sift the flour and salt well.

Break eggs into mixing bowl and beat in the sugar gradually. Remove the pan from the heat, place the bowl on top and whisk the eggs and sugar together until thick and mousse-like. This will take at least 5 minutes and the mixture will increase in volume and lighten in colour. When dropped from whisk it will make a 'ribbon' on

Sponge drops

2½ oz plain flour
pinch of salt
3 eggs (separated)
3 oz caster sugar
1 teaspoon orange flower water,
   or lemon juice
icing sugar (for dredging)

*Forcing bag; ½-inch plain éclair
nozzle*

This recipe makes about 24 sponge drops.

Method
Set the oven at 350°F or Mark 4 and grease and flour a baking sheet.

Sift the flour and salt well. Place the egg yolks in a basin, add the sugar gradually and cream them together with a wooden spoon or heavy whisk until very thick and light in colour. Add the orange flower water or lemon juice.

Whisk the egg whites until stiff and dry, add 1 teaspoon to the yolk mixture and then fold in the flour. Using a metal spoon, and with great care, cut and fold in the remaining egg white to the flour and yolks.

Put the mixture into a forcing bag and shape into drops about 1½ inches in diameter (or shape with teaspoons) on to the baking sheet. Dredge them with icing sugar and bake in the pre-set oven for about 15–20 minutes. Leave to cool.

Biscuit milanaise

2 oz plain flour
2 oz fécule (potato flour), or
   arrowroot
pinch of salt
4 eggs (2 separated)
8 oz caster sugar
grated rind of 1 lemon
1 oz currants (cleaned)

7½–8-inch diameter cake tin

Method
Set the oven at 350°F or Mark 4 and prepare tin.

Sift flours and salt well together. Put 2 whole eggs and 2 egg yolks into a mixing bowl, add the sugar gradually and whisk it over gentle heat until thick and white (about 15 minutes).

Whisk the 2 egg whites until stiff and, using a metal spoon, fold into the mixture with the sifted flours, grated lemon rind and the currants.

Put in the prepared tin and bake in pre-set oven for about 1 hour. Lower heat after the first 30 minutes if cake is getting too brown. Turn out and cool.

Small sponge cakes

2½ oz plain flour
pinch of salt
3 eggs
3 oz caster sugar (plus extra for
   dredging)

8–12 small sponge cake tins

Method
Set oven at 350°F or Mark 4, grease and flour tins. Make mixture as for sponge cake (1) (see page 233) and put into greased and floured tins. Dredge the top of each cake with caster sugar and bake in the pre-set oven for about 20 minutes. Leave to cool.

Flavourings for sponge cakes

Orange flower water, obtainable at a chemist, is the traditional flavouring for sponge cakes.

Alternatively grated lemon or orange rind can be used but do not overdo it. The grated rind of ½ a small orange or lemon is quite enough; too much will result in a sticky sponge.

Another way of flavouring is to place 2–3 leaves of sweet (rose) geranium or lemon verbena leaves on the bottom of the prepared cake tin before pouring in the mixture. This gives a delicious flavour to a plain sponge cake.

The first of the two swiss roll recipes is quicker and simpler than the second one, and has a different flavouring.

Swiss roll (1)

2 oz plain flour
¼ teaspoon baking powder
pinch of salt
2 eggs (beaten)
4 oz caster sugar
2 tablespoons water
2–3 drops of vanilla essence
icing, or caster, sugar (for
   dusting)

For filling
3 tablespoons warm jam

*Swiss roll tin, or paper case, 8 inches
by 12 inches*

Method
Set the oven at 375°F or Mark 5; grease and flour swiss roll tin or paper case.

Sift the flour well with baking powder and salt. Beat the eggs with a whisk until thick, add the sugar gradually and continue beating until white.

Stir in the water and vanilla essence and add the flour to the mixture all at once. Beat with the whisk until just smooth and turn at once into the prepared tin or paper case. Spread it evenly and bake in pre-set oven for 12–15 minutes.

To turn out the cake: loosen the edges and turn immediately on to a tea towel or sheet of greaseproof paper, dusted with icing or caster sugar. Quickly and carefully remove the paper case (if used), trim the side edges of the swiss roll with a knife and spread with the warm jam. Roll the cake up at once and leave it to cool in the towel. Sprinkle liberally with sugar before serving.

Swiss roll (2)

2 oz plain flour
1 dessertspoon cornflour
½ teaspoon baking powder
pinch of salt
4 oz caster sugar
2 eggs (separated)
1 dessertspoon orange flower
   water
icing, or caster, sugar (for
   dusting)

For filling
3 tablespoons warm jam

*Swiss roll tin, or paper case, 8 inches
by 12 inches*

The paper case is torn away in two pieces, quickly and carefully, from the swiss roll

Sides of swiss roll sponge are trimmed to give a neat edge and to remove browned parts

After filling has been spread on, sponge is rolled up by gently tilting the paper, or tea towel (For how to make a paper case, see page 162)

This sponge rises well and has a thick spongy texture.

Method

Set the oven at 350°F or Mark 4; grease and flour swiss roll tin or paper case.

Sift the flour with the cornflour, baking powder and salt four times. Set aside 2 tablespoons sugar ready to be added to the egg whites. Whisk the egg yolks until thick, adding a large portion of remaining sugar, then the orange flower water gradually, with rest of the caster sugar.

Whisk the egg whites until stiff, add the 2 tablespoons of reserved sugar and continue whisking until the mixture stands in peaks. Fold the whites into the yolks and lastly fold in the flour. Pour mixture into prepared tin or paper case, spread it evenly and bake in the pre-set oven for about 12 minutes.

Turn the cake at once on to a sugared tea towel and remove the paper case very quickly (if used). Trim swiss roll edges with a knife, spread cake with warm jam and roll up quickly. Sprinkle with sugar before serving.

Strawberry or banana cream roll

ingredients as for Swiss roll (2)

icing sugar (for dusting)

For filling
¼ pint double cream
caster sugar (to taste)
vanilla essence (to taste)
8 oz ripe strawberries, or 2–3 bananas

Swiss roll tin, or paper case, 8 inches by 12 inches

Method

Make swiss roll as in previous recipe. Shape the cake by rolling it up in the sugared tea towel, but roll the towel in with the cake to prevent it sticking. Leave to cool in the towel.

Whip the cream until thick, add caster sugar and vanilla essence to taste. Slice strawberries or bananas. Unroll the cake and spread with the cream; sprinkle with strawberries or bananas, and roll up again.

Chill before serving. Dust the cake with icing sugar.

Chocolate swiss roll

1 oz plain flour
1 dessertspoon cocoa
pinch of salt
3 eggs (separated)
large pinch of cream of tartar

4 oz caster sugar
2–3 drops of vanilla essence
icing sugar (for dusting)

For filling

icing sugar
Chantilly cream (see page 274), or coffee butter cream (see page 239)

Swiss roll tin, or paper case, 8 inches by 12 inches

Method

Set oven at 325°F or Mark 3; grease and flour swiss roll tin or paper case.

Sift the flour well with cocoa and salt. Separate the eggs and whisk the whites with the cream of tartar until stiff; then gradually beat in half the sugar. Continue whisking until the mixture looks very glossy and will stand in peaks.

Cream the egg yolks until thick, then beat in the remaining sugar and add the vanilla essence. Stir the flour into the yolks and pour this mixture over the whites. Using a metal spoon, cut and fold carefully until thoroughly blended.

Turn the mixture into the prepared tin or paper case, bake in the pre-set oven for 20–25 minutes. Turn at once on to a sugared tea towel, trim the cake's edges and roll it up, with the towel inside the cake.

When cool, unroll cake carefully and fill with the chosen cream; roll up again and dust with icing sugar before serving.

Gâteaux and Pâtisseries

This branch of cookery requires a certain amount of expertise, but with care and attention to detail you can get a professional result.

In pâtisseries, two or three foundations are used, from which several varieties of cakes can be made. All these small cakes (pâtisseries), as well as the large gâteaux, follow tradition strictly where names and decoration are concerned; any deviation from this is frowned upon as the gâteaux or pâtisseries are then not identical to their traditional form.

A special pastry called French flan pastry (pâte sucrée, or sèche) is largely used for pâtisseries and certain gâteaux, as well as for flans and tartlets, because it stands up better than shortcrust to being filled with fruit and glazed. French flan pastry is best made at least an hour before rolling out and baking, or it can be made up and stored in a polythene bag in the refrigerator, where it will keep satisfactorily for two to three days.

BASIC FOUNDATIONS

French flan pastry (Pâte sucrée)

French flan pastry is made with plain flour, butter, caster sugar and egg yolks, and no liquid of any kind. The method of making is completely different from English shortcrust pastry and, for this reason, the resulting paste should be firm and completely non-elastic. This means that the pastry keeps its shape during baking and when cooked is slightly short and melt-in-the-mouth. It should be made 1–2 hours before using, then chilled. Take it out of refrigerator 15–20 minutes before you use it and keep at room temperature.

You will see that the baking temperature for French flan pastry is a little lower than for English shortcrust pastry, owing to its high proportion of sugar.

French flan pastry is cooked when it is a delicate biscuit-colour; if over-cooked, it becomes hard and tasteless.

Basic foundation recipes are given, right, for easy reference, rather than repeating them in the recipes on the following pages.

Basic recipe 1

4 oz flour
pinch of salt
2 oz butter
2 oz caster sugar
2–3 drops of vanilla essence
2 egg yolks

This quantity is sufficient to line a 7-inch diameter flan ring or 9–12 individual tartlet tins, according to size.

Note: 2 oz vanilla sugar may be used instead of caster sugar and vanilla essence.

Method
Sieve the flour with a pinch of salt on to a marble slab or pastry board, make a well in the centre and in it place the butter, sugar, vanilla essence and egg yolks. Using the fingertips of one hand only, pinch and work these last three ingredients together until well blended. Then draw in the flour, knead lightly until smooth.

Use as directed in the recipes.

Basic recipe 2

6 oz flour
pinch of salt
3 oz butter
3 oz caster sugar
2–3 drops of vanilla essence
3 egg yolks

This quantity is sufficient to line an 8–9-inch diameter flan ring or a 7-inch one, if a lattice of pastry is called for.

Method
Make pastry as for the basic recipe 1 above.

Gâteau au chocolat is decorated with scrolls of chocolate caraque and then icing sugar (see page 242)

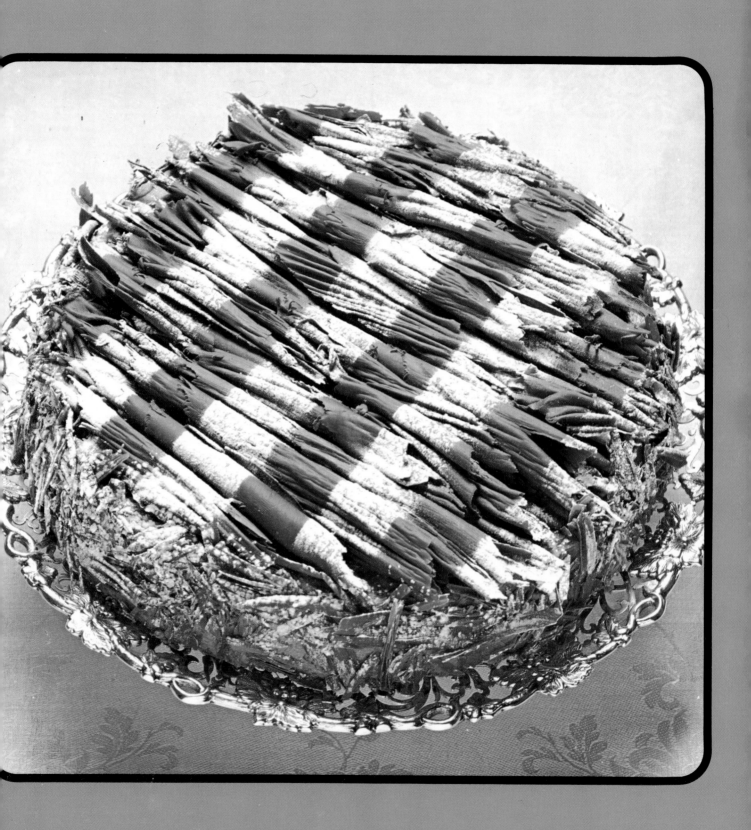

Genoese pastry (Pâte génoise commune)

Basic recipe 1

4¼ oz flour
pinch of salt
2 oz butter
4 eggs
4¼ oz caster sugar

8½–9 inch diameter moule à manqué

Basic recipe 2

3 oz flour
pinch of salt
1½ oz butter
3 eggs
3¼ oz caster sugar

7½–8 inch diameter moule à manqué

This recipe makes a rich, firm type of sponge cake foundation, lighter than the English kind. Although it is called pâte (pastry), it is not a true pastry but traditionally comes under the heading of pâtisseries because it is widely used in this particular field.

Method
Set the oven at 350–375°F or Mark 4–5; grease mould, line bottom only with a disc of greaseproof paper to fit exactly, grease again, dust with caster sugar, then flour.

Sift the flour 2 or 3 times with the salt. Warm the butter gently until just soft and pourable, taking great care not to make it hot or oily. Have ready a large saucepan half full of boiling water over which the mixing bowl will rest comfortably without touching the water.

Break the eggs into the bowl and beat in the sugar gradually. Remove the saucepan from the heat, place the bowl on top and whisk the eggs and sugar until thick and mousse-like. This will take quite 7–8 minutes and the mixture will increase in volume and lighten in colour; when lifted on the whisk a little will fall back, forming a ribbon on the mixture in the bowl. Remove the bowl from the heat and continue whisking for 5 minutes until mixture is cold. Now, using a metal spoon, very gently cut and fold in two-thirds of the flour, then the butter, quickly followed by the remaining flour.

Watchpoint If you have an electric mixer, there is no need to place the mixing bowl over hot water but do add the flour by hand, cutting and folding it in as described in the recipe.

Turn the mixture immediately into prepared mould, bake in a pre-set oven for 30–35 minutes.

For genoese pastry, fold in flour by hand, add melted butter and remaining flour before baking in the lined mould

Frangipane

4 oz butter
4 oz caster sugar
2 eggs
4 oz ground almonds
1 oz flour
orange flower water, or lemon juice, or kirsch, or vanilla essence (to flavour)

Use this recipe for pâtisseries and gâteaux, or as a plain cake.

Method
Soften the butter with a wooden spoon, add the sugar and beat together until light and fluffy. Beat in the eggs gradually, then stir in the almonds and flour. Flavour and use as required.

Frangipane is thought to have been invented by an Italian perfumer named Frangipani, who had a very sweet tooth. He lived in Paris during the reign of Louis XIII.

A variety of moulds: from top left, moule à manqué, brioche, a six-madeleine tray, tartlet and boat moulds in two sizes

MOULDS

Some gâteaux and pâtisseries are made in special moulds or tins. The French tartlet mould is best for pâte sucrée. It is fairly deep, measures from 2–2½ inches in diameter and is obtainable from any good kitchen ironmonger.

A boat mould can also be used for pâte sucrée. Here a medium-size mould, eg. 2½–3 inches long, is best, especially one with a slightly wide base, rather than one that is too long and narrow.

Moule à manqué
This is similar to a deep sandwich tin, has sloping sides and is usually plain, although some have a classic pattern on the bottom. They are used for genoese, sponges and other cakes, especially those to be iced. For icing, the cake is inverted so that icing runs down the sloping sides.

Mixtures to be served plain, such as frangipane, and cream sweets look attractive in these moulds.

Using a rolling pin to lay the pastry over the boat moulds

Cut off a small piece of pastry, and roll into a floury ball; use this to press pastry into moulds

When moulds are well lined, roll off pastry edges with rolling pin, first one way, then the other

Lining French flan pastry into moulds

Tartlet moulds. Take half the given paste and roll it out very thinly. Set 4–5 moulds on your work surface. Lift up pastry on rolling pin and lay over the moulds. Cut off a small piece of paste, roll it into a small ball (about the size of a marble). Dip this ball lightly into flour and use it to pat and press the paste into the moulds, easing it gently in. When moulds are well lined, roll off the pastry edges with the rolling pin, first one way, then the other.

Add the trimmings to remaining paste and line remaining moulds in the same way.

Flan ring. Prepare pastry as above and roll it out ¼ inch thick. Place the flan ring on a baking sheet and proceed as for tartlet moulds.

FILLINGS AND DECORATION

There are two types of butter cream (crème au beurre) used in pâtisseries and gâteaux. The first one, given below, has a whipped egg mousse added to the creamed butter, the second one has a meringue added. Unless specified, either butter cream may be used in the following recipes.

Butter cream 1

2 oz granulated sugar
4 tablespoons water
2 egg yolks
6 oz unsalted butter

For flavourings (optional)
chocolate
coffee essence
zest of orange, or lemon, rind

Method
Dissolve the sugar in water in a saucepan over gentle heat, then boil it steadily until the syrup forms a slim 'thread' between the finger and thumb (216–218°F on a sugar thermometer).
Watchpoint To test between the finger and thumb, remove a little syrup from the pan, off the heat, with the handle of a teaspoon; cool it and then test.

When bubbles subside, pour the syrup on to the egg yolks and whisk until mixture is thick and mousse-like. Cream the butter until soft and add the egg mousse gradually. Flavour to taste with melted sweetened chocolate, or coffee essence, or the zest of orange or lemon rind and use as required.

Butter cream 2

2 egg whites
4 oz icing sugar
8 oz unsalted butter

This butter cream is particularly suitable for tinting to pastel shades.

Method
Whisk the egg whites and icing sugar in a basin over a pan of simmering water until the mixture holds its shape. Cream the butter until soft, then add the meringue mixture to it, a little at a time. Flavour as for butter cream 1, colour and use as required.

Pastry cream (Confectioner's custard or crème pâtissière)

1 egg (separated)
1 egg yolk
2 oz caster sugar
¾ oz flour
½ oz cornflour
½ pint milk

For flavouring (optional)
1 vanilla pod
2–3 oz plain chocolate
1–1½ tablespoons coffee essence

This recipe gives a firm cream that holds its shape and is suitable for filling all types of pâtisseries.

Method
Cream the two egg yolks and sugar together until white, add the flours and a little of the cold milk to make a smooth paste. Scald the remaining milk with the vanilla pod, or if flavouring cream with chocolate, simmer it in remaining milk until melted, then pour it on to egg mixture, blend and return it to pan.

Stir over gentle heat until the mixture boils.

Watchpoint The pastry cream must be smooth before it boils; if lumps form as it thickens, draw pan off heat, beat cream until smooth. If it is too stiff, add a little extra milk.

Whip the egg white until stiff, turn a little of the boiling cream into a bowl and fold in egg white. Return this to the pan and stir carefully for 2–3 minutes over the heat to set the egg white. Turn cream into a bowl to cool. If flavouring cream with coffee essence, stir it into the cooled cream.

This recipe is for ½ pint pastry cream.

GATEAUX

Gâteau moka

(see photograph, opposite)

4 egg quantity of genoese pastry
6 oz butter cream (coffee-flavoured, page 239)

To decorate
2 oz almonds (browned and ground, or finely chopped)
icing sugar (for dredging)

8½-inch diameter moule à manqué, or deep 8½–9 inch diameter cake tin

Method
Set oven at 350°F or Mark 4. Prepare the mould or tin by lining the bottom only with a disc of greaseproof paper, grease again, dust first with caster sugar, then with flour.

Fill the genoese into mould or tin, then bake in pre-set oven for approximately 35–40 minutes or until firm to the touch. Turn gâteau out and, when cool, cut in 2–3 layers. Fill with coffee-flavoured butter cream, then reshape.

Spread the top and sides of the gâteau with a layer of butter cream, press almonds round the sides only. Decorate the top of gâteau by piping on remaining butter cream, using a rose pipe. **Note:** as a variation, this cake can be split in half and filled with butter cream. After reshaping, the top and sides of the cake are spread with more butter cream and decorated all over with shredded almonds. The top is then dredged with icing sugar; top edge can be piped with rosettes of butter cream.

Gâteau Cendrillon

3 oz flour
pinch of salt
3 eggs
scant 3¼ oz caster sugar
1 tablespoon coffee essence
1½ oz butter (softened)
coffee-flavoured butter cream
apricot jam glaze (see page 208)
coffee-flavoured fondant icing
8–10 hazelnuts, or split almonds

9-inch diameter layer cake tin

Method
Grease and flour the cake tin. Set oven at 350–375°F or Mark 4–5.

Sift the flour with the salt. Break the eggs into a bowl, add the sugar and coffee essence and whisk mixture over gentle heat until the mixture is thick and mousse-like. Remove the bowl from the heat and continue whisking until the mixture is cold. Fold in two-thirds of the flour, then the melted butter and lastly the remaining flour.

Turn the mixture quickly into the tin and bake in pre-set oven for 30–35 minutes.

When cake is cool, split it in two and sandwich the halves together with a layer of coffee-flavoured butter cream. Reshape the cake and brush over the top and sides with a thin coating of hot apricot glaze. When glaze is set, ice cake with coffee-flavoured fondant icing, pipe 8–10 rosettes of butter cream around (one for each portion/slice of cake) and decorate each one with a browned hazelnut (or a split almond).

Gâteau aux groseilles (Redcurrant cake)

(see photograph, opposite)

3 egg quantity of genoese pastry
redcurrant jelly
apricot jam glaze
white fondant icing (see page 228)
frosted redcurrants

8½-inch diameter layer cake tin

Method
Set oven at 350–375°F or Mark 4–5. Grease and flour cake tin.

Fill the genoese into the tin and bake in pre-set oven for about 25–30 minutes. When cool, split the cake in two, sandwich the halves with redcurrant jelly and then reshape cake; brush it with apricot glaze, ice with white fondant and decorate with frosted redcurrants.

Frosted redcurrants
Choose good sprays of clean, fresh redcurrants; brush them sparingly with slightly-beaten egg white and dip each spray in caster sugar. Leave sprays on a sieve or wire rack to dry.

Gâteau St. Honoré

2 oz quantity of French flan pastry (page 236)
1 egg (beaten)
3 egg quantity of choux pastry (see page 218)
2 oz granulated sugar
2 tablespoons water
crème St. Honoré

To decorate
glacé cherries
few diamonds of angelica

Forcing bag, ½-inch plain nozzle

From top to bottom: gâteau aux groseilles, gâteau moka and gâteau St. Honoré (see recipes

Method

Set the oven at 400°F or Mark 6.

Chill French flan pastry well, roll it out, ⅛ inch thick, and cut out a round the size of a dessert plate. Place the round on a baking sheet, prick pastry well and damp or brush a ½-inch wide band around the edge with beaten egg.

Fill the choux pastry into a forcing bag, and make a circle around edge of French flan pastry. Brush the choux pastry with beaten egg and bake in pre-set oven for about 25 minutes.

Pipe also, on to a baking sheet, 10–15 small rounds of choux pastry about the size of a nut, brush with beaten egg and bake until crisp in pre-set

oven for approximately 12–15 minutes.

When choux pastry is cool, dissolve the sugar in the water in a small pan and boil it briskly to the crack stage, (300°F or until the syrup just begins to turn a pale straw-colour). Dip the bottom of each ball of choux pastry into the sugar syrup and place them close together around the top of cake. Fill the centre of the cake with the crème St. Honoré and decorate with glacé cherries and diamonds of angelica.

Crème St. Honoré

4 egg yolks
4 oz caster sugar
1 oz flour
scant ½ pint milk
vanilla pod
6 egg whites

Method

Cream egg yolks and sugar together until white, add the flour and a little cold milk to make a smooth paste. Scald remaining milk with vanilla pod, then pour this on to egg mixture, blend and return it to pan. Stir over gentle heat until the mixture boils.

Whip egg whites until stiff, turn a little of boiling cream into a bowl and fold in egg whites. Return this to pan and stir carefully for 2–3 minutes over heat to set egg whites. Turn cream into a bowl to cool.

241

Gâteau au chocolat

(see photograph on page 237)

2¼ oz flour
pinch of salt
2 oz chocolate (unsweetened)
about 2½ fl oz water
3 eggs
4½ oz caster sugar
2 oz plain chocolate
6 oz butter cream
chocolate caraque
a little icing sugar (to decorate)

9½-inch diameter layer cake tin

Method

Set oven at 350°F or Mark 4. Grease and flour the cake tin.

Sift the flour with the salt. Grate or slice the unsweetened chocolate, melt it in the water over gentle heat until it is a thick cream, then set it aside to cool.

Whisk the eggs and sugar together over gentle heat until thick and mousse-like, remove the bowl from the heat and continue whisking until the mixture is cold. Fold the flour into the mixture, then add the melted chocolate. Turn the mixture into the prepared tin and bake in pre-set oven for about 35 minutes.

While the cake is cooking, melt the plain chocolate on a plate over a pan of hot water; when it is quite smooth, beat it into the butter cream.

When cake is cool, split it in two halves and sandwich together with a thin layer of the chocolate butter cream. Re-shape the cake, spread the top and sides with the same cream and press chocolate caraque over and around it, then sprinkle with icing sugar.

Chocolate caraque

Grate 3 oz plain chocolate or chocolate couverture (cooking chocolate). Melt on a plate over hot water and work with a palette knife until smooth. Spread this thinly on a marble slab or laminated surface and leave until nearly set. Then, using a long sharp knife, shave it off the slab, slantwise, using a slight sawing movement and holding the knife almost upright. The chocolate will form long scrolls or flakes. These will keep in an airtight tin but look better when they are freshly made.

For chocolate caraque, spread melted chocolate on marble slab. Shave off in long scrolls or flakes with palette knife

Spread gâteau au chocolat with chocolate butter cream, lay the caraque scrolls on top

Doboz torte

5 oz plain flour
pinch of salt
4 eggs
6 oz caster sugar
8 oz quantity butter cream
  (flavoured with 4 oz plain
  chocolate)

For caramel
5 oz loaf sugar
¼ pint water

To finish
crushed caramel or grated
  chocolate (optional)
chocolate butter cream (for
  rosettes)

This cake is of Austrian origin.

Method

Prepare 6 baking sheets by brushing them with melted lard or oil and dusting lightly with flour; then mark an 8-inch circle on each one, using a plate or pan lid as a guide. Set the oven at 375°F or Mark 5.

Sift the flour with the salt. Break the eggs in a bowl, add the sugar. Place bowl over pan of hot water on gentle heat and whisk mixture until it is thick and white. Remove bowl from the heat and continue whisking

until it is cold. Lightly fold the flour into the mixture, using a metal spoon. Divide mixture into 6 portions and spread each over a circle on the prepared sheets (this can be done, using fewer sheets in rotation, but each time the baking sheet to be re-used must be wiped, re-greased and floured). Bake in a pre-set moderate oven for about 5–6 minutes.

Trim each round with a sharp knife while still on the baking sheet, then lift on to a wire rack to cool. Take 1 round, lay it on an oiled sheet ready to coat with the caramel.

To prepare caramel: melt the sugar in the water over a very low heat without boiling. When completely dissolved, increase the heat and cook it rapidly to a rich brown caramel. Pour this at once over the single cake round and, when caramel is just about set, mark it into portions with an oiled knife and trim edges.

Sandwich the six rounds together with chocolate butter cream, putting the caramel-covered round on top. Spread the sides with more butter cream and press round crushed caramel or grated chocolate. Pipe a rosette of butter cream on each portion.

The finished cake is shown on the back of the cover.

Marking the caramelised round of Doboz torte into portions

Gâteau d'ananas (Pineapple cake)

3 egg quantity of genoese pastry
butter cream (flavoured with
  kirsch, or lemon juice)
apricot jam glaze
candied pineapple
white fondant icing

8-inch diameter cake tin

Method

Prepare tin by greasing it, lining bottom only with a disc of greaseproof paper, greasing

242

again and dusting first with caster sugar, then with flour.

Set oven at 350°F or Mark 4.

Fill genoese into tin and bake in pre-set oven for about 30 minutes. When cool, split cake in two and sandwich halves with the kirsch (or the lemon) flavoured butter cream. Reshape the cake and brush the top and sides with a thin coating of the hot apricot glaze, then leave it to set. Arrange the slices of candied pineapple over the top of the cake and coat the top and sides with a very thin layer of fondant icing.

Candied pineapple

Take one small can of pineapple slices and divide each slice horizontally, if very thick. Put half the juice from the can into a frying pan with 2 rounded tablespoons of granulated sugar. Allow this to dissolve over a slow heat, add the pineapple and cook gently until the fruit is transparent. Do not allow the sugar to caramelise, and turn the slices from time to time. Use the candied pineapple when cold.

Note: treat fresh pineapple in the same way but substitute water for canned pineapple juice.

Gâteau praliné

4 egg quantity of genoese pastry
6 oz butter cream
apricot jam glaze
2 oz ground almonds (browned)

For praline
2 oz caster sugar
2 oz almonds (unblanched)

9½-inch diameter deep cake tin

Method

Set oven at 350°F or Mark 4. Prepare tin as for gâteau genoese; fill into the prepared tin and bake in pre-set oven for about 35 minutes.

Take 2 oz praline, crush and sieve it, then pound it to a smooth paste and add it to the butter cream.

When the cake is cold, split it in two and sandwich the halves together with a thick layer of butter cream. Reshape

---

cake and brush the top and sides with well-reduced apricot glaze. Cover cake with the almonds, pressing them on well with a palette knife.

To prepare praline: put almonds and sugar into a small pan and cook slowly to a nut-brown; stir well with a metal spoon when sugar starts to brown. Then turn praline on to an oiled tin to cool.

Gâteau flamande

4 oz quantity of French flan
    pastry
2 oz crystallised cherries
2–3 tablespoons kirsch

For frangipane
4 oz butter
4 oz caster sugar
2 eggs
4 oz ground almonds
1 oz flour (sifted)
1 tablespoon kirsch

To decorate
2 oz flaked almonds
4 tablespoons thick glacé icing

8-inch diameter flan ring

Method

Make up the pastry, chill and then line into flan ring. Slice cherries, reserving a few for decoration and macerate in the kirsch. Set oven at 375°F or Mark 5.

Gâteau flamande is decorated with glacé icing and cherries

Soften the butter, add the sugar and beat until light and fluffy. Beat in the eggs a little at a time, then stir in the almonds, flour and kirsch.

Place the cherries at the bottom of the flan, cover with frangipane and place the almonds on top. Bake gâteau in pre-set oven for about 45 minutes. When cool, brush gâteau with glacé icing and decorate with reserved cherries.

PATISSERIES

Bateaux Célestins

4 oz quantity of French flan
    pastry
2 tablespoons apricot jam
¼ quantity of madeleine mixture
    (see overleaf)
rind of 1 orange (grated)
apricot jam glaze
orange glacé, or fondant icing

12–16 boat moulds

Method
Set oven at 375°F or Mark 5.

Line moulds with pastry. Place a little apricot jam at the bottom of each pastry case, then fill each one with the madeleine mixture flavoured with grated orange rind. Bake cakes in pre-set oven for about 10 minutes, then turn moulds upside down on to a rack to cool.

Brush the tops with hot apricot glaze and, when set, coat top of each cake with an orange glacé or fondant icing.

Selection of pâtisseries: from left to right, chocolatines, madeleines, tartelettes amandines, bateaux de miel, mirlitons, bateaux de miel, tartelettes amandines and gâteaux St. André

Chocolatines

2 egg quantity of genoese
   pastry
6 oz butter cream 1, flavoured
   with 4 oz chocolate (melted)
finely-chopped browned, or
   ground, almonds

6-inch square cake tin

Method
Bake the genoese in the pre-pared tin (see basic recipe) and, when cool, split and sandwich with a thin layer of chocolate butter cream. Reshape the cake, trim and cut into 2-inch squares. Spread the top and sides of each cake with the butter cream and press the almonds round the sides only. Decorate tops with rosettes of the same chocolate-flavoured butter cream.

Madeleines

2 oz flour
2 eggs
2 oz caster sugar
2 oz butter (softened – see
   genoese pastry)

12–18 madeleine moulds

These traditional French made-leines (shaped like shallow, oval shells with fluted tops) are different from the English ones given on page 224 and are served quite plain.

Method
Butter and flour the tins and set oven at 375°F or Mark 5.

Sift the flour. Place the eggs and sugar in a basin and whisk together until thick and mousse-like (*not* over hot water), then fold in the sifted flour and the softened butter.

Fill the tins with the mixture and bake in pre-set oven for about 10 minutes.

Tartelettes amandines (Almond tartlets)

4 oz quantity of French flan
   pastry
½ quantity of frangipane recipe
2 oz almonds (flaked)
apricot, or redcurrant, jam glaze
2 tablespoons ground almonds
   (for decoration)

12 tartlet moulds

Method
Set oven at 375°F or Mark 5.

Line moulds with pastry, prick pastry bottoms with a fork and fill each case with frangi-pane. Scatter the flaked almonds over the tops and bake for 12–15 minutes in pre-set oven. As soon as the tartlets are cooked, remove them from the moulds, brush the tops with hot glaze and decorate the outside edges with a thin line of ground almonds.

Note: it is quicker and easier to fill the tartlet moulds if the frangipane is put into a piping bag fitted with a plain pipe.

Bateaux de miel (Almond and honey cakes)

4 oz quantity of French flan
   pastry

For filling
3 oz butter (unsalted)
3 oz caster sugar
3 oz ground almonds
1 tablespoon honey
coffee essence (to taste)
coffee fondant icing

12–16 boat moulds

Method
Set oven at 375°F or Mark 5.

Line the ungreased moulds with pastry and bake blind in

pre-set oven for 5–7 minutes, then remove and leave to cool.

Meanwhile cream the butter and sugar together until light, stir in the ground almonds and honey and flavour with the coffee essence to taste. When pastry cases are cold, fill with coffee almond cream, doming it well and shaping it with a small, sharp knife. Leave filled cases in a cool place to set, then ice with the coffee fondant and leave undecorated.

Mirlitons

4 oz quantity of French flan
   pastry
2 tablespoons apricot jam

For filling
4 macaroons
2 eggs
3½ oz caster sugar
2–3 drops of vanilla essence

To decorate
halved blanched almonds
icing sugar

10–12 tartlet moulds

Mirlitons are a speciality of the French town of Rouen.

Method
Set oven at 300°F or Mark 2.

Line the moulds, prick the pastry bottoms with a fork and place a little apricot jam at the bottom of each one.

To prepare the filling: break the macaroons in small pieces and bake in pre-set oven for about 10–15 minutes, or until quite dry, then crush them with a rolling pin and put through a sieve. Increase the oven to 350°F or Mark 4.

Whip the eggs and sugar together until very thick and mousse-like, add the sieved macaroons and flavour with vanilla essence. Fill the mixture into the moulds, decorate each top with three almond halves, dredge with icing sugar and bake in pre-set oven for about 15 minutes.

Gâteaux St. André

4 oz quantity of French flan
   pastry
apple marmelade (made from
   1 lb cooking apples)—see page
   266
For royal icing
5 oz icing sugar
1 egg white
pinch of flour

12 boat moulds

Method
Set oven at 375°F or Mark 5.

Line the moulds with pastry and fill with the apple marmelade (well reduced and very cold). Reserve the pastry scraps to decorate.

To make royal icing: sift the icing sugar. Whisk the egg white until frothy, then add to the icing sugar, 1 tablespoon at a time, beating well between each addition. Add the flour. Continue beating until the mixture will stand in peaks. Cover the apple marmelade with the royal icing and place two bands of pastry, ¼ inch wide, on the tops to form a St. Andrew's cross. Bake in the pre-set oven for about 10 minutes.

Mokatines

2 egg quantity of genoese
   pastry
3 oz coffee-flavoured butter
   cream 1
apricot glaze
8 oz quantity of coffee-flavoured
   fondant icing

6-inch square cake tin

Method
Bake the genoese in the prepared tin (see basic recipe) and, when cool, split and sandwich with a thin layer of coffee butter cream. Reshape the cake, trim and cut into neat oblongs 2½ inches long and 1 inch wide. Brush the top and sides with hot apricot glaze, ice with the fondant icing and decorate with piped butter cream.

Note: as a variation this cake can be cut into small rounds. Split these and fill with a thin layer of coffee butter cream. Reshape and spread the top and sides with butter cream, roll in chopped browned almonds, and pipe in small rosette of coffee butter cream in the centre.

Printaniers

2 egg quantity of genoese
   pastry
8 oz butter cream 2
vanilla essence
coffee essence
a little fresh strawberry purée,
   or sieved strawberry jam
carmine, or cochineal (for
   colouring)
8 oz quantity of fondant icing

Swiss roll tin, or paper case, 12 inches
   by 8 inches; forcing bag and ⅝-inch
   plain pipe

Method
Bake the genoese (see basic recipe) in a prepared swiss roll tin or paper case. When cool, split cake and sandwich halves with a little vanilla-flavoured butter cream. Trim the cake and cut it into long strips, 1½ inches wide.

Divide remaining butter cream into three portions; flavour one vanilla, another coffee and the last portion strawberry, adding a few drops of carmine, to colour it a delicate pink.

Fill forcing bag and pipe on the top three lines of butter cream; first the vanilla and coffee, side by side, then the strawberry on the top. Place cakes in a refrigerator to harden butter cream. Then coat with white fondant icing and, when set, cut diagonally into sections about ¾ inch wide.

Bateaux bruxellois

4 oz quantity of French flan
   pastry
½ quantity of pastry cream
   recipe
2 oz ground almonds

For decoration
6 glacé cherries
strip of angelica (cut into
   24 diamonds)
icing sugar

Approximately 12 boat moulds

Method
Set oven at 375°F or Mark 5.

Line moulds with pastry, prick bottoms, fill with pastry cream and ground almonds mixed together. Decorate each one with a half cherry and two diamonds of angelica. Dust with icing sugar and bake in pre-set oven for 10–12 minutes.

Home Baking and Yeast Cookery

YEAST

Yeast is a living plant, needing warm and moist conditions in which to grow. It is affected by extremes of temperatures: excess cold will retard or check (but not kill) the growth, while strong heat will kill it completely. This explains why bread dough can be mixed and stored before rising either in the refrigerator for a short period, or in a deep-freeze for a longer time.

After a long and slow rising process, the risen dough is baked in a hot oven to kill the yeast which has done its work.

Sugar helps yeast to grow, so if creaming it with yeast take care not to overmix as it will reduce its qualities; just stir in enough to bring it to a liquid.

Salt retards its growth if mixed with the yeast, so it is usually sifted with the flour or dissolved in part of the liquid in the recipe.

The proportion of yeast to flour varies with the type of bread. Household breads use 1 oz yeast to 3 lb flour; light or milk breads, $\frac{1}{2}$ oz yeast to 1 lb flour; rolls and buns, $\frac{3}{4}$ oz yeast to 1 lb flour.

The proportion of yeast to flour also affects the time allowed for rising. The smaller the quantity of yeast the longer the rising will take; the greater the quantity the shorter the time.

You can use either fresh compressed yeast or dried yeast. The former is not always easy to obtain, but you can probably buy some from a baker who bakes on the premises. Full directions for using dried yeast are always given on the tin; it must soak in some of the liquid from the recipe for a given time before being mixed with remaining liquid and flour.

If you want to store fresh yeast, it will keep in a screw-top jar in the refrigerator for more than a week. For longer periods store in the deep-freeze. If you haven't a refrigerator, press into a small jar or pot until three-quarters full, then invert jar in a saucer of cold water. Yeast will then keep fresh and moist for several days.

> **Note:** the amount of yeast specified in all these recipes is for fresh yeast. In all cases dried yeast (usually half the amount) may be substituted, but it is essential to check the quantity and to read the instructions given on the tin.

Flour A special bread flour should be used for white bread. It is called 'strong' flour and has a high gluten content. If you find this impossible to obtain, use plain flour. However, some makes of plain flour are stronger than others, so do ask your grocer's advice.

There are also various grades of flour from fine white to coarse wholemeal for different types of bread and certain firms produce stone-ground flour which is ideal for bread-making.

BREAD

There are four distinct stages in bread-making.

1 Sponging This helps to speed up the general rising of the dough and produces a fine grain in the finished bread. The flour is sifted into a warm bowl with the salt, a well made in the centre and the total quantity of liquid, with the yeast dissolved in it, is poured in.

Draw in enough flour from the sides of the well to make a thick batter. Liberally sprinkle the top of the batter with flour taken from the sides, cover with a damp cloth and set in a warm place to rise; a fairly cool airing cupboard or a cupboard in a warm kitchen is suitable, where the temperature is 75°F–80°F.

Leave for about 15–20 minutes, or until bubbles start to break through on the surface, which indicates that the batter has started to rise. The batter or sponge, as it has now become, is ready for the next stage.

2 Rising The rest of the flour is then drawn into the spongy dough which is kneaded well on a board or table and transferred

From the left: refrigerator rolls, wholemeal loaves and cottage loaves (see pages 248–250) are shown here

to a greased bowl. Turn the dough over in the bowl so that the top surface is lightly greased. This will prevent a skin forming.

Cover the bowl with a damp cloth. Set in a warm, draught-free place until double in bulk. A steamy atmosphere helps the rising and the temperature should be between 70°F–80°F The dough is then ready for shaping.

3 Proving This next stage is a short period of rising carried out after shaping dough, when it is put in a slightly warmer place than for general rising; for example over the stove or in a warming drawer, at about 80°F–85°F and left there for 10–15 minutes until the dough begins to swell.

4 Baking Immediately it is clear the dough is rising, the loaves or buns (in their loaf tins or on baking sheets) should be put into a pre-heated oven. As a general rule all yeast mixtures are baked in a hot oven, but if the dough is rich the temperature is lower.

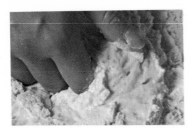

Sponging: the yeast liquid is worked into the warmed flour

When dough is doubled in size, turn out of bowl on to a board

Shape the dough as wanted and then line it into the bread tins

Baking temperatures

Type of Bread	Electric and solid fuel	Gas
Bread	425°F–400°F	7–6
Rolls	425°F	7
Buns (small)	450°F	8
Tea cakes	450°F–425°F	8–7
Bun loaf, brioche and savarin	400°F	6

Household bread

2 lb plain flour
1 dessertspoon salt
½–¾ oz fresh yeast
½ teaspoon sugar
1 pint water
lard (for greasing bowl)

2 loaf tins, 9 inches by 5 inches by 3 inches

Method
Sift flour with the salt into a warm mixing bowl. Cream yeast and sugar, add to the water.

Make a well in the centre of the flour, warm the water, pour it in and draw in enough flour to make a thick batter. Well sprinkle top with flour from the sides, cover bowl with a damp cloth and leave to rise in a warm place 15–20 minutes.

When bubbles have broken through the floured surface work up to a dough with the hand. Turn on to a floured board or table and knead until dough is no longer sticky. Dust occasionally with flour.

Put back into a clean and lightly-greased warm bowl, turn dough over and make a shallow cross-cut on the top. Cover with the cloth and leave to rise 1–1½ hours until double in bulk. Grease the tins and set the oven at 425°F or Mark 7.

Turn dough out on to the floured board and knead lightly for a few seconds. Then cut in half, shape and put each piece into a tin. Stand these on a baking sheet, cover with the cloth and prove for 10–15 minutes. Then bake for 35–40 minutes in pre-set oven. Lower heat slightly after 20–25 minutes to 400°F or Mark 6.

When well browned and shrinking slightly from the sides of the tins, tip the loaves out on to a rack to cool. Tap the bottom of the loaf and if it sounds hollow it is a good sign that the bread is done.

Cottage loaf

Make as for household bread, but divide dough in two pieces, one twice the size of the other. Knead each piece lightly into a bun shape. Set the large piece on a baking sheet, put the small one on top and push your finger right through the centre down to the sheet. Prove and bake as for previous recipe.

Wholemeal bread

3 lb coarse wholemeal flour
2 tablespoons salt
1¼ oz fresh yeast
1 tablespoon Barbados sugar
1¼ pints milk and water (mixed)
lard (for greasing tins)

2 loaf tins, 9 inches by 5 inches by 3 inches, or sandwich tins (optional)

Method
Sift salt thoroughly with flour in a warm mixing bowl and make a well in the centre. Cream sugar and yeast together, warm the milk and water, add to yeast and stir well to mix.

Pour liquid into the well and with your hand mix the flour into the liquid, gradually drawing it from round the sides of the bowl. It should be a soft dough, so quantity of liquid may need slight varying. Cover bowl with a thick cloth and leave to rise in a warm place 1–1½ hours.

Set oven at 400°F or Mark 6.

Turn dough on to a floured board; knead until it leaves board and hands are clean. Divide dough into two, knead each piece until there's no trace of stickiness.

Shape each piece into a round loaf and put on a floured baking sheet, or into greased tins, but do not let sides of loaf touch the tin. Prove for a further 30 minutes. Bake in the pre-set oven for 1 hour.

Fine wholemeal bread

1½ lb wholemeal flour
8 oz plain white flour
1 dessertspoon salt
1 oz butter, or lard
¾–1 oz fresh yeast
1 teaspoon sugar
¾–1 pint warm water
lard (for greasing tins)

2 loaf tins, 9 inches by 5 inches by 3 inches, or sandwich tins (optional)

Method
Mix flours and salt together in a bowl, rub in butter or lard. Continue as for wholemeal bread.
Watchpoint Wholemeal flour absorbs slightly less liquid than a finer flour; this should be taken into account when mixing the dough.

Bun loaf

A simple bun loaf can be made from a bread dough with dried fruit, butter, sugar and eggs worked in before proving.

When making a batch of bread use a portion of the dough for this. To 1 lb of dough add 2 oz creamed butter, sugar, 1–2 eggs (depending on size) and dried fruit to taste.

Crust finishes

For a crisp crust leave the loaves as they are. **For a softer crust** rub with buttered paper; when turned out cover with a cloth for 5–10 minutes.

Ordinary bread is made with water, which gives a crisp crust. Light bread is made with milk and a small quantity of fat, which give a soft crust and a spongy texture to the crumb.

The Sally Lunn is sliced into three rounds. Each side is toasted, then buttered; the cake is then reshaped and sliced for serving

Baps

1 lb plain flour
1 teaspoon salt
½ pint milk and water (mixed)
2 oz shortening, or butter
½ oz fresh yeast
1 teaspoon sugar

This is a quick, light bread, suitable for either breakfast or dinner rolls.

Method
Sift flour with salt into a warm bowl, warm the milk and water, add the fat and stir until dissolved. Cream yeast and sugar, add to the liquid and pour it all into the centre of the flour. Mix to a soft dough and knead until smooth and elastic.

Cover with a damp cloth and leave to rise in a warm place for 1–1½ hours. Set the oven at 425°F or Mark 7.

Knead dough lightly on a board and divide into 6 pieces. Roll each piece on a floured board to an oval, or flatten with the heel of the hand. Set on a floured baking sheet, dust with flour, prove and then bake in the pre-set oven for 10–15 minutes. Lower heat slightly after 5 minutes to 400°F or Mark 6. When cooked, the baps should be pale brown in colour.

Sally Lunn

7½ fl oz milk
1 oz butter
12 oz plain white flour (warmed)
½ teaspoon salt
1 egg
¾ oz fresh yeast
1 teaspoon sugar
1 tablespoon sugar dissolved in 1 tablespoon milk (for glazing)
lard (for greasing tins)

Two 5-inch diameter cake tins

This is a typical and popular English teacake.

Method
Set oven at 425°F or Mark 7. Warm and grease the tins.

Heat the milk in a pan, dissolve the butter in it and allow mixture to cool until tepid. Sift the warmed flour and salt in a bowl. Beat the egg and add to the milk. Cream the yeast and sugar together and add to this the milk and egg mixture.

Make a well in the flour and strain in the liquid. Mix to a dough. Turn on to a floured board and knead lightly for a few minutes. Put half of the dough into each warmed tin.

Cover with a cloth and set in a warm place to rise until doubled in bulk (about 30 minutes). Bake in a pre-set oven for 20–25 minutes. Brush with sweetened milk and put back in oven to dry the glaze.

Refrigerator rolls

6 oz potatoes
1 lb plain white flour
2 oz butter
1 teaspoon salt
¾ oz fresh yeast
1 dessertspoon sugar
½ pint milk and water (mixed)
1 large egg
beaten egg mixed with ½
   teaspoon of salt (for glazing)
   – optional
lard (for greasing)

The potatoes help the fermentation and make these rolls especially light. The dough keeps very well in the refrigerator, or for longer in the deep-freeze, and a little at a time can be used from this stock.

Method
Boil potatoes in their skins. Peel and crush well with the masher, or put through a sieve. Put into a warm bowl, sift in the flour, rub in the butter and add salt.

Set oven at 425°F or Mark 7.

Cream yeast with the sugar, warm the milk and water and add to yeast together with the beaten egg. Pour into a well in the flour mixture and work up to a dough. Knead until the dough has no trace of stickiness, dusting occasionally with a little flour.

If storing this dough, put it in a basin covered with a plate in the refrigerator. After 12 hours the dough will have risen to the top. Push it down and turn it over. Make a cross-cut on the top, cover and leave until wanted. It will keep for at least a week in the fridge. If dough rises to top of the bowl, push it down with the back of your hand.

When wanted for use, knead lightly and leave to rise in a warm place until double in bulk. The longer the dough has been kept, the longer rising time it will need here.

If using immediately, turn into a greased basin and leave to rise until double in bulk (1–1½ hours). Then knead lightly and shape into rolls. Prove and bake on a greased baking sheet in pre-set oven. Brush with beaten egg mixed with salt if you like a glazed finish.

PIZZAS

Pizzas are popular party dishes. Choose from several different fillings: smoked haddock and mushroom (at back), ham (centre), napolitana (front left) and Cordon Bleu (front right)

Basic pizza dough

1 lb flour
1 teaspoon salt
1 oz yeast
2 teaspoons sugar
about ¼ pint milk (warmed)
3–4 eggs (beaten)
4 oz butter (creamed)

Method
Sift the flour and salt into a warmed basin. Cream yeast and

sugar and add to the warmed milk with the beaten eggs : add this liquid to the flour and beat thoroughly. Work the creamed butter into the dough. Cover and leave for 40 minutes to rise. **Note:** for the best pizza, it is wise to use a flan ring to keep the dough in position. It has the added advantage of enabling you to cover the entire surface with topping without it running and sticking to your baking sheet.

Patting out the pizza dough to the size of the flan ring

Pizza napolitana

¼ quantity of basic dough

For topping
4–6 anchovy fillets
2 tablespoons milk
1 lb ripe tomatoes
1–2 tablespoons olive oil
1 small onion (finely chopped)
1 dessertspoon chopped marjoram, or basil
salt and pepper
4 oz Bel Paese, or Mozzarella, cheese (sliced)

8-inch diameter flan ring

Method
Flour the dough lightly and pat it out with the palm of your hand on floured baking sheet to a round 8 inches in diameter. Then place greased flan ring over it.

Split the anchovy fillets in two lengthways and soak them in the milk ; set aside.

Scald and skin the tomatoes, cut away the hard core, squeeze gently to remove seeds, then slice. Heat the oil in a frying pan ; add chopped onion and, after a few minutes, the sliced tomatoes. Draw pan aside and add the herbs ; season well.

Set oven at 400°F or Mark 6. Cover dough with tomato mixture, place cheese slices on this and arrange anchovies lattice-wise over the top. Prove pizza for 10–15 minutes, then bake in pre-set oven for 30–35 minutes. Lift off flan ring and slide pizza on to a bread board or wooden platter to serve.

Smoked haddock and mushroom pizza

¼ quantity of basic dough

For topping
1 lb smoked haddock
béchamel sauce (made with 1 oz flour, 1 oz butter, ¼ pint

flavoured milk)
1 oz butter
1 shallot (finely chopped)
6 oz mushrooms (quartered)
salt and pepper

8-inch diameter flan ring

Method
Cover the smoked haddock with water, bring it slowly to the boil ; cover, turn off heat and leave for 10 minutes.

Meanwhile make béchamel sauce in the usual way.

Remove skin and bones from the haddock and flake flesh carefully. Melt 1 oz butter, add shallot, cook for 2–3 minutes, then add quartered mushrooms and sauté briskly for 2–3 minutes. Add béchamel sauce and haddock ; season to taste.

Set oven at 400°F or Mark 6. Pat out the dough as before, cover with topping, prove and bake in pre-set hot oven.

Ham pizza

¼ quantity of basic dough

For topping
2 oz butter
1 large Spanish onion (about ½ lb) – finely sliced
6 oz ham (shredded)
2 oz mortadella sausage (shredded)
2–3 tablespoons mango, or tomato, chutney

Method
Melt butter, add onion and cook slowly until very brown. Add shredded ham and mortadella, moisten with chutney.

Set oven at 400°F or Mark 6. Pat out the last quarter of dough as before, cover with the topping, prove and bake in pre-set hot oven.

Spooning the prepared ham topping on to the pizza dough

Pizza Cordon Bleu

¼ quantity of basic dough

For topping
2 shallots (finely chopped)
1 wineglass white wine
1 lb scampi
4 oz mushrooms (chopped)
1 oz butter
¾ oz flour
1 clove of garlic (crushed with
    ½ teaspoon salt)
¼ pint chicken stock
1 teaspoon tomato purée
4 tomatoes
salt and pepper

8-inch diameter flan ring

Method
Simmer shallot in white wine until reduced to half the quantity. Add scampi and mushrooms and cook very slowly for 5 minutes; set pan aside.

Melt butter, add flour and when coloured add the garlic, stock and tomato purée, stir until boiling, then cook for 3–4 minutes. Scald tomatoes, skin, quarter, and remove seeds, cut flesh again into strips. Add scampi mixture to tomatoes and sauce. Season to taste.

Set oven at 400°F or Mark 6. Pat out the dough as before and cover with the topping; prove and bake in pre-set hot oven.

The name **Pizza** originated from the area around Naples. It is not certain, however, that the nearby village of Pizza, where the flour for the best pizza dough is grown and ground, can claim to be its creator. A pizza may first have been made to use up left-over bread dough and tomato sauce, plus whatever sausage, ham or cheese happened to be available.

SCONES AND SODA BREAD

A selection of scones and soda bread. Left to right at back: fly bread, soda, treacle and girdle scones; large white and brown soda breads; in front: buttered soda scones and drop scones

When you are short of time for baking, try making soda bread or baking powder bread; the same dough can also be turned into a variety of scones. The dough must be mixed quickly and handled lightly, and can be cooked on a girdle or baked in the oven. A girdle or griddle is a thick, round, iron plate with a semi-circular (half-hoop) handle, and it is used on top of the stove. The lightness of the finished bread depends on attention to the following points.

General points

The raising agent should be bicarbonate of soda used with an acid such as buttermilk or sour milk. The two together release the carbon dioxide necessary to make bread light.

If neither of these acids are available and fresh (sweet) milk is used, you will need to add twice the amount of cream of tartar to bicarbonate of soda. A tablespoon of black treacle,

which is also an acid, helps rising in this case.

Plain flour is best, but if using self-raising flour, you must still add bicarbonate of soda with an acid. This is because the proportion of raising agent for scone dough should be greater than that of the raising agent present in self-raising flour.

Mixing and handling. Sufficient liquid should be added to dry ingredients to make a soft dough. Avoid any delay between mixing and baking.

Baking. Scones should be baked quickly to prevent them from getting overbrown on the bottom; cook on shiny, ungreased baking sheets (a shiny surface reflects heat).

If cooked on a girdle, scones or soda bread should be rolled thinner than for baking or they will be too brown before the middle is sufficiently cooked. Cook more slowly on a girdle than when baking.

Watchpoint A girdle must be pre-heated to the right heat. A frequent mistake is to have it too hot at first and in consequence the outside crust becomes too brown, leaving the centre uncooked. This applies especially to bread.

A good test is to sprinkle the girdle with flour; if this becomes light-brown in colour in 3 minutes, the girdle is at the correct temperature. Alternatively sprinkle a few drops of water on to the girdle. If it is heated to the right temperature, they will dance around. If possible turn loaves or scones once only (this may have to be disregarded it girdle was a little too hot in the first place).

Soda bread

1½ lb plain flour
1½ teaspoons salt
1½ teaspoons bicarbonate of soda
scant 1½ oz butter
about ¾ pint buttermilk, or fresh milk with 1 dessertspoon cream of tartar

Method
If not using a girdle, set the oven at 400°F or Mark 6.

Sift the flour with salt and bicarbonate of soda into a mixing bowl. Rub in the butter and mix with the buttermilk to a soft dough. Turn the dough on to a floured board and shape into a large round about 2 inches thick.

Score or cut into quarters, place on a floured baking sheet in a circle and bake in pre-set oven for about 25–30 minutes (or cook on a girdle) until the bread sounds hollow when tapped on the bottom.

Scoring the soda bread into quarters before baking; it may be cut instead of scored

Testing the cooked soda bread; it should sound hollow when tapped on the bottom

Fly bread

Bake as for soda bread, adding a handful of cleaned currants to the dry ingredients.

Baking powder bread

Bake as for soda bread, but use self-raising flour.

Brown soda bread

Bake as for soda bread but use half wholemeal flour and half white flour. Bake or cook on a girdle.

Turning quartered girdle scones; cooking them only takes about five minutes on each side

Girdle scones

8 oz plain flour
large pinch of salt
1 level teaspoon bicarbonate of soda
1 rounded teaspoon caster sugar
2 oz butter, or margarine, or lard
1 tablespoon currants (optional)
1 teaspoon cream of tartar with ¼ pint buttermilk, or fresh milk with 2 teaspoons cream of tartar

Girdle, or very thick frying pan

This recipe makes approximately 8 scones.

Method
Heat girdle. Sift flour with salt and sugar into a bowl, rub in the butter. Dissolve cream of tartar in the buttermilk. Add currants and buttermilk to bowl and mix quickly to a firm dough.

Turn dough on to a floured board, divide in half and shape into two rounds, ½-inch thick; cut each round into quarters. Dust with flour and cook on the hot girdle, in thick frying pan or direct on a solid hot plate, until risen and lightly brown (about 5 minutes). Turn and cook on the other side. Split, butter and serve scones immediately.

Soda scones

1 lb plain flour
1 teaspoon salt
1 teaspoon bicarbonate soda
1½ oz butter
½ pint buttermilk, or sour milk (or fresh milk with 2 teaspoons cream of tartar)

2-inch diameter plain cutter

This recipe makes approximately 8 scones.

Method
Set oven at 425°F or Mark 7. Sift flour with salt and soda into a bowl. Rub in butter. Mix quickly to a soft dough with buttermilk. Turn on to a floured board, knead lightly then roll

Stamping out soda scones with a two-inch plain cutter; the trimmings can be cut into triangles

Taking soda scones out of the oven; they should be well risen and golden-brown

out about ¾-inch thick. Stamp out into 2-inch rounds with a plain cutter or cut into triangles.

Bake on lightly floured baking sheet for 12–15 minutes until risen and golden-brown.

Wholemeal scones

8 oz plain flour
large pinch of salt
2 teaspoons bicarbonate of soda
2 teaspoons cream of tartar
8 oz wholemeal flour
4 teaspoons caster sugar
4 oz butter, or margarine, or lard
½ pint buttermilk, or fresh milk with 3 teaspoons baking powder

This recipe makes approximately 8 scones.

Method
Set oven at 425°F or Mark 7. Sift the plain flour with the salt, bicarbonate of soda and cream of tartar into a mixing bowl, add the wholemeal flour and caster sugar and mix well. Rub in the fat until evenly distributed, stir in the buttermilk and mix quickly to a soft dough.

Turn dough on to a floured board, divide it into two, knead lightly and then pat or roll it into two rounds.

Cut each round into four and place them on a baking sheet, fitting pieces together to make two rounds again. Dust with flour and bake in pre-set oven for about 12 minutes.

Treacle scones

¾ lb plain flour
½ teaspoon salt
1 teaspoon bicarbonate soda
1 teaspoon cream of tartar
2 oz butter, or margarine
2 tablespoons black treacle
¼ pint sour, or fresh, milk

This recipe makes approximately 8 scones.

Method
Set oven at 425°F or Mark 7. Sift flour with salt, bicarbonate of soda and cream of tartar. Rub in butter or margarine. Mix treacle with the milk, then stir into the dry ingredients.

Knead the scone mixture lightly on a floured board, then roll out and cut into triangles. Bake in pre-set oven for about 7–10 minutes, or cook on a girdle as for drop scones.

Drop scones

5 oz plain flour
large pinch of salt
2 teaspoons baking powder
caster sugar (to taste)
1 oz melted butter
1 egg
¼ pint fresh milk

Girdle

This recipe makes approximately 30 scones.

Method
Heat girdle over a moderate heat while mixing the batter. Sift all the dry ingredients (plus up to 1 tablespoon sugar to taste) into a mixing bowl, make a well in the centre and drop in egg and melted butter. Add milk gradually and beat well with a wooden spoon.

Grease the girdle very lightly and pour the mixture from the point of a spoon or from a jug, to give perfectly round cakes. As soon as the 'pancakes' are puffed and full of bubbles, and the undersides golden-brown, lift them with a palette knife, turn and brown on other side. Serve immediately or place between folds of a clean, warm tea towel until wanted. Serve with butter and honey or jam.

Potato scones

1½ lb floury, freshly-boiled potatoes
salt
6 oz plain flour

Girdle

This recipe makes approximately 12 scones.

These scones, which are different in shape and texture to drop scones, are equally good eaten cold or fried with the breakfast bacon. Made in large farls (large rounds marked in four), they are thin and flexible.

Method
Crush or sieve potatoes on to a floured board. Add salt to taste, work in the flour gradually, kneading it lightly and carefully.

Roll out mixture as thinly as possible. Cut into rounds the size of a dinner plate, then cut each round into quarters. Bake scones on a moderately hot girdle for 7–10 minutes, turning them once only.

CONTINENTAL DOUGHS AND PASTRIES

These doughs may be divided into three sections: for 'coffee' breads, a rich dough including eggs, milk, yeast and butter; for brioches, a dough using the same ingredients as 'coffee' breads but with a completely different method of introducing the yeast; for French croissants and Danish pastries, where yeast is added to a flour and water dough and then butter rolled in as for flaky, or puff, pastry. Many of these doughs or pastes have a high proportion of yeast which, with the butter and eggs, gives a rich spongy texture and a soft crust. When trying out these recipes for the first time, it is wise to start with the less rich doughs because you do need more skill to make the very rich ones.

COFFEE BREADS

These are so called because they are often served with coffee on the Continent, but they are all suitable for teatime. Eaten with butter or curd cheese, they make an excellent lunchtime alternative to a pudding. The basic dough can be made either by hand or in a mixer, and can be used for many different recipes.

Foundation dough for coffee breads

1 lb flour
large pinch of salt
7 fl oz milk
1 oz yeast
4 oz butter
4 oz caster sugar
2 eggs (beaten)

Method
Sift the flour with the salt into a mixing bowl. Warm the milk carefully to blood heat, add to the yeast and butter, stir until dis- solved and then mix in the sugar and beaten eggs. Make a well in the centre of the flour, pour in the liquid ingredients and mix until smooth, first with a wooden spoon and then with your hand. When the dough comes away cleanly from the sides of the bowl, turn it on to a floured board and knead until it becomes elastic. Place the dough in a greased bowl (turn it in the bowl so that it is lightly greased all over), cover with a damp cloth and set the dough in a warm place to rise for 45–50 minutes, or until it has doubled in bulk.

Knock down the dough, pull sides to the centre, turn it over, cover and let it rise again for 30 minutes before shaping and baking it. Add fruit when indi- cated in recipe.

If the dough is not for im- mediate use, omit the last rising, ie. 30 minutes. Merely knock down the dough, pull sides to centre and turn it over. Cover the top of the basin with a large plate or lid and put into the refrigerator. Keep like this overnight, or longer if wished. Once the dough comes to the top of the bowl, push it down again. When wanted for use, take out of the bowl and leave at room temperature for at least 1 hour, by which time the dough should start to rise. At this stage, dry fruit, or whatever ingredient is called for in the recipe being followed, is added.

The shaping, proving and baking should now take place. The basic method for home- baked bread is given on pages 246–8. Refer to this for in- formation on the various stages.

Stollen

½ quantity of foundation dough
1½ oz almonds
1 oz glacé cherries
about ¾ oz citron peel
1½ oz seeded raisins
1½ oz sultanas
grated rind of ½ lemon
1½ oz butter
soft, or glacé icing (made with 3 tablespoons icing sugar mixed with 1–2 tablespoons syrup, or water), or icing sugar

Method
Blanch and chop the almonds, quarter the cherries, shred the peel and mix it with the raisins, sultanas and lemon rind. After the dough has risen twice, turn it on to a floured board and knead in the fruit, pat or roll it out to an oval about 8 inches by 10 inches and spread with about 1 oz softened butter. Fold in two lengthwise and shape into a crescent. Press in the double edges firmly together.

Place the stollen on a greased baking sheet, melt the remain- ing butter and brush the top of the stollen with it. Prove dough in a warm place for about 30 minutes. Bake in a hot oven set at 400°F or Mark 6 for 30–35 minutes.

Make the icing and while the stollen is still warm pour it over the top. Or simply dredge the stollen with icing sugar.

> **Note:** the amount of yeast specified in all these recipes is for fresh yeast. In all cases dried yeast (usually half the amount) may be sub- stituted, but it is essential to check the quantity and to read the instructions given on the tin.

Easter tea ring

½ quantity of foundation dough
1 oz butter (softened)
2 oz caster sugar
2 oz raisins
1 teaspoon ground cinnamon
(optional)

For decoration
soft icing (as for stollen)
about 1 oz walnut kernels
1 oz glacé cherries
1 oz angelica

If making this tea ring for a party, double the quantities and it will then be sufficient to serve 8–10 people.

Method
Have the foundation dough ready after the second rising. Turn on to a floured board and roll out to an oblong approximately 9 inches by 6 inches. The dough should be ¼–½ inch thick. Cover surface with pats of butter, sprinkle with sugar, raisins and cinnamon. Then roll up the dough tightly, beginning at the wide side, and seal

by pinching the edges well together. Curl the dough round into a ring, joining the ends together well, and place on a greased baking tin. Snip the ring at 1-inch intervals with scissors, making each cut or snip two-thirds through the ring. Cover with a cloth and prove for about 15–20 minutes.

Bake until golden-brown in a hot oven set at 400°F or Mark 6, for about 25 minutes. Pierce the roll with a thin skewer at the end of this time to test if the ring is done. Mix the icing and brush this over the tea ring while still warm. Decorate with the nuts, cherries and angelica and then lightly brush again with icing.

Easter tea ring, decorated with soft icing, walnuts, glacé cherries and angelica

Snipping the dough after it has been rolled up and made into a ring before proving

Rolling up dough covered with the butter, sugar, raisins and cinnamon for Easter tea ring

Decorating the cooked tea ring; the icing should be spread on while ring is warm

A kugelhopf is baked in a special fluted tin with a tube in the centre

Kugelhopf

about 7 fl oz milk
scant 1 oz yeast
12 oz flour
pinch of salt
1 oz caster sugar
2 large, or 3 small, eggs (well
  broken with a fork)
4 oz butter (melted)
2 oz currants (washed and
  dried)
2 oz raisins, or sultanas (washed
  and dried)
about 24 almonds (blanched)
icing sugar (optional)

7–8 inch diameter kugelhopf tin

A kugelhopf is generally eaten with coffee, but not tea. It is baked in a special fluted tin with a tube in the centre, known as a kugelhopf tin.

Method
Butter the tin well. Warm the milk to blood heat, pour on to the yeast and stir until dissolved. Sift the flour and salt into a warm bowl, make a well in the centre, pour in the warm milk and yeast, add the sugar and eggs and the melted (but not hot) butter. Mix thoroughly together, then add the cleaned, dried fruit. Press the blanched almonds round the sides and bottom of the buttered tin. Turn the dough into it so that it is three-quarters full, then stand

it in a warm place for about 20–30 minutes, or until the mixture is about 1 inch below the top of the tin.

Meanwhile set the oven at 375–400°F or Mark 5–6. Stand the tin on a thick baking sheet, then put into the centre of the pre-set oven and bake for 50–60 minutes. If the top tends to colour too much, lower the heat until the kugelhopf is done. Leave for a few minutes before turning out and dust with icing sugar if wanted.

Turning the kugelhopf dough, mixed with dried fruit, into the kugelhopf tin before proving

Streusel kuchen

1 quantity of foundation dough

For streusel
2½ oz brown sugar
¾ oz flour
1 teaspoon cinnamon
1 oz butter (melted)
2 oz walnuts (chopped)

2 lb cake, or loaf, tin

Method
Grease the tin well. Set the oven at 400°F or Mark 6. After the second rising divide the dough into two. Put half into the prepared tin and push it down with your fist. Mix the ingredients for the streusel together, put half of this on top of the dough, then cover with the other half of the dough, and scatter the rest of the streusel mixture over the top.

Prove for 10–15 minutes, then bake for about 45–50 minutes. Test with a thin skewer before taking it out of the oven.

Apple streusel kuchen

½ quantity of foundation dough

For apple mixture
1–1½ lb dessert apples
  (preferably Laxton)
1–2 oz butter (melted)
streusel (as for streusel kuchen)

*Deep 7-inch diameter sandwich tin,
  or spring-form mould*

It is important that the apples should not be too watery, ie. cooking apples such as Bramley are not suitable for this. Use dessert apples, such as Laxton, which have a sub-acid content.

Method
Have the dough ready after second rising, knead the dough lightly and press on to the bottom of sandwich tin or mould. Set aside. Peel, core and quarter the apples, cut each quarter in half lengthwise then sauté quickly in the butter for about 3–4 minutes, turning them frequently with a slice. Draw aside, cool and then spoon the apple slices on top of the dough.

Prepare the streusel by mixing the ingredients together, scatter over the top of the apple and dough and prove for about 10–15 minutes. Then bake in a hot oven set at 400°F or Mark 6 for about 45 minutes. If the streusel browns too quickly, lower the heat to 375°F or Mark 5 and cook for the same length of time. Take out and cool slightly before serving. This may alternatively be served warm as a pudding.

Putting dough in brioche tins to rise again before baking

BRIOCHES

Brioche dough is rich, light-textured and has a soft brown crust when cooked. The dough can vary in richness according to the proportion of eggs and butter. The kind of dough which is given here makes the well known brioches.

Brioches

8 oz flour
scant ½ oz yeast
2–3 tablespoons tepid water
1 tablespoon caster sugar
1 teaspoon salt
2 eggs
about 2–4 tablespoons milk (if
  necessary)
4 oz butter
extra flour (for sprinkling)
1 egg (beaten) – mixed with 1
  tablespoon milk and a large
  pinch of salt (for brushing)

8–9 fluted brioche tins

Method
Sift the flour; dissolve yeast in water and mix it well with about a quarter of the flour to make a small ball of dough. Cut a cross on top of the dough to en-courage it to rise, and drop it into a large bowl of hand-hot water. When the ball is nearly double in size and has risen to the surface it is ready to mix with the other ingredients.

Meanwhile, make a well in the remaining flour and place the sugar, salt and eggs in it; mix together to a slack dough using 2–4 tablespoons of milk if necessary. Beat the dough until it is elastic in texture and looks like chamois leather.

Cream the butter until soft and work it into the dough; then drain the yeast ball and cut and fold it into the mixture very carefully. Knead the dough into a large ball, place it in a greased bowl, sprinkle with flour, cover with a cloth and leave to rise at room temperature for 1½–2 hours. When the dough has doubled its bulk knock it down, pull the sides to the centre and turn it over. Sprinkle again with flour, cover with a cloth and put in a cool larder or refrigerator overnight or for 6–7 hours.

The next day grease the tins, and divide the dough into 8–9 even-size pieces. Knead and shape them with the hand, place in brioche tins, or half fill the brioche tins, cut a cross on the top and crown with a small ball or 'head' of dough.

Let the brioches rise in a warm place for 15–20 minutes, then brush carefully with beaten egg. Bake in oven, set at 425°F or Mark 7, for 15–20 minutes.

French croissants

8 oz flour
¼ oz yeast
2–3 tablespoons tepid water
½ teaspoon salt
1 tablespoon sugar
4 oz butter
about 3 tablespoons milk
1 egg (beaten)

This quantity will make 18 croissants.

Method
Sift the flour. Dissolve the yeast in the water and mix with a quarter of the flour to make a small ball of dough. Cut a cross on top and drop this yeast cake into a large bowl of warm water.

Meanwhile mix the remaining flour with the salt, sugar, half the butter and sufficient milk to give a soft, but not slack, dough. The dough for croissants should not be as soft as for brioches. Beat the dough on the pastry board until it is smooth and elastic. When the yeast cake has risen to the surface of the water and is almost double its size, drain carefully and mix into the dough thoroughly. Put the dough into a floured bowl, cover and leave overnight in a cool larder or refrigerator.

Shape the remaining butter into a flat cake. Turn the dough on to a floured board, roll it out to an oblong and place the butter in the centre. Fold one third of the dough over the butter and fold the other third of the dough on top to make 3 layers. Turn the folded dough so that one of the open ends faces front. Roll out again, fold over as before and turn. Repeat once more. Wrap in a cloth and leave for 15 minutes in a cool place. Repeat the rolling and folding twice more.

To shape the croissants: roll the dough to an oblong, ⅛ inch thick, divide lengthways and cut each strip into triangles. Roll up, starting from the base, curl and place on a lightly floured baking sheet. Cover with a cloth and prove in a warm place for 15–20 minutes. Brush with beaten egg and bake in a hot oven, set at 425°F or Mark 7, for 5 minutes, then reduce the heat to 375°F or Mark 5 and continue cooking for about 10 minutes, until the croissants are browned.

A selection of Danish pastries: top left to right: cartwheels, envelope, comb; centre: pinwheels; bottom: crescents

DANISH PASTRIES

Danish pastries are made in various traditional shapes — the most usual are cartwheels and pinwheels. They are filled with almond paste, jam, sultanas and raisins, apples, etc.

Danish pastries (basic recipe)

12 oz flour
large pinch of salt
1 oz yeast
2 oz caster sugar
1 teacup lukewarm milk
9 oz butter
1 egg (beaten)
little extra egg (beaten) — for brushing
soft icing (see stollen, page 256)

This quantity will make 12 pastries of any shape.

Method
Sift the flour with the salt into a mixing bowl, cream the yeast with the sugar until liquid, add a good teacup of lukewarm milk and 2 oz of the butter, stir until dissolved; then add the beaten egg. Pour these liquid ingredients into the flour and mix to a smooth dough. Cover the dough and leave at room temperature for about 1 hour or until double in bulk. Punch down the dough, turn it on to a floured board and knead lightly. Roll out to an oblong and cover two-thirds of the dough with half the remaining butter, divided in small pieces the size of a walnut. Fold and roll as for flaky pastry. Fold in three and roll again. Put on the remaining butter, cut into pieces, fold and leave for 15 minutes. Roll and fold twice more and leave again for 15 minutes. Chill the dough for a little while.

Then roll pastry until it is ½ inch thick, shape as described right, prove and brush with beaten egg and bake in a hot oven, set at 400°F or Mark 6, for 25 minutes. Ice the finished pastries while they are still warm.

Dotting two-thirds of Danish pastry dough with butter

Folding dough into three, with unbuttered portion first

Half turn the dough round on the board and then roll it

Shaping dough into pinwheels; other shapes in foreground

CARTWHEELS

Roll out the Danish pastry dough as thinly as possible to a large oblong, spread carefully with a very thin layer of almond filling, then sprinkle with raisins and roll it up as for a swiss roll. Cut the roll into ¼-inch slices, and place the slices, cut side down, on a greased baking tin. Prove, brush with beaten egg and sprinkle flaked almonds on the top before baking.

PINWHEELS

Roll out dough thinly and cut it into 4-inch squares. Cut the dough from each corner to within a ½ inch of the centre. Fold four alternate points to the centre, pressing them down firmly. Put a little jam or almond filling in the centre, then prove and bake.

CRESCENTS

Roll dough into a large circle ⅛ inch thick and cut it into triangles or wedges. Pour a little almond filling on each triangle and roll them up loosely, starting at the base of the triangle, and then shape into crescents. Prove and bake.

ENVELOPES

Roll out the dough thinly and cut into 4-inch squares. Spread with vanilla cream and fold the corners in towards the middle. Press the edges down lightly. Prove, then bake for 12–15 minutes in a hot oven set at 400°F or Mark 6, then brush lightly with soft icing.

COMBS

Roll out the dough fairly thinly and cut into strips about 5 inches wide. Place an apple or almond filling in the middle and fold both sides over. Brush lightly with beaten egg and roll in crushed lump sugar and chopped almonds. Cut into

pieces about 4 inches long and gash about four or five times on one side; open out the slits slightly. Prove, then bake for 12–15 minutes in a hot oven at 400°F or Mark 6. These combs can be brushed slightly with beaten egg before baking to give them a glazed finish.

FILLINGS FOR DANISH PASTRIES

Vanilla cream

1 tablespoon flour
1 teaspoon cornflour
1 egg yolk
1 tablespoon sugar
¼ pint milk
2–3 drops of vanilla essence

Method
Work the flours, egg yolk and sugar together, adding a little milk. Bring the rest of the milk to the boil, pour on to the mixture, blend and return to the pan. Stir until boiling. Allow to cool then flavour with a few drops of vanilla essence.

Almond filling

2 oz almonds (ground)
2 oz caster sugar
little beaten egg

Method
Mix the almonds and sugar together and bind with enough egg to bring to a firm paste.

Apple filling

1 lb cooking apples
½ oz butter
grated rind and juice of ½ lemon
3–4 tablespoons granulated sugar

This can be used for any shape of Danish pastries and the pastries can either be finished with a soft icing or brushed with a little apricot glaze.

Method
Wipe the apples, quarter and core them, but do not peel. Rub the butter round a saucepan, slice in the apples and add the grated rind and lemon juice. Cover and cook them slowly to a pulp.

Rub pulp through a nylon strainer, return to the rinsed-out pan with the sugar. Cook gently until thick. Turn out and allow to get quite cold before using. This can be turned into a jam jar and used as required.

Fruit Dishes and Desserts

FRUIT DISHES

Strawberries Cordon Bleu

1 lb strawberries
1 large orange
6–8 sugar lumps
1 small glass brandy (2 fl oz)

Method

Hull the strawberries and place them in a bowl. Rub the lumps of sugar over the rind of the orange until they are soaked with oil, then squeeze the juice from the orange. Crush the sugar cubes and mix them with the orange juice and brandy. Pour this syrup over the strawberries, place a plate on top and chill thoroughly (2–3 hours) before serving.

Pineapple charlotte

1 pint milk
4 egg yolks
1 teaspoon arrowroot
2 rounded tablespoons caster sugar
1 medium-size can pineapple rings
½ pint double cream
scant ¾ oz powdered gelatine
2 egg whites
1 packet langues de chats biscuits

7-inch diameter spring-form cake tin (a catch unclips to open sides)

Method

Scald milk in a pan. Cream egg yolks in a bowl with arrowroot and sugar, pour on milk and return to pan. Stir over heat to thicken, but do not boil. Strain custard and cool.

Drain pineapple (keep juice); chop up 2 rings (to give 3–4 tablespoons of chopped pineapple) and keep rest for decoration. Lightly whip cream.

Soak gelatine in 4 tablespoons pineapple juice, dissolve over heat, then add to custard with three-quarters of cream. Whisk egg whites until stiff.

As custard begins to thicken, fold in egg whites with chopped pineapple using a metal spoon. Turn at once into cake tin. When set, turn out and spread sides of charlotte with remaining cream; arrange biscuits on cream, overlapping slightly. Decorate top with rest of pineapple and additional cream.

Oranges en surprise

5–6 large seedless oranges
4–5 oz glacé fruit
2–3 tablespoons Grand Marnier
2 egg quantity of meringue cuite
little caster sugar (for dusting)

Any glacé fruit — including stem ginger, angelica and cherries — can be used. The liqueur can be omitted, but it does give a good flavour.

Method

Set the oven at 400°F or Mark 6. Slice or dice the glacé fruit and macerate pieces in the Grand Marnier. Slice off the flower end of the oranges and, using a grapefruit knife, scoop out the flesh. Take out the core, and remove as many membranes as possible.

Mix the orange flesh with the glacé fruit and replace in the skins. Have ready the meringue and pipe this on each orange; place them in a roasting tin containing ice cubes. Dust with sugar and put into the pre-set hot oven until just coloured (5–10 min-

utes), then take out and serve cool.

Watchpoint. The meringue should be browned quickly because if the oranges are allowed to cook in any way they will get a marmalade taste. The ice cubes in the roasting tin help to keep the oranges from cooking.

Cherry and raspberry jelly

½ lb cherries
1 lb raspberries
½ lb redcurrants, or blackcurrants
1 pint water
2 oz fine sago
4–6 oz granulated sugar (to taste)

Ring mould (1½ pints capacity)

Method

Stone the cherries and crack kernels; string currants. Put the fruit and kernels into a pan with the water. Cover and simmer gently until currants split and give out their juice; then rub mixture through a nylon strainer. Return to pan, add sago and sugar.

Boil mixture carefully until sago is cooked (about 3–5 minutes), taking care that it doesn't stick to the bottom of the pan. Pour into wet mould, leave to cool. Turn out and serve cold with clotted cream.

Oranges en surprise are filled with glacé fruits in a liqueur-flavoured syrup and topped with meringue cuite

Summer pudding 1

5–6 rounds of stale white
  sandwich loaf
1½ lb mixed fruit – currants,
  raspberries, stoned red cherries, etc. (picked over)
4–6 oz granulated sugar

Pudding basin (1½ pints capacity)

Use an uncut sandwich loaf, if possible, rather than sliced bread which is too doughy and makes for a sodden pudding.

The fruit should weigh 1½ lb when picked over. To allow for the stalks etc. begin with 2 lb mixed fruit.

Method

Remove crusts from bread and cut 1–2 slices to fit the bottom of the basin. Arrange slices to line the sides, cutting them if necessary and reserving two slices. Put the fruit and sugar into a shallow pan, cover and set on a low heat for 10–15 minutes, shaking pan occasionally. By this time the juice will have run and the fruit will be tender. Cool a little and adjust sweetening, if necessary.

Half fill the bread-lined basin with fruit, then put in one layer of bread and fill up with the fruit. Cover the fruit with bread and then spoon in just enough juice to fill the basin. Put a small plate on top, pressing it down on the bread and place a 2 lb weight on top. Stand basin on a plate to catch any juice that spills over. Refrigerate overnight, then turn out and serve with cream.

Summer pudding 2

1½–2 lb blackcurrants, or raspberries, or loganberries, or
  blackberries (picked over)
¼ pint water
approximately ½ sandwich loaf
  (thinly sliced)
granulated sugar (to taste)
arrowroot (slaked with fruit
  juice or water)

6-inch diameter top (No. 2 size)
soufflé dish, or pudding basin
(1½ pints capacity)

Method

Put the fruit and water into a pan, cover and simmer for 4–5 minutes (1–2 minutes longer for currants); strain. Work the fruit in an electric blender with a little of the juice, or rub

Summer pudding 2, served with sauce and cream

through a Mouli sieve. If blended, strain the pulp through a strainer to get rid of any tiny pips. Add the rest of the juice to the purée, sweeten well. Remove the crusts from the bread. Pour a little fruit purée into bottom of dish or bowl, put 1–2 slices of bread on top and add more of the purée. Continue like this until the dish is very full, making sure that each layer is well soaked with the purée. Reserve a good ¼ pint of purée for the sauce. Put a plate and a 2 lb weight on top of the pudding and leave overnight.

Add a little water to the reserved purée, add arrowroot, bring to the boil, stirring continuously, pour off and cool. Turn out pudding, spoon this sauce over it and serve with cream.

Raspberry and red-currant cheese

1 lb raspberries
½ lb redcurrants
¾ lb granulated sugar
gelatine (see method)
¼ pint double cream (whipped)

Ring mould (1½–2 pints capacity)

Method
Put the raspberries and redcurrants into a saucepan with the sugar and ½ pint of water. Stir over gentle heat until sugar is dissolved, then rub through a nylon strainer. Measure fruit purée and allow ¾ oz of gelatine to each pint of purée.

Soak gelatine in a little water (use 3 tablespoons water for every ¾ oz). Add the soaked gelatine to the hot fruit purée and stir until gelatine is dissolved. Pour into a wet ring mould and leave to set. Turn out and serve with whipped cream piled in the centre.

Gooseberry cream

1 lb gooseberries
½ pint water
3 tablespoons granulated sugar
scant 1 oz gelatine
½ pint double cream
1½ tablespoons caster sugar
2–3 drops edible green colouring

For decoration
1 pint lemon jelly
pistachio nuts, or small
    diamonds of angelica

6–7 inch diameter cake tin, or charlotte tin

Method
Top and tail the gooseberries and poach them until tender in a syrup made from the water and granulated sugar; then drain and rub fruit through a nylon sieve. Set this purée and ½ pint of the syrup on one side.

Line the mould with the cold but still liquid jelly, decorate the bottom with pistachio nuts (or angelica), setting the decoration in sufficient jelly to cover.

Add half of the reserved syrup to the gelatine, allow it to soak and then dissolve it over gentle heat. Half whip the cream in a bowl, add the fruit purée, remaining syrup, sugar and colouring. Add the melted gelatine, stir gently with the bowl set on ice cubes until cream begins to thicken, then pour it at once into the prepared mould. Leave it to set firm.

Gooseberry cream, with the angelica set in layer of lemon jelly

265

APPLES AND PEARS

To make a syrup for apples and pears (cookers and eaters), whole or quartered, prepare in the following way: dissolve 3–4 tablespoons granulated sugar in ½ pint water for every lb of fruit. Then boil rapidly for 2 minutes. Flavour syrup with a strip of lemon rind or a piece of vanilla pod.

To cook in syrup: only eating apples of the pippin variety can be kept whole when cooked this way. Peel and core fruit. Leave whole or quartered, according to recipe, and then put into syrup with thick part of fruit at bottom of pan. Allow syrup to boil up over fruit, then reduce heat, cover pan and leave to cook very gently until fruit looks transparent. Leave to cool in the syrup.

To make a purée of cooking apples: thinly peel, quarter and core apples. Slice into a saucepan, add 2 tablespoons of granulated sugar per lb of apples, 1 tablespoon water and grated rind of ½ lemon. Cover with buttered paper and lid and cook gently to a pulp, stirring occasionally. Crush with a potato masher or beat well with a wooden spoon.

For special recipes, this purée is sometimes rubbed through a strainer or worked in a blender.

To make a 'marmelade' purée: wash cooking apples, wipe, quarter and core. Rub ½ oz butter over sides and bottom of a large pan. Slice apples into pan, add a strip of lemon rind, cover with buttered paper and a lid and cook gently until soft. Stir occasionally. Rub through a sieve or strainer.

Rinse out pan, return purée to it and add sugar to sweeten. Allow 4 oz granulated sugar to 1 pint purée. Cook rapidly, stirring all the time, until mixture is of dropping consistency. When cold, this marmelade (not to be confused with marmalade) sets firmly and is used to fill flans and cakes.

Before baking apples, score the skins round the middles to stop them splitting

Baked apples

Choose firm, large cooking apples without blemishes (1 per person). Wipe, core them with the end of a potato peeler. In this way you can scoop out the core without making a hole right through the apple. Cut horizontally through skin round the middle of each apple.

Fill each cavity with white or soft brown sugar and sultanas, and place apples in an oven-proof dish with 2–3 tablespoons of water. Top each apple with ½ oz butter and bake for about 40 minutes until tender in an oven at 375°F or Mark 5. The cooking time will vary with the type of apple. Baste once or twice with the juices in the pan.

Eve's pudding

3 large cooking apples
2 tablespoons granulated sugar
grated rind and juice of ½ lemon
1 tablespoon water
3 oz butter
3 oz caster sugar
1 large egg
5 oz self-raising flour
pinch of salt
2–3 tablespoons milk
custard, or cream (optional)

6-inch diameter pie dish

Method
Peel and core the apples, cut in thick slices and put in a pan with granulated sugar, lemon juice and water; cook until apple is tender. Place at the bottom of a pie dish.

Soften the butter with the lemon rind in a bowl, add the caster sugar and work until light and fluffy. Beat in the egg and then with a metal spoon fold in the flour sifted with the salt (this is to avoid losing any of the air beaten into the egg). Stir in enough milk to give a mixture of dropping consistency.

Spread the mixture over the apple and bake for about 40 minutes in an oven at 375°F or Mark 5. Serve hot with custard or cream, if wished.

Apple brown Betty

2 lb cooking apples
4–5 slices stale bread (thickly buttered, thinly sliced)
3 tablespoons golden syrup
custard, or cream (optional)

6-inch diameter pie dish

Method
Remove crusts from the bread and cut each slice into four. Peel, core and thinly slice apples. Place a layer of bread at the bottom of the pie dish, cover with about half the apple slices and 1 tablespoon of syrup. Cover with a second layer of bread and then fill with remaining apple slices and a second tablespoon of syrup.

Arrange the rest of the squares of the bread overlapping to cover the whole surface of the fruit and spread this with the remaining tablespoon of syrup. Bake for 40–50 minutes until golden-brown and crisp in an oven at 375°F or Mark 5.

Serve with custard or cream.

Apples and pears with almond meringue

2 lb cooking apples
½ oz butter
rind and juice of 1 lemon
sugar (to sweeten)
4 ripe dessert pears
½ pint vanilla-flavoured sugar syrup
little icing sugar (for dusting)

For almond meringue
2 egg whites
small pinch of salt
4 oz icing sugar
2–3 oz almonds (sliced and blanched)
6-inch diameter pie dish

Method
Cook the apples to a marmelade (see opposite), adding the lemon juice with rind; peel, quarter and poach the pears (by cooking extremely gently in syrup).

To make the meringue: whisk the egg whites, salt and icing sugar together in a basin over gently simmering water until the mixture stands in peaks. Then fold in the blanched, sliced almonds with a metal spoon. Place the apple purée in a buttered, ovenproof dish, arrange the drained pears on top and then cover with the meringue. Dust with icing sugar and bake for about 20 minutes in an oven at 350°F or Mark 4.

Pears in red wine

5–6 ripe dessert pears
5 oz lump sugar
¼ pint water
¼ pint red wine (claret or burgundy)
strip of lemon rind
small piece of stick cinnamon
1 teaspoon arrowroot
1 oz almonds (shredded and browned)
whipped cream (optional)

Method
To make syrup: dissolve sugar, water, wine and flavourings slowly in a pan. Bring to boil and boil for 1 minute.

Keeping stalks on pears, remove peel and the 'eye' from each base and place in the pre-pared syrup. Poach pears in the pan, covered, until tender. Even if pears are ripe, you must allow at least 20–30 minutes to prevent them discolouring around cores. Remove pears and strain syrup, which should be reduced to ½ pint in the cooking.

Mix the arrowroot with a little water before adding to syrup and stir until boiling; then cook until liquid is clear. (Lump sugar gives a crystal-clear liquid.) Arrange pears in a serving dish. Spoon over the wine sauce and finish by scattering the browned and shredded almonds on top.

Serve cold, hand round a bowl of whipped cream separately.

To shred and brown almonds: blanch, skin and split; cut each half lengthways in fine pieces and brown quickly in the oven at 350°F or Mark 4.

COMPOTES

A compote is the term for fresh or dried fruit which is cooked, whole or cut into quarters, in a thick or thin syrup; various flavourings may be added to this syrup. So often fruit is just put in a pan with water to cover, an unknown or variable amount of sugar is thrown in and the whole is then cooked rather haphazardly. The resulting dish is usually dismissed as 'only stewed fruit', a justified criticism if it is overcooked and mushy, with a watery syrup. Fruits best suited for making compotes are apricots, plums and forced rhubarb.

Preparation of fruit

Pick over fruit to remove any damaged or mouldy flesh, then wash it in a colander under a running tap.

Apricots and large plums. Split by running a stainless steel knife round the fruit from the stalk end, following the slight indentation and cutting through to the stone. By giving the fruit a slight twist the halves should separate easily and the stone can be removed. A few stones can be cracked and the kernels added to the compote.

If the stone will not come away, cook fruit whole and detach stone after cooking.

Place fruit, rounded side down, in a pan with syrup and bring very slowly to boil. Allow syrup to boil up and over fruit and then reduce heat, cover pan and leave to simmer very gently until tender.

Even fully ripe fruit must be thoroughly cooked to allow the syrup to penetrate, sweeten and prevent discolouration.

Rhubarb. Wash and dry 1–1½ lb rhubarb and cut into even lengths. Spread 2 tablespoons of redcurrant jelly or strained raspberry jam over the bottom and sides of a casserole. Put the rhubarb on this and put 1 more tablespoon of jelly or jam on top. Cover and cook in a moderate oven at 350°F or Mark 4 for about 45 minutes, or until tender.

Rhubarb can also be cut in even lengths and cooked as for apricots and plums.

Syrup. The most important point to remember when cooking fruit is that the water and sugar should first be made into a syrup (see opposite).

Plum suédoise

1½ lb red plums (stoned)
sugar syrup (made with ½ pint water, and 4 rounded tablespoons granulated sugar)
1 tablespoon gelatine
a few almonds (blanched)

6-inch diameter deep cake tin, or charlotte tin (1½ pints capacity)

Method
Make the sugar syrup, then halve plums and poach them in it, making sure that they cook for at least 15 minutes to develop the flavour. Drain the fruit and keep a few of the best halves on one side; reserve syrup. Rub remaining halves through a nylon strainer into a bowl.

Measure ¾ pint of the syrup and pour ½ pint into the fruit purée. Soak and dissolve the gelatine over heat in the remaining ¼ pint of syrup and mix with purée. Put half a blanched almond in each reserved plum half and arrange at the bottom of wet tin, cut sides to the base of the tin.

When purée is on point of setting, carefully pour into wet tin; leave in a cool place to set.

Turn out and serve with crème à la vanille (see page 186) or whipped fresh cream.

Rhubarb fool – fold whipped cream into the custard mixture to leave a marbled effect

Rhubarb fool

1 lb rhubarb
sugar syrup (made with ¼ pint water and 2 tablespoons granulated sugar)
1 tablespoon caster sugar
¼ pint thick custard (made with ¼ pint milk and 3 egg yolks, or 1 dessertspoon custard powder to ¼ pint milk)
¼ pint double cream

For serving

sponge fingers, or crisp biscuits

Method
Make sugar syrup. Prepare the rhubarb and cook in the syrup. Drain and rub through a strainer into a bowl. Sweeten to taste.

To prepare the custard: beat egg yolks in bowl; gently heat milk in a pan (do not boil). Pour on to egg yolks and mix. Strain back into rinsed pan. Stir gently over low heat until mixture thickens (about 15 minutes), set aside to cool. If using custard powder, follow instructions on packet.

When the custard is cold mix into the purée. Whip the cream lightly and fold into the rhubarb mixture, leaving it with a marbled effect.

Serve in glasses or in a bowl, with a few sponge fingers or crisp biscuits handed separately.

Cherry compote

1 lb red cherries (preferably Morellos)
2 tablespoons caster sugar
pinch of powdered cinnamon
1 wineglass port
grated rind and juice of 1 orange
4 tablespoons redcurrant jelly

Method
Stone cherries and place in a pan with sugar and cinnamon, cover and cook slowly for 5 minutes. Remove from heat and leave to cool.

Meanwhile, reduce wine by half, adding orange rind and juice and cherry juice. Then add redcurrant jelly; when mixture has melted, add to the cherries.

CHOCOLATE DESSERTS

Chocolate roulade

6 oz block chocolate
5 eggs
8 oz caster sugar
3–4 tablespoons water

For filling
½ pint double cream (lightly whipped and flavoured with vanilla essence, or rum, or brandy)
icing sugar (for dusting)

Shallow swiss roll tin (12 inches by 8 inches), or roulade paper case

Method
Line tin with oiled greaseproof paper, or brush the paper case with oil or melted shortening.

Set the oven at 350°F or Mark 4.

Separate the eggs, add the yolks gradually to sugar, beating until the mixture is lemon-coloured. Melt chocolate in water in a pan over gentle heat and, when it is a thick cream, draw pan aside. Whip the egg whites to a firm snow, then add chocolate to egg yolks mixture; cut and fold egg whites into the mixture and turn it into the prepared tin or case. Place in pre-set moderate oven and bake for 10–15 minutes or until firm to the touch.

Have ready a clean cloth, wrung out in cold water. Take out the roulade, cool it slightly, then cover with the cloth. (This is to prevent any sugary crust forming.) Leave it in a cool place for 12 hours or in a refrigerator overnight.

Lay a piece of greaseproof paper on a table, dust it well with icing sugar. Remove the cloth and turn the roulade upside down on to the prepared paper; strip paper case off the roulade carefully, (or remove swiss roll tin), spread with the whipped cream and roll it up like a swiss roll. Lift on to a serving dish and dust well with icing sugar.

Note: for serving at Christmas, the cream filling can be mixed with a little dry, sieved chestnut; otherwise serve the roulade as it is.

Above: chocolate roulade (left), and nègre en chemise – two attractive party dishes

Stirring melted chocolate into egg yolk mixture for roulade

Nègre en chemise

12 oz block chocolate
about 4 fl oz water
3 oz butter (unsalted)
4 oz praline
rum, or brandy (to taste)
7½ fl oz double cream
7½ fl oz–½ pint double cream (to decorate)
chocolate buttons

Bombe mould (1 pint capacity); forcing bag with rose pipe

Method

Break up the chocolate, put it into a pan with the water over gentle heat and melt until it is a thick cream. Draw pan aside, cool chocolate a little then cream butter in a bowl, add the chocolate and gradually beat in the praline. Flavour with rum (or brandy).

Lightly oil the mould. Then partially whip 7½ fl oz cream, and cut and fold it into the mixture. Turn the mixture into the mould and leave to set in a cool place for 2–3 hours. Turn it out by dipping the mould quickly into hot water.

Whip the remaining cream, fill into forcing bag and pipe a ruff of cream around the base of the mould. Decorate the cream with chocolate buttons (bought, or made at home as squares for decoration).

Arranging chocolate buttons around the nègre en chemise

CUSTARDS

Custards play an important part in cooking. They not only form the basis of many sweets and some savoury dishes, but can also accompany cooked fruit and hot puddings. The basic ingredients are eggs and milk used in varying proportions, with different flavours according to recipe.

Making custards

There are two types of custard. The first is when eggs and milk are mixed together and baked, or steamed, to set to a firm consistency, eg. as for caramel custard. The second type of custard is when egg yolks and milk are cooked over a gentle heat to a creamy consistency. This is a soft custard and forms the basis of cold creams and soufflés set with gelatine.

Important points to note. Egg whites will set a custard and egg yolks will give it a creamy consistency. For a cooked custard, eg. baked or steamed, the proportion of eggs to milk should be 2 whole eggs and 2 egg yolks to 1 pint of milk. For a soft custard take 4 egg yolks to 1 pint of milk. More yolks can be added if a very rich custard is called for. Whites tend to curdle the mixture. Eggs and milk will curdle if allowed to get too hot. For baking a custard in the oven, it is wise to use a bain marie. For a soft custard scald milk by bringing up to boiling point. You can use a double saucepan, the lower pan containing hot water, but if care is taken, the custard can be thickened on direct, but gentle heat. When eggs are scarce, 1 teaspoon of corn-flour can replace 1 egg yolk in a custard sauce.

Custard tart

For rich shortcrust pastry
6 oz flour
4 oz butter
1 rounded dessertspoon caster sugar
1 egg yolk
2 tablespoons water

For custard filling
3 eggs
1 tablespoon caster sugar
½ pint milk
2–3 drops of vanilla essence
nutmeg (grated)
6-inch diameter flan ring, or cake tin, or deep small moulds

Method
First prepare pastry (see recipe on page 204) and set aside to chill. Then roll out and line into the flan ring (or small moulds) and set on a baking sheet. Prick the bottoms very lightly, then put baking sheet into the refrigerator while the custard is made.

Break eggs into a bowl, mix with a fork, add sugar, milk and vanilla essence. Strain mixture, then pour into the flan ring. Fill to about ¼ inch below the top. Grate a little nutmeg over top.

Set the oven at 400°F or Mark 6, and put a second baking sheet on the top shelf to heat. When thoroughly hot set first baking sheet (from refrigerator) with the flan ring or moulds on top of the second one which will heat it up quickly; this helps to cook bottom of pastry. Bake for about 15–20 minutes, or until the custard is set. After 7 minutes reduce the heat to 350°F or Mark 4. When set, take custard out and cool. Lift the flan ring off carefully or turn custard tarts out of the moulds. Serve cold.

Bavarian cream (Bavarois à la crème)

3 egg yolks
2 tablespoons caster sugar
1 vanilla pod, or 2–3 drops of vanilla essence
½ oz gelatine
5 tablespoons water
¼ pint double cream

Plain mould (1½ pint capacity)

Method
Cream yolks thoroughly with sugar in a bowl. Infuse pod in milk until well flavoured, or add vanilla essence to the yolk mixture. Pour milk on to the yolks, first taking out the vanilla pod. Blend well and return to the pan. Stir continually over the heat until the custard coats back of the spoon. Strain into bowl to cool.

Put the gelatine into a small pan, add the water, leave to soak for 4–5 minutes. Partially whip the cream. When the custard is cold, dissolve the gelatine over heat. It should be quite hot before pouring into the custard. Turn into a thin pan and stand in a bowl of cold water (for quickness add a little ice to the water). Stir until beginning to thicken creamily, then add 2 tablespoons of the partially-whipped cream.

Turn custard into a lightly-oiled mould, leave to set. Then turn out carefully and spread over the rest of the cream. If wished, additional cream can be used for decorating. In this case use the whole ¼ pint for the mixture.

For a coffee bavarois: add 1 tablespoon instant coffee to the milk while bringing it to scalding point, then pour on to the yolks.

For a chocolate bavarois: break up 4 oz plain dessert chocolate and cook for 3–4 minutes in the milk.

For a good party sweet for 6–8 people, make two lots of bavarois, say a vanilla and a chocolate one. Pour the vanilla into a large plain cake tin and, when just about to set, pour in the chocolate. Gently stir round once or twice to marble the colours. Leave to set, turn out and edge with cream (or pipe a ruff of cream) round the base.

Caramel cream (Crème caramel)

1 pint milk
2 eggs
2 egg yolks
1½ tablespoons caster sugar

For caramel
4 oz lump, or granulated, sugar
½ cup water

6-inch diameter soufflé dish, or cake tin

Method
Scald milk. Break eggs into a bowl, then add the extra yolks.

Beat well with a fork but do not allow to get frothy. Add sugar and milk, mix and set aside until needed.

Put sugar and water for caramel into a small pan, dissolve sugar over a gentle heat, then boil rapidly without stirring until a rich brown in colour. Stop boiling by dipping bottom of pan into a basin of cold water and, when still, pour three-quarters of caramel into a dry and warm soufflé dish or cake tin; pour rest on to an oiled plate or tin. Turn soufflé dish or cake tin carefully round to coat the caramel evenly over the bottom and sides.

Strain in the custard mixture, cover with foil or a piece of buttered paper. Cook in a bain marie in the oven at 375°F or Mark 5 for 40–50 minutes until just set; take out and leave until cool before turning out. Crush the rest of the caramel and put round the dish.

Watchpoint A certain amount of caramel will always be left in the mould after turning out; this can be lessened by adding 1 teaspoon boiling water to caramel before pouring it into soufflé dish or cake tin. For a more creamy-textured result, use an extra egg yolk.

Petits pots de crème (Small pots of cream)

1½ pints milk
vanilla pod
3 eggs
3 egg yolks
1 tablespoon vanilla sugar
  (see Vanilla cream ice 1, method on page 277)
2 tablespoons caster sugar
2 teaspoons instant coffee
2 oz plain chocolate

deep mousse pots, or ramekin pots

Made in a variety of flavours and arranged on a large dish, these 'petits pots' look good on a buffet table.

Method
Warm all the milk with the vanilla pod, remove from heat and leave to infuse 5–10 minutes until well flavoured. Meanwhile, break 1 of the eggs into a bowl, add 1 yolk and 1

Chocolate- and vanilla-flavoured petits pots de crème

tablespoon vanilla sugar, and beat well with a fork, but do not allow to get frothy. Remove the vanilla pod from milk, and pour ½ pint on to eggs and sugar. Blend well, strain and pour into pots.

Using the same bowl, beat 1 egg, 1 egg yolk and 1 tablespoon caster sugar. Warm the remaining milk slightly, and pour ½ pint of it on to eggs and sugar. Blend in the coffee, making sure it has thoroughly dissolved, strain and pour into pots.

Again using the same bowl

(any leftover coffee will improve the flavour of the chocolate), beat the remaining egg, egg yolk and sugar. Simmer the chocolate in remaining ½ pint milk for 2–3 minutes. Pour on to the eggs and sugar, blend, strain and pour into pots.

Place the filled pots in water in a bain marie, or in a deep ovenproof dish on a baking sheet, covered with buttered paper. Cook in oven at 350°F–375°F or Mark 4–5 for 12–15 minutes until just set. Take out and chill. Serve plain or with cream.

MERINGUES

Meringue, a mixture of egg white and sugar, is thought to have been invented in the early 18th century by Gasparini, a Swiss pastrycook, in the town of Mehrinyghen — hence 'meringue'. There are three distinct types of meringue used for various sweet course dishes, gâteaux and pâtisseries: suisse, cuite and italienne.

1 Meringue suisse is the one most frequently made. The proportion of sugar to egg white never varies, being 2 oz caster sugar to each egg white, which is stiffly whipped before the sugar is folded in. The number of egg whites varies according to the recipe.

This meringue is used in sweets such as **vacherin** (large rounds of meringue filled with whipped cream, fruit, chestnuts etc.), or as a **topping** for pies (see page 209, lemon meringue pie for example).

The most simple way to use this type is with **meringue shells** which are then filled with whipped cream (see recipe for meringue Chantilly on this page).

2 Meringue cuite (cooked) is a slight misnomer as it is not actually cooked in the making. It is firmer than meringue suisse and used mainly for **meringue baskets** and **pâtisserie**.

Proportions are 2 oz icing sugar to each egg white (you can be generous with the weight of sugar), and it can be made in large quantities with an electric whisk (but not over heat). If whisking by hand, it is quicker to put the bowl of egg whites over a pan of hot water, as the heat quickens up the thickening process.

3 Meringue italienne is really more for professionals and those engaged in pâtisserie work. It is similar to meringue cuite but a lighter and finer mixture. It takes some skill to make as the lump sugar is made into a syrup and boiled to a certain degree before being poured on to the egg whites. It is essential to use a sugar thermometer for this meringue.

Small meringue baskets are perhaps the nicest form of meringue to eat, as well as being an attractive way of serving a small amount of choice fruit with cream. We think they are best cooked in a hotter oven than is often advised and not for too long. In this way the meringue basket is crisp on the outside and rather marshmallow-like inside.

There are certain sweets which use variations of meringue suisse and meringue cuite. These contain a small proportion of cream of tartar, resulting in a soft and somewhat sticky consistency.

Though the sugar for meringues can be measured by the tablespoon it is wiser to use scales as accuracy ensures a uniform result.

For meringue shells or a vacherin-type sweet, a special copper bowl and a balloon whisk is best, but not essential. The shape of the bowl and slightly-rounded whisk make for greater bulk of egg whites.

There is also less risk of overbeating which so often happens when an electric mixer or rotary whisk is employed. If you don't have a copper bowl, whisk whites to a froth only with a rotary whisk or mixer, then whisk by hand with a balloon whisk until a firm snow.

For meringue cuite and meringue italienne use a rotary whisk in a pudding basin, rather than a mixing bowl — larger and more suitable for mixing or beating — or use electric mixer.

Meringue Chantilly

For meringue suisse
4 egg whites
8 oz caster sugar (plus extra for dredging)
½ pint Chantilly cream (see page 274)
salad oil (for baking sheets)
flour (for dredging)

These are meringue shells filled with vanilla-flavoured whipped cream. This quantity will make 12–16 shells (6–8 filled meringues). Unfilled shells may be stored for up to 2 days in an airtight container.

Method
Set oven at 250°F–275°F or Mark ½–1. Brush 2 baking sheets lightly with oil and dredge with flour. Bang sheets on the table to distribute the flour evenly, or line the sheets with non-stick (silicone) cooking paper.

Whisk the egg whites until quite stiff; they should look smooth and when a little is lifted on the whisk it should remain in position when shaken. For each egg white whisk in 1 teaspoon of sugar for 1 minute only. Fold in remaining sugar with a metal spoon.

Put meringue into a forcing bag with a plain nozzle and pipe shells on to prepared baking sheets (or put out in spoonfuls). Dredge with caster sugar and leave for a few minutes before putting into oven to allow the sugar to melt slightly, giving a crystallised effect to the meringues when cooked.

Taking up meringue mixture with two spoons to form shell shape

Laying shells on to baking sheet before dredging with sugar

Alternatively, piping out shells with plain nozzle before baking in the oven for about 1 hour

Bake for about 1 hour, changing round the trays halfway through (top shelf being warmer than second shelf).

A strawberry meringue basket, filled, and decorated with cream and whole strawberries

When meringues are set, carefully lift them from the sheet with a sharp knife, or peel off the non-stick paper.

Gently press underneath to form a hollow, put back on the sheets on their sides, and replace in the oven to allow the undersides to dry for 20–30 minutes. Lift on to a rack to cool.

The shells are hollowed so that they can hold a fair proportion of cream and the two halves will not slip when sandwiched together.

A meringue of this type should be delicate beige in colour, crisp in texture and slightly sticky.

Serve within 1–2 hours of filling with Chantilly cream.

Large meringue basket

For a 7-inch diameter basket that will give 6–8 portions, you will need double the quantity of ingredients in recipe for meringue cuite (on page 274). Also include 6 drops of vanilla essence. Make it in two batches.

Method
Set the oven at 275°F or Mark 1, line 2 baking sheets with non-stick (silicone) cooking paper.

Make up first batch of meringue cuite and put about half in a forcing bag fitted with a ½-inch éclair pipe. Use about two-thirds of this to shape one round, 6 inches in diameter, and one hoop of the same size. Bake for 45–50 minutes until dry and crisp. During this baking time

keep the basin of remaining meringue mixture covered with a damp cloth to stop it from hardening in the basin.

When the round and hoop are ready, turn on to a wire rack to cool and peel off the non-stick paper. Turn this paper over, put back on to the baking sheets and pipe two more hoops of the meringue to the same size as before. Bake and cool as before.

Make up the second batch of meringue and use a little of this uncooked mixture to mount the hoops on the round, one on top of the other. Now put the rest of mixture in a forcing bag fitted with an 8-cut vegetable rose pipe and cover the plainly-piped hoops with a decorative pattern (see photographs below). Bake again at the same temperature for 45-50 minutes until set and crisp.

This meringue case can be made at least a week before a party and stored in an airtight container. Fill with fresh fruit and cream, or ice-cream, just before serving.

Draw 6-inch circle on non-stick (silicone) cooking paper to act as piping guide for a meringue basket. Use ½-inch éclair pipe

Pipe three hoops of the same diameter (in two batches). When baked and cool, mount on circular base of the basket

With more meringue mixture, pipe decoration on to hoops; bake again, fill with fruit and cream as shown above left

273

Meringue topping

For meringue suisse
2 egg whites
4 oz caster sugar (plus extra for dredging)

This quantity of meringue suisse will be sufficient for a pudding or pie for 4–6 people.

Method
Set oven at 300°F or Mark 2. Make meringue suisse, as in Meringue Chantilly on page 272, and pile on to the pudding or pie. Dredge with caster sugar and leave for a few minutes before putting in oven.

Cook for about 30 minutes, until the meringue is a delicate brown and crisp on the top. The inside should have the consistency of a marshmallow – white, firm and easy to cut.

Meringue cuite

8½ oz icing sugar
4 egg whites

Method
Sift the icing sugar through a fine sieve and tip it into a basin containing beaten egg whites. Place the basin over a pan of simmering water and whisk the whites and sugar together until thick and holding their shape.

Flavour the meringue and use according to recipe.

Meringue italienne

8 oz lump sugar
6–7 tablespoons water
4 egg whites

Sugar thermometer

Method
First prepare sugar syrup by putting sugar and water in pan; dissolve sugar over gentle heat and then cook quickly without stirring to 260°F.

Meanwhile beat egg whites until stiff and, when sugar syrup is ready, pour it steadily on to egg whites, mixing quickly with a whisk. Continue whisking until all sugar has been absorbed.

When cold this meringue is used as a topping and/or filling for cakes, or to replace cream.

Chantilly cream

Turn ½ pint of double cream into a cold basin and, using a fork or open wire whisk, whisk gently until it thickens. Add

3–4 teaspoons caster sugar to taste and 2–3 drops of vanilla essence and continue whisking until the cream will hold its shape.

For a delicate flavour, instead of the essence, sweeten with vanilla sugar (see Vanilla cream ice 1, method, on page 277), and a few of the seeds scraped from a vanilla pod.

ICES

Methods of freezing

In refrigerator or home-freezer. Use the ice trays of a refrigerator or a stainless steel bowl in a home-freezer. In both these cases, the mixture must be well stirred about every hour and, as it thickens, stirred and beaten more frequently until it barely holds its shape. Then smooth over the top and cover with foil. Leave for at least an hour to 'ripen' before serving.

For freezing a water ice in the refrigerator, see lemon water ice (basic recipe) on page 276.
Churn freezer. This type can be manual or electric. The former is more generally used, and it consists of a wooden bucket with a metal container fitted with a dasher. The bucket is first packed with a combination of ice and salt, and the ice-cream mixture is poured into the container. A handle is then turned which revolves the dasher, and so not only gradually scrapes away the mixture from round the sides as it freezes, but also churns, or beats, it at the same time.

The electric churn machines, of which there are two types, operate on the same principle. One type is set in the ice-making compartment of the refrigerator (so that there is no necessity for extra ice), with the flex leading to an electric plug outside the refrigerator. The other variety requires a quantity of ice.

The hand churn freezer is moderate in price and, if well cared for, will last for several

years. The electric churn freezers are naturally more expensive. The hand churn freezer is made in different sizes from 1 quart upwards (ice-cream being measured by the quart). A 2-quart machine is the most convenient size for the average household.

The mixture to be frozen must not come more than half to three-quarters of the way up the sides of the container. This allows for what is called 'swell', ie. when the cream mixture is churned the quantity increases and rises in the container. A water ice has slightly less swell, and it is not apparent until the egg white has been added (see lemon water ice, page 276).

To obtain a low freezing temperature a mixture of ice and salt is used. The salt should be coarse rock salt (known as freezing salt), obtainable from some fishmongers and from big stores. The ice is best chipped off from a block rather than ice made by an ice-maker. The latter is in pellets (or small cubes), which are uneconomical as churn freezers require constant refilling. Being small, the pellets melt very quickly. As they are usually square, they do not, therefore, fit well around the machine.

Unfortunately, with the wider use of refrigerators and home-freezers, many fishmongers only stock ice made by an ice-maker. Those who are fortunate enough to possess a roomy home-freezer can freeze water in any suitable container, break or chip it into convenient-sized pieces, then store it in polythene bags for future use.

To chip ice, use an ice pick, consisting of a single spike fitted into a wooden handle. To break the ice, put the block on several layers of newspaper on the floor, or if more convenient in the sink. Give short sharp jabs at the piece or block of ice with the pick; avoid going right through down to the paper.

Watchpoint The pieces of ice should not be so large that the salt trickles through the gaps between them, as would certainly happen if ice cubes from the refrigerator were used. This can be prevented if the pieces are well jabbed down with the pick when filling them into the bucket.

Care of churn freezer

After use the container, lid and dasher must be washed well, then scalded with boiling water. Dry container thoroughly before putting it away with its lid off. Keep the ratchet well oiled to ensure smooth running and to avoid squeaking. Rinse the bucket well in cold water, then dry. If the machine has a wooden bucket which has not been used for some time it is wise, when you start using it again, **to** immerse the bucket in cold water for a few hours to enable the wood to swell and so keep it comparatively water-tight.

A selection of home-made ices: pineapple water ice, served in pineapple halves on a bed of green leaves; plum pudding ice decorated with a ruff of flavoured, whipped cream; two coupes of vanilla cream ice, and one of grapefruit with mint ice

WATER ICES

A water ice is essentially a fruit-flavoured, light syrup, either lemon or orange, or a fruit purée with syrup added. This type is best churned in a freezer, but it can be made in a refrigerator if a small quantity of gelatine is added.

Water ice is frozen to a slush before a very small quantity of egg white, whipped to a firm snow, is added and the freezing is continued until the ice is firm. The addition of egg white binds the ice together and makes for a smooth, yet firm, consistency.

Lemon water ice

1¼ pints water
pared rind and juice of 3 large and juicy lemons
7 oz cube sugar
½ egg white (whisked)
1 dessertspoon gelatine (see method)

This recipe gives the basic method for making water ices.

Method

Put the water, lemon rind and sugar into a scrupulously clean pan, bring slowly to the boil, simmer for 5 minutes, then strain into a jug. Strain the lemon juice and add to jug, mix well and taste for sweetness. Chill well before freezing.

Pour mixture into the packed freezer, leave for 5 minutes, then start to churn. When a slush, whip white to a firm snow and add 1 dessertspoon to 1 table-spoon of this, then churn it until firm. Remove dasher and pack down as directed in the general instructions.

Note: if freezing the ice in a refrigerator, dissolve 1 dessert-spoon of gelatine in a small quantity of the sugar syrup after straining it. Add to the jug with the lemon juice. Chill before pouring into the ice trays. Turn the refrigerator down to the maximum freezing temperature, freeze to a slush, then beat in the required amount of white. Return to the ice compartment, freeze until just firm, then beat again, cover with foil and return to the ice compartment. At this stage the refrigerator can be turned back to normal and the ice left until required.

Watchpoint The quantity of egg white varies according to consistency desired for indi-vidual recipes. Half a white is the smallest quantity it is pos-sible to whisk, but it may not be necessary to use it all.

Grapefruit with mint ice

3 grapefruit
¾ pint water

Crystallised mint leaves decorate grapefruit with mint ice

pared rind and juice of 2 large lemons
4 oz cube sugar
2 large handfuls of mint leaves (picked from the stalk)
2–3 drops of green colouring (optional)
½ egg white (whisked)

To garnish

caster sugar
freshly chopped mint, or 1–2 leaves of crystallised mint

Method

First prepare the ice. Put the water into a pan with the pared rind of the lemons and the sugar. Bring to the boil and cook for 4–5 minutes. Draw pan aside, add the well-washed mint leaves and the juice of the lemons.

Watchpoint Leave pan on the side of the stove for liquid to infuse; do not boil as this would spoil the flavour.

After 10–12 minutes, strain liquid into a jug, taste for sweet-ness and add colour, if wished. Chill and then freeze ice, either in a churn or in the ice-making compartment of the refrigerator. When the ice is just frozen to a slush, add 1 teaspoon of whisked egg white.

Prepare the grapefruit in the usual way and hollow out the centres a little to hold the ice. Dust with caster sugar and chill.

To serve, put a scoop of the ice on the centre of each grape-fruit and sprinkle with a little freshly-chopped mint or 1–2 crystallised mint leaves.

Crystallised mint leaves

Pick some fresh mint leaves, brush them very lightly with lightly broken egg white. Dust with caster sugar and place on greaseproof paper or a cake rack to dry for 1–2 hours. These will not keep for more than a day.

Pineapple water ice
(see photograph on page 275)

1 large pineapple
soft fruits (see method)

For ice

6 oz cube sugar
1 pint water
pared rind and juice of 1 large lemon
½ egg white (whisked)

To garnish

vine, or strawberry, leaves

Method

Dissolve the sugar in the water with the pared rind of the lemon and boil for 4–5 minutes; then add the lemon juice, strain, and leave liquid to cool.

Split the pineapple in two, lengthways, and slice out the pulp with a grapefruit knife, removing the large centre core. With a fork break the flesh of the pineapple into shreds and

ICES

measure this. There should be ¾–1 pint. Add this pulp to the cold syrup and freeze as for lemon water ice (opposite), adding 1 tablespoon whisked egg white when it forms a slush.

Chill the pineapple halves and, when ready to serve, put the fresh soft fruits, eg. raspberries, strawberries or currants, in the bottom of the pineapple halves and set the ice on top. Arrange the pineapple halves on a silver dish lined with green leaves, such as vine leaves or strawberry leaves.

CREAM ICES

Cream ices are made on a base of either egg mousse or custard, with a proportion of egg white added. When the mousse or custard is cold, cream is folded into the mixture.

For cream ices made on an egg mousse base, single cream can be used. If using double cream, partially whip it to give the ice a smoother and richer consistency, especially when freezing ice in refrigerator.

As with water ices, freezing diminishes the flavour and colour of cream ices, so this must always be taken into consideration when tasting the unfrozen mixture.

Vanilla cream ice 1

2 eggs
2 egg yolks
3 oz caster sugar
1 pint milk
1 vanilla pod, or 2–3 drops of vanilla essence
¼ pint single cream, or double cream (lightly whipped)

This is the basic method for making cream ices on a custard base.

The caster sugar may be flavoured with a vanilla pod. This is done by leaving a dry pod in a small jar of caster sugar for a few days. The vanilla in the recipe may then be omitted.

Method
Break the whole eggs into a bowl, add the separated egg yolks, then the sugar and whisk to mix well, but not so that the

mixture becomes slushy.

Scald the milk (if using a vanilla pod, split it and add to the milk). When it is at boiling point, pour on the egg mixture, stirring vigorously. Strain custard and allow to cool. If using vanilla essence, add it at this point.

When custard is quite cold, add the cream, then freeze it in the refrigerator ice tray, or in a churn freezer.

Vanilla cream ice 2

1 vanilla pod, or vanilla essence
1¼ pints single, or double, cream
3 oz granulated sugar
4 fl oz water
4 egg yolks (well beaten)

This ice is made on an egg mousse base, and is thus more suitable for making in a refrigerator than vanilla cream ice 1. To obtain a quicker, creamier result, when making a cream ice in this way, it is better to have the mixture thicker than that for making in a churn freezer.

Method
Split the vanilla pod and scoop out a few seeds. Put the cream into a pan with the vanilla pod. Leave it to infuse, covered, for about 7–10 minutes on a low heat until the cream is well scalded, ie. just below simmering point. Strain cream, cover with greaseproof paper to prevent a skin from forming and leave to cool.

Put the sugar and the water into a small pan, stir over gentle heat until the sugar is dissolved, then boil steadily without shaking or stirring until the syrup reaches the 'thread' stage. Have the well-beaten egg yolks ready, then draw pan of syrup aside and, when the bubbles have subsided, pour it on to the yolks and whisk well with a rotary whisk until the mixture is thick and mousse-like. Add the cream and vanilla essence, if used, and mix well. Chill mixture thoroughly before freezing it.
Note: if wished, the cream need not be scalded, but you should then use half double and half single cream. Partly whip the double cream before adding it to the mousse with the single cream. If whipping the cream it cannot be scalded as well.

Chocolate cream ices

Chocolate cream ices can be made using the vanilla cream ice 1 recipe. Take 7 oz plain block chocolate, and dissolve in the milk, then add mixture to egg yolks. A chocolate cream ice is usually flavoured with vanilla, unless rum or brandy is added.

Plum pudding ice
(see photograph on page 275)

2 oz currants
4 oz stoned raisins
½ oz blanched almonds
½ oz candied orange peel
1 oz glacé cherries
½ wineglass brandy, or rum

For cream ice mixture
6 oz plain block chocolate, or 2 oz cocoa and 2½ fl oz cold water
1 pint single, or ½ pint single and ½ pint double, cream
2 oz granulated sugar
2½ fl oz water
3 egg yolks

To decorate
whipped double cream, flavoured with brandy, or rum

Method
First prepare the fruit. Wash the currants and raisins well, finely shred the almonds and candied orange peel and rinse the cherries to get rid of some of the heavy syrup. Pour over the brandy (or rum) and leave fruit to macerate for 1–2 hours.

To prepare the cream ice mixture: dissolve chocolate in the single cream over gentle heat. If using cocoa, mix with the cold water and cook to a thick cream, then add this to the single cream and scald.

Make an egg mousse with the sugar, water and yolks (see vanilla cream ice 2) and add to the cream; if using double cream, whip it lightly.

When the mixture is chilled, turn it into a churn freezer and churn until very thick. Then add the fruit and continue to churn until really firm. Remove the dasher and pack down.

Serve cream ice on a chilled serving dish scooped out in the form of a plum pudding. Decorate, if wished, with a ruff of whipped cream, flavoured with brandy (or rum).

277

Metrication

The metric system of measurements is now in use and these tables are provided as a guide. It is important to remember the following points:

1. The exact conversions from Imperial to metric frequently give inconvenient working quantities, and so, for convenience, the ounce is converted to 25 grams, and this conversion gives good results for almost all recipes.

2. When using the 25 gram unit for one ounce, you will find that the size of the cooked dish will be slightly smaller; remember, if eggs are included in the converted recipe, that you should use small ones in order to keep the proportions correct.

WEIGHT

Imperial ounces	Approximate grams to the nearest whole figure	Recommended conversion to the nearest unit of 25 grams
1	28	25
2	57	50
3	85	75
4	113	100
5	142	150
6	170	175
7	198	200
8 (½lb)	226	225
9	255	250
10	283	275
11	311	300
12	340	350
13	368	375
14	396	400
15	428	425
16 (1lb)	456	450
32 (2lb)	907	900
35 (2lb 3oz)	997	1 kilogram

OVEN TEMPERATURE

This table compares oven thermostats marked in °C with those marked in °F and with gas marks. These are dial markings and not exact conversions.

°C	°F	Gasmark
290	550	
270	525	
250	500	
240	475	9
230	450	8
220	425	7
200	400	6
190	375	5
180	350	4
170	325	3
150	300	2
140	275	1
130	250	½
110	225	¼
100	200	Low
80	175	
70	150	

LIQUID MEASUREMENT

Imperial fluid ounces	Approximate ml. to nearest whole figure	Recommended conversion to nearest unit of 25 ml.
1	28	25
5 (¼pt)	142	150
10 (½pt)	283	275
15 (¾pt)	428	425
20 (1pt)	569	575
35 (1¾pt)	992	1 litre

Index